Kamisama Kiss

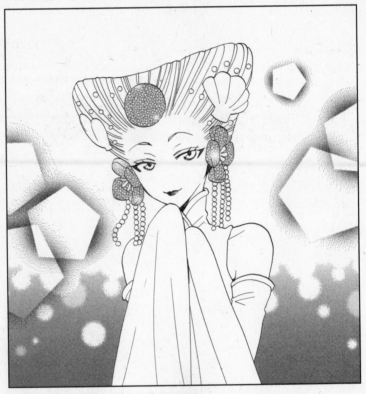

Story & Art by
Julietta Suzuki

CHARACTERS

Mamoru

Nanami's shikigami.

Nanami Momozono

A high school student who was turned into a kamisama by the tochigami Mikage.

Tomoe

The shinshi who serves Nanami now that she's the new tochigami. Originally a wild fox ayakashi.

Mizuki

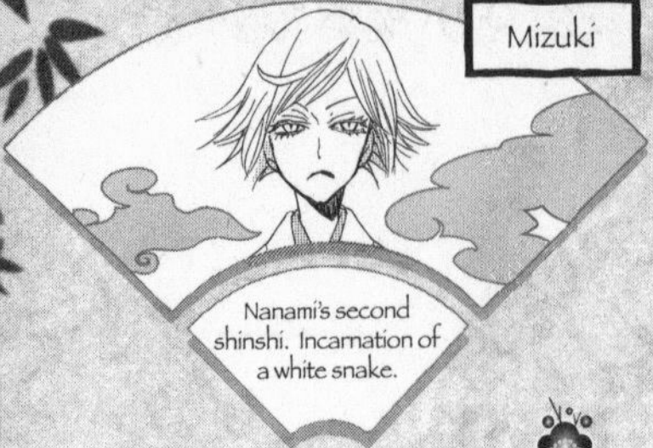

Nanami's second shinshi. Incarnation of a white snake.

Kotetsu

Onikiri

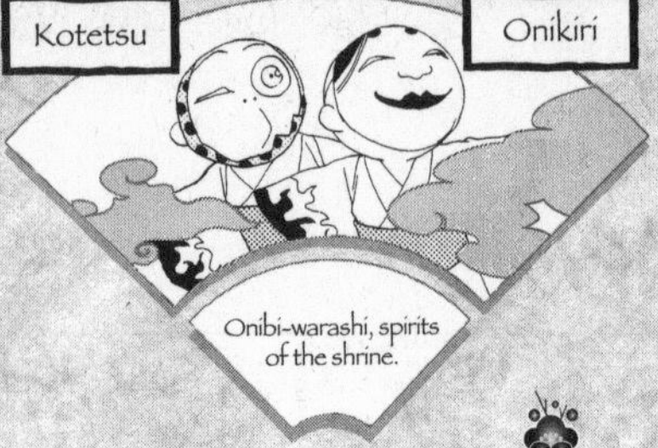

Onibi-warashi, spirits of the shrine.

Kotaro Urashima

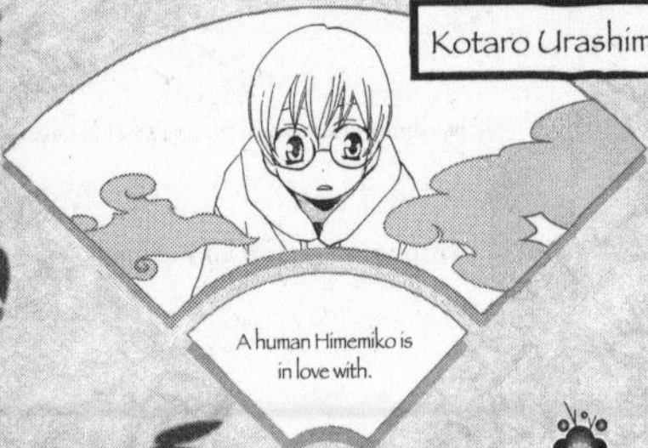

A human Himemiko is in love with.

Himemiko

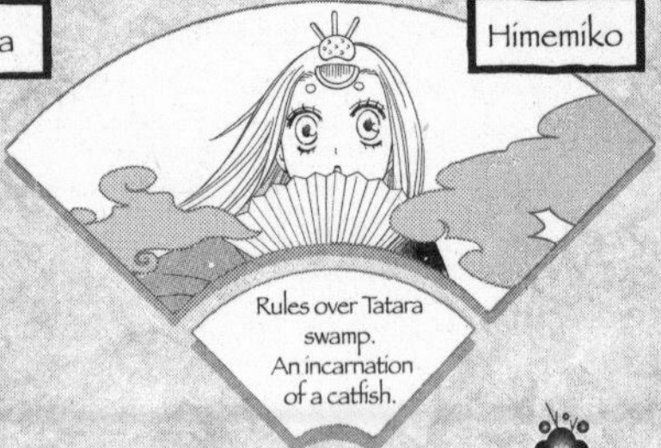

Rules over Tatara swamp. An incarnation of a catfish.

Sukuna

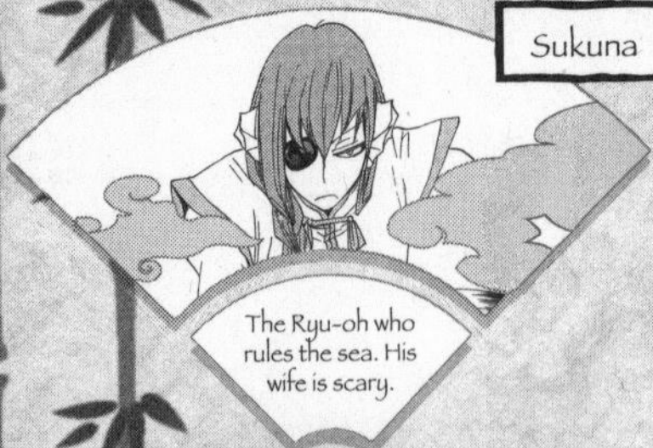

The Ryu-oh who rules the sea. His wife is scary.

Aotake

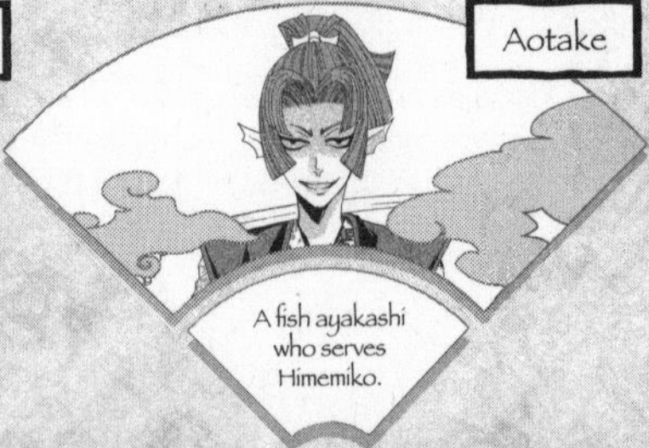

A fish ayakashi who serves Himemiko.

Story so far

Nanami Momozono is a high school student who was evicted from her home when her dad skipped town.
She meets the tochigami Mikage in a park, and he leaves his shrine and his kami powers to her.
Now Nanami spends her days with Tomoe and Mizuki, her shinshi, and with Onikiri and Kotetsu, the onibi-warashi spirits of the shrine.
Nanami has been slowly gaining powers as a kamisama by holding a festival at her shrine, attending a big kami conference, and getting embroiled in the succession fight at the tengu village.
Nanami's love for Tomoe is growing daily, while Tomoe is becoming aware of his feelings for Nanami. The Mikage shrine is slowly gaining respectability thanks to them and has finally properly celebrated the new year, but...?!

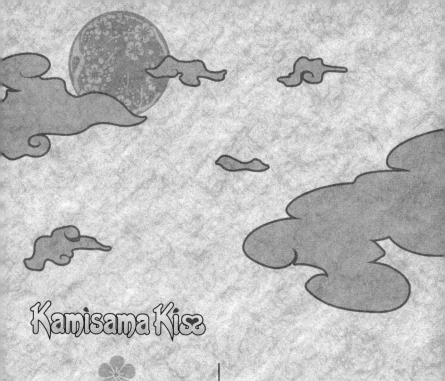

Kamisama Kiss

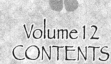

Volume 12
CONTENTS

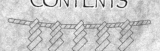

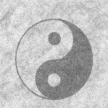

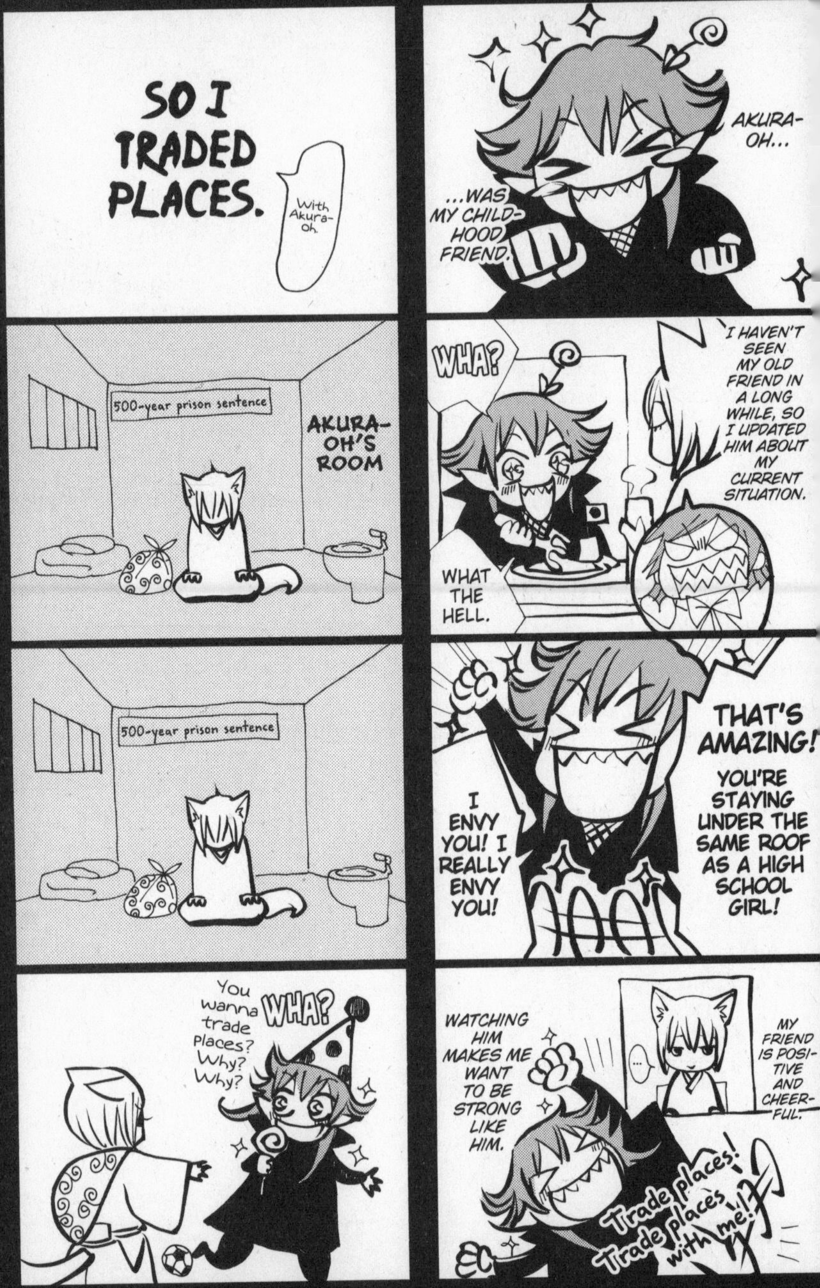
AKURA-OH...
...WAS MY CHILDHOOD FRIEND.
I HAVEN'T SEEN MY OLD FRIEND IN A LONG WHILE, SO I UPDATED HIM ABOUT MY CURRENT SITUATION.
WHA?
WHAT THE HELL.
THAT'S AMAZING!
YOU'RE STAYING UNDER THE SAME ROOF AS A HIGH SCHOOL GIRL!
I ENVY YOU! I REALLY ENVY YOU!
MY FRIEND IS POSITIVE AND CHEERFUL.
...
WATCHING HIM MAKES ME WANT TO BE STRONG LIKE HIM.
Trade places! Trade places with me!
SO I TRADED PLACES.
With Akura-oh.
500-year prison sentence
AKURA-OH'S ROOM
500-year prison sentence
WHA?
You wanna trade places? Why? Why?

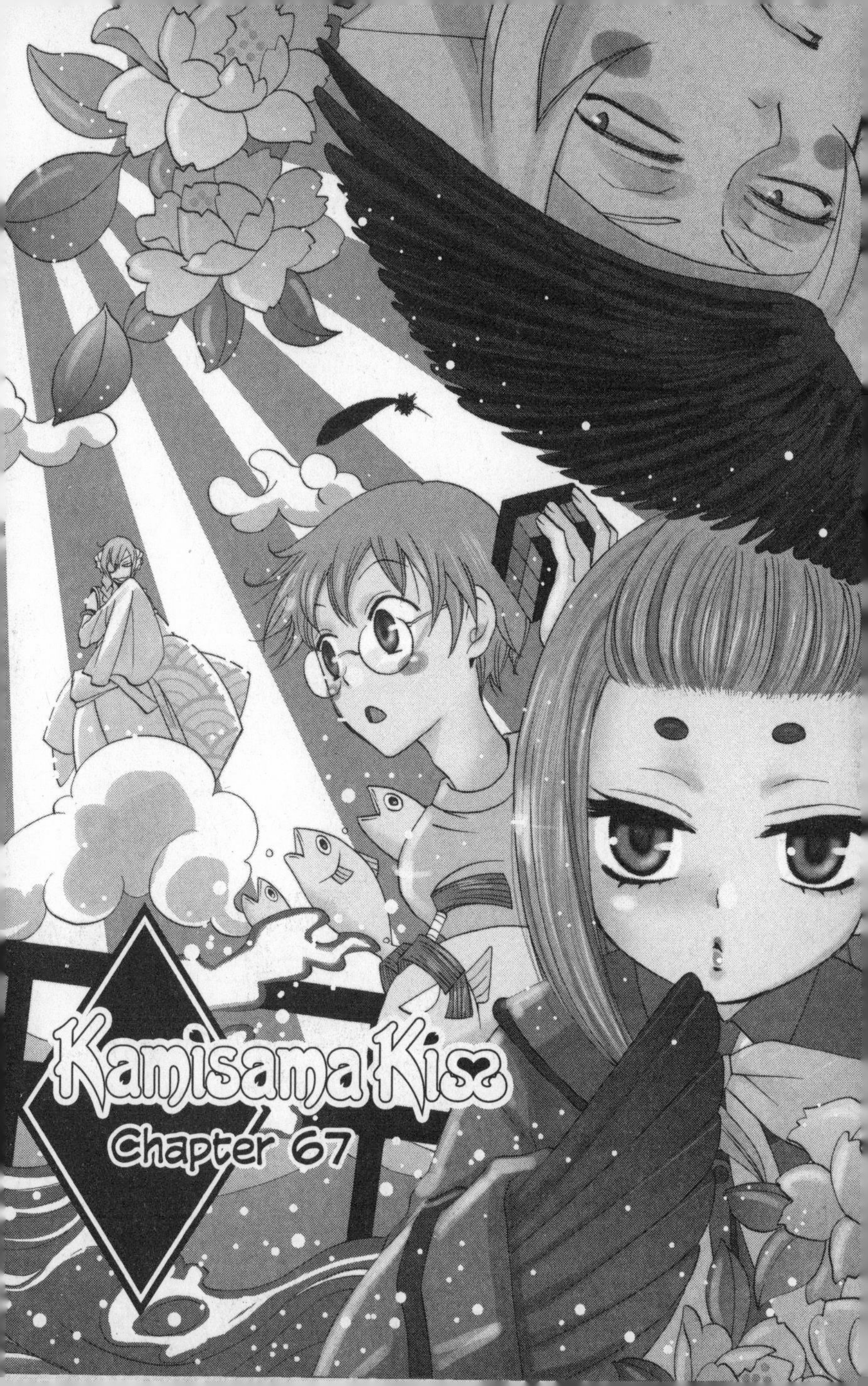
Kamisama Kiss
Chapter 67

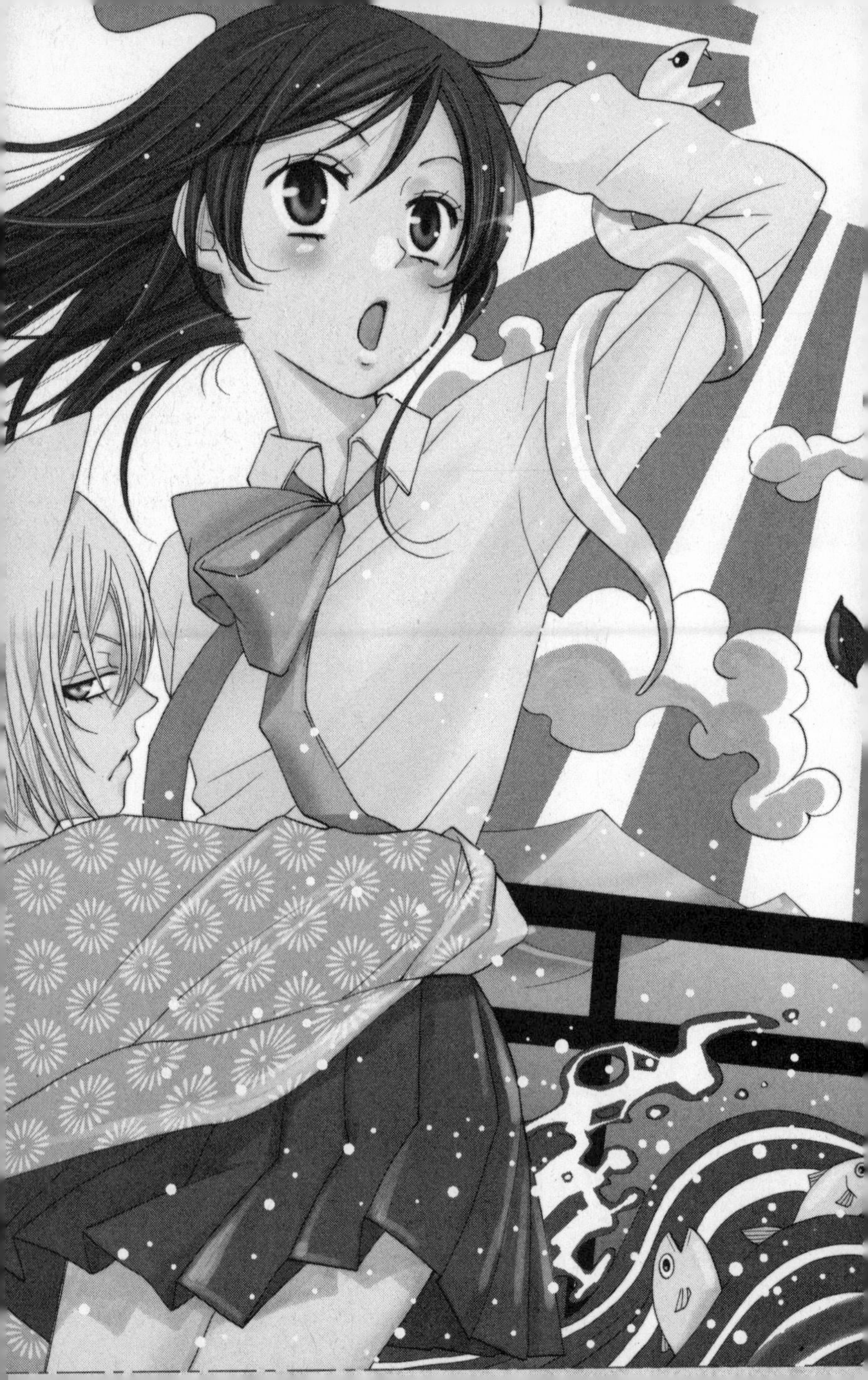

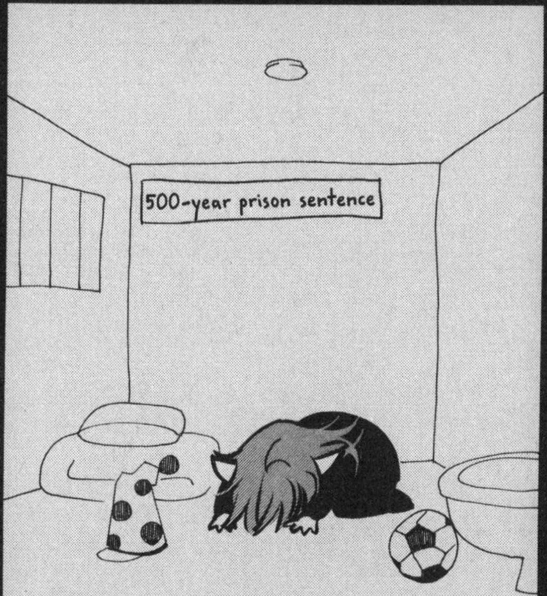
500-year prison sentence

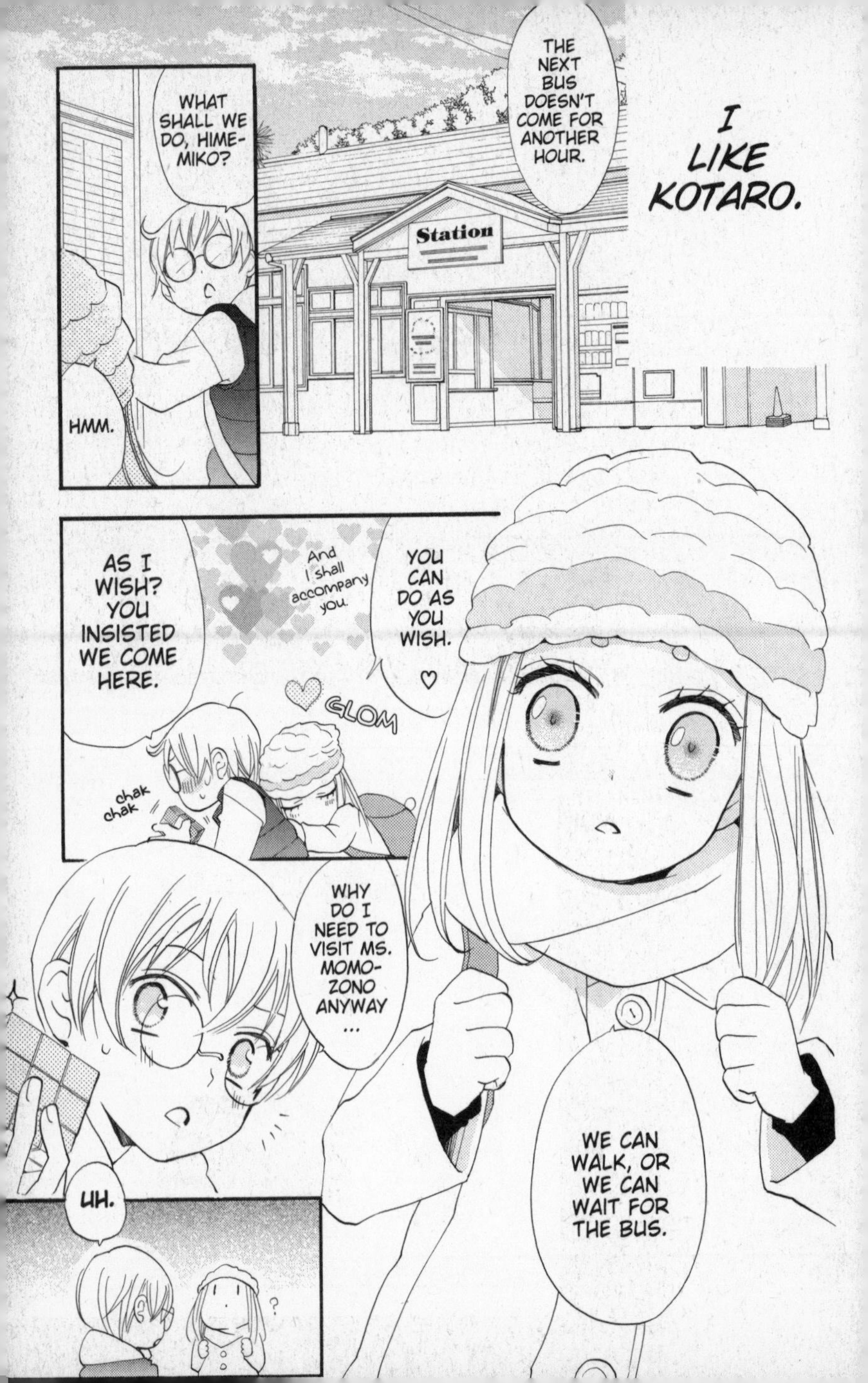
I LIKE KOTARO.
THE NEXT BUS DOESN'T COME FOR ANOTHER HOUR.
Station
WHAT SHALL WE DO, HIME-MIKO?
HMM.
WE CAN WALK, OR WE CAN WAIT FOR THE BUS.
YOU CAN DO AS YOU WISH. ♡
And I shall accompany you.
GLOM
AS I WISH? YOU INSISTED WE COME HERE.
chak chak
WHY DO I NEED TO VISIT MS. MOMO-ZONO ANYWAY ...
UH.
?

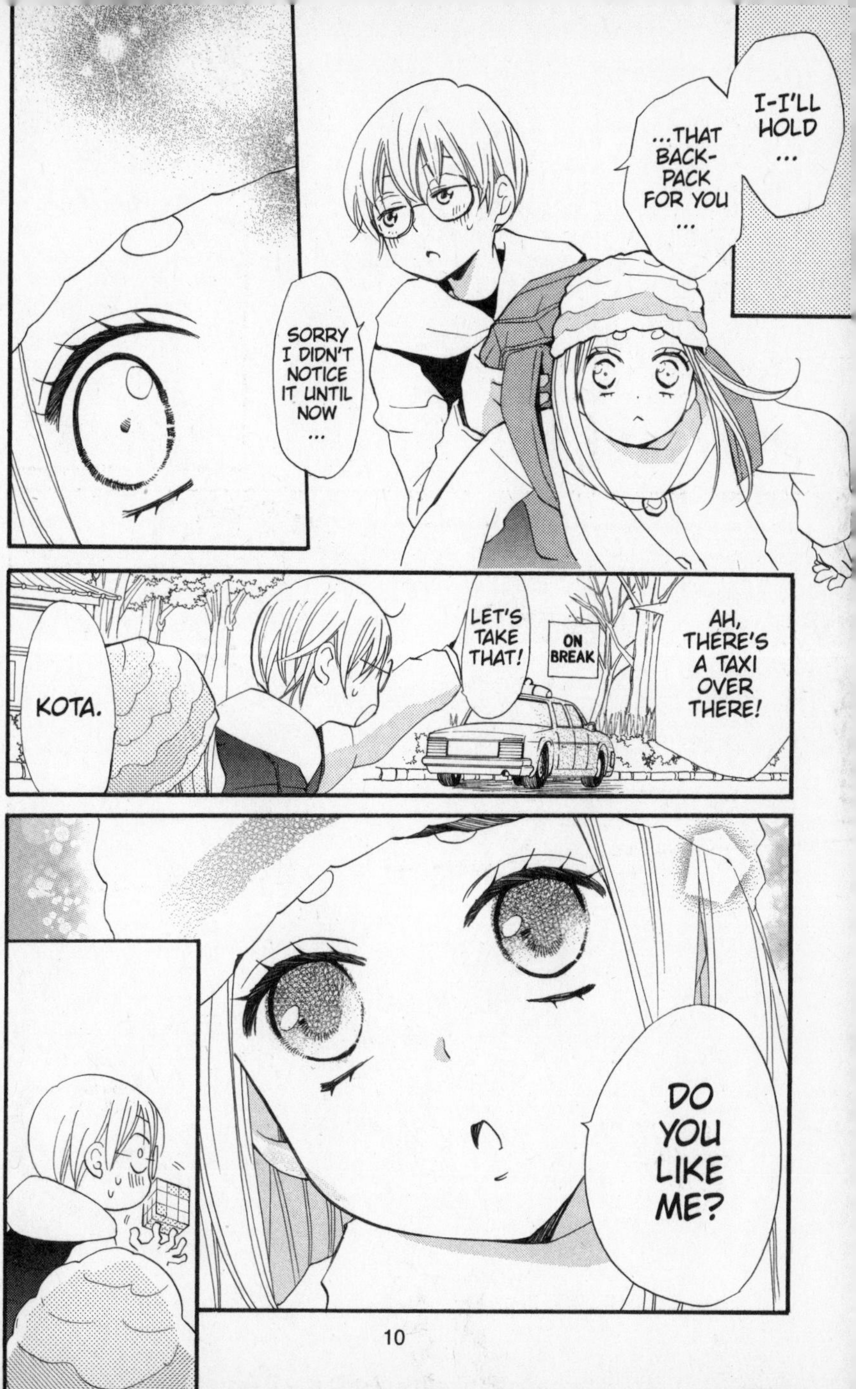
I-I'LL HOLD ...
...THAT BACK-PACK FOR YOU ...
SORRY I DIDN'T NOTICE IT UNTIL NOW ...
AH, THERE'S A TAXI OVER THERE!
ON BREAK
LET'S TAKE THAT!
KOTA.
DO YOU LIKE ME?

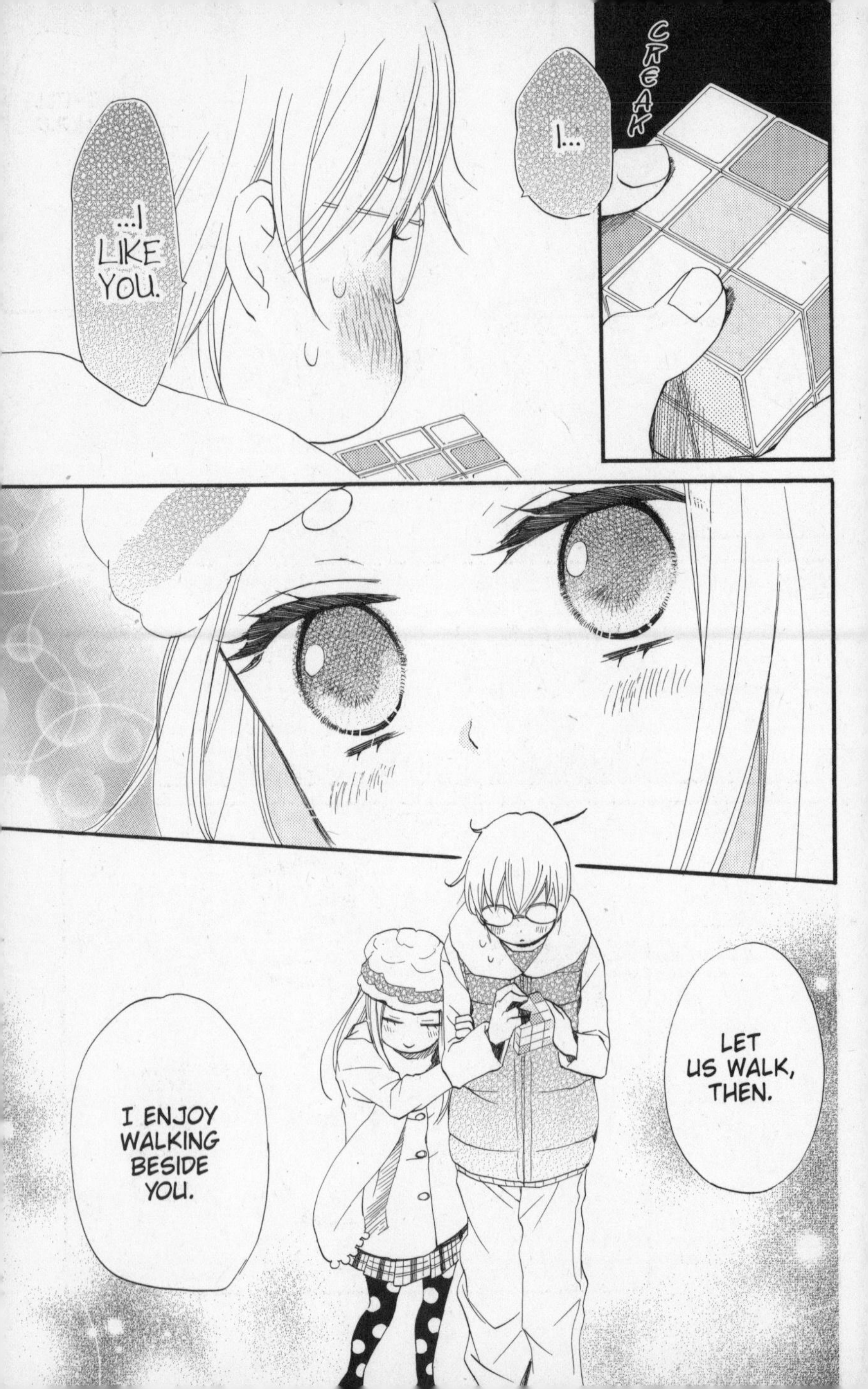
CREAK
I...
...I LIKE YOU.
LET US WALK, THEN.
I ENJOY WALKING BESIDE YOU.

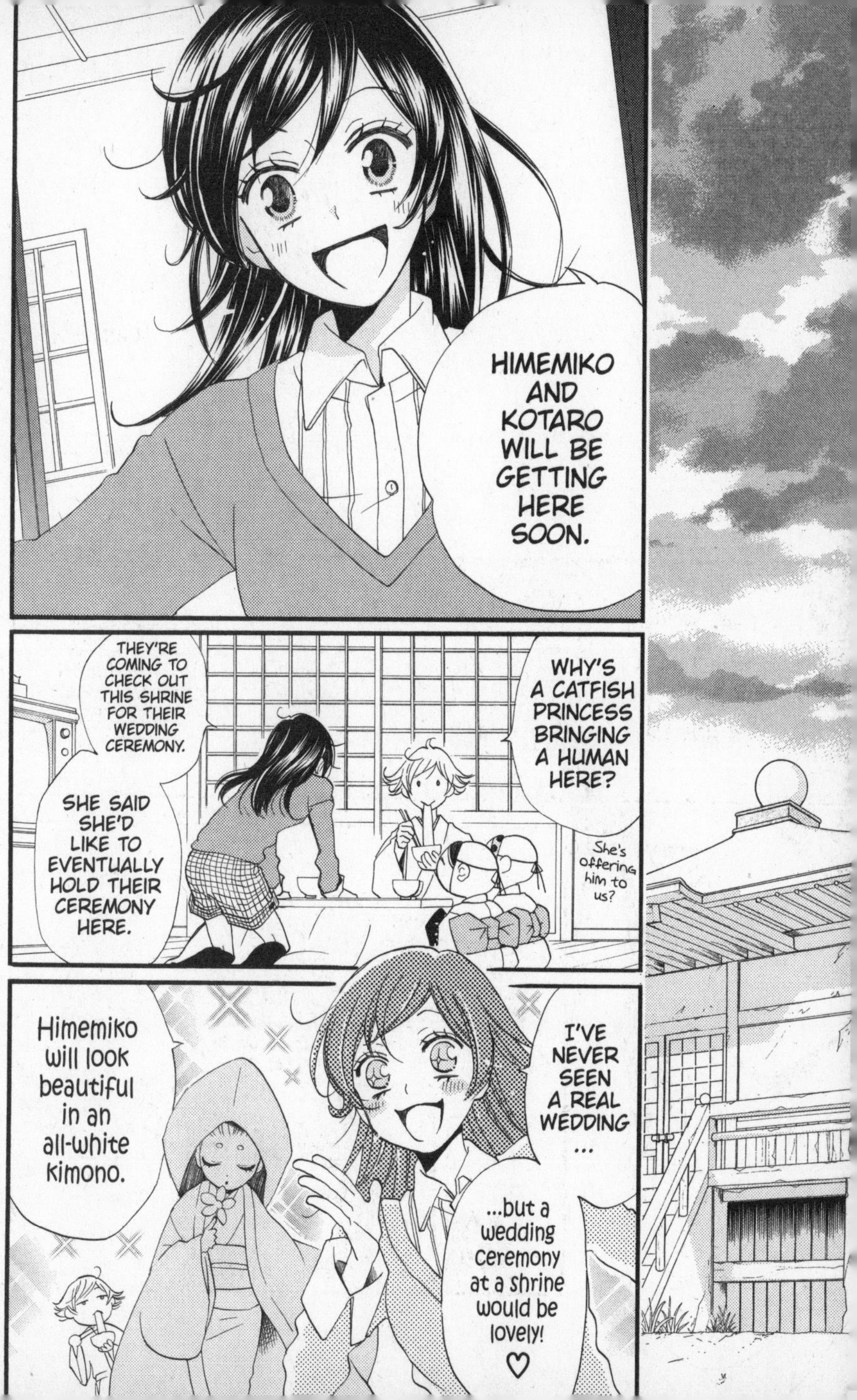
HIMEMIKO AND KOTARO WILL BE GETTING HERE SOON.
WHY'S A CATFISH PRINCESS BRINGING A HUMAN HERE?
THEY'RE COMING TO CHECK OUT THIS SHRINE FOR THEIR WEDDING CEREMONY.
SHE SAID SHE'D LIKE TO EVENTUALLY HOLD THEIR CEREMONY HERE.
She's offering him to us?
I'VE NEVER SEEN A REAL WEDDING...
...but a wedding ceremony at a shrine would be lovely! ♡
Himemiko will look beautiful in an all-white kimono.

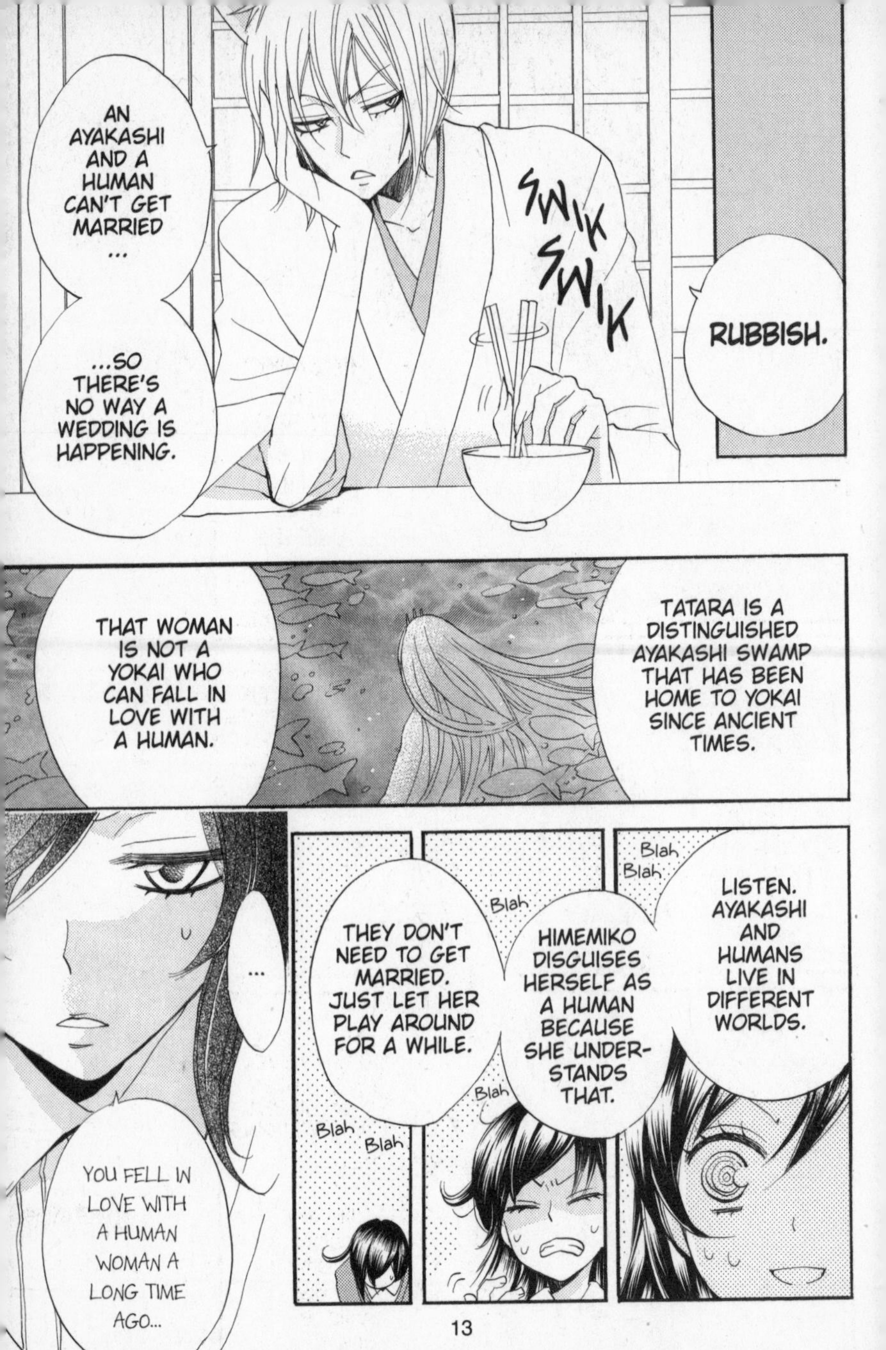
RUBBISH.
SWIK SWIK
AN AYAKASHI AND A HUMAN CAN'T GET MARRIED...
...SO THERE'S NO WAY A WEDDING IS HAPPENING.
TATARA IS A DISTINGUISHED AYAKASHI SWAMP THAT HAS BEEN HOME TO YOKAI SINCE ANCIENT TIMES.
THAT WOMAN IS NOT A YOKAI WHO CAN FALL IN LOVE WITH A HUMAN.
Blah Blah
LISTEN. AYAKASHI AND HUMANS LIVE IN DIFFERENT WORLDS.
Blah
HIMEMIKO DISGUISES HERSELF AS A HUMAN BECAUSE SHE UNDER-STANDS THAT.
Blah
THEY DON'T NEED TO GET MARRIED. JUST LET HER PLAY AROUND FOR A WHILE.
Blah Blah
...
YOU FELL IN LOVE WITH A HUMAN WOMAN A LONG TIME AGO...

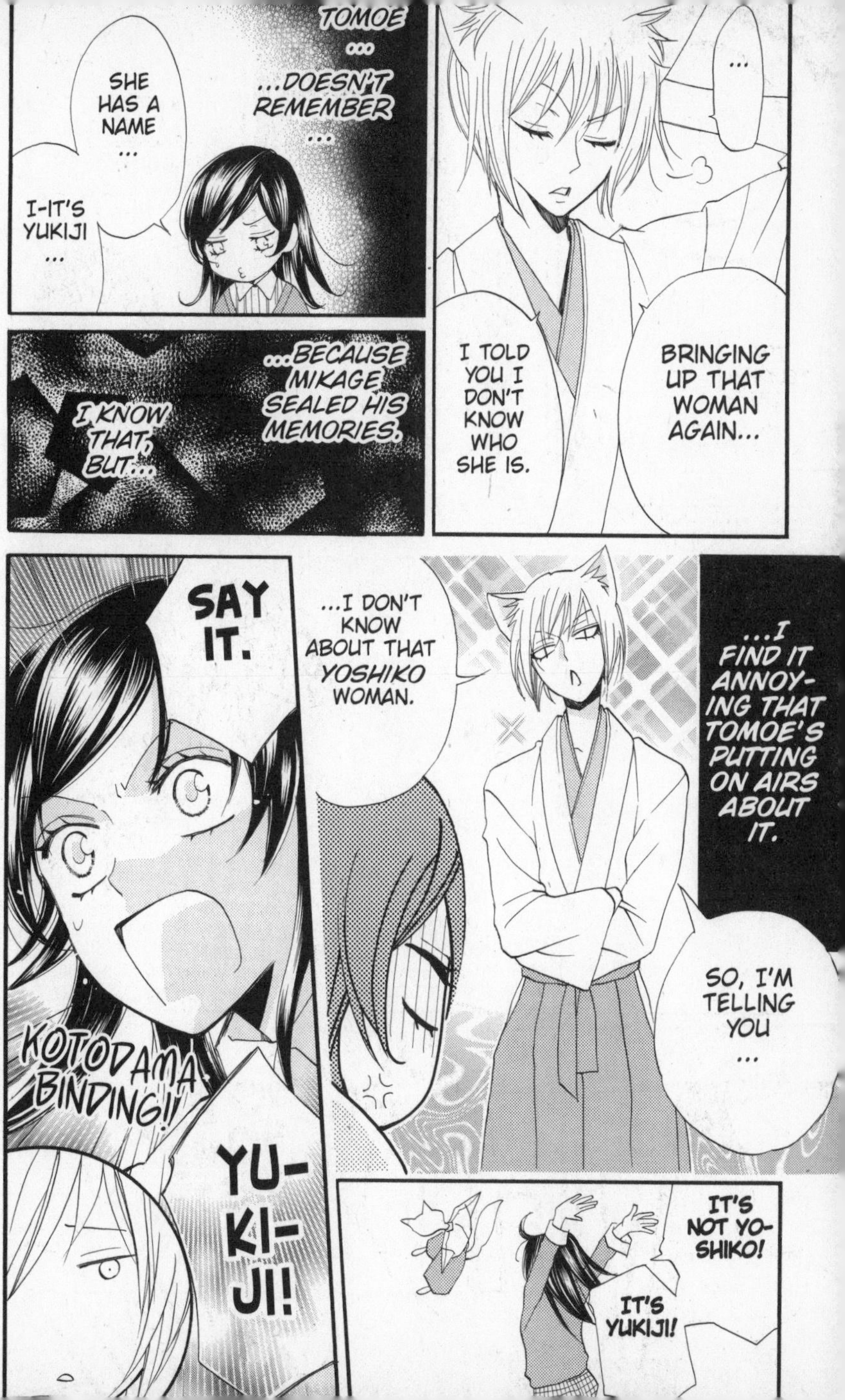
...
BRINGING UP THAT WOMAN AGAIN...
I TOLD YOU I DON'T KNOW WHO SHE IS.
TOMOE ... ...DOESN'T REMEMBER ...
SHE HAS A NAME ...
I-IT'S YUKIJI ...
...BECAUSE MIKAGE SEALED HIS MEMORIES.
I KNOW THAT, BUT...
...I FIND IT ANNOYING THAT TOMOE'S PUTTING ON AIRS ABOUT IT.
...I DON'T KNOW ABOUT THAT YOSHIKO WOMAN.
SO, I'M TELLING YOU ...
IT'S NOT YO-SHIKO!
IT'S YUKIJI!
SAY IT.
KOTODAMA BINDING!!
YU-KI-JI!

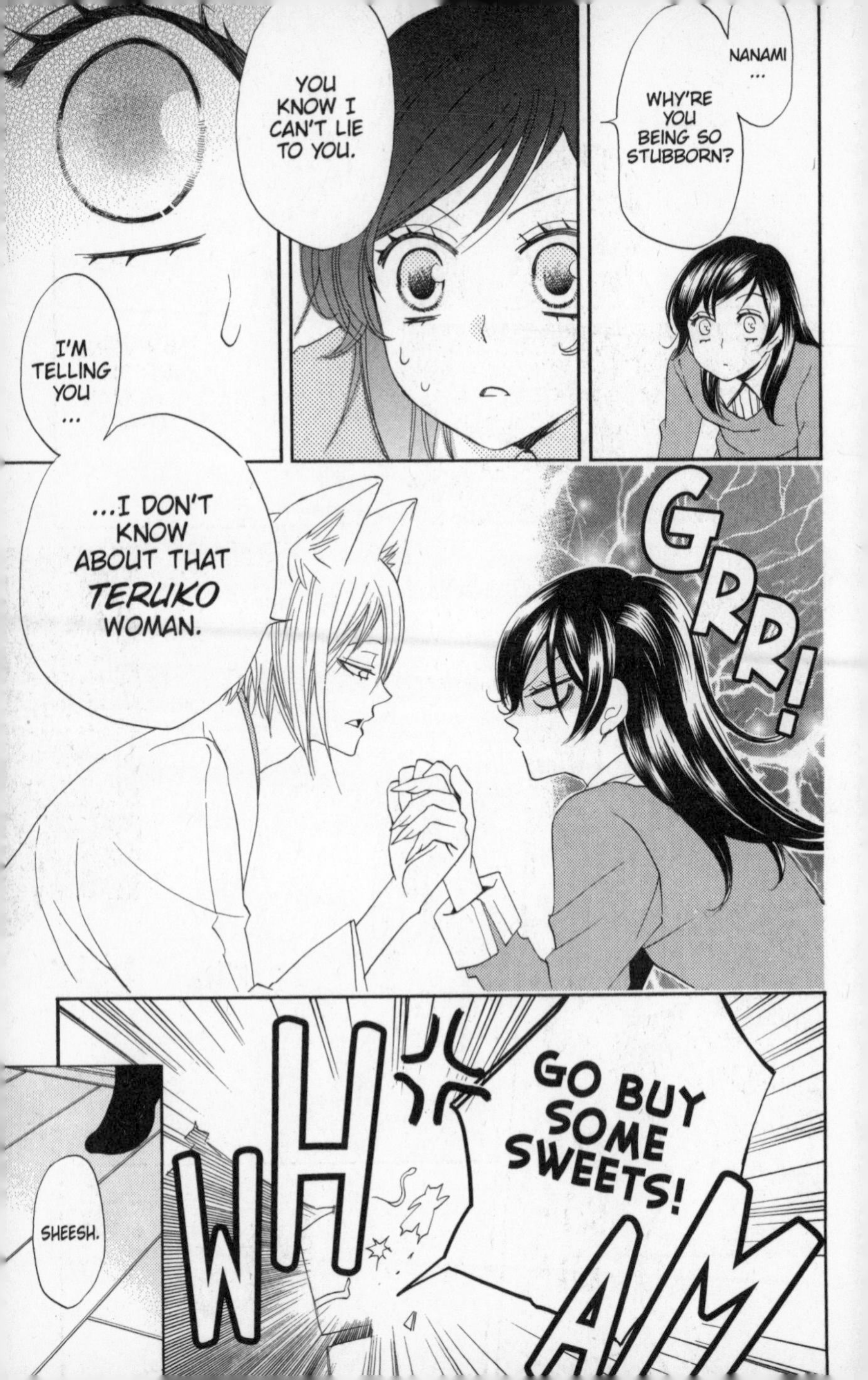
NANAMI...
WHY'RE YOU BEING SO STUBBORN?
YOU KNOW I CAN'T LIE TO YOU.
I'M TELLING YOU...
...I DON'T KNOW ABOUT THAT *TERUKO* WOMAN.
GRRR!
GO BUY SOME SWEETS!
WHAM
SHEESH.

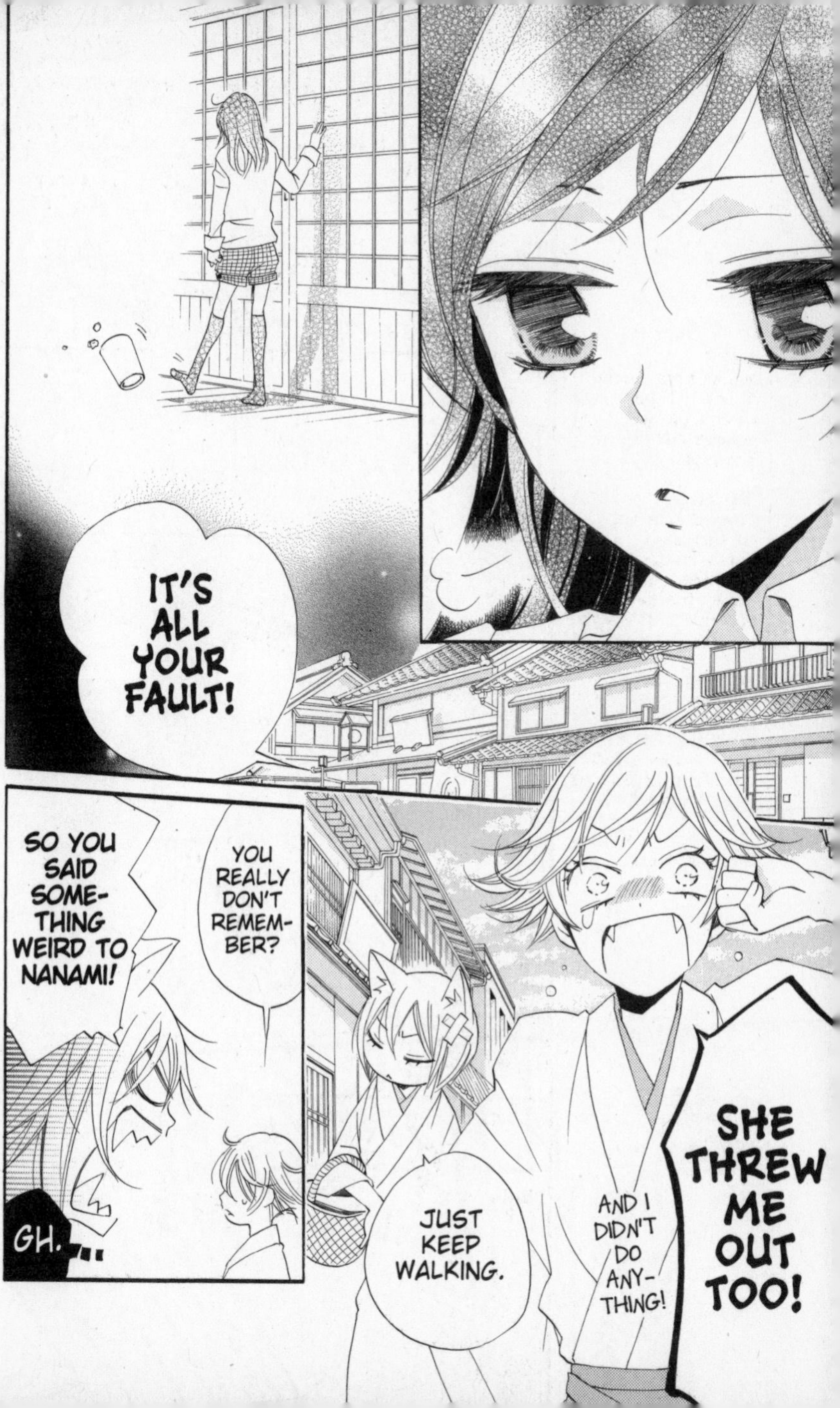
IT'S ALL YOUR FAULT!
SHE THREW ME OUT TOO!
AND I DIDN'T DO ANY-THING!
JUST KEEP WALKING.
YOU REALLY DON'T REMEM-BER?
SO YOU SAID SOME-THING WEIRD TO NANAMI!
GH....

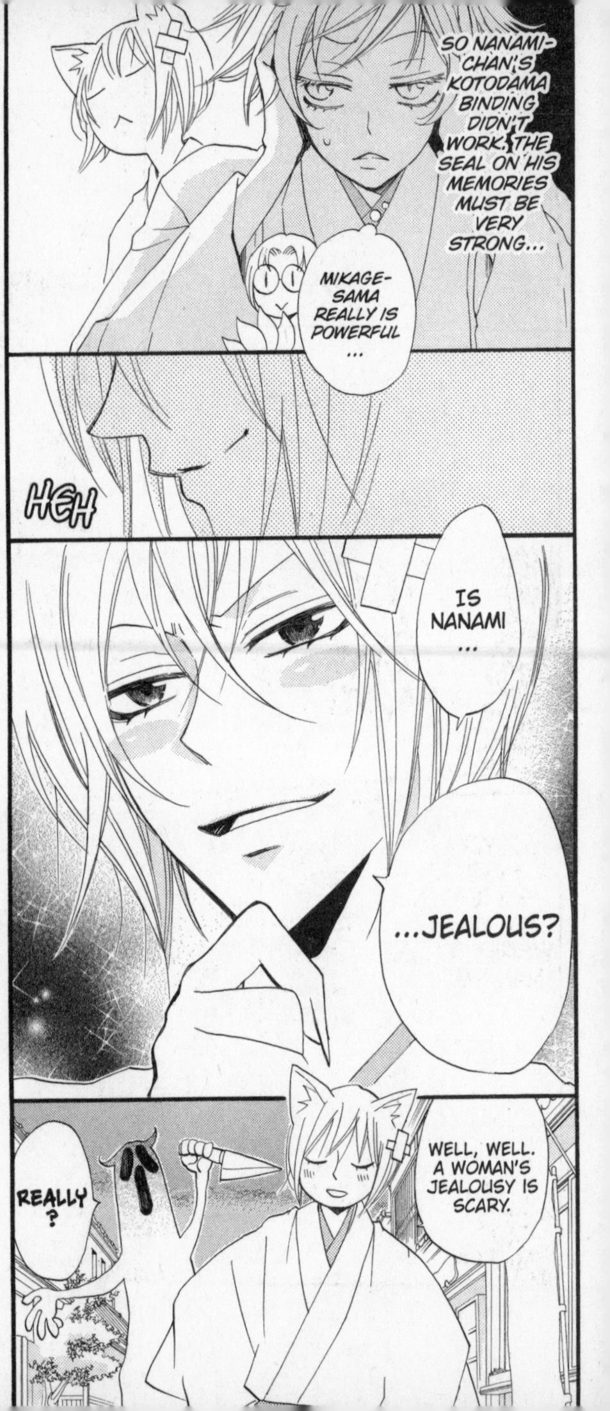
SO NANAMI-CHAN'S KOTODAMA BINDING DIDN'T WORK. THE SEAL ON HIS MEMORIES MUST BE VERY STRONG...
MIKAGE-SAMA REALLY IS POWERFUL ...
HEH
IS NANAMI ...
...JEALOUS?
WELL, WELL. A WOMAN'S JEALOUSY IS SCARY.
REALLY ?

Hello!
I'm Julietta Suzuki.
Thank you for picking up this volume of Kamisama Kiss!

This is the twelfth volume of Kamisama. This is the Himemiko arc I've had in the back of my mind. I hope you enjoy reading it.

And the Ryu-oh who hasn't been around in a long while (?) appears. If you're wondering who he is, please read volume four. ☺

See you later!

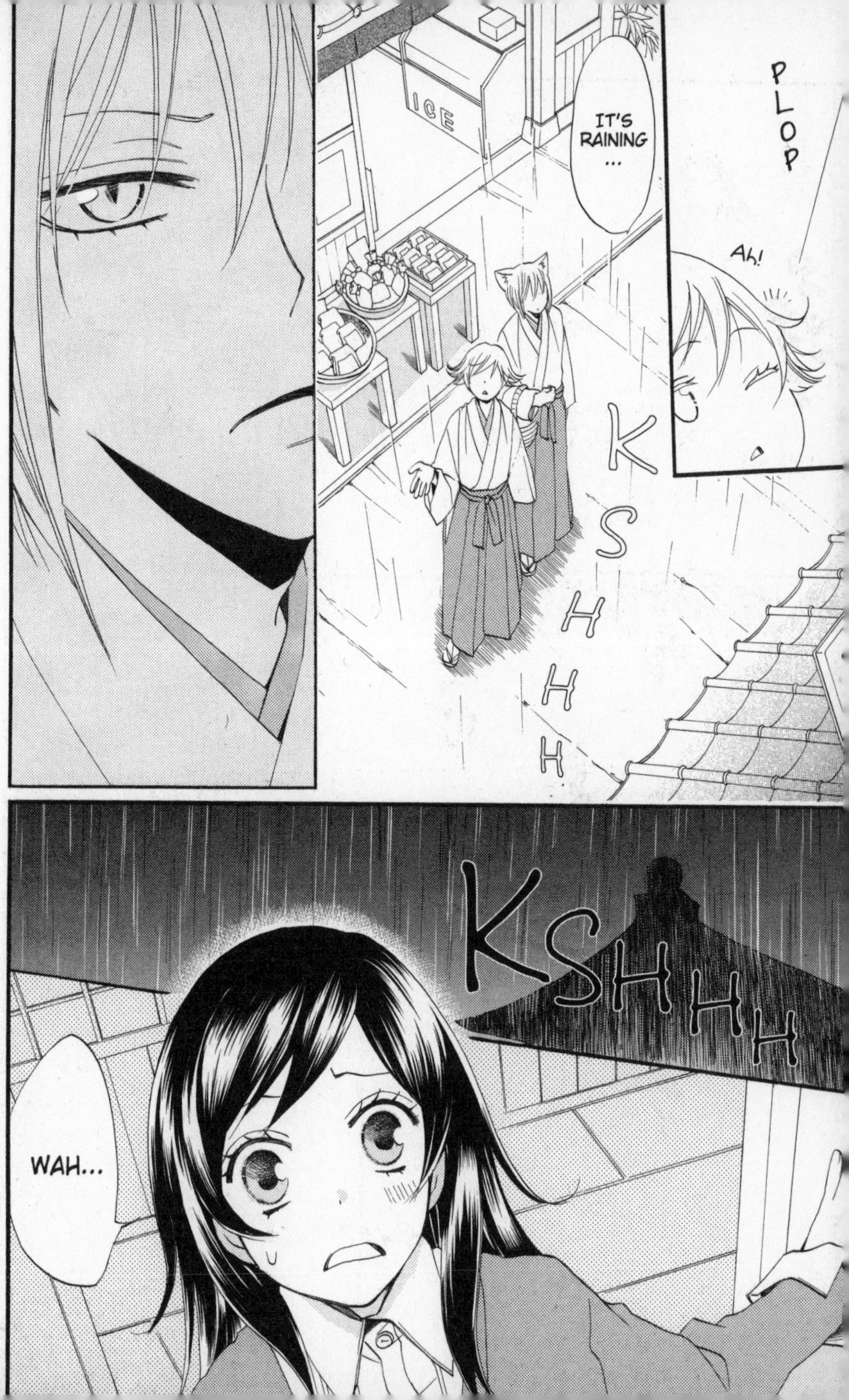
PLOP
Ah!
IT'S RAINING ...
KSHHHH
KSHHH
WAH...

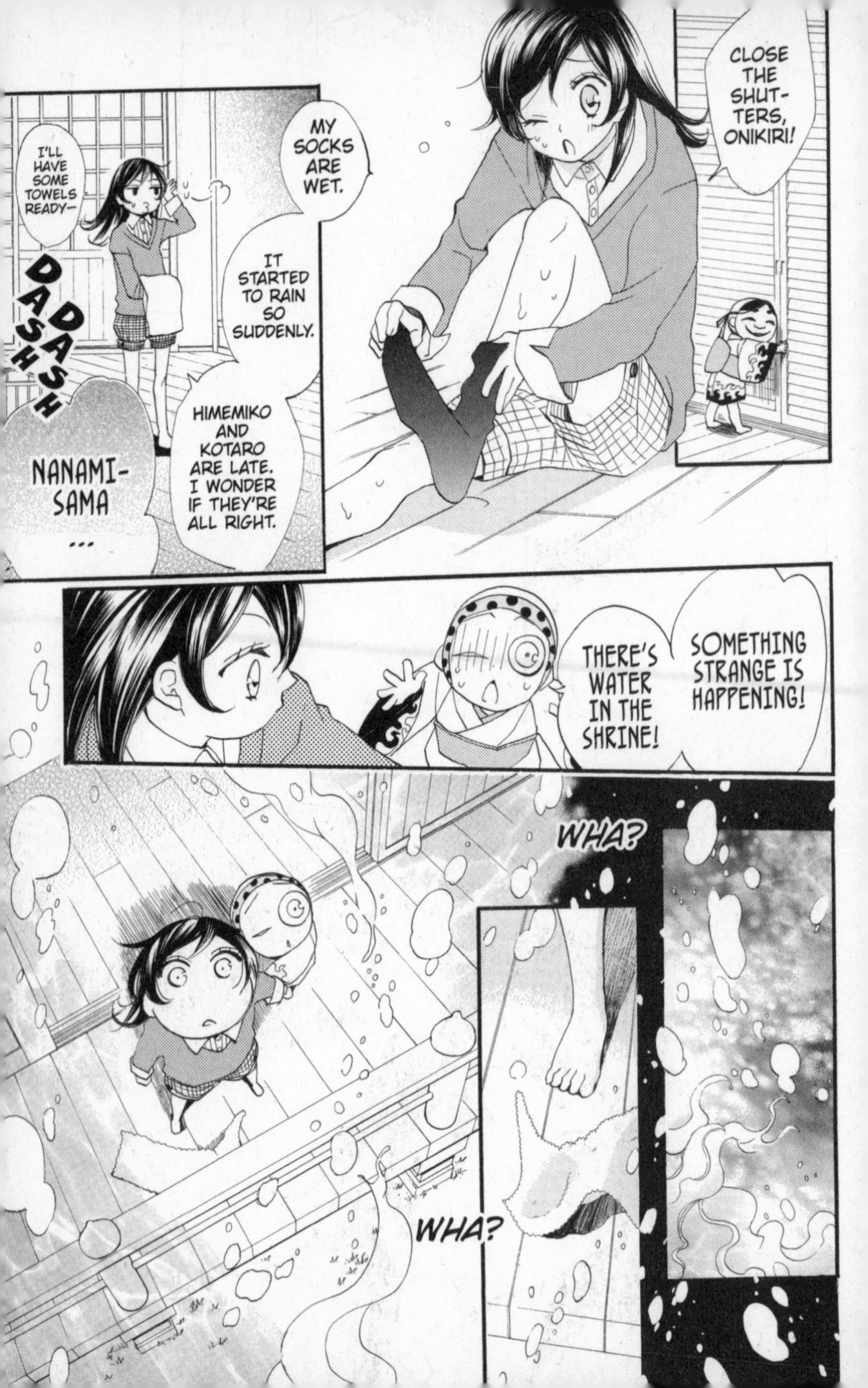
CLOSE THE SHUTTERS, ONIKIRI!
MY SOCKS ARE WET.
IT STARTED TO RAIN SO SUDDENLY.
HIMEMIKO AND KOTARO ARE LATE. I WONDER IF THEY'RE ALL RIGHT.
I'LL HAVE SOME TOWELS READY—
DASH DASH
NANAMI-SAMA ...
SOMETHING STRANGE IS HAPPENING!
THERE'S WATER IN THE SHRINE!
WHA?
WHA?

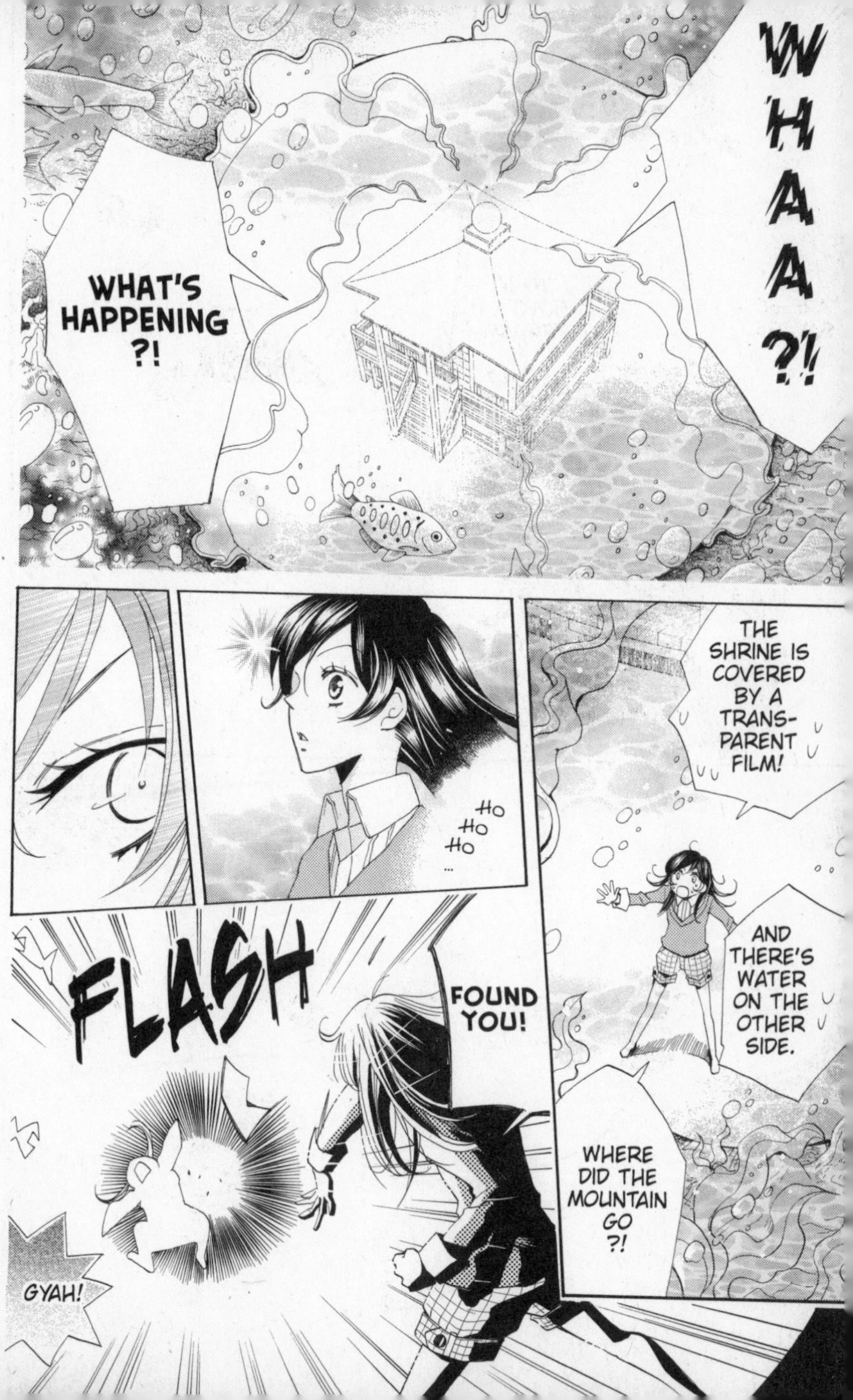
WHAA?!
WHAT'S HAPPENING?!
THE SHRINE IS COVERED BY A TRANSPARENT FILM!
AND THERE'S WATER ON THE OTHER SIDE.
WHERE DID THE MOUNTAIN GO?!
HO HO HO ...
FOUND YOU!
FLASH
GYAH!

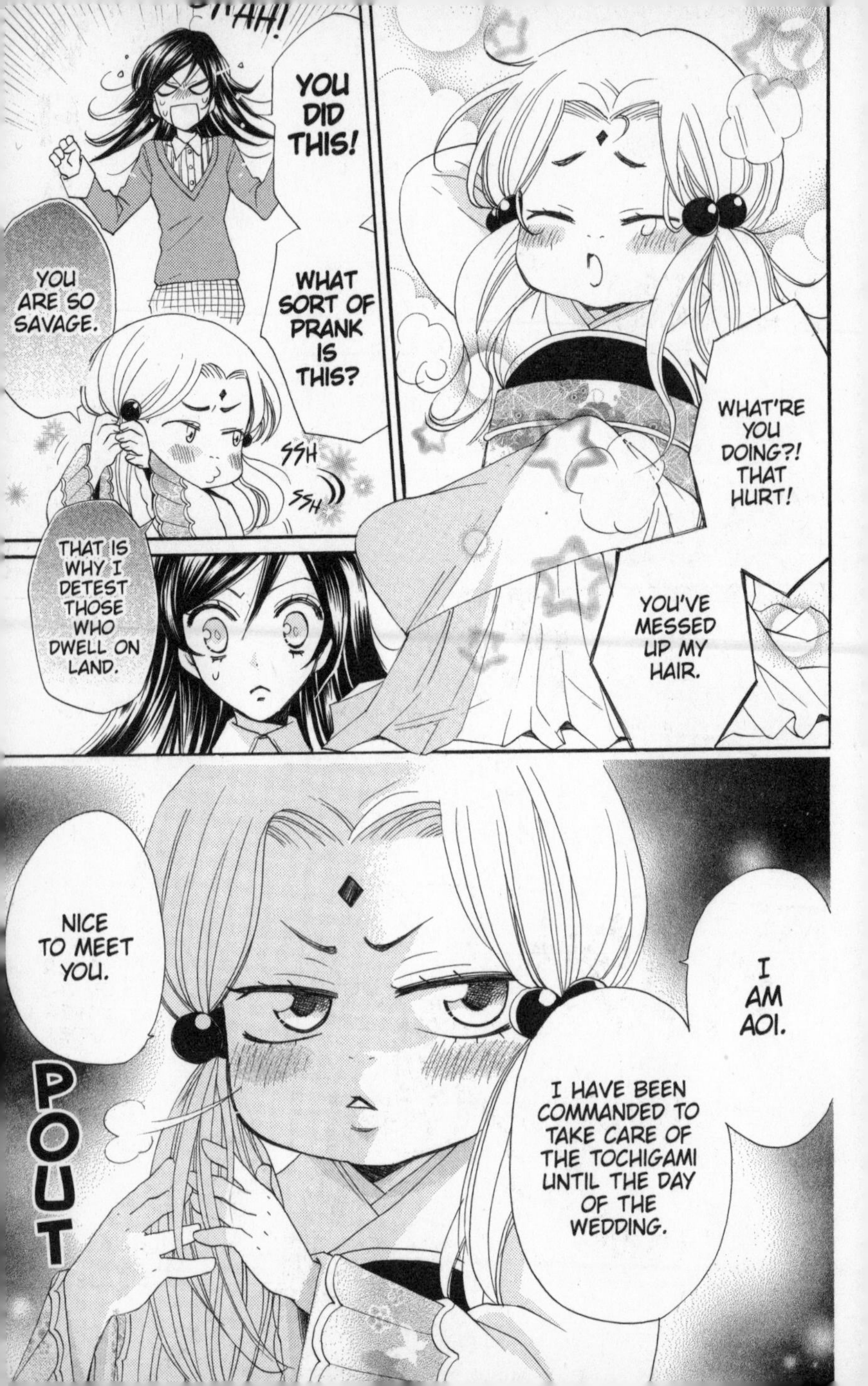
WHAT'RE YOU DOING?! THAT HURT!
YOU'VE MESSED UP MY HAIR.
YOU DID THIS!
WHAT SORT OF PRANK IS THIS?
YOU ARE SO SAVAGE.
SSH
SSH
THAT IS WHY I DETEST THOSE WHO DWELL ON LAND.
I AM AOI.
I HAVE BEEN COMMANDED TO TAKE CARE OF THE TOCHIGAMI UNTIL THE DAY OF THE WEDDING.
NICE TO MEET YOU.
POUT

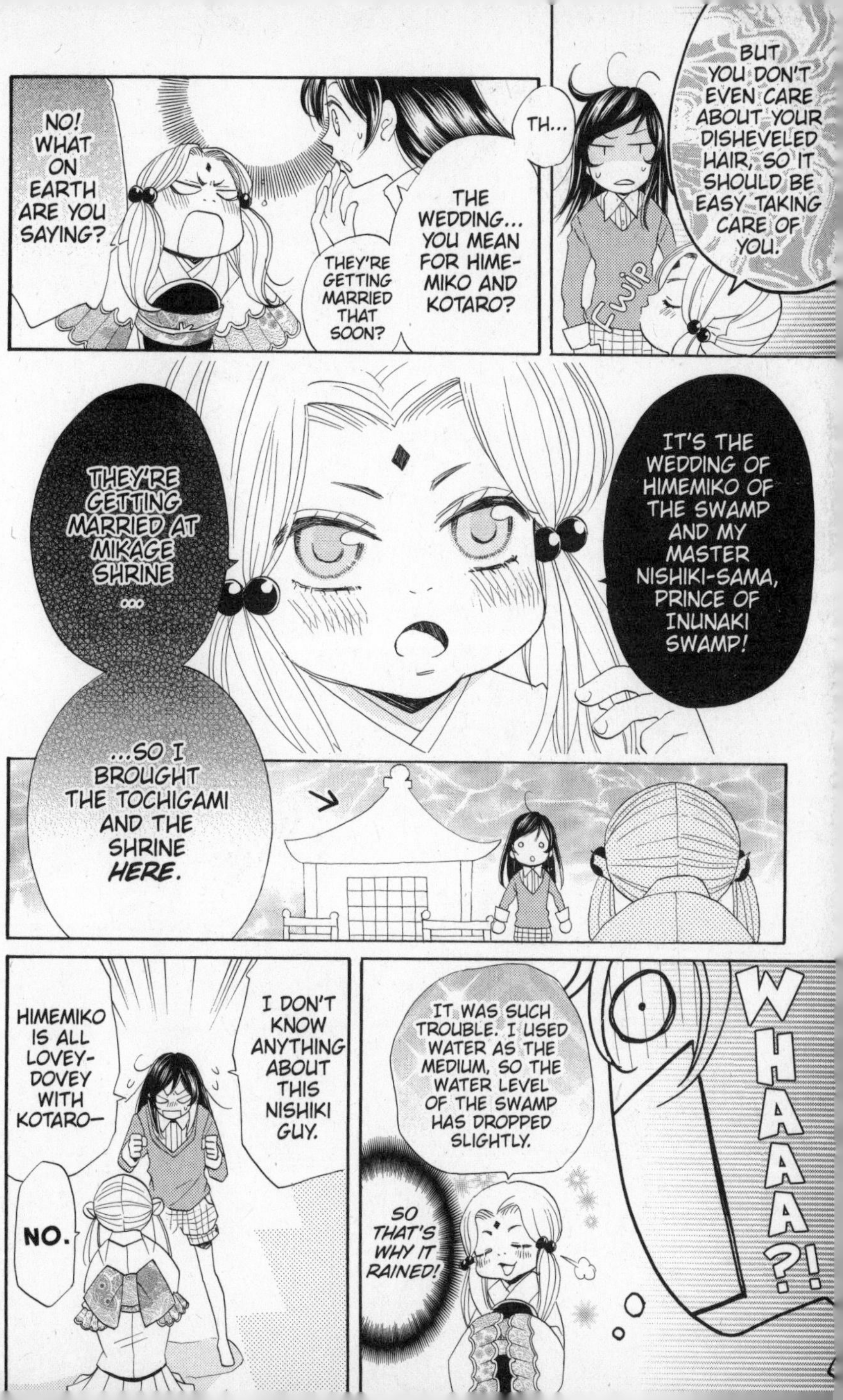
BUT YOU DON'T EVEN CARE ABOUT YOUR DISHEVELED HAIR, SO IT SHOULD BE EASY TAKING CARE OF YOU.
Fwip
TH...
THE WEDDING... YOU MEAN FOR HIME-MIKO AND KOTARO?
THEY'RE GETTING MARRIED THAT SOON?
NO! WHAT ON EARTH ARE YOU SAYING?
IT'S THE WEDDING OF HIMEMIKO OF THE SWAMP AND MY MASTER NISHIKI-SAMA, PRINCE OF INUNAKI SWAMP!
THEY'RE GETTING MARRIED AT MIKAGE SHRINE...
...SO I BROUGHT THE TOCHIGAMI AND THE SHRINE HERE.
WHAAAA?!
IT WAS SUCH TROUBLE. I USED WATER AS THE MEDIUM, SO THE WATER LEVEL OF THE SWAMP HAS DROPPED SLIGHTLY.
SO THAT'S WHY IT RAINED!
I DON'T KNOW ANYTHING ABOUT THIS NISHIKI GUY.
HIMEMIKO IS ALL LOVEY-DOVEY WITH KOTARO—
NO.

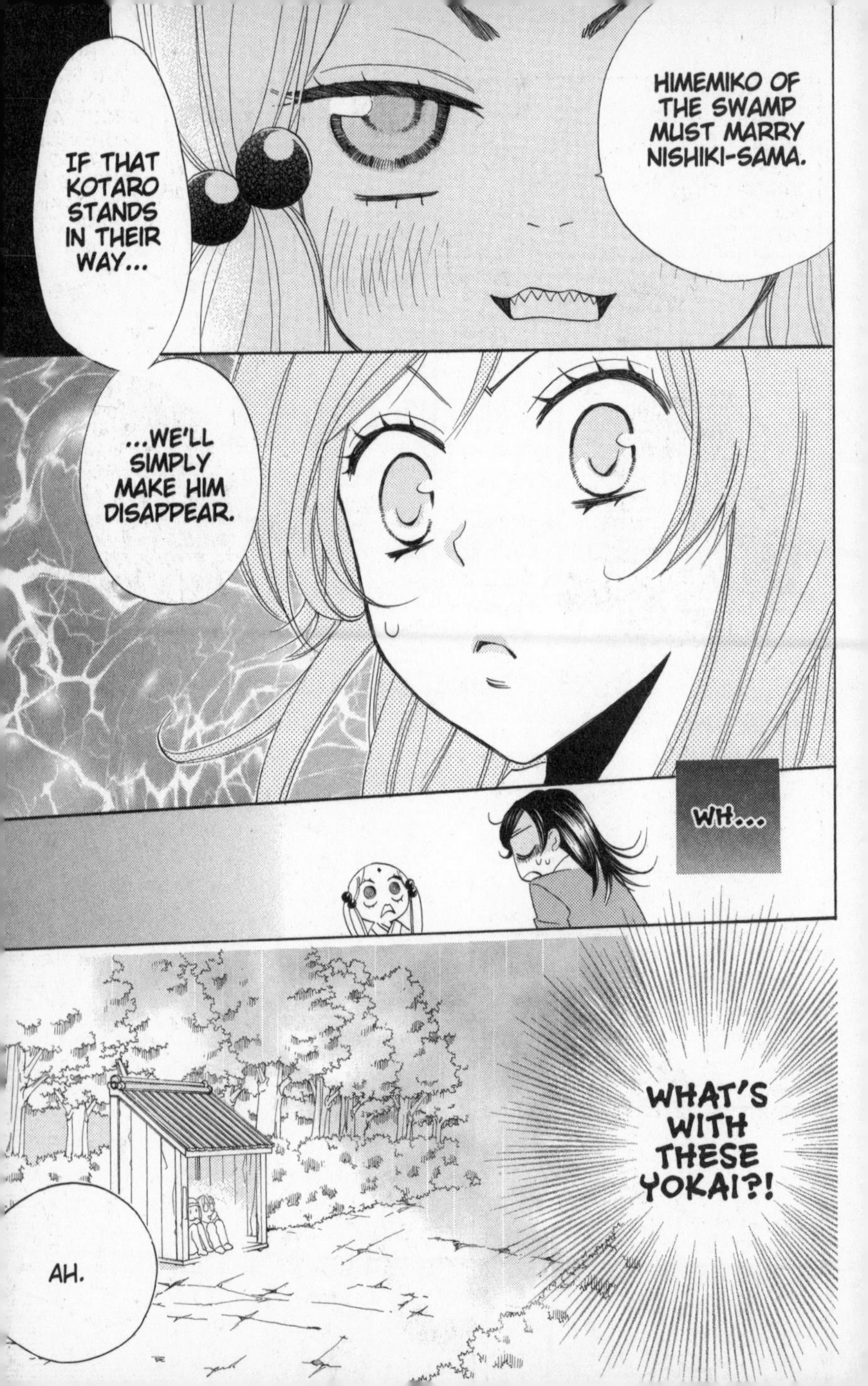
HIMEMIKO OF THE SWAMP MUST MARRY NISHIKI-SAMA.
IF THAT KOTARO STANDS IN THEIR WAY...
...WE'LL SIMPLY MAKE HIM DISAPPEAR.
WH...
WHAT'S WITH THESE YOKAI?!
AH.

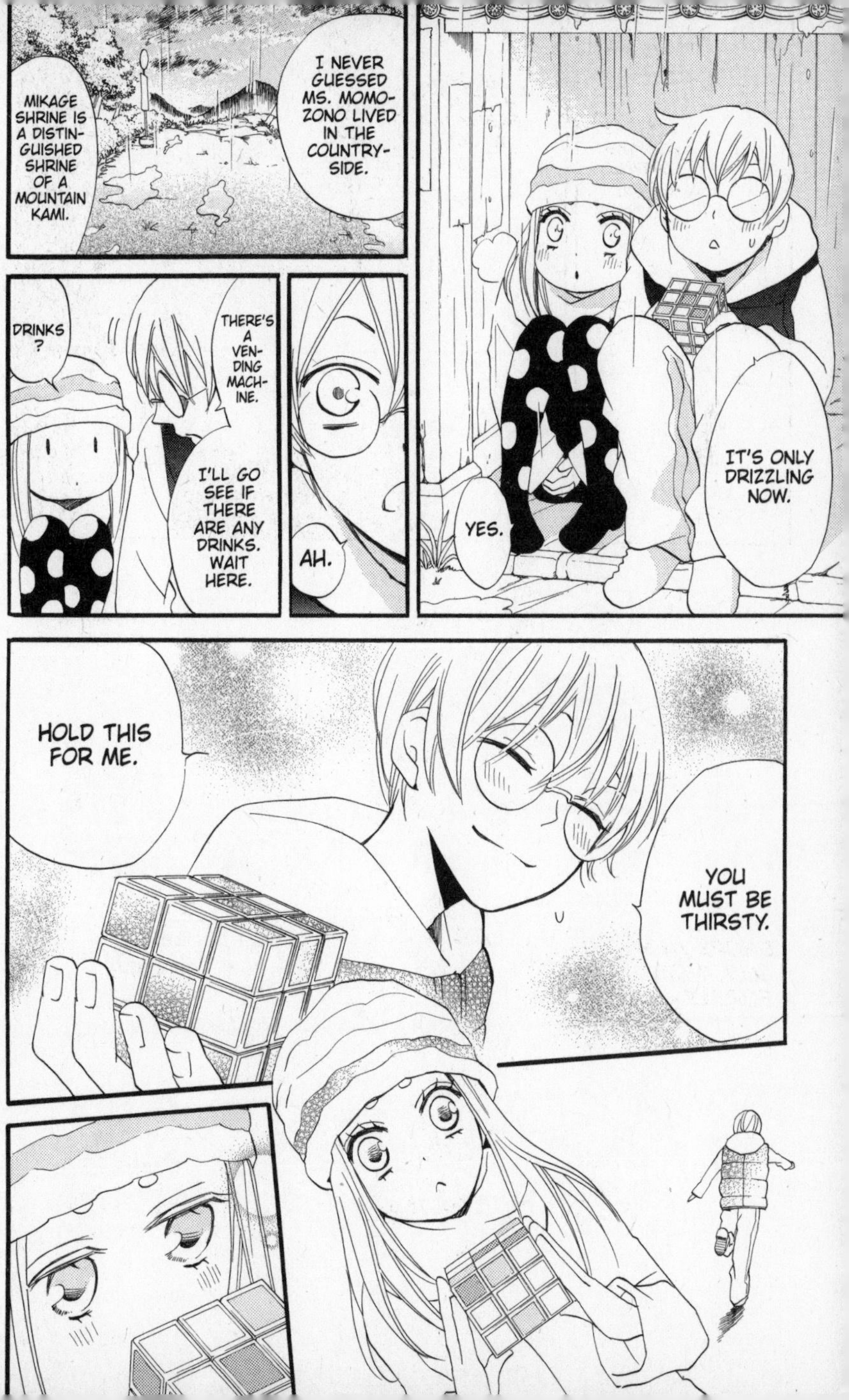
IT'S ONLY DRIZZLING NOW.
YES.
I NEVER GUESSED MS. MOMOZONO LIVED IN THE COUNTRYSIDE.
MIKAGE SHRINE IS A DISTINGUISHED SHRINE OF A MOUNTAIN KAMI.
AH.
THERE'S A VENDING MACHINE.
I'LL GO SEE IF THERE ARE ANY DRINKS. WAIT HERE.
DRINKS?
YOU MUST BE THIRSTY.
HOLD THIS FOR ME.

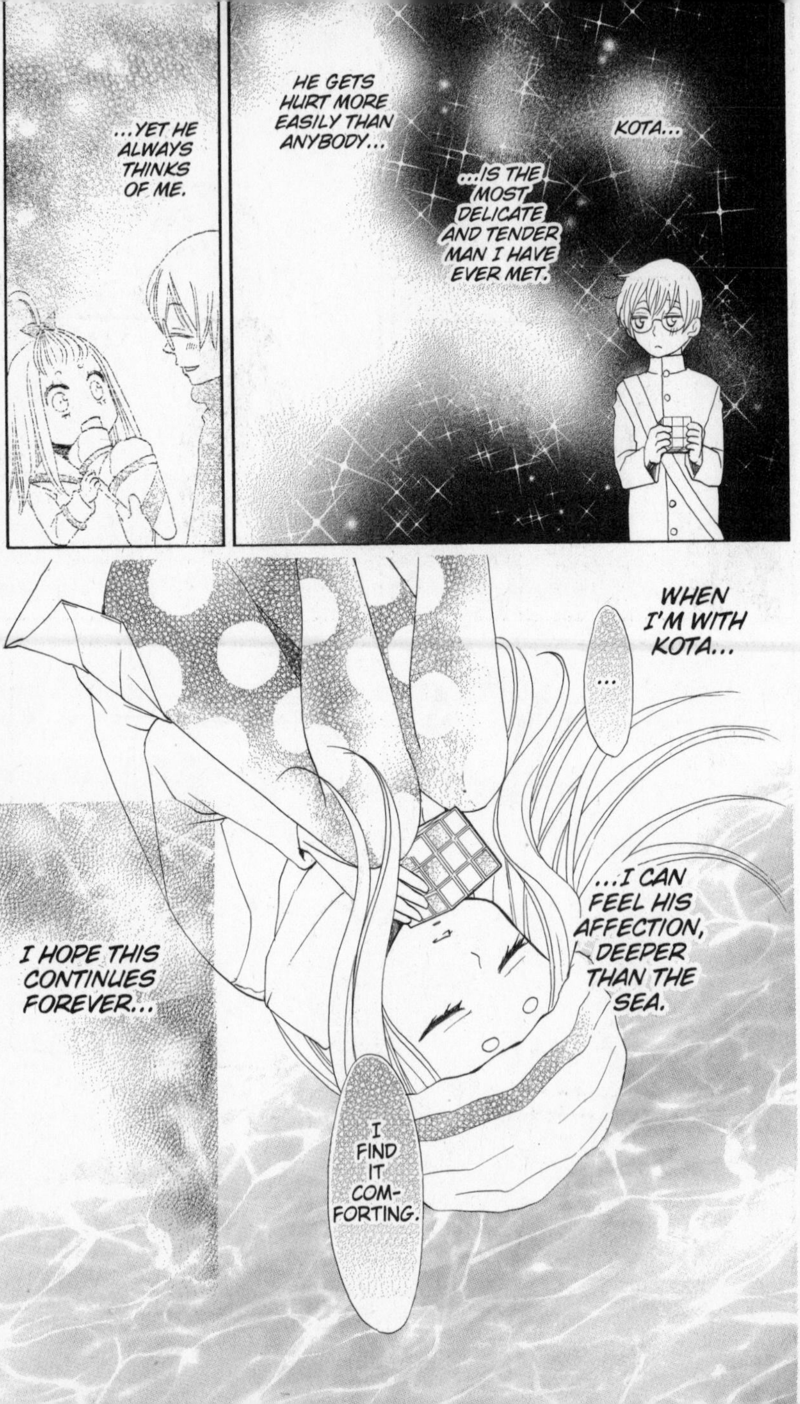
KOTA...
...IS THE MOST DELICATE AND TENDER MAN I HAVE EVER MET.
HE GETS HURT MORE EASILY THAN ANYBODY...
...YET HE ALWAYS THINKS OF ME.
WHEN I'M WITH KOTA...
...
...I CAN FEEL HIS AFFECTION, DEEPER THAN THE SEA.
I FIND IT COM-FORTING.
I HOPE THIS CONTINUES FOREVER...

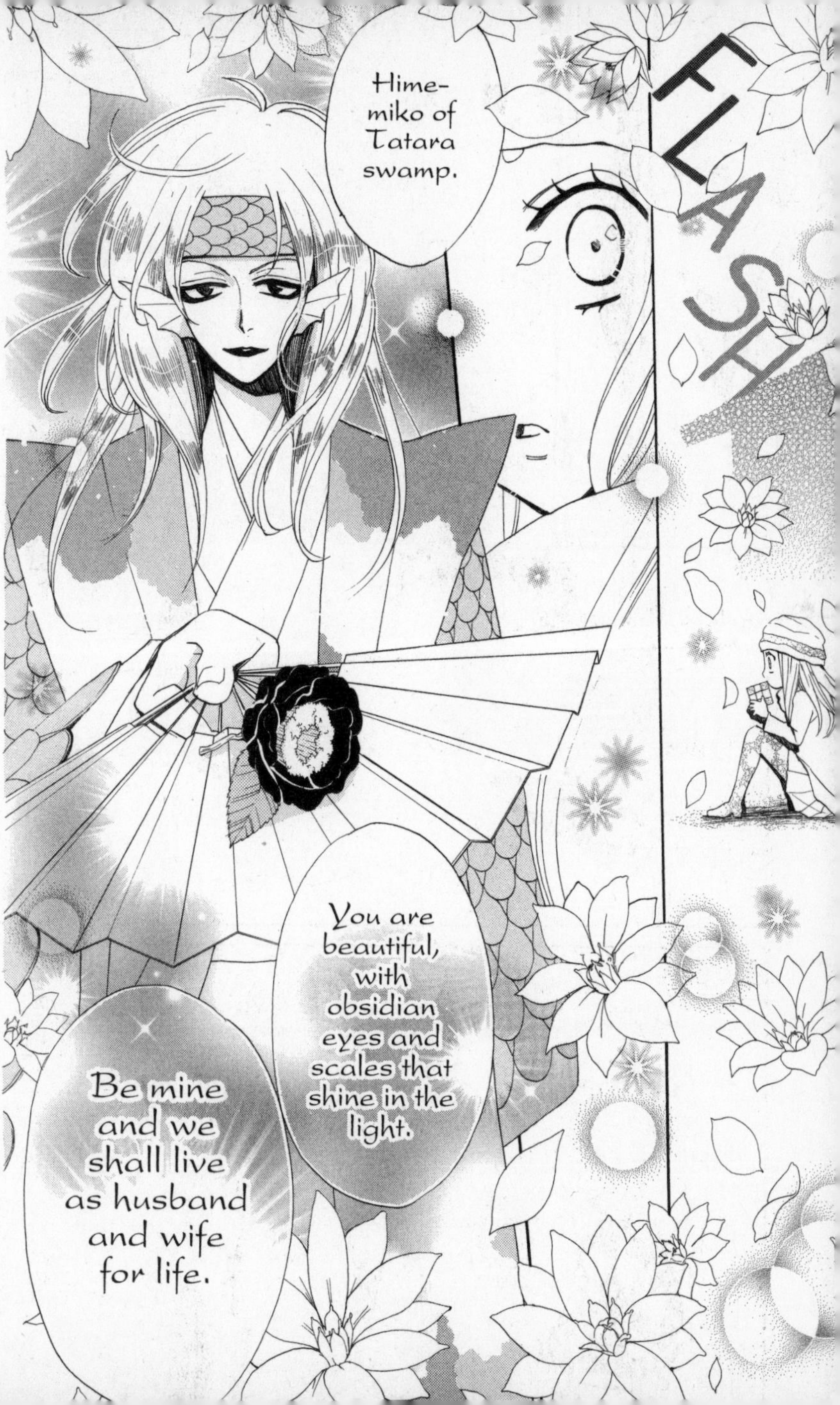
FLASH
Hime-miko of Tatara swamp.
You are beautiful, with obsidian eyes and scales that shine in the light.
Be mine and we shall live as husband and wife for life.

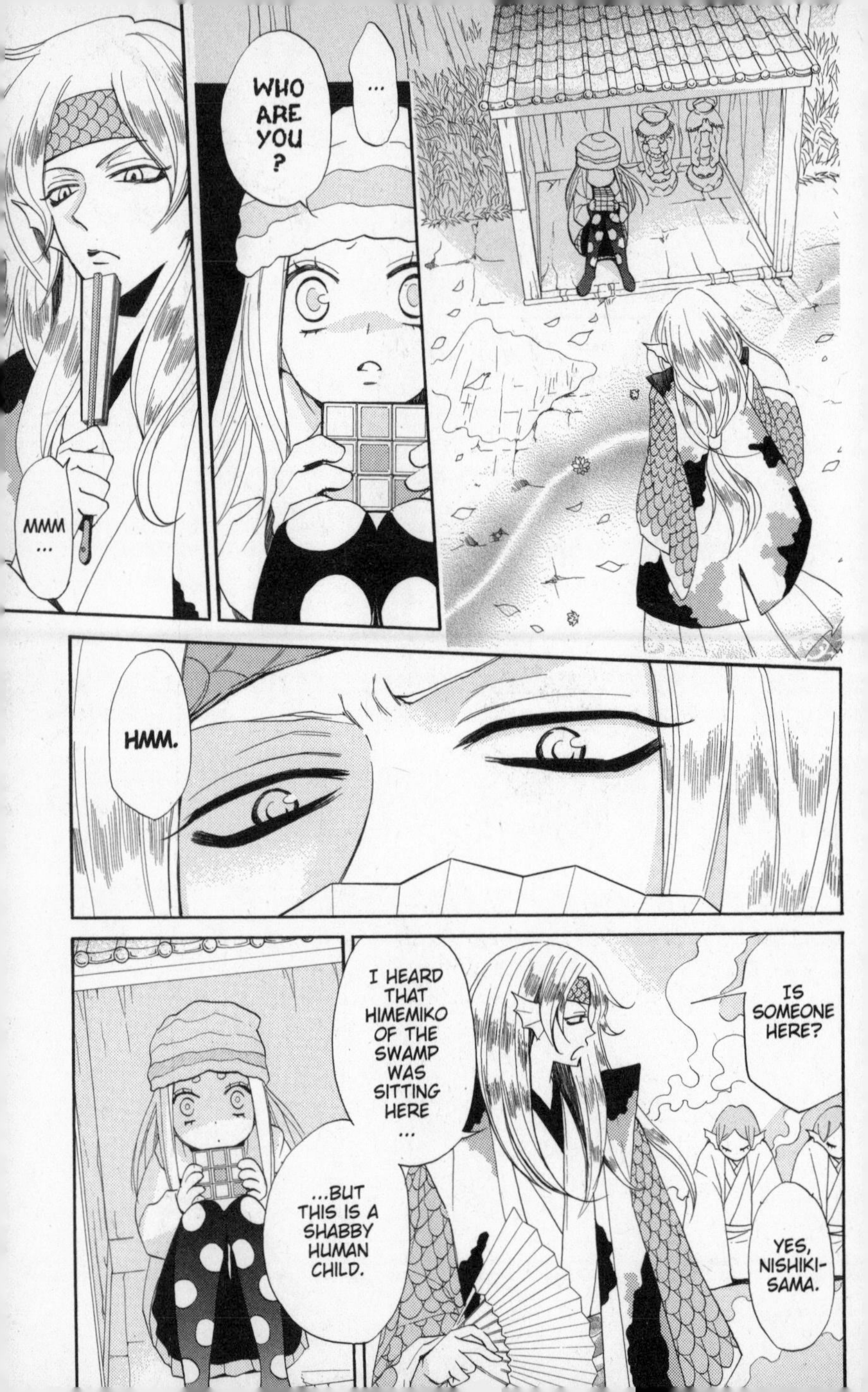
...
WHO ARE YOU?
MMM...
HMM.
IS SOMEONE HERE?
YES, NISHIKI-SAMA.
I HEARD THAT HIMEMIKO OF THE SWAMP WAS SITTING HERE...
...BUT THIS IS A SHABBY HUMAN CHILD.

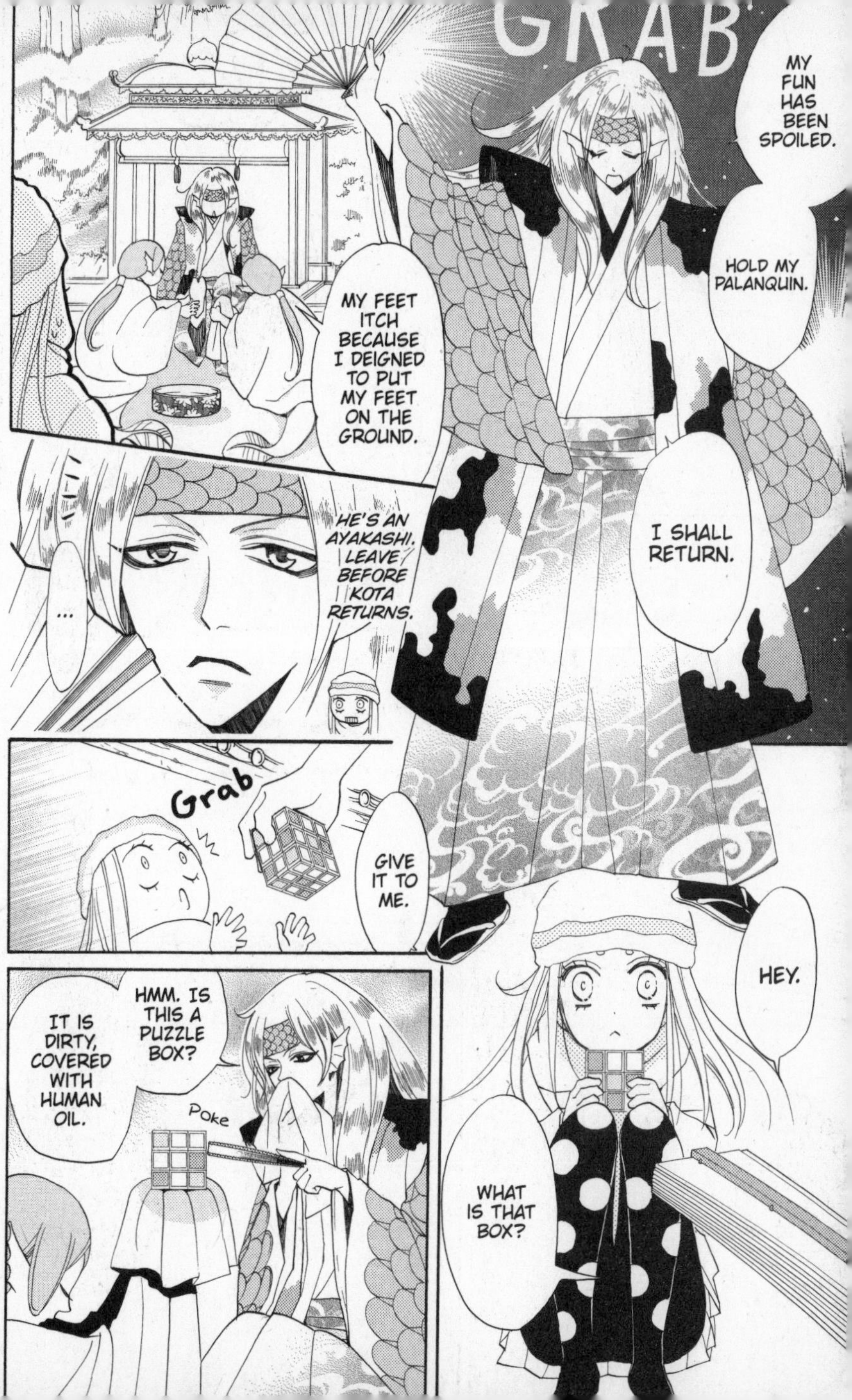
GRAB
MY FUN HAS BEEN SPOILED.
HOLD MY PALANQUIN.
MY FEET ITCH BECAUSE I DEIGNED TO PUT MY FEET ON THE GROUND.
I SHALL RETURN.
HE'S AN AYAKASHI. LEAVE BEFORE KOTA RETURNS.
...
HEY.
WHAT IS THAT BOX?
Grab
GIVE IT TO ME.
HMM. IS THIS A PUZZLE BOX?
IT IS DIRTY, COVERED WITH HUMAN OIL.
Poke

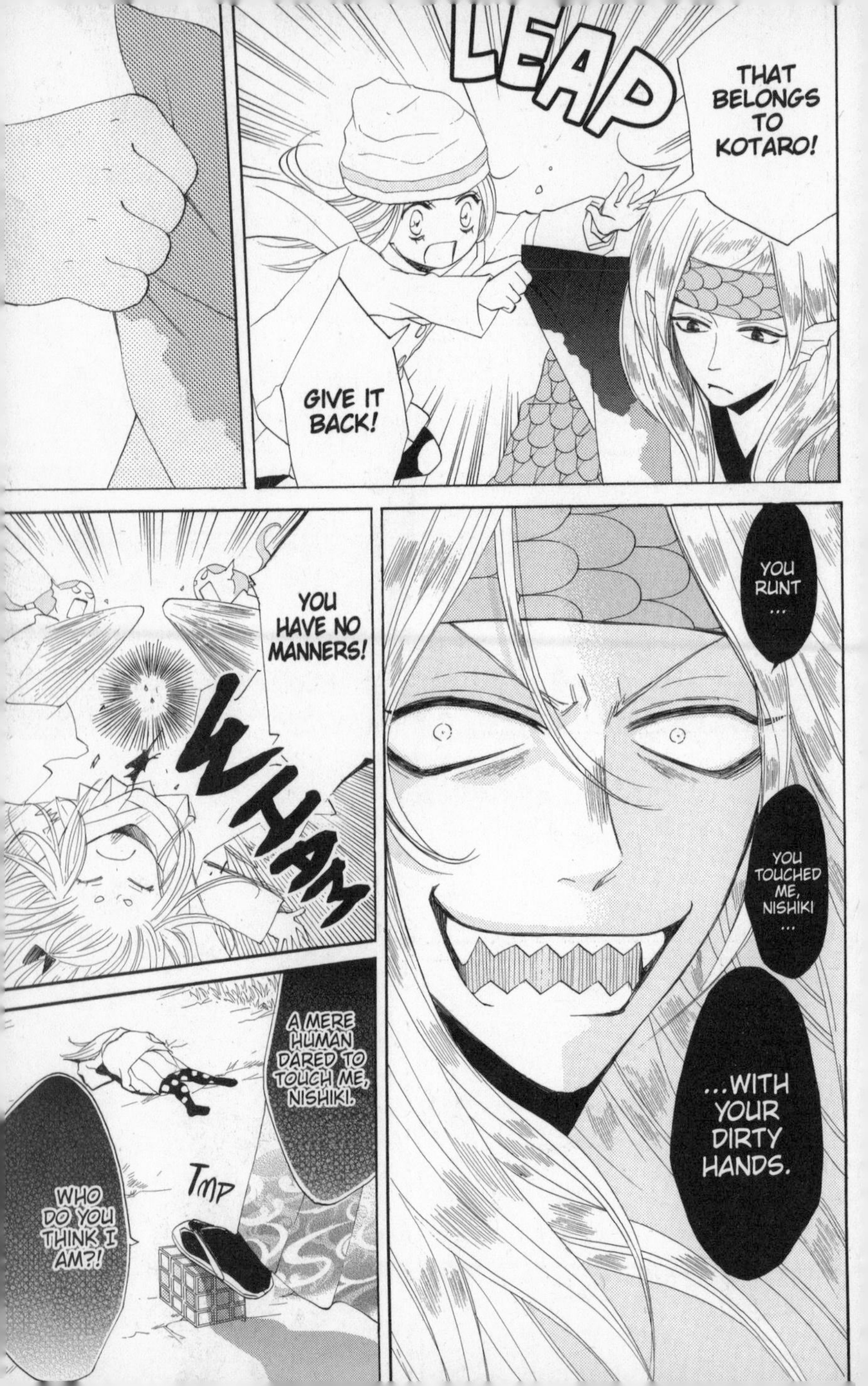
LEAP
THAT BELONGS TO KOTARO!
GIVE IT BACK!
YOU RUNT...
YOU TOUCHED ME, NISHIKI...
...WITH YOUR DIRTY HANDS.
YOU HAVE NO MANNERS!
WHAM
A MERE HUMAN DARED TO TOUCH ME, NISHIKI.
TMP
WHO DO YOU THINK I AM?!

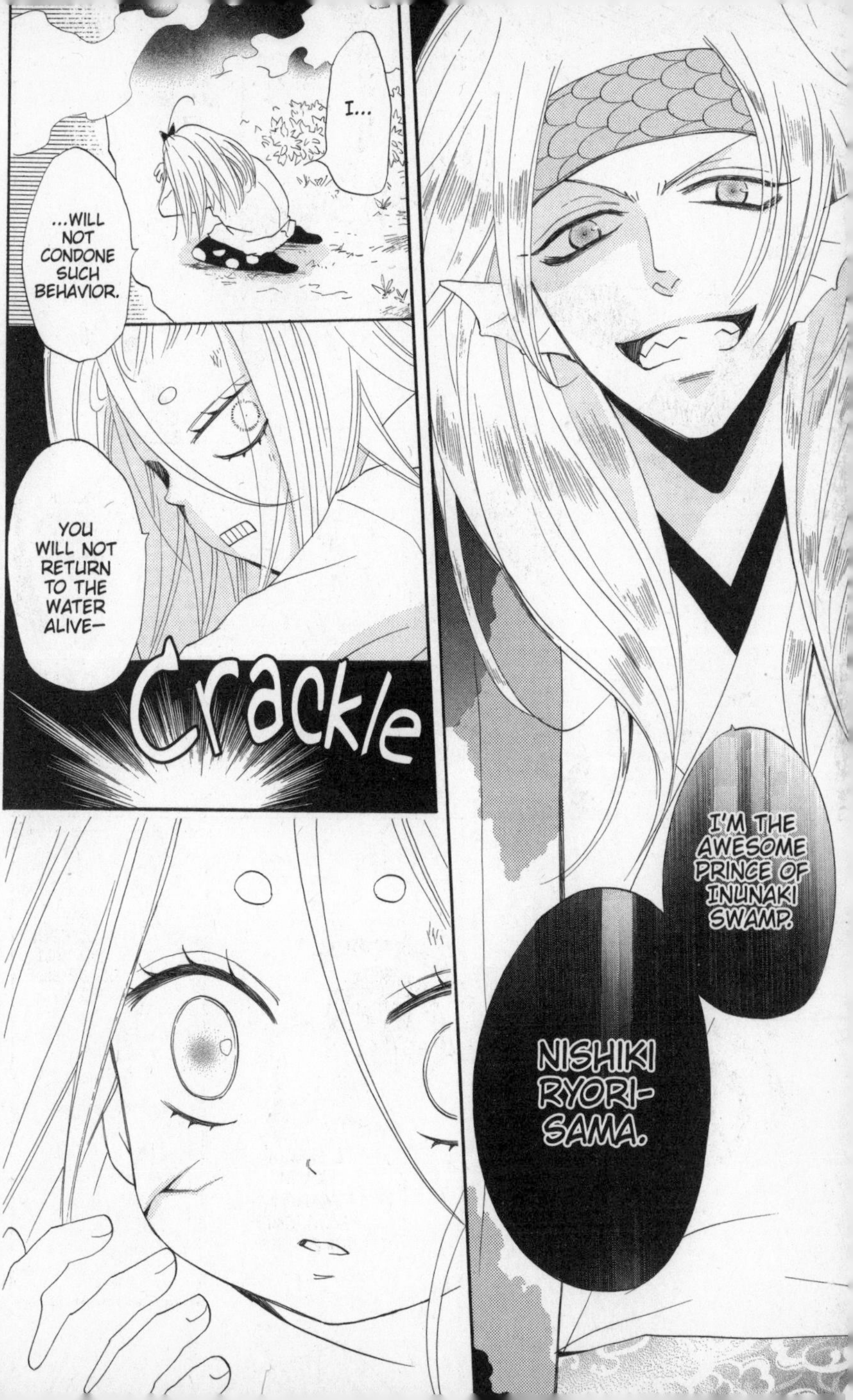
I'M THE AWESOME PRINCE OF INUNAKI SWAMP.
NISHIKI RYORI-SAMA.
I...
...WILL NOT CONDONE SUCH BEHAVIOR.
YOU WILL NOT RETURN TO THE WATER ALIVE—
Crackle

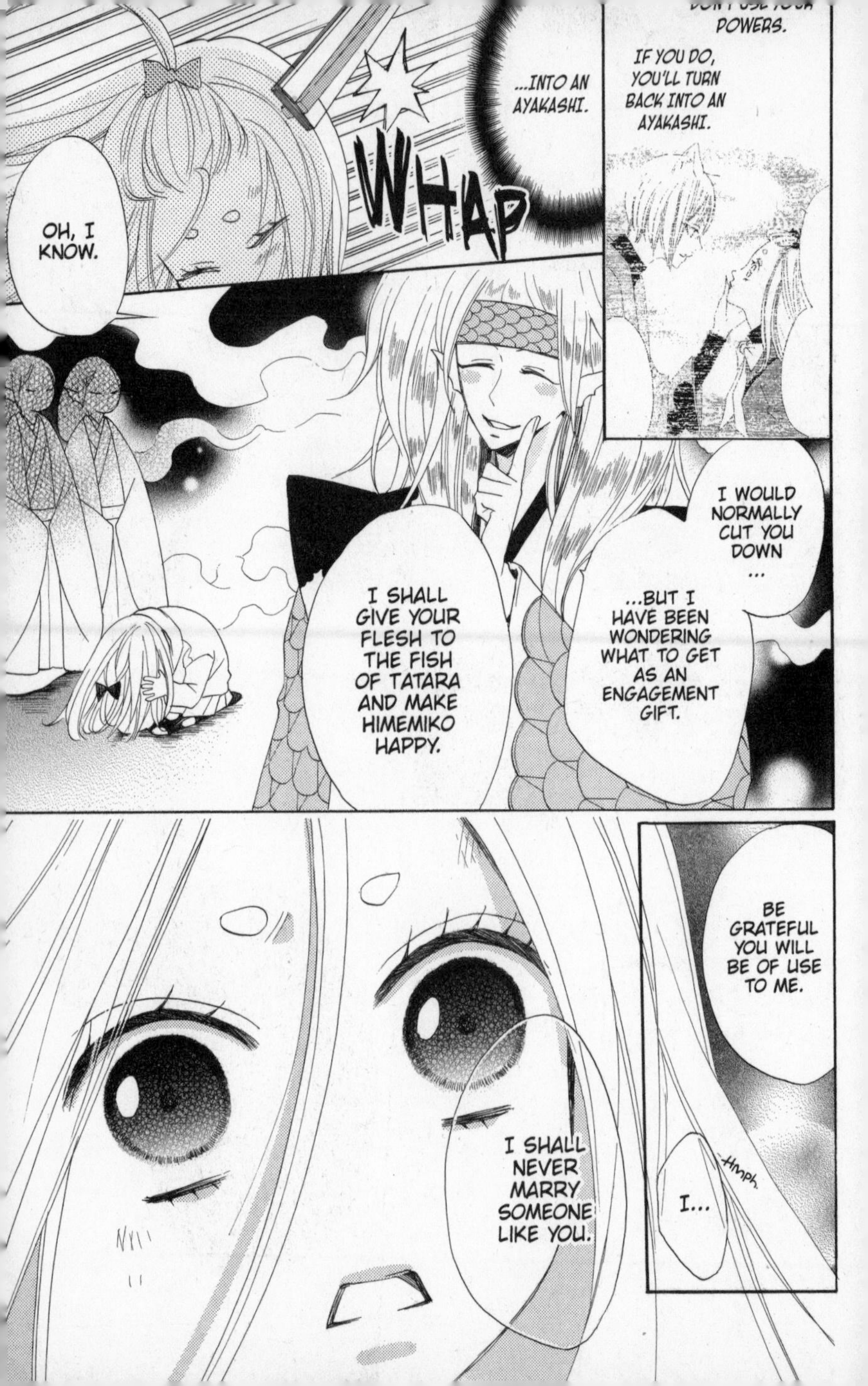
POWERS.
IF YOU DO, YOU'LL TURN BACK INTO AN AYAKASHI.
...INTO AN AYAKASHI.
WHAP
OH, I KNOW.
I WOULD NORMALLY CUT YOU DOWN ...
...BUT I HAVE BEEN WONDERING WHAT TO GET AS AN ENGAGEMENT GIFT.
I SHALL GIVE YOUR FLESH TO THE FISH OF TATARA AND MAKE HIMEMIKO HAPPY.
BE GRATEFUL YOU WILL BE OF USE TO ME.
Hmph.
I...
I SHALL NEVER MARRY SOMEONE LIKE YOU.

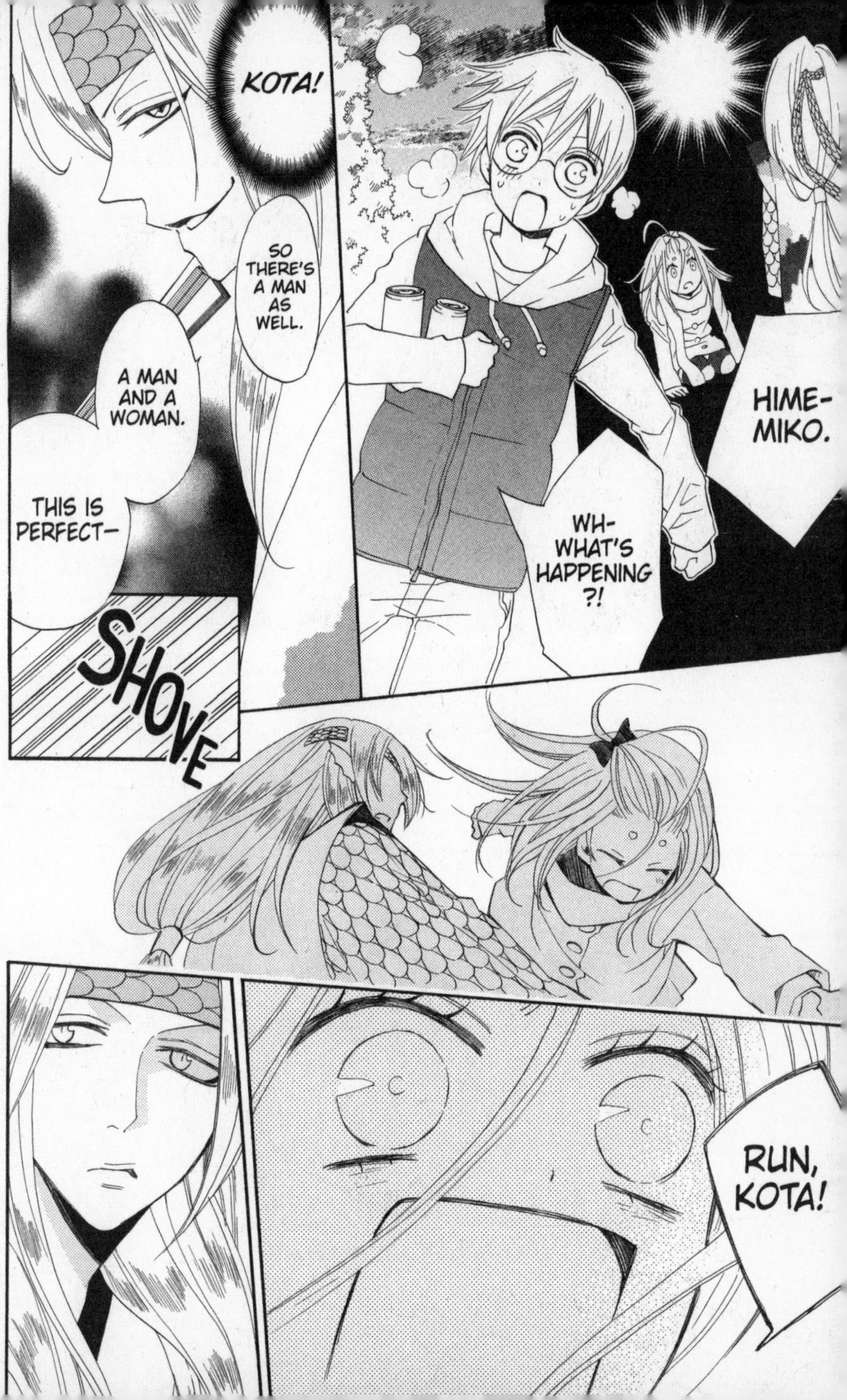
HIME-MIKO.
WH- WHAT'S HAPPENING ?!
KOTA!
SO THERE'S A MAN AS WELL.
A MAN AND A WOMAN.
THIS IS PERFECT-
SHOVE
RUN, KOTA!

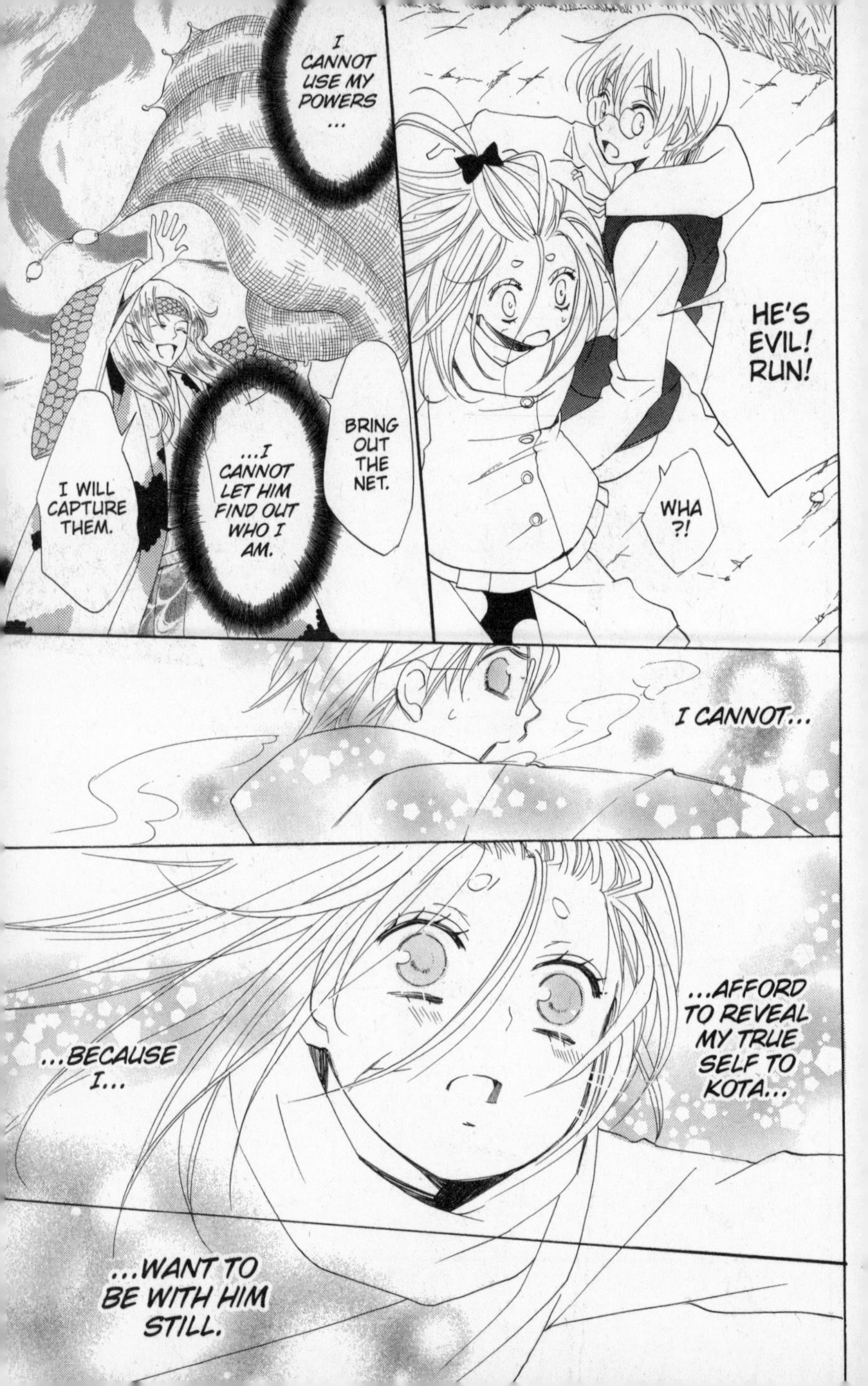
HE'S EVIL! RUN!
WHA?!
I CANNOT USE MY POWERS...
BRING OUT THE NET.
...I CANNOT LET HIM FIND OUT WHO I AM.
I WILL CAPTURE THEM.
I CANNOT...
...AFFORD TO REVEAL MY TRUE SELF TO KOTA...
...BECAUSE I...
...WANT TO BE WITH HIM STILL.

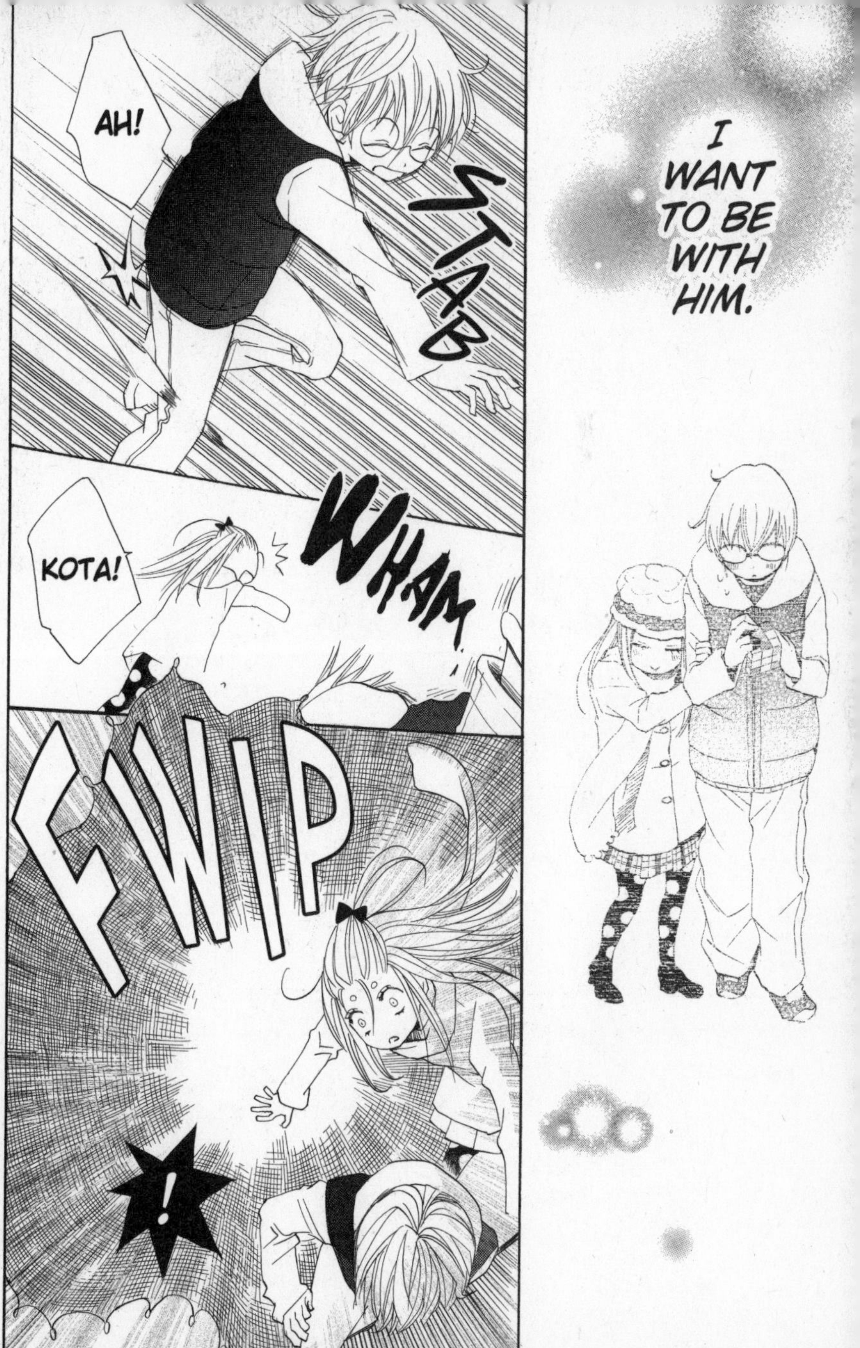
I WANT TO BE WITH HIM.
AH!
STAB
KOTA!
WHAM
FWIP
!

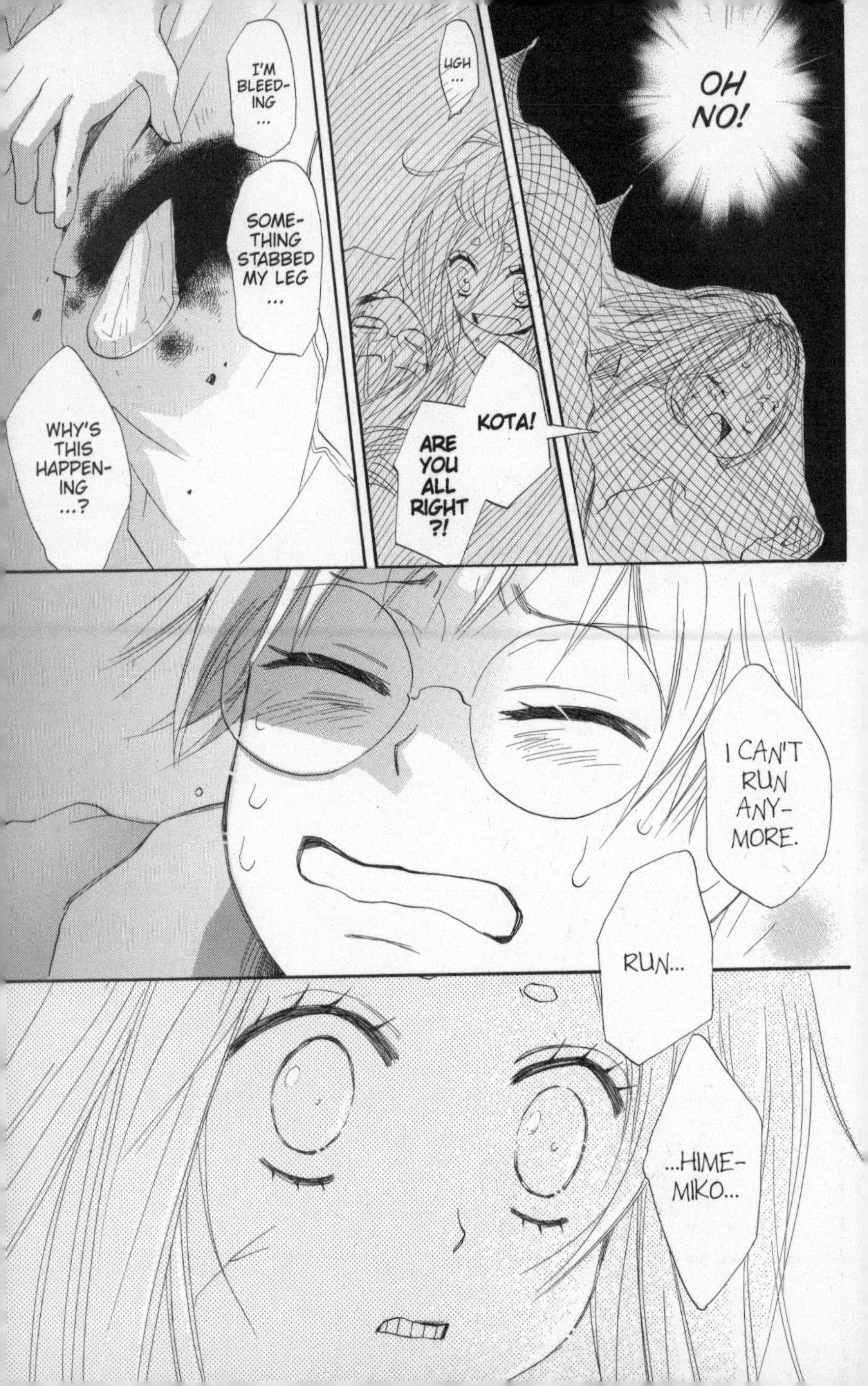
OH NO!
UGH...
KOTA!
ARE YOU ALL RIGHT?!
I'M BLEEDING...
SOMETHING STABBED MY LEG...
WHY'S THIS HAPPENING...?
I CAN'T RUN ANYMORE.
RUN...
...HIME-MIKO...

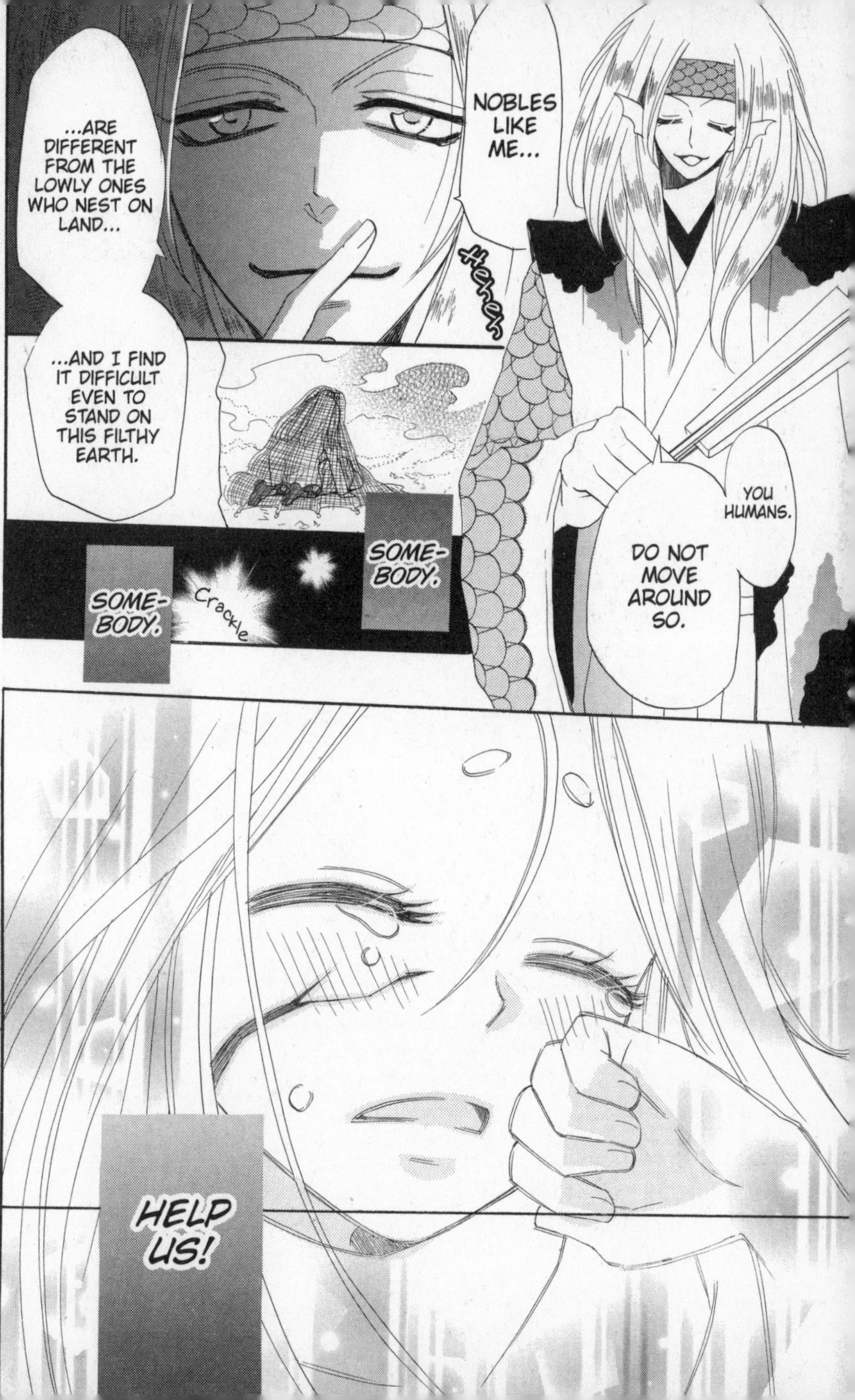
NOBLES LIKE ME...
Hehe
YOU HUMANS.
DO NOT MOVE AROUND SO.
...ARE DIFFERENT FROM THE LOWLY ONES WHO NEST ON LAND...
...AND I FIND IT DIFFICULT EVEN TO STAND ON THIS FILTHY EARTH.
SOME-BODY.
Crackle
SOME-BODY.
HELP US!

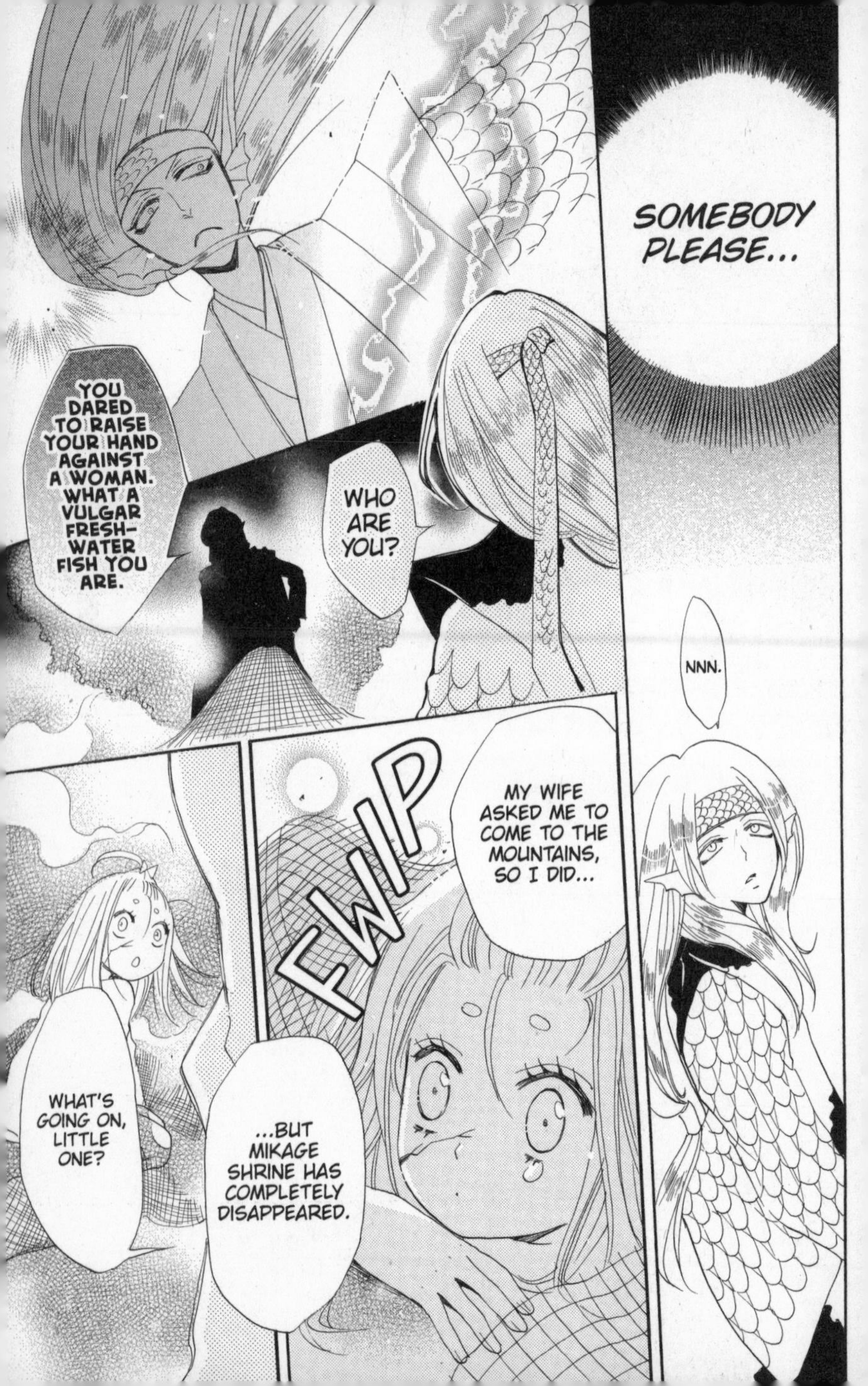
SOMEBODY PLEASE...
NNN.
WHO ARE YOU?
YOU DARED TO RAISE YOUR HAND AGAINST A WOMAN. WHAT A VULGAR FRESH-WATER FISH YOU ARE.
MY WIFE ASKED ME TO COME TO THE MOUNTAINS, SO I DID...
FWIP
...BUT MIKAGE SHRINE HAS COMPLETELY DISAPPEARED.
WHAT'S GOING ON, LITTLE ONE?

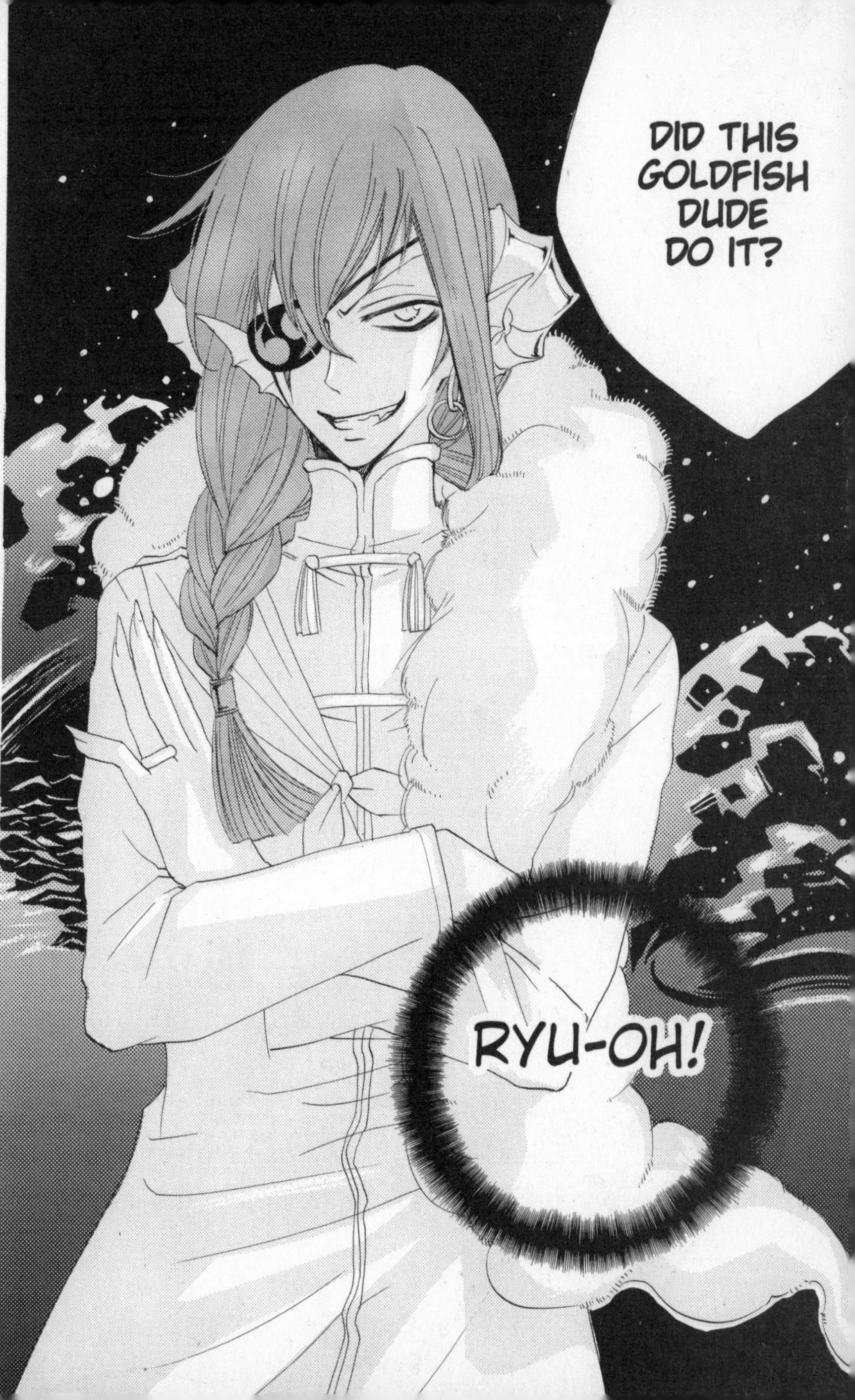
DID THIS GOLDFISH DUDE DO IT?
RYU-OH!

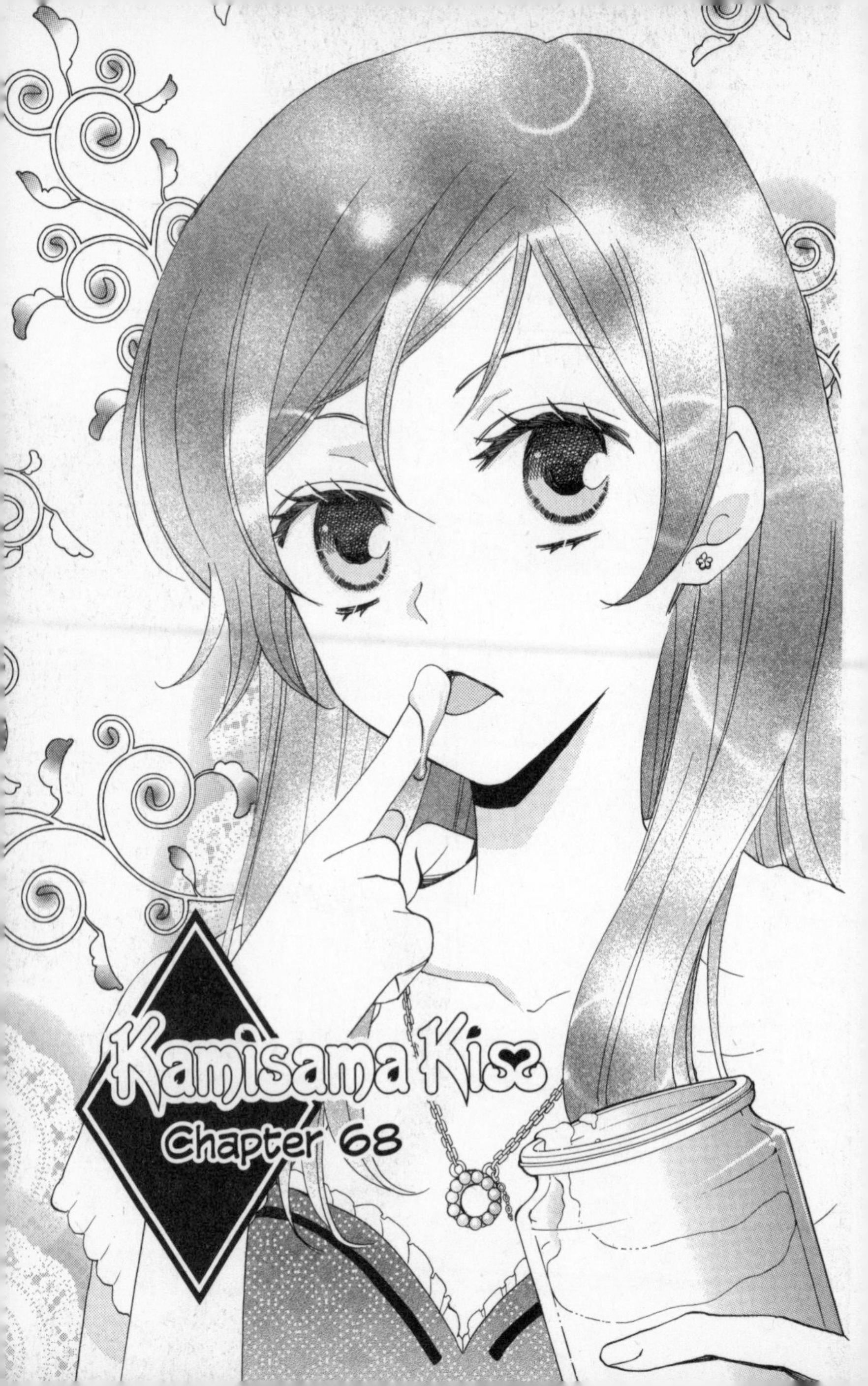
Kamisama Kiss
Chapter 68

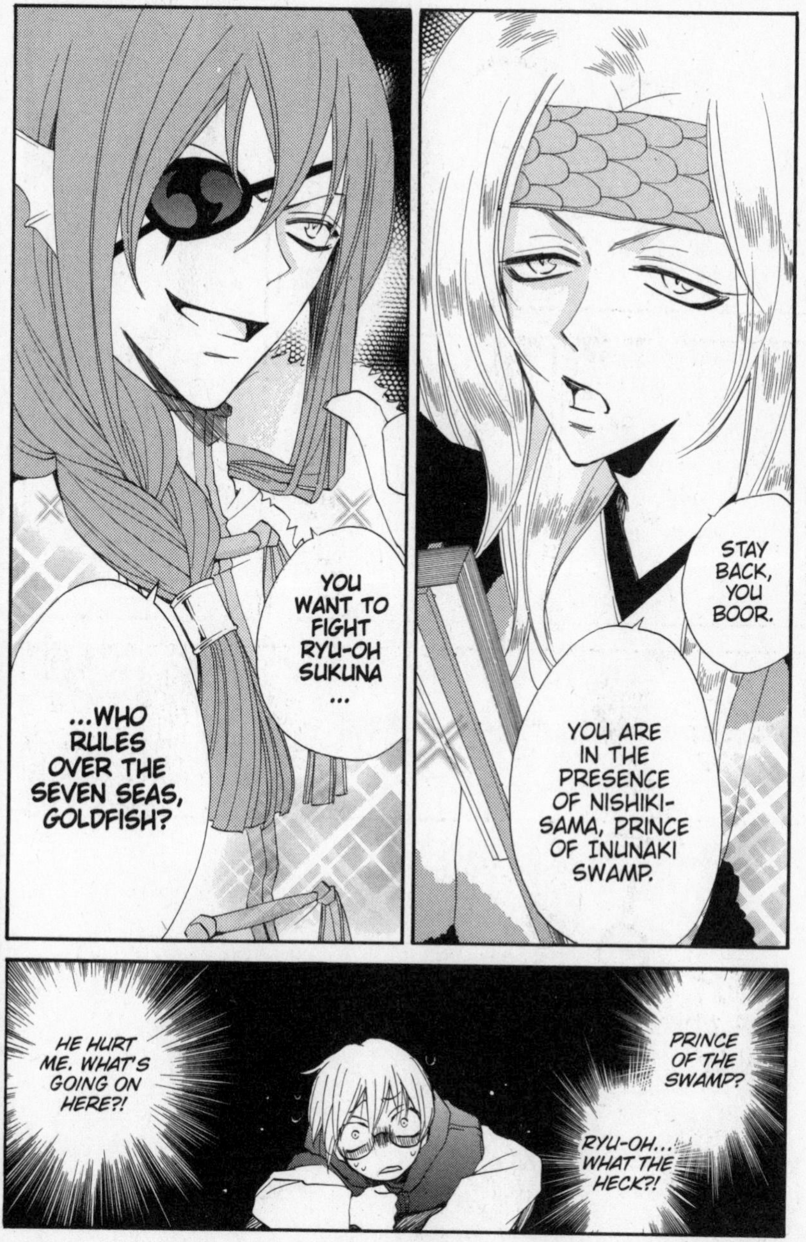
STAY BACK, YOU BOOR.
YOU ARE IN THE PRESENCE OF NISHIKI-SAMA, PRINCE OF INUNAKI SWAMP.
YOU WANT TO FIGHT RYU-OH SUKUNA ...
...WHO RULES OVER THE SEVEN SEAS, GOLDFISH?
PRINCE OF THE SWAMP?
RYU-OH... WHAT THE HECK?!
HE HURT ME. WHAT'S GOING ON HERE?!

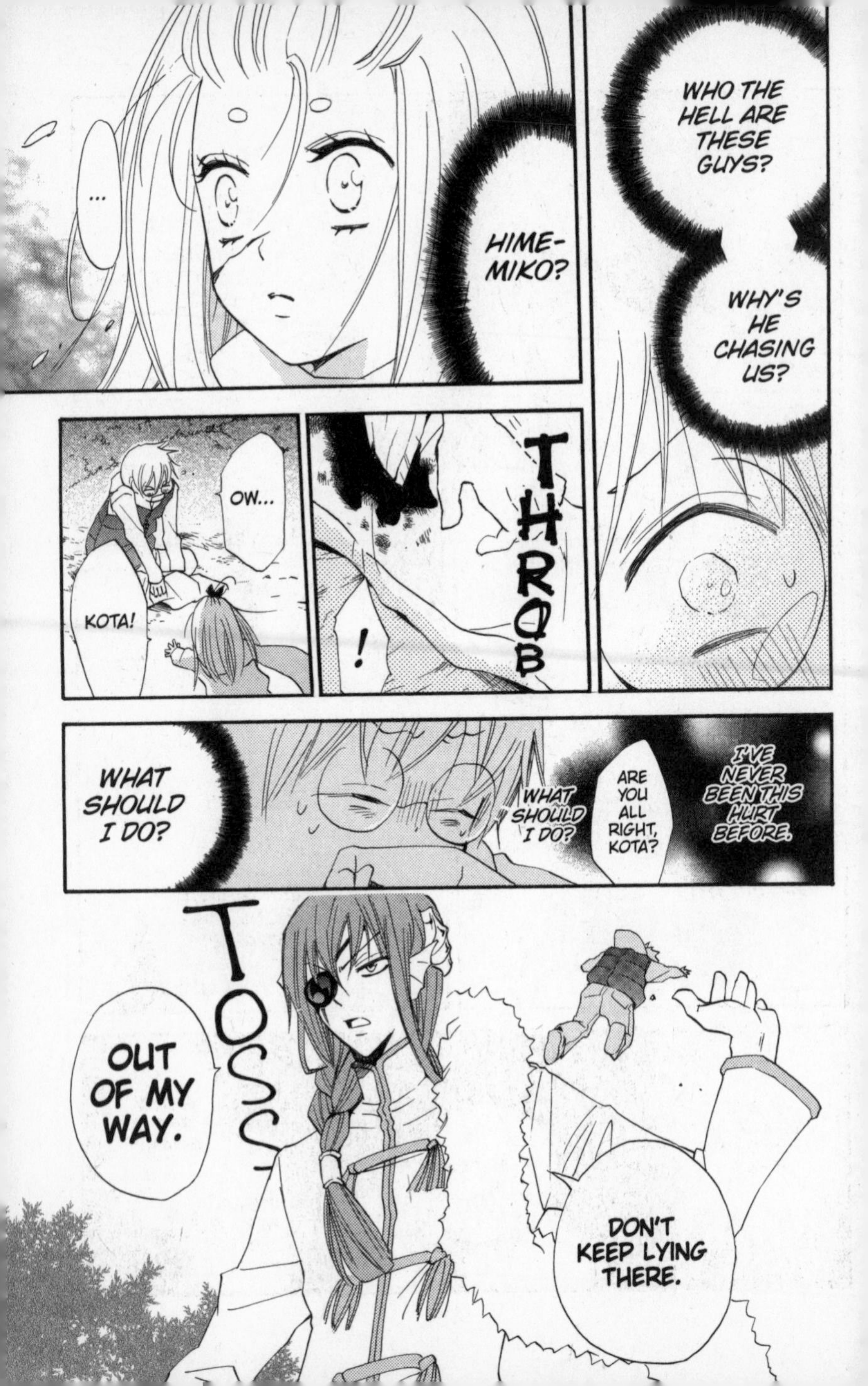
WHO THE HELL ARE THESE GUYS?
WHY'S HE CHASING US?
HIME-MIKO?
...
THROB
!
OW...
KOTA!
I'VE NEVER BEEN THIS HURT BEFORE.
ARE YOU ALL RIGHT, KOTA?
WHAT SHOULD I DO?
WHAT SHOULD I DO?
TOSS
DON'T KEEP LYING THERE.
OUT OF MY WAY.

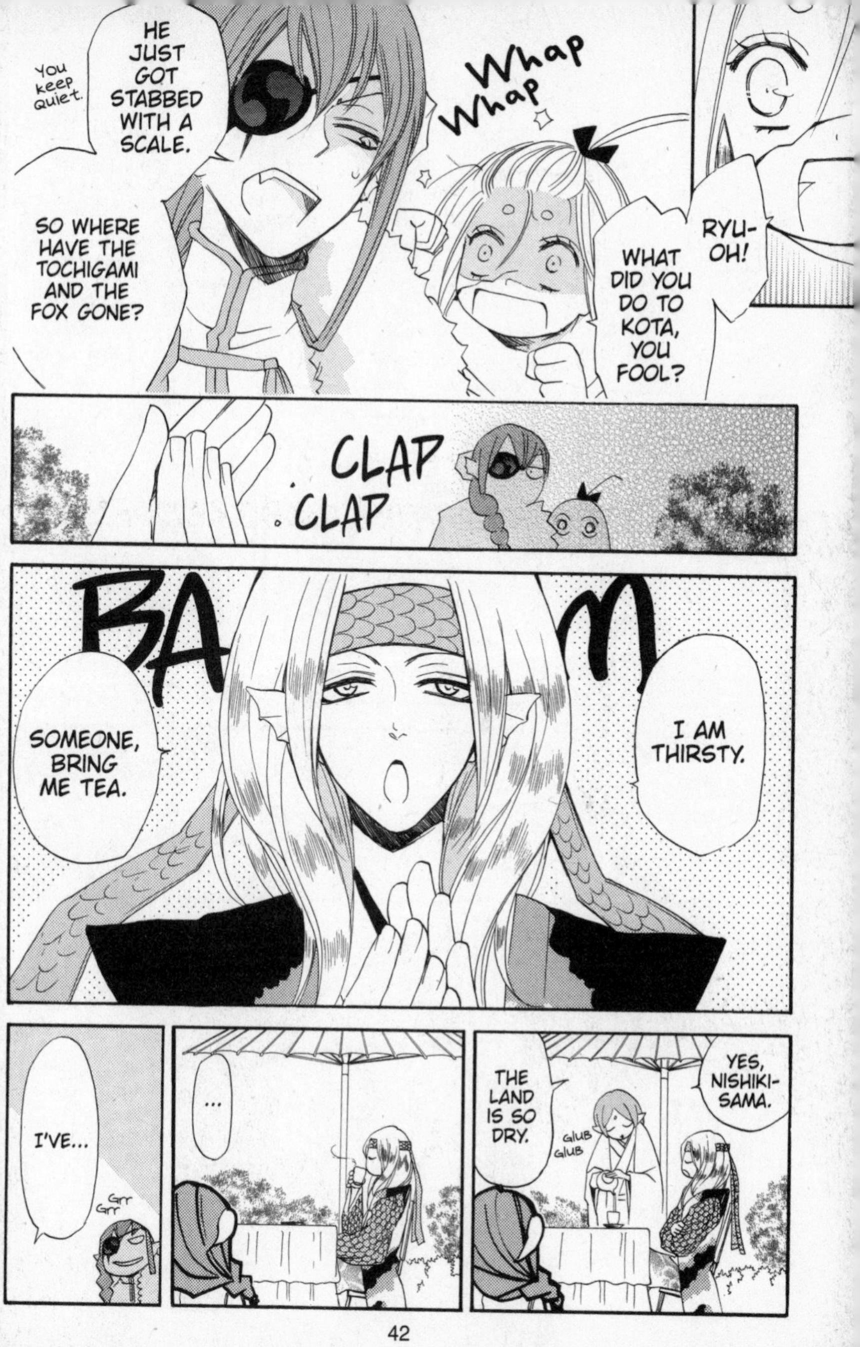
RYU-OH!
Whap Whap
WHAT DID YOU DO TO KOTA, YOU FOOL?
HE JUST GOT STABBED WITH A SCALE.
You keep quiet.
SO WHERE HAVE THE TOCHIGAMI AND THE FOX GONE?
CLAP CLAP
I AM THIRSTY.
BAM
SOMEONE, BRING ME TEA.
YES, NISHIKI-SAMA.
THE LAND IS SO DRY.
Glub Glub
...
I'VE...
Grr Grr

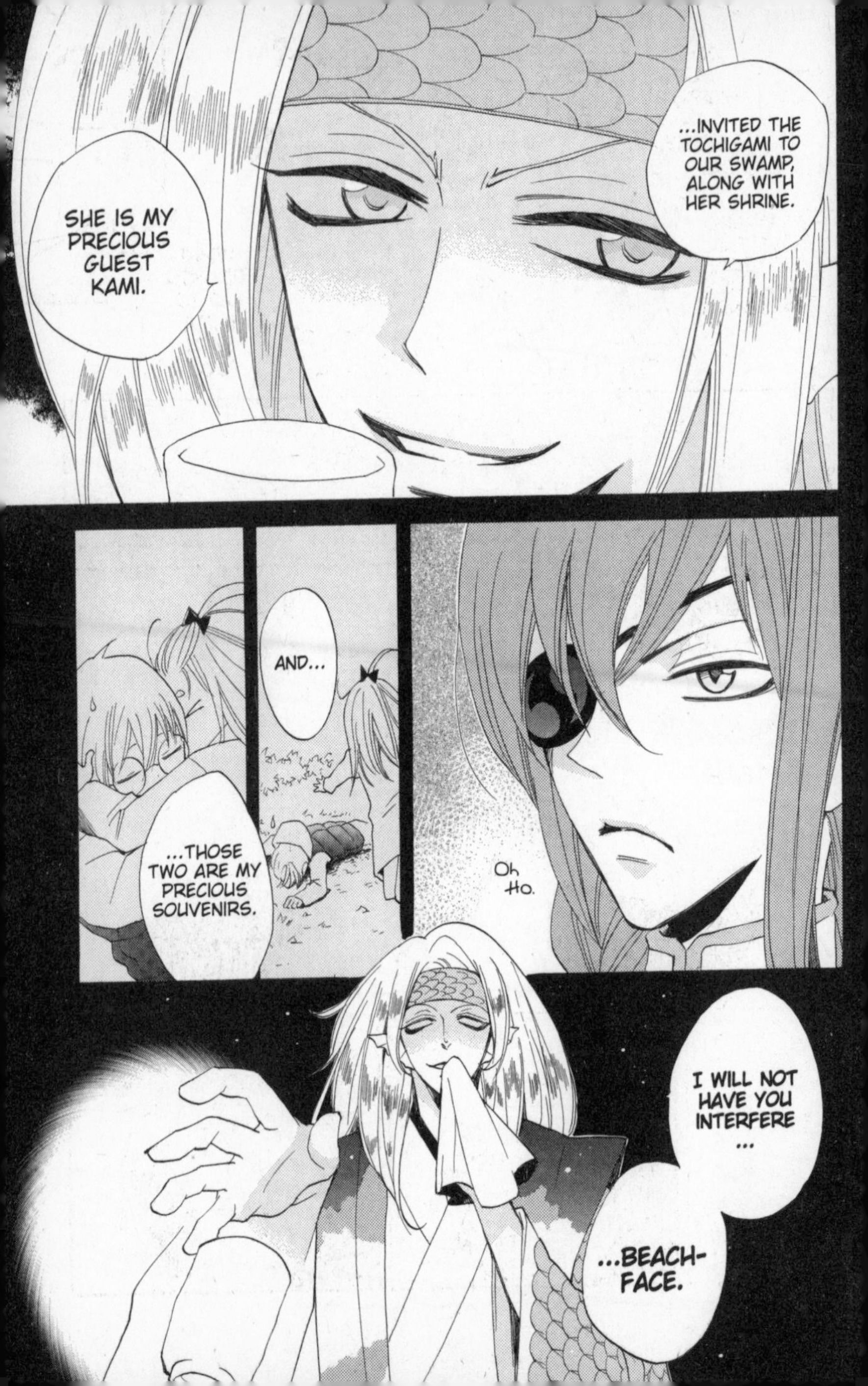
...INVITED THE TOCHIGAMI TO OUR SWAMP, ALONG WITH HER SHRINE.
SHE IS MY PRECIOUS GUEST KAMI.
Oh Ho.
AND...
...THOSE TWO ARE MY PRECIOUS SOUVENIRS.
I WILL NOT HAVE YOU INTERFERE ...
...BEACH-FACE.

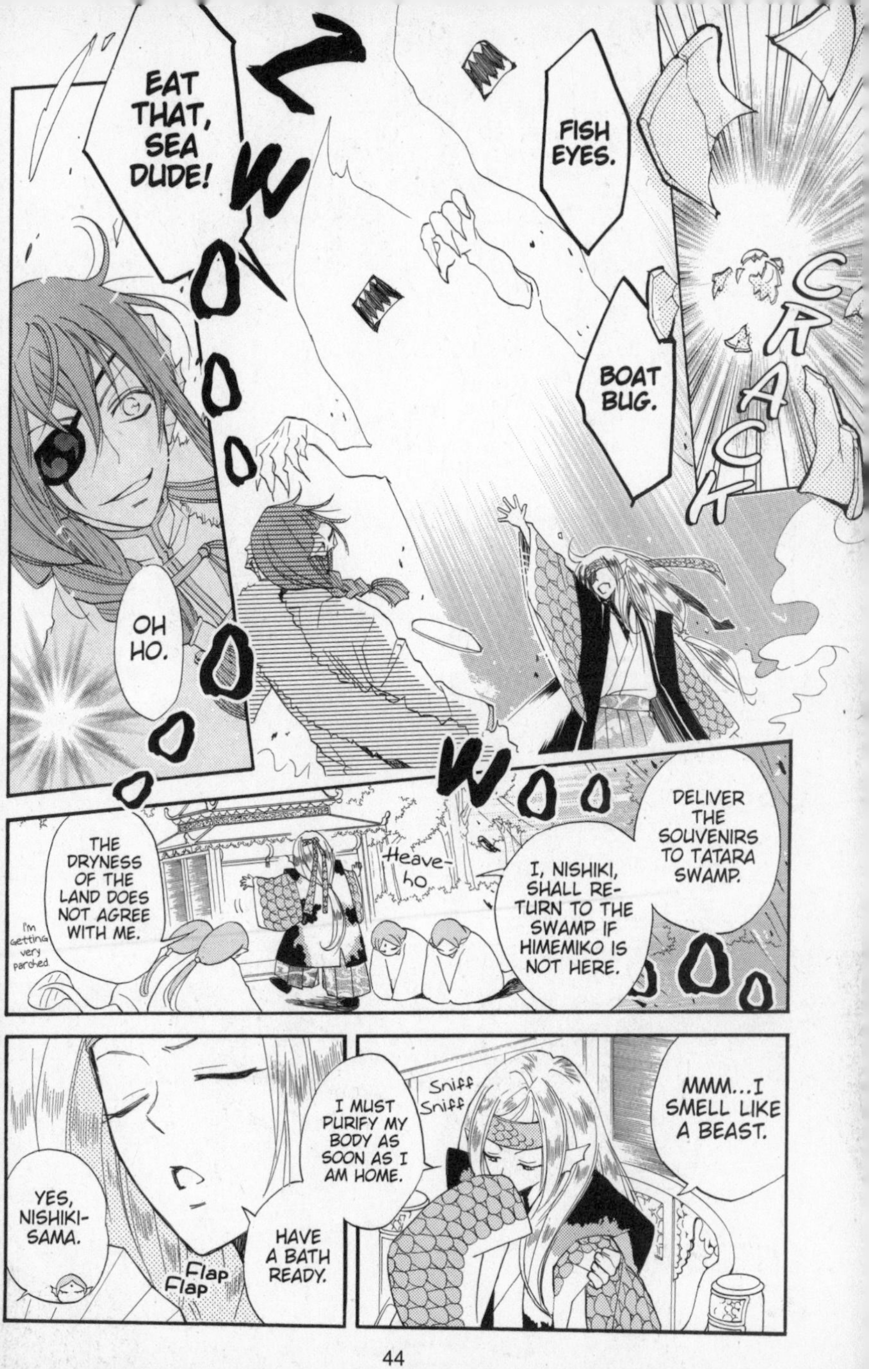
FISH EYES.
BOAT BUG.
CRACK
EAT THAT, SEA DUDE!
WOOOOOOOO
OH HO.
WOOOOO
DELIVER THE SOUVENIRS TO TATARA SWAMP.
I, NISHIKI, SHALL RE-TURN TO THE SWAMP IF HIMEMIKO IS NOT HERE.
Heave-ho
THE DRYNESS OF THE LAND DOES NOT AGREE WITH ME.
I'm getting very parched
MMM...I SMELL LIKE A BEAST.
Sniff Sniff
I MUST PURIFY MY BODY AS SOON AS I AM HOME.
HAVE A BATH READY.
YES, NISHIKI-SAMA.
Flap Flap

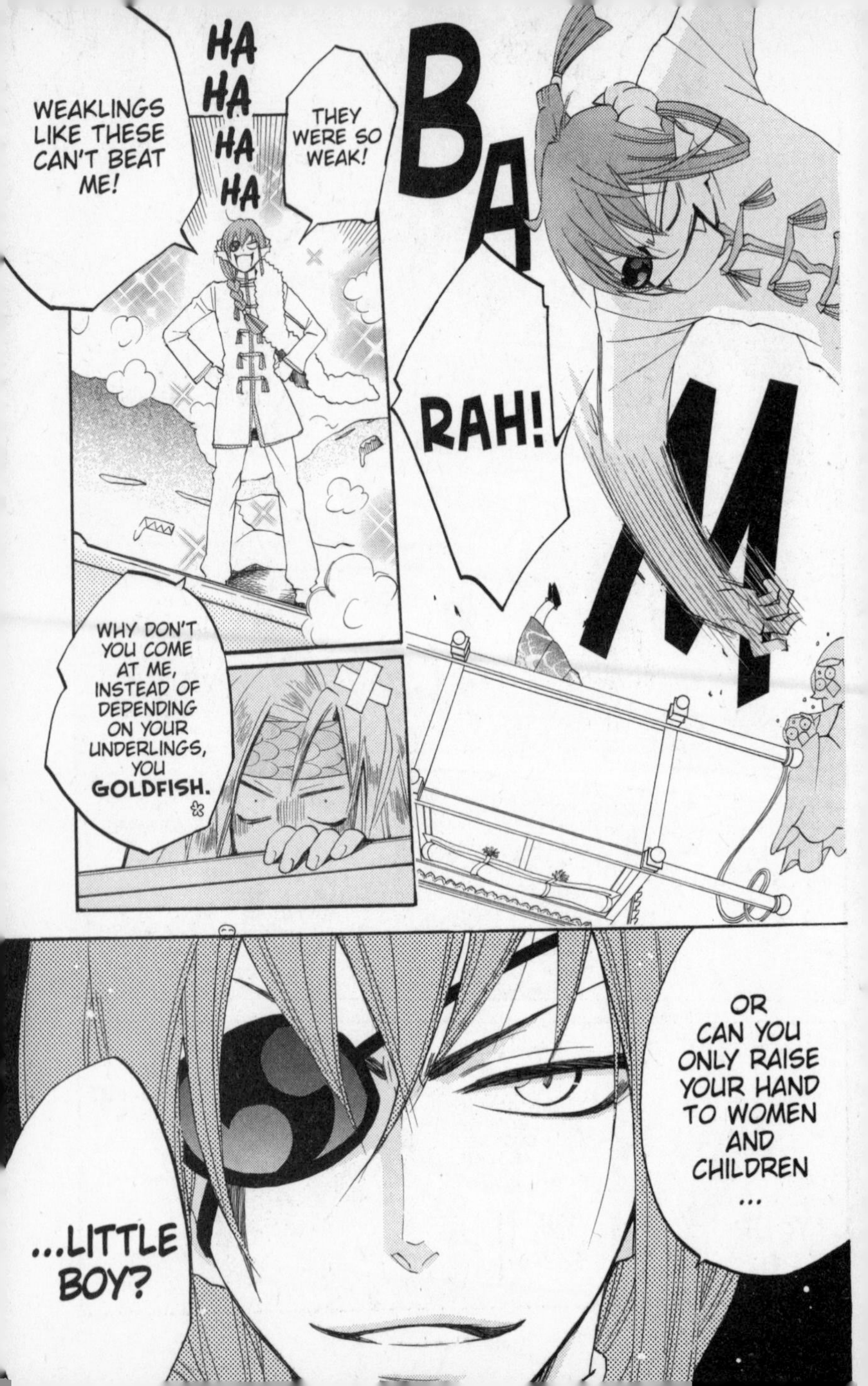
BAM
RAH!
THEY WERE SO WEAK!
HA HA HA HA
WEAKLINGS LIKE THESE CAN'T BEAT ME!
WHY DON'T YOU COME AT ME, INSTEAD OF DEPENDING ON YOUR UNDERLINGS, YOU GOLDFISH.
OR CAN YOU ONLY RAISE YOUR HAND TO WOMEN AND CHILDREN ...
...LITTLE BOY?

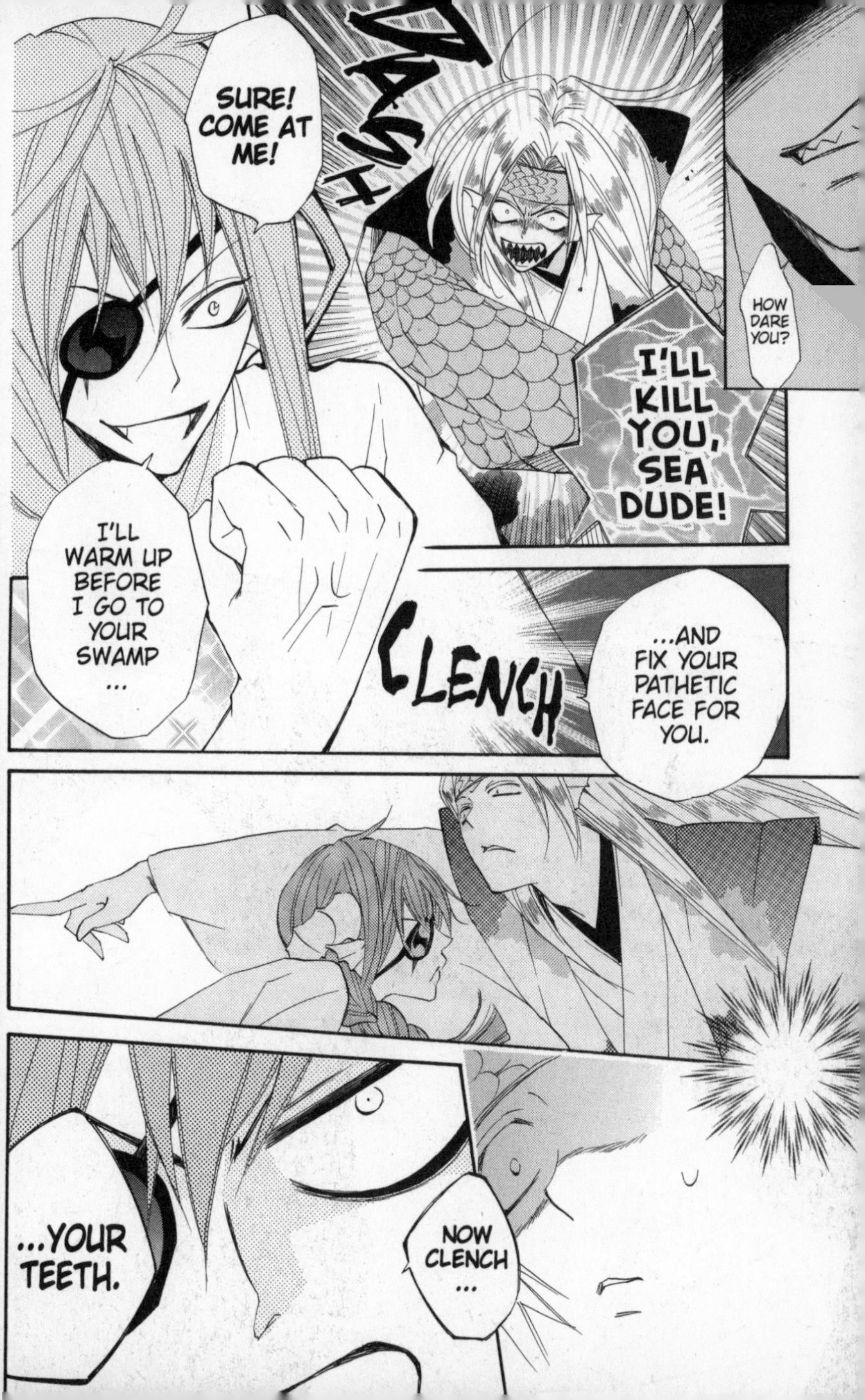
HOW DARE YOU?
ZASH
I'LL KILL YOU, SEA DUDE!
SURE! COME AT ME!
I'LL WARM UP BEFORE I GO TO YOUR SWAMP ...
CLENCH
...AND FIX YOUR PATHETIC FACE FOR YOU.
NOW CLENCH ...
...YOUR TEETH.

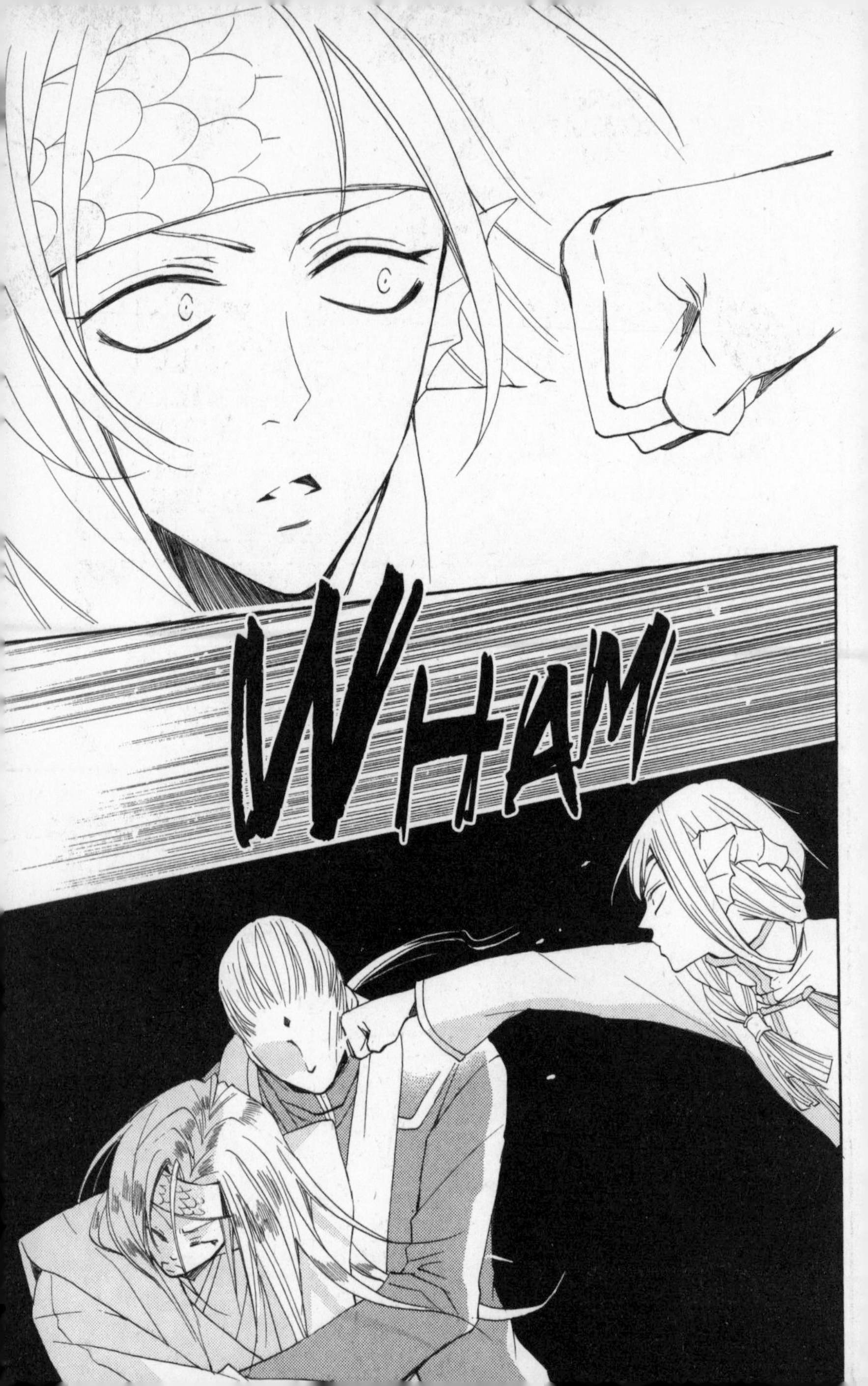
WHAM

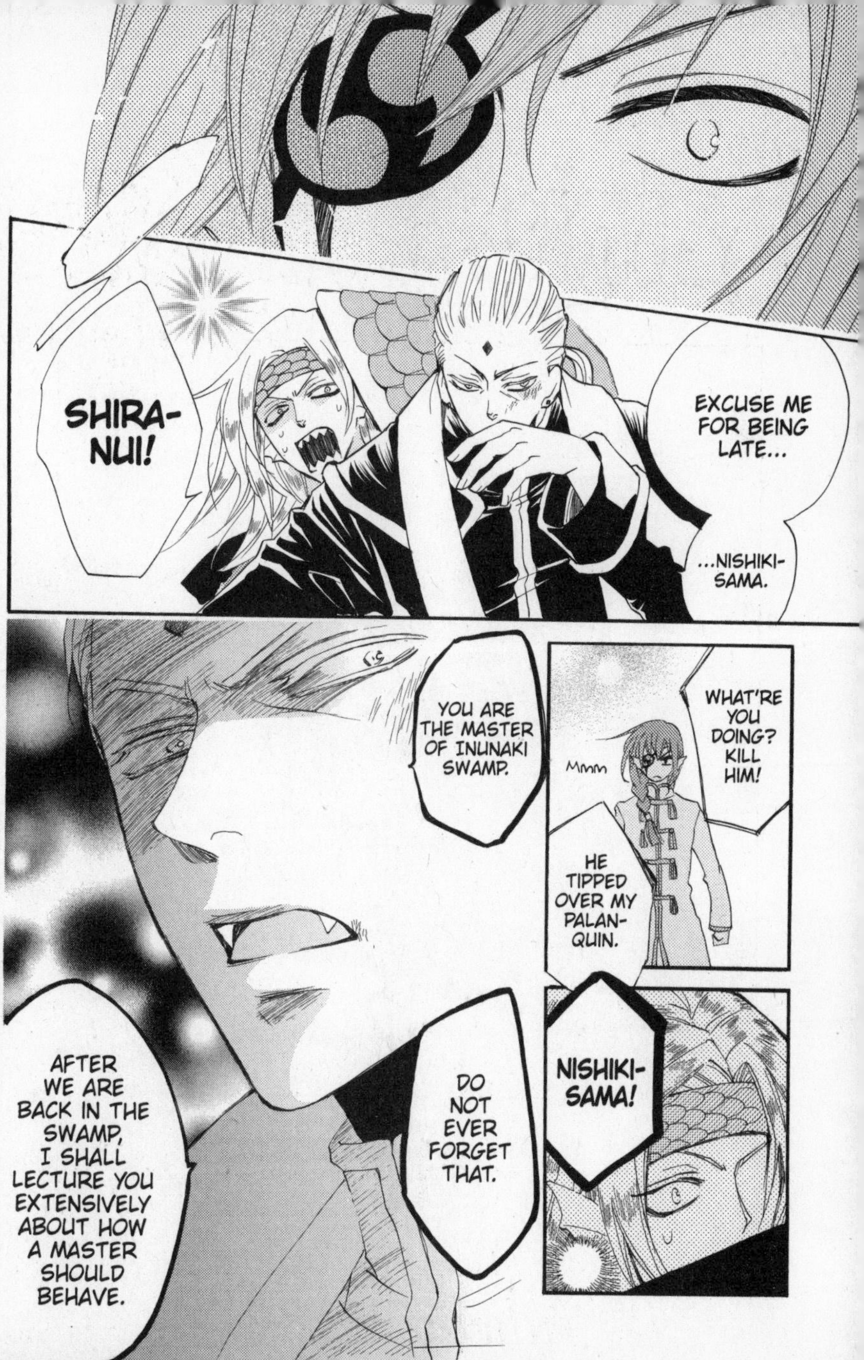
EXCUSE ME FOR BEING LATE...
...NISHIKI-SAMA.
SHIRA-NUI!
WHAT'RE YOU DOING? KILL HIM!
Mmm
HE TIPPED OVER MY PALAN-QUIN.
NISHIKI-SAMA!
YOU ARE THE MASTER OF INUNAKI SWAMP.
DO NOT EVER FORGET THAT.
AFTER WE ARE BACK IN THE SWAMP, I SHALL LECTURE YOU EXTENSIVELY ABOUT HOW A MASTER SHOULD BEHAVE.

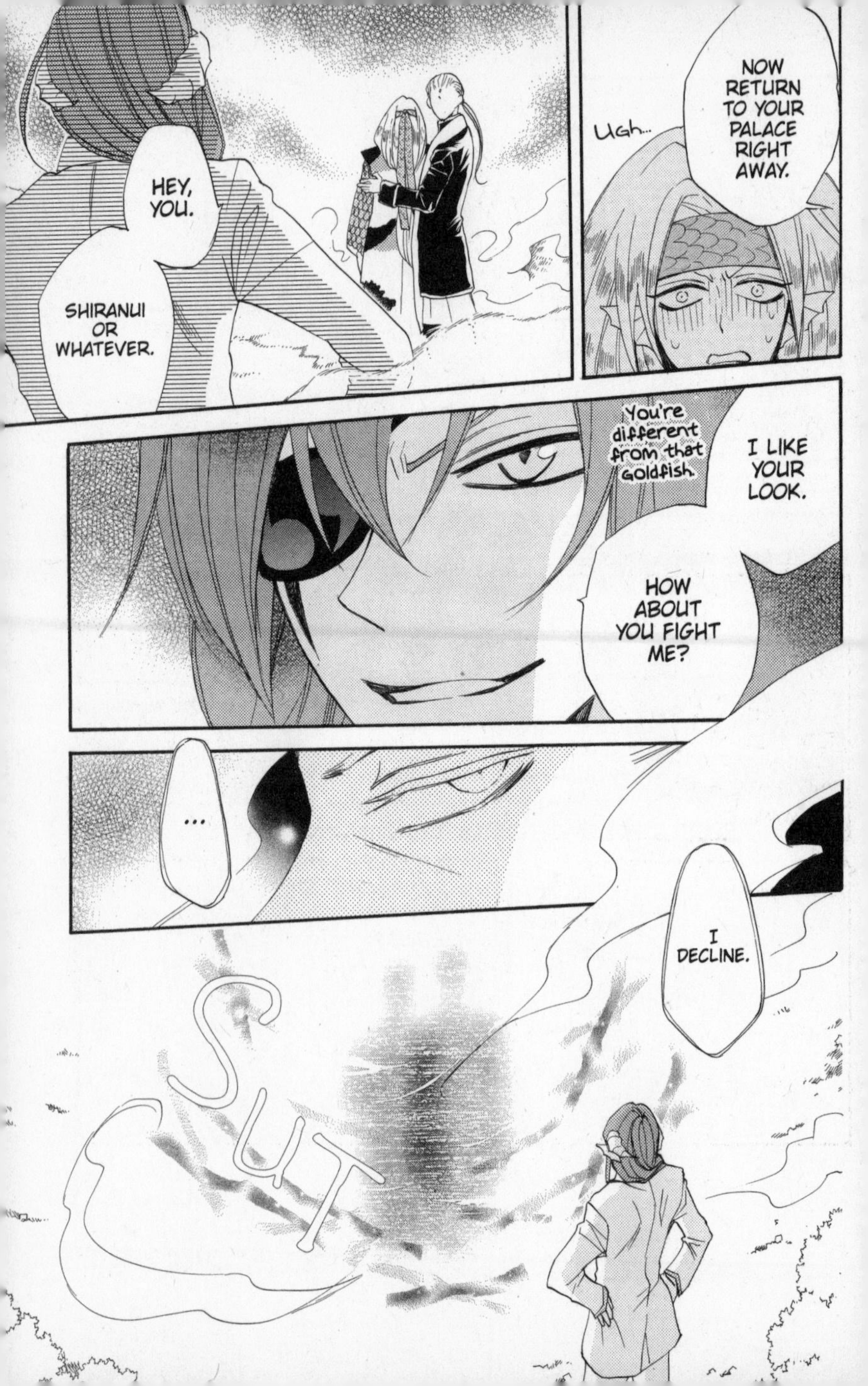
NOW RETURN TO YOUR PALACE RIGHT AWAY.
Ugh...
HEY, YOU.
SHIRANUI OR WHATEVER.
I LIKE YOUR LOOK.
You're different from that goldfish.
HOW ABOUT YOU FIGHT ME?
...
I DECLINE.
SUT

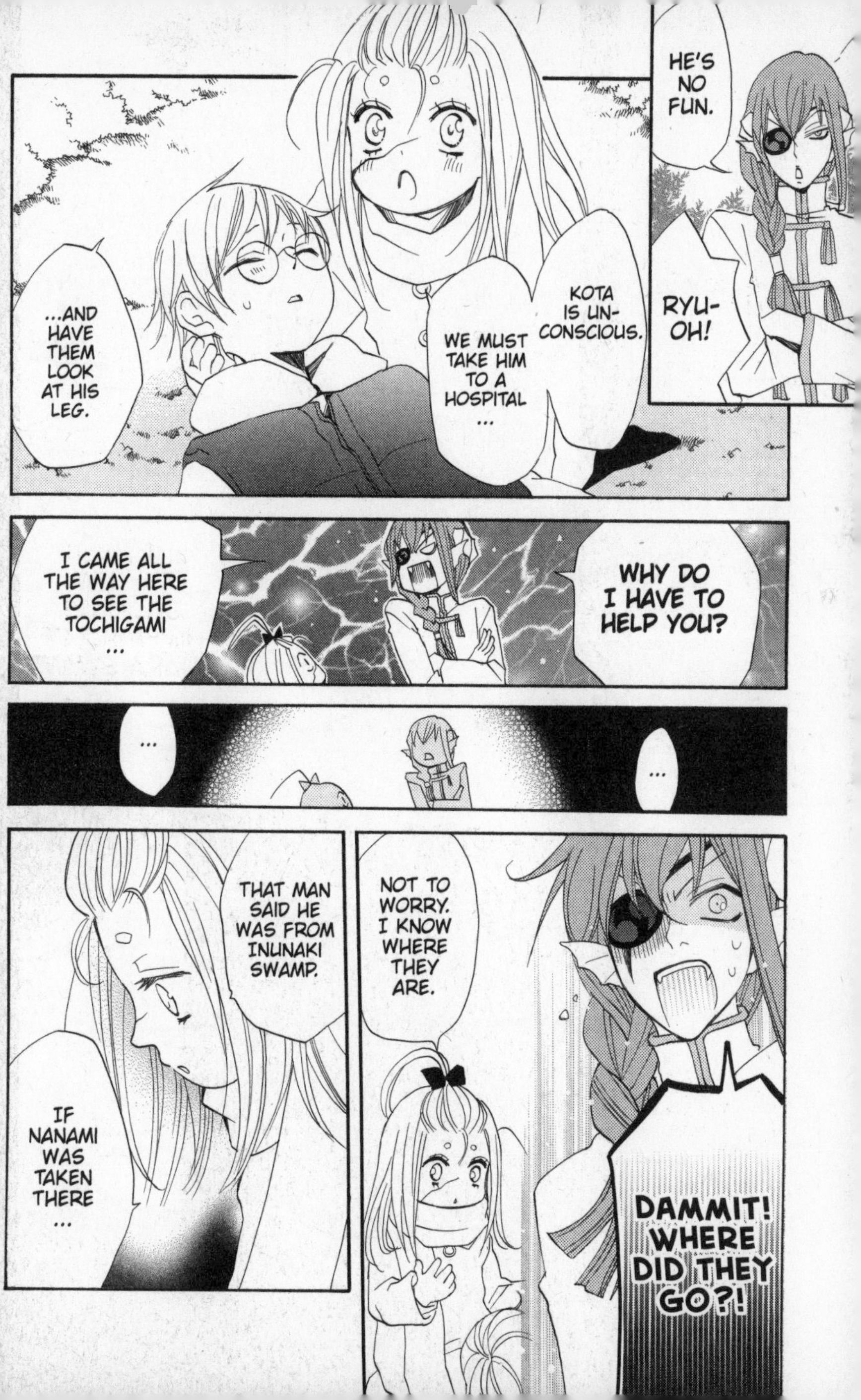
HE'S NO FUN.
RYU-OH!
KOTA IS UN-CONSCIOUS.
WE MUST TAKE HIM TO A HOSPITAL ...
...AND HAVE THEM LOOK AT HIS LEG.
WHY DO I HAVE TO HELP YOU?
I CAME ALL THE WAY HERE TO SEE THE TOCHIGAMI ...
...
...
DAMMIT! WHERE DID THEY GO?!
NOT TO WORRY. I KNOW WHERE THEY ARE.
THAT MAN SAID HE WAS FROM INUNAKI SWAMP.
IF NANAMI WAS TAKEN THERE ...

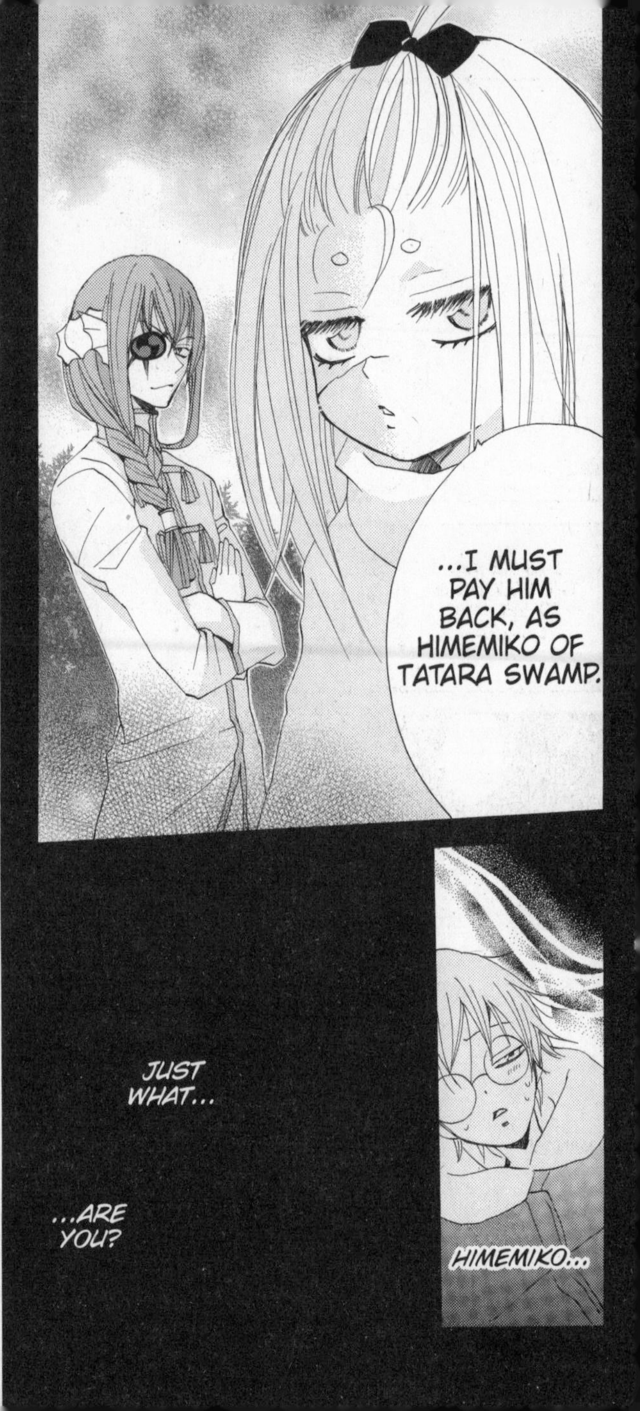

...I MUST PAY HIM BACK, AS HIMEMIKO OF TATARA SWAMP.
HIMEMIKO...
JUST WHAT...
...ARE YOU?

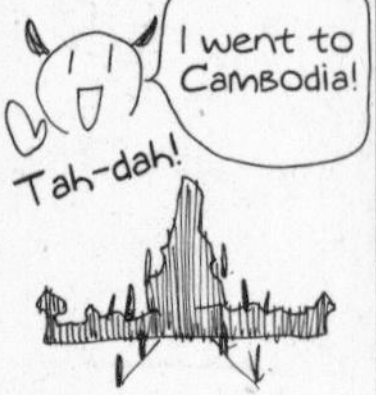

I went to Cambodia!
Tah-dah!

I went to see Angkor Wat! I only stayed for three days, but Cambodia was a good place! The people were nice and delightful. At the airport...

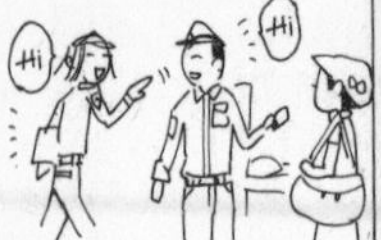

Hi
Hi
B

...the airport staff kept greeting each other in a friendly manner and everyone was smiling. I felt very good about it.

There were many ruins! I'm scared of high places, so there were places I couldn't climb, but I took a very thorough look at the lower places instead. The food was good too!

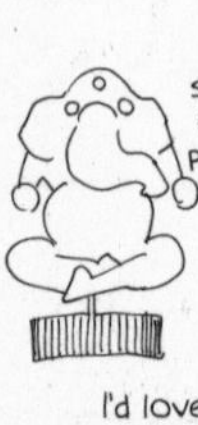

For a souvenir I bought a papercraft of Ganesha.

I'd love to go again!

Love Love

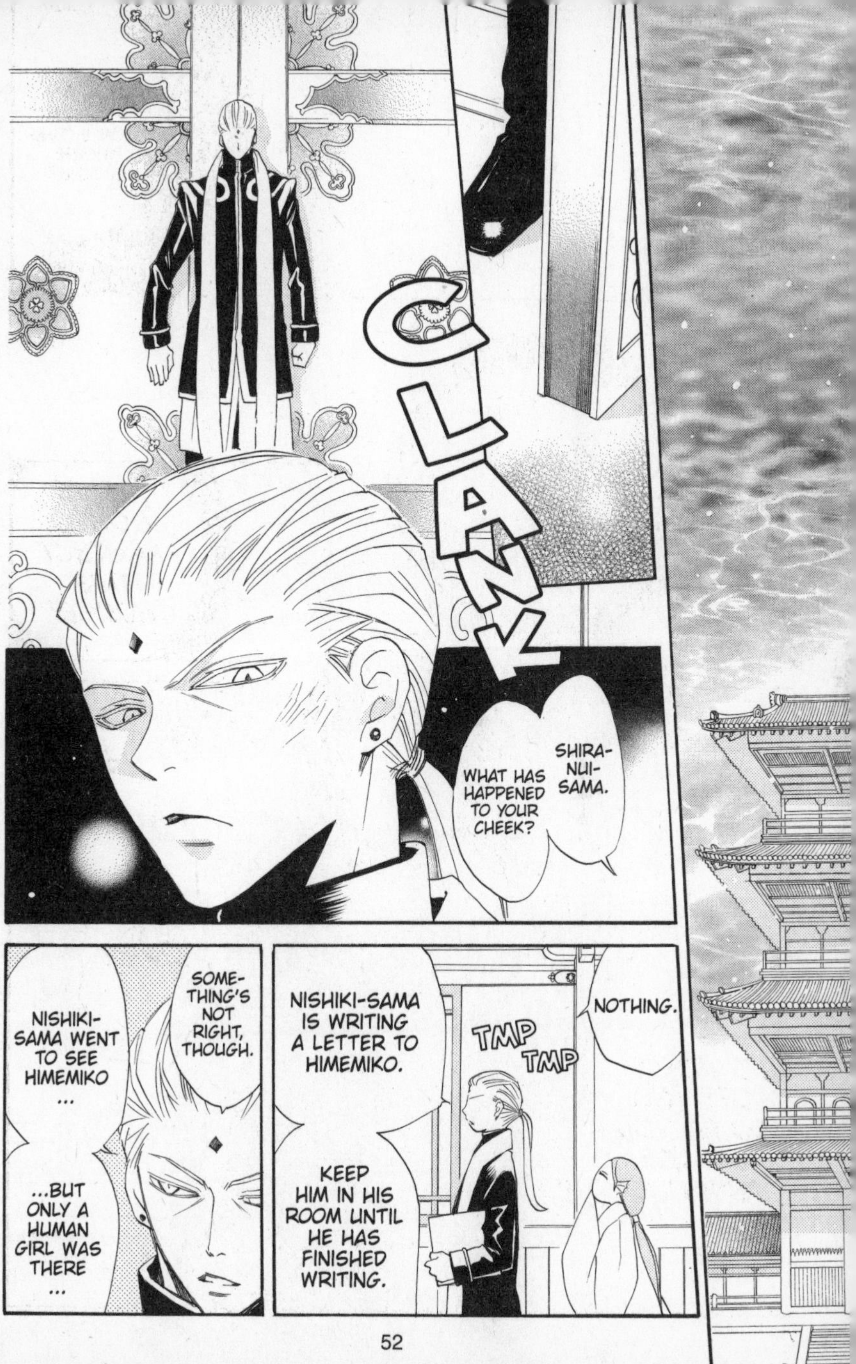
CLANK
SHIRANUI-SAMA.
WHAT HAS HAPPENED TO YOUR CHEEK?
NOTHING.
TMP TMP
NISHIKI-SAMA IS WRITING A LETTER TO HIMEMIKO.
KEEP HIM IN HIS ROOM UNTIL HE HAS FINISHED WRITING.
SOMETHING'S NOT RIGHT, THOUGH.
NISHIKI-SAMA WENT TO SEE HIMEMIKO ...
...BUT ONLY A HUMAN GIRL WAS THERE ...

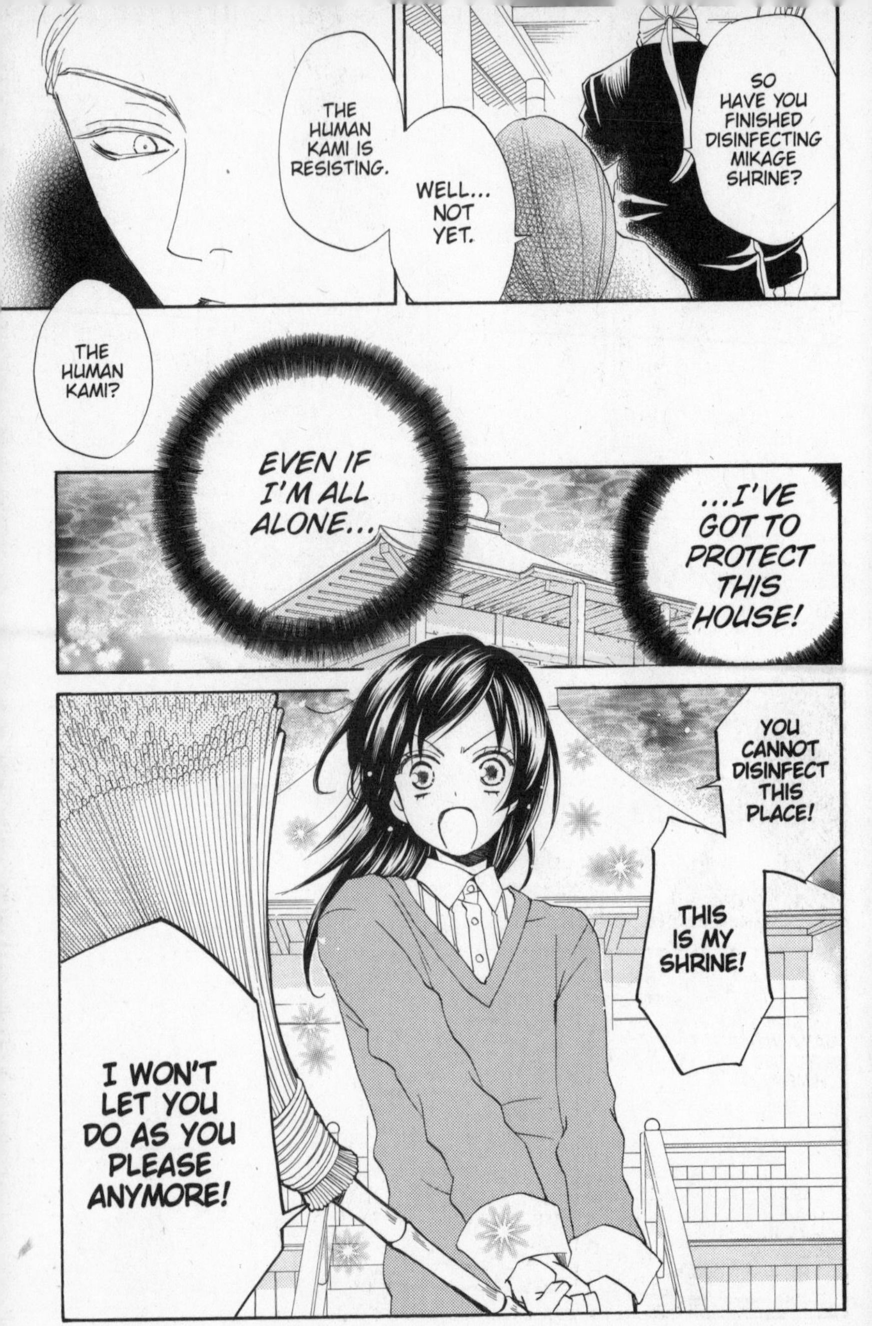
SO HAVE YOU FINISHED DISINFECTING MIKAGE SHRINE?
WELL... NOT YET.
THE HUMAN KAMI IS RESISTING.
THE HUMAN KAMI?
EVEN IF I'M ALL ALONE...
...I'VE GOT TO PROTECT THIS HOUSE!
YOU CANNOT DISINFECT THIS PLACE!
THIS IS MY SHRINE!
I WON'T LET YOU DO AS YOU PLEASE ANYMORE!

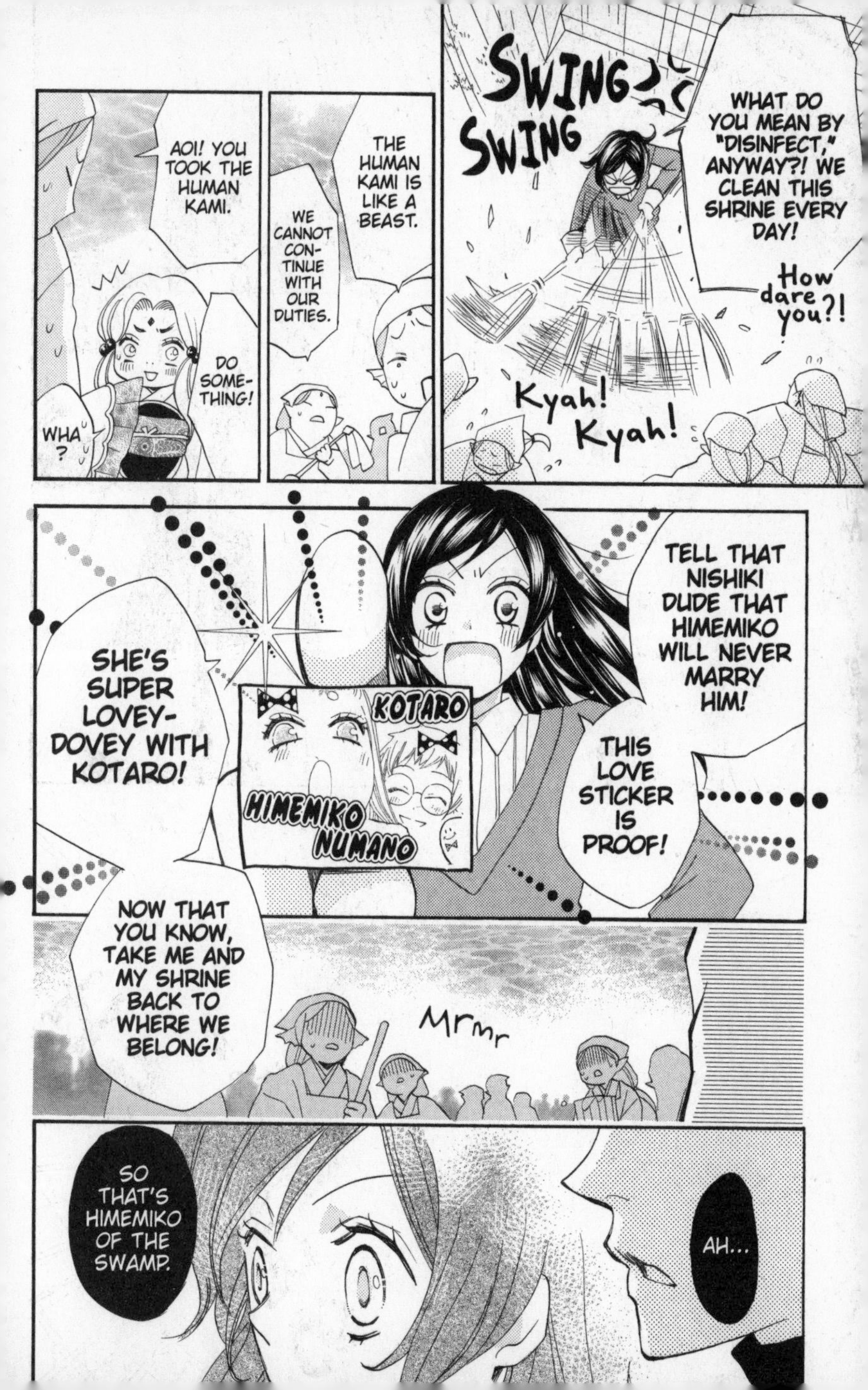
SWING SWING
WHAT DO YOU MEAN BY "DISINFECT," ANYWAY?! WE CLEAN THIS SHRINE EVERY DAY!
How dare you?!
Kyah! Kyah!
THE HUMAN KAMI IS LIKE A BEAST.
WE CANNOT CONTINUE WITH OUR DUTIES.
AOI! YOU TOOK THE HUMAN KAMI.
DO SOMETHING!
WHA?
TELL THAT NISHIKI DUDE THAT HIMEMIKO WILL NEVER MARRY HIM!
THIS LOVE STICKER IS PROOF!
KOTARO
HIMEMIKO NUMANO
SHE'S SUPER LOVEY-DOVEY WITH KOTARO!
NOW THAT YOU KNOW, TAKE ME AND MY SHRINE BACK TO WHERE WE BELONG!
Mrmr
AH...
SO THAT'S HIMEMIKO OF THE SWAMP.

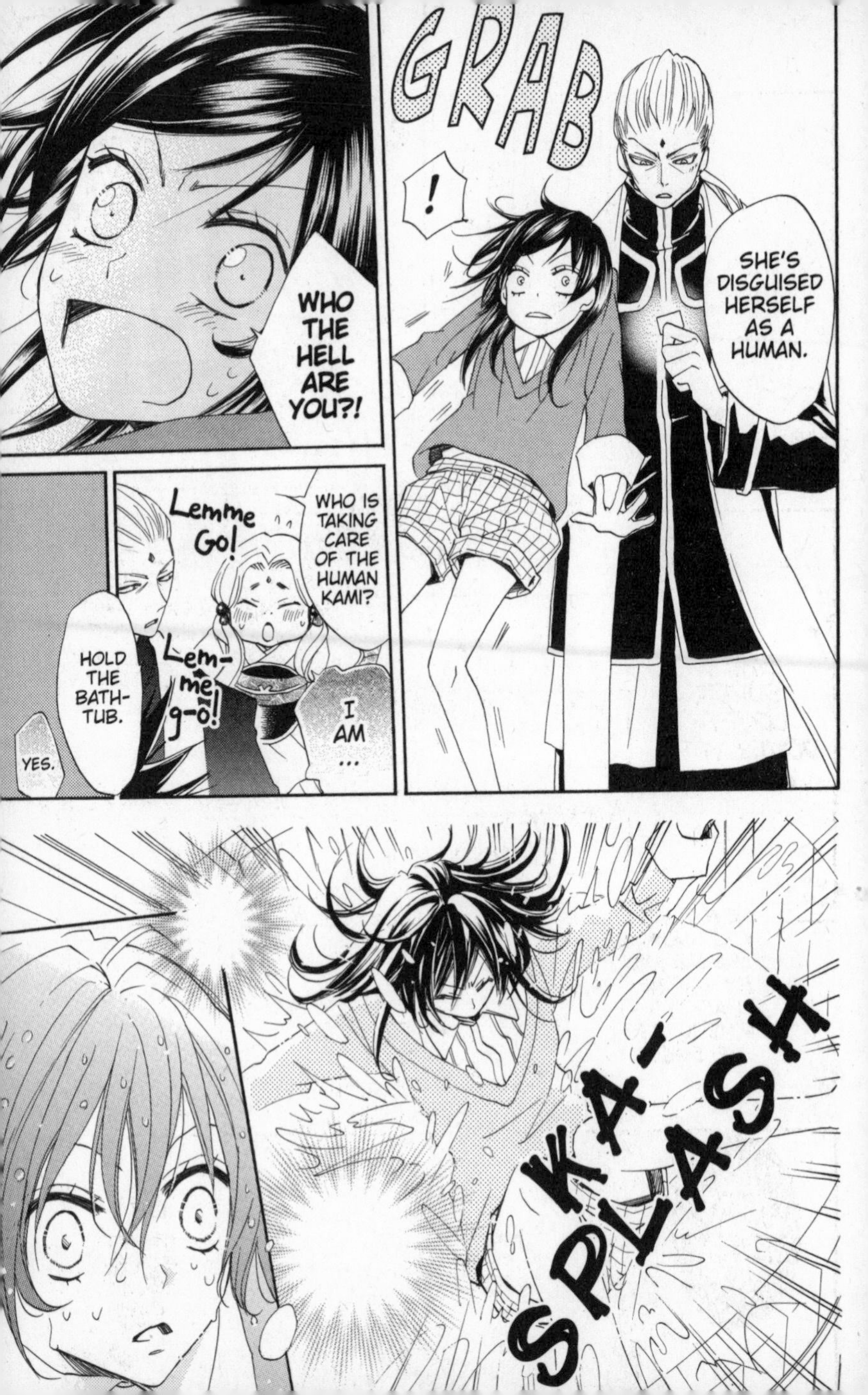
GRAB
!
SHE'S DISGUISED HERSELF AS A HUMAN.
WHO THE HELL ARE YOU?!
WHO IS TAKING CARE OF THE HUMAN KAMI?
I AM...
Lemme Go!
Lem-me g-o!
HOLD THE BATH-TUB.
YES.
KA-SPLASH

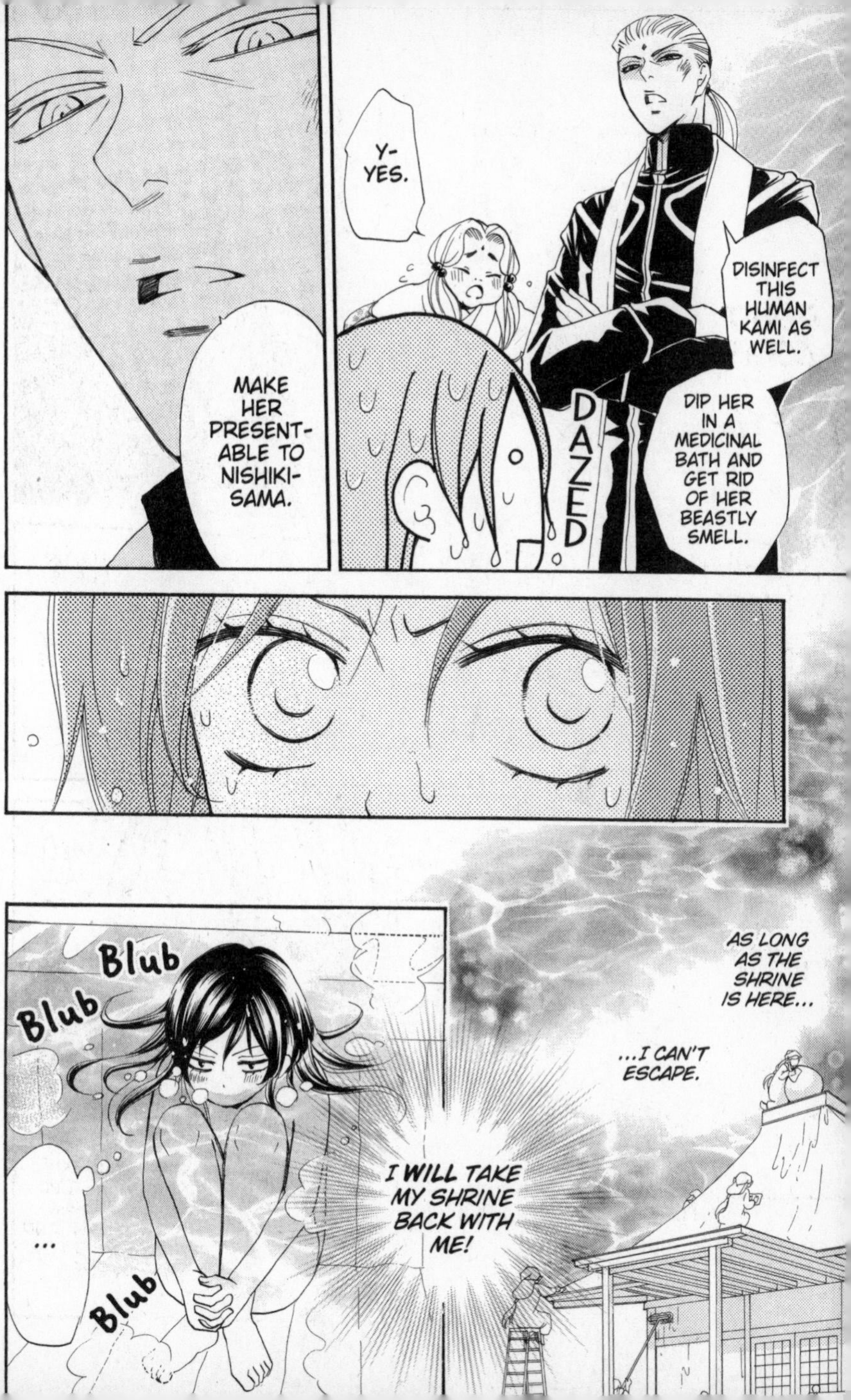

DISINFECT THIS HUMAN KAMI AS WELL.
DIP HER IN A MEDICINAL BATH AND GET RID OF HER BEASTLY SMELL.
Y- YES.
DAZED
MAKE HER PRESENT-ABLE TO NISHIKI-SAMA.
AS LONG AS THE SHRINE IS HERE...
...I CAN'T ESCAPE.
I WILL TAKE MY SHRINE BACK WITH ME!
Blub
Blub
...
Blub

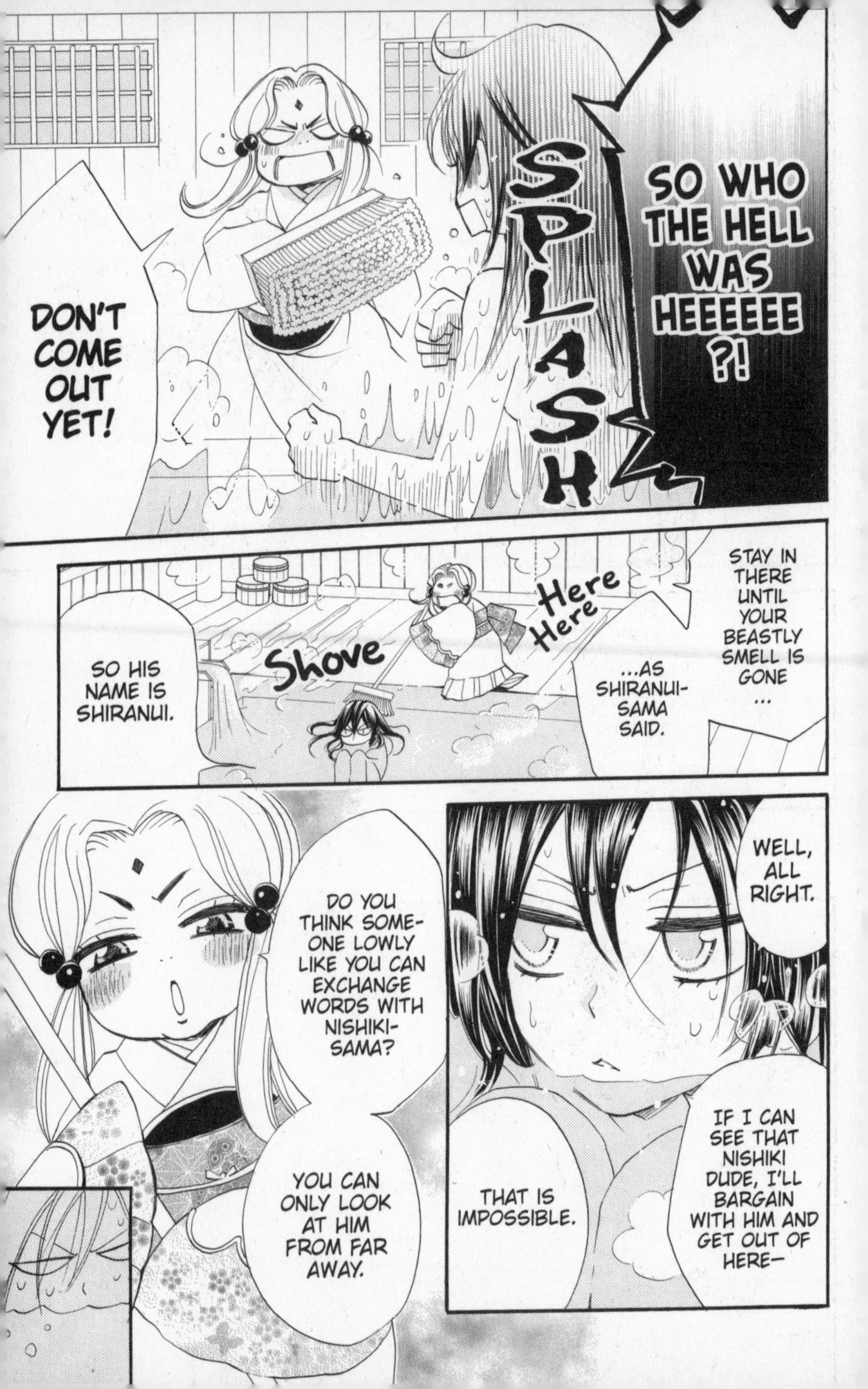
SO WHO THE HELL WAS HEEEEEE?!
SPLASH
DON'T COME OUT YET!
STAY IN THERE UNTIL YOUR BEASTLY SMELL IS GONE ...
...AS SHIRANUI-SAMA SAID.
Here Here
Shove
SO HIS NAME IS SHIRANUI.
WELL, ALL RIGHT.
IF I CAN SEE THAT NISHIKI DUDE, I'LL BARGAIN WITH HIM AND GET OUT OF HERE–
THAT IS IMPOSSIBLE.
DO YOU THINK SOME-ONE LOWLY LIKE YOU CAN EXCHANGE WORDS WITH NISHIKI-SAMA?
YOU CAN ONLY LOOK AT HIM FROM FAR AWAY.

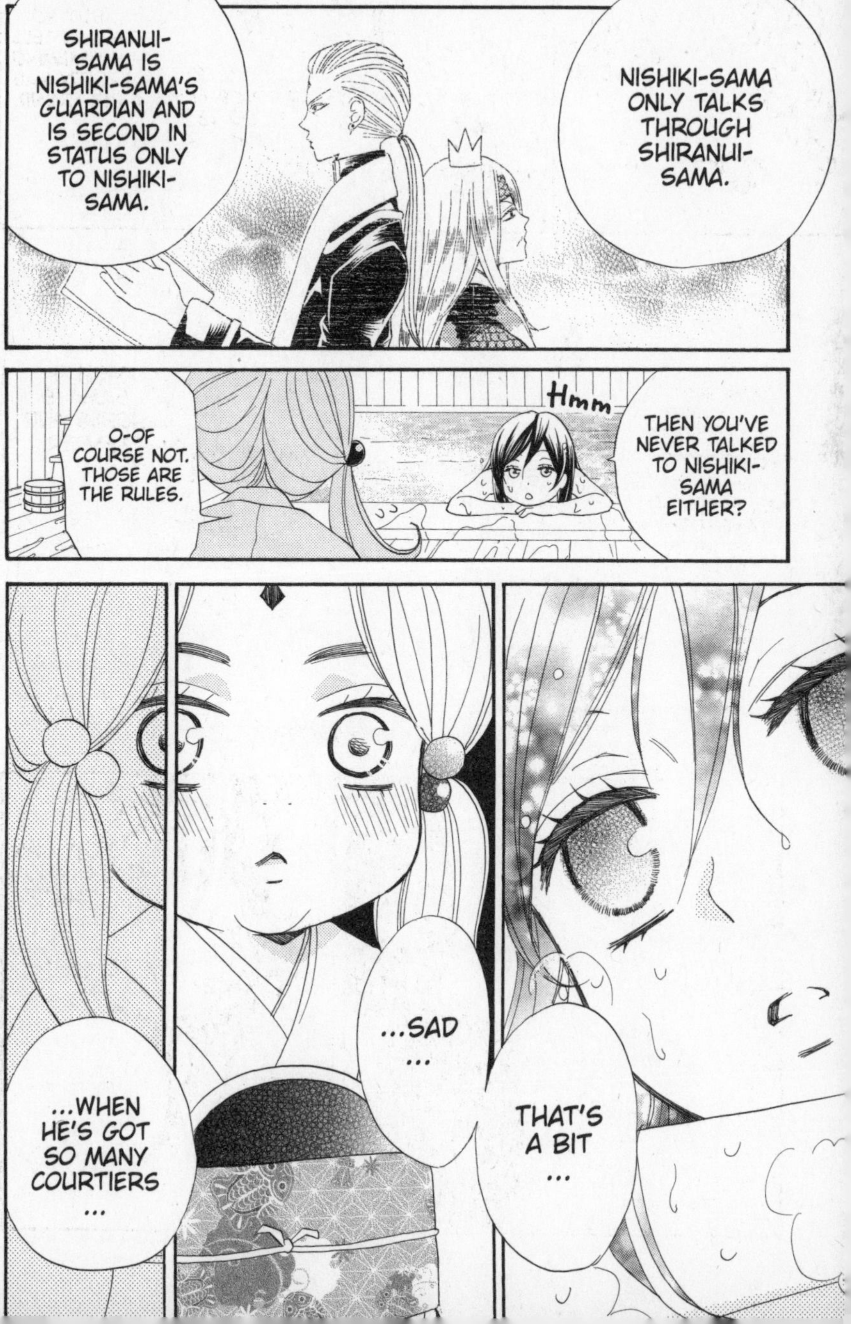
NISHIKI-SAMA ONLY TALKS THROUGH SHIRANUI-SAMA.
SHIRANUI-SAMA IS NISHIKI-SAMA'S GUARDIAN AND IS SECOND IN STATUS ONLY TO NISHIKI-SAMA.
Hmm
THEN YOU'VE NEVER TALKED TO NISHIKI-SAMA EITHER?
O-OF COURSE NOT. THOSE ARE THE RULES.
THAT'S A BIT ...
...SAD ...
...WHEN HE'S GOT SO MANY COURTIERS ...

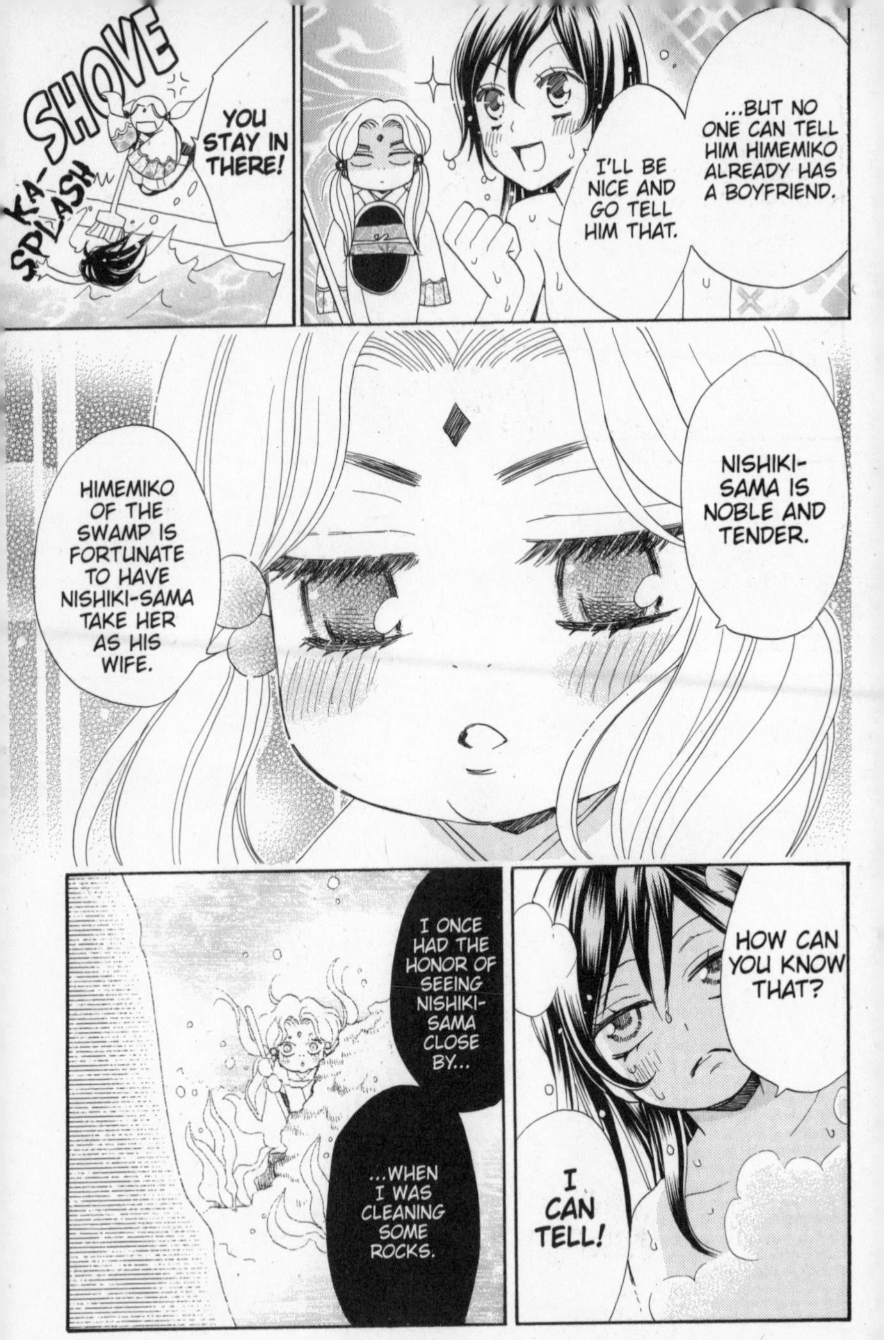
...BUT NO ONE CAN TELL HIM HIMEMIKO ALREADY HAS A BOYFRIEND.
I'LL BE NICE AND GO TELL HIM THAT.
YOU STAY IN THERE!
SHOVE
KA-SPLASH
NISHIKI-SAMA IS NOBLE AND TENDER.
HIMEMIKO OF THE SWAMP IS FORTUNATE TO HAVE NISHIKI-SAMA TAKE HER AS HIS WIFE.
HOW CAN YOU KNOW THAT?
I CAN TELL!
I ONCE HAD THE HONOR OF SEEING NISHIKI-SAMA CLOSE BY...
...WHEN I WAS CLEANING SOME ROCKS.

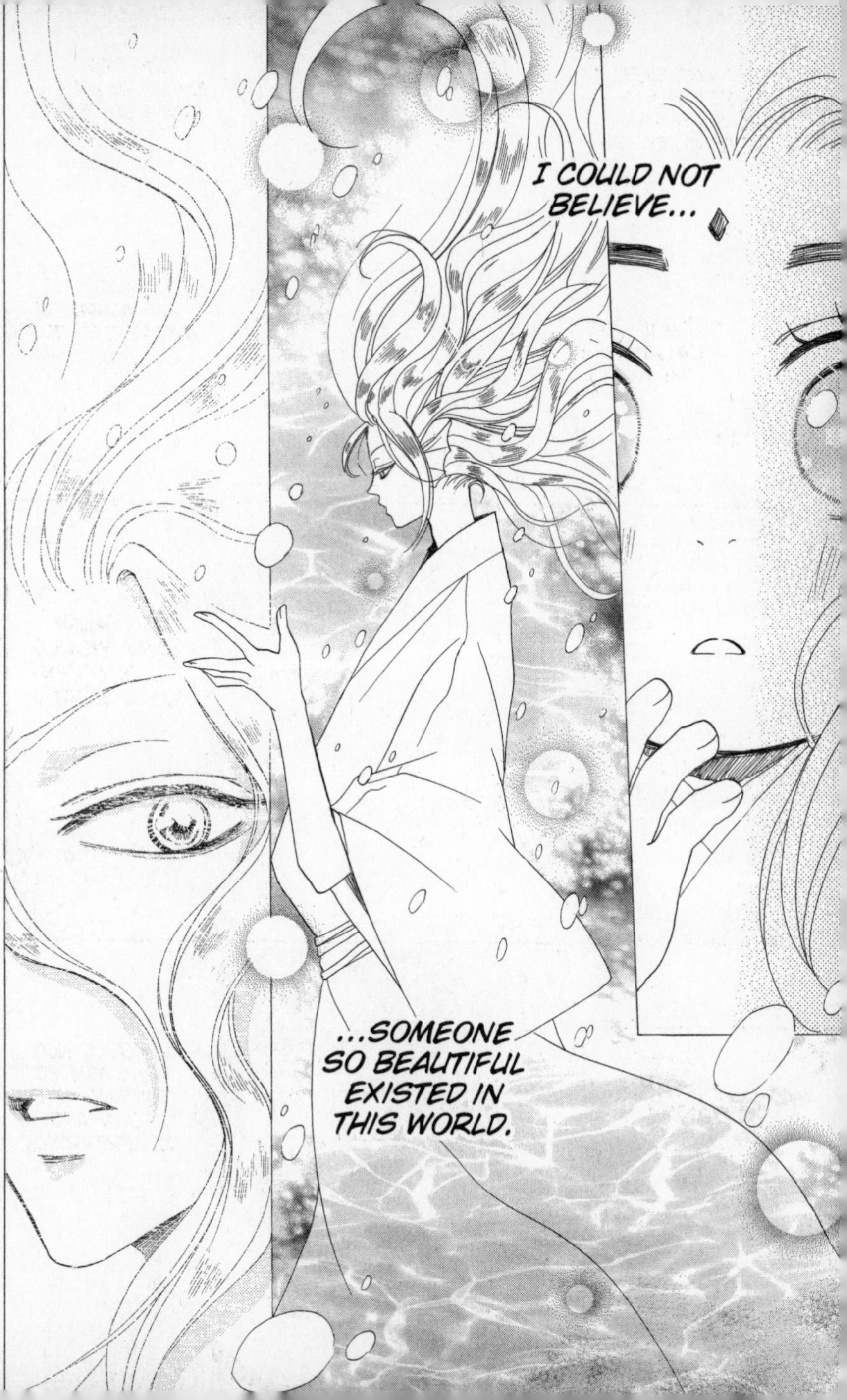
I COULD NOT BELIEVE...
...SOMEONE SO BEAUTIFUL EXISTED IN THIS WORLD.

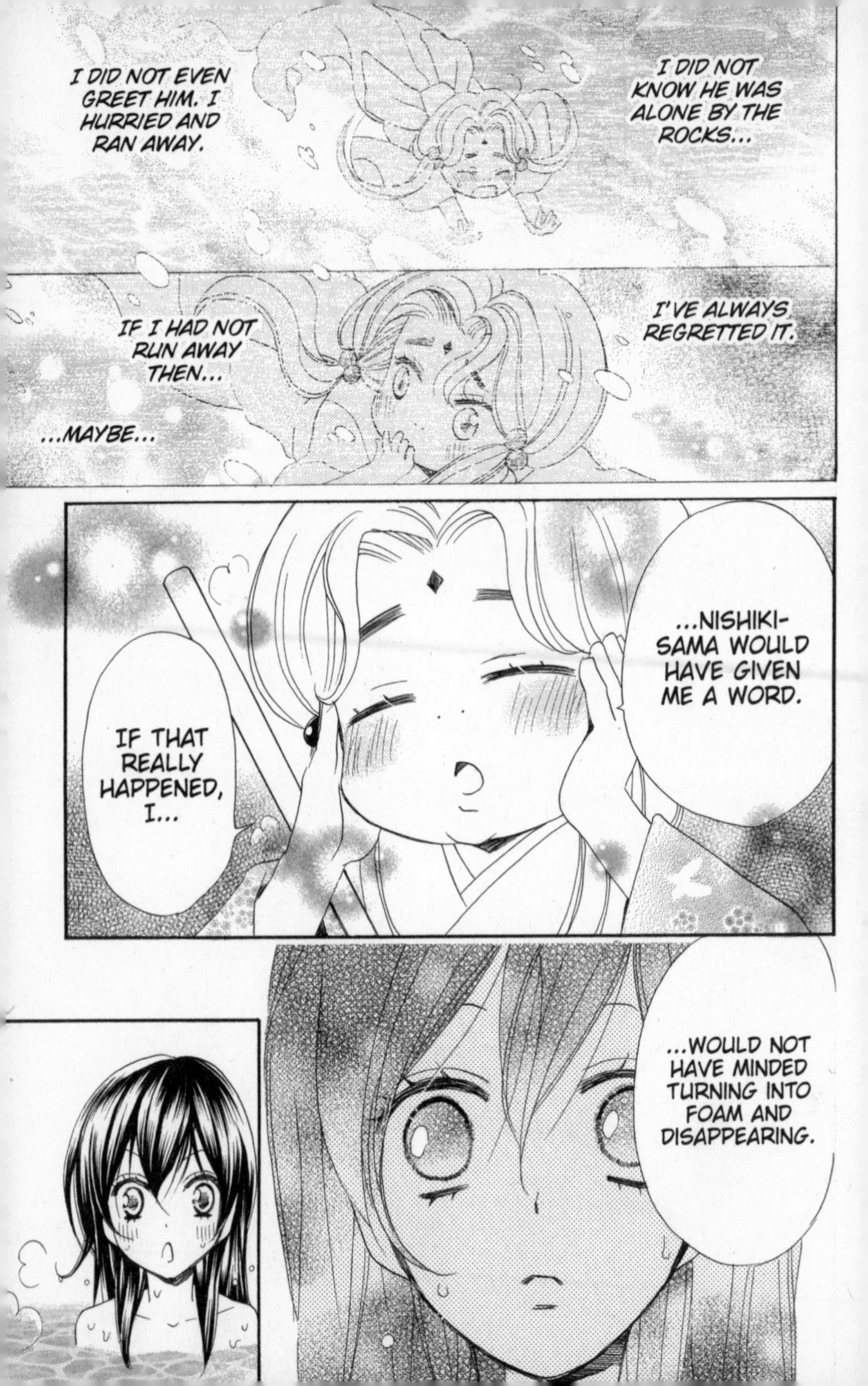
I DID NOT KNOW HE WAS ALONE BY THE ROCKS...
I DID NOT EVEN GREET HIM. I HURRIED AND RAN AWAY.
I'VE ALWAYS REGRETTED IT.
IF I HAD NOT RUN AWAY THEN...
...MAYBE...
...NISHIKI-SAMA WOULD HAVE GIVEN ME A WORD.
IF THAT REALLY HAPPENED, I...
...WOULD NOT HAVE MINDED TURNING INTO FOAM AND DISAPPEARING.

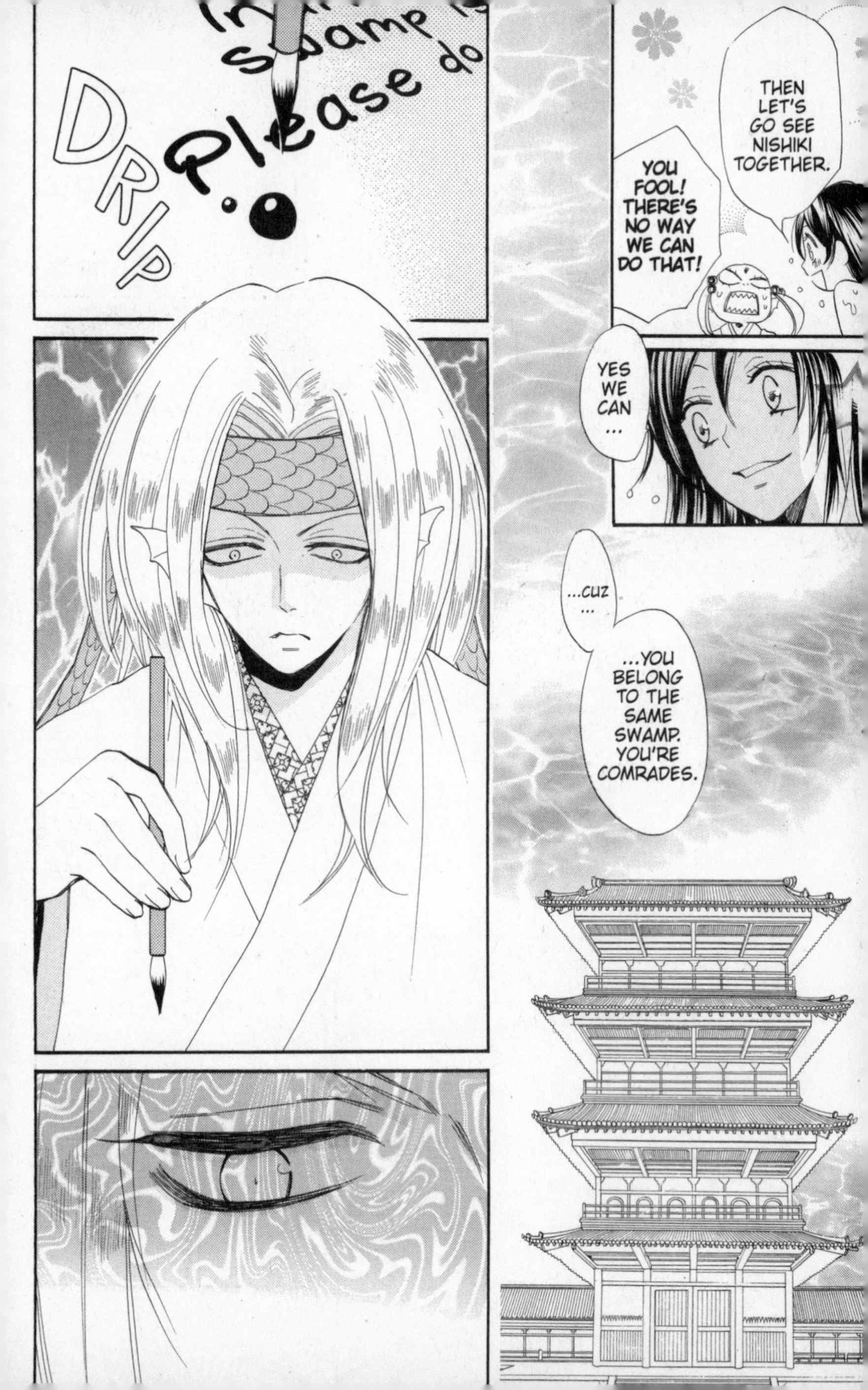
THEN LET'S GO SEE NISHIKI TOGETHER.
YOU FOOL! THERE'S NO WAY WE CAN DO THAT!
YES WE CAN ...
...CUZ ...
...YOU BELONG TO THE SAME SWAMP. YOU'RE COMRADES.
Please do
DRIP

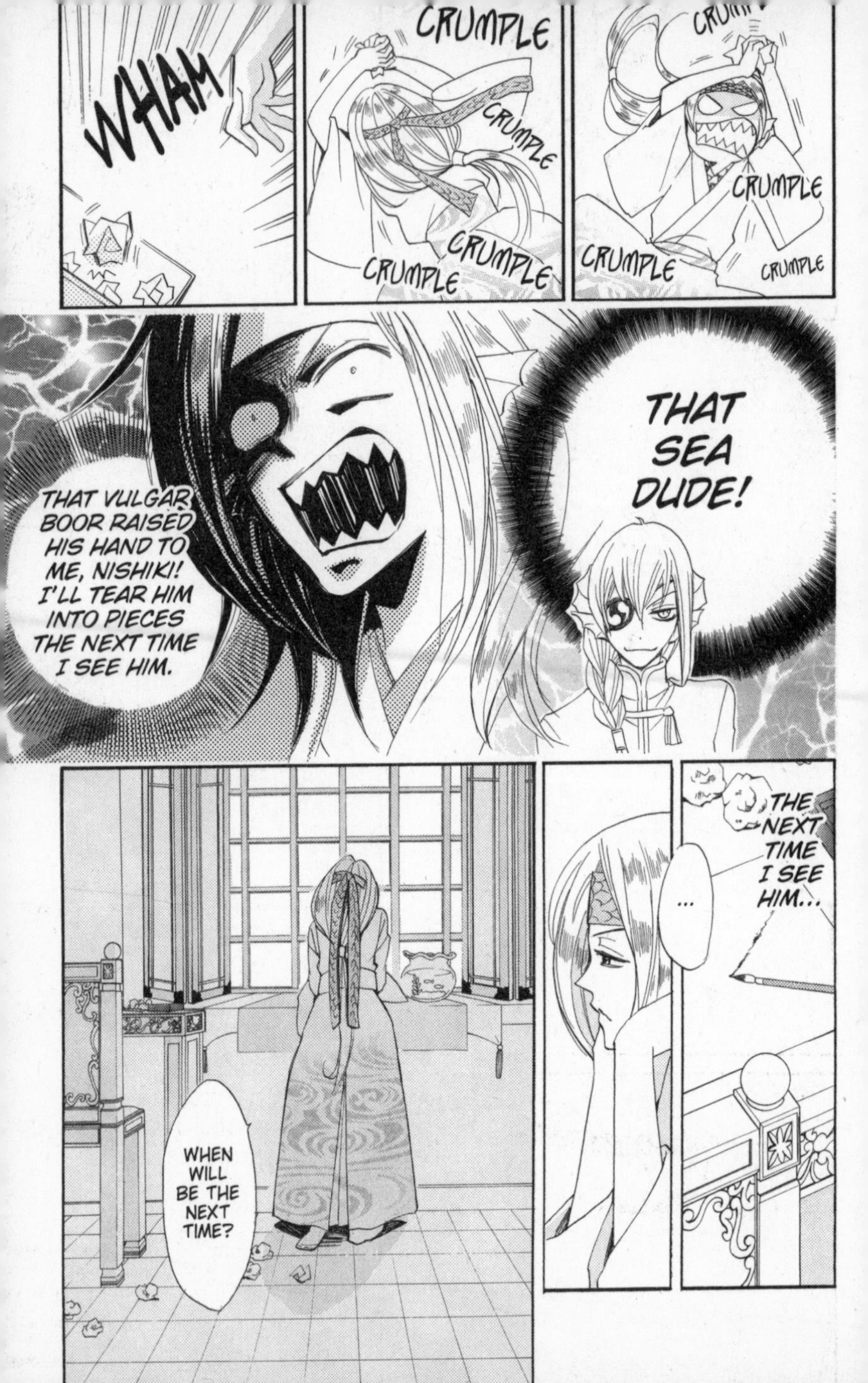
CRUMPLE
CRUMPLE
CRUMPLE
CRUMPLE
CRUMPLE
CRUMPLE
CRUMPLE
CRUMPLE
WHAM
THAT SEA DUDE!
THAT VULGAR BOOR RAISED HIS HAND TO ME, NISHIKI! I'LL TEAR HIM INTO PIECES THE NEXT TIME I SEE HIM.
THE NEXT TIME I SEE HIM...
...
WHEN WILL BE THE NEXT TIME?

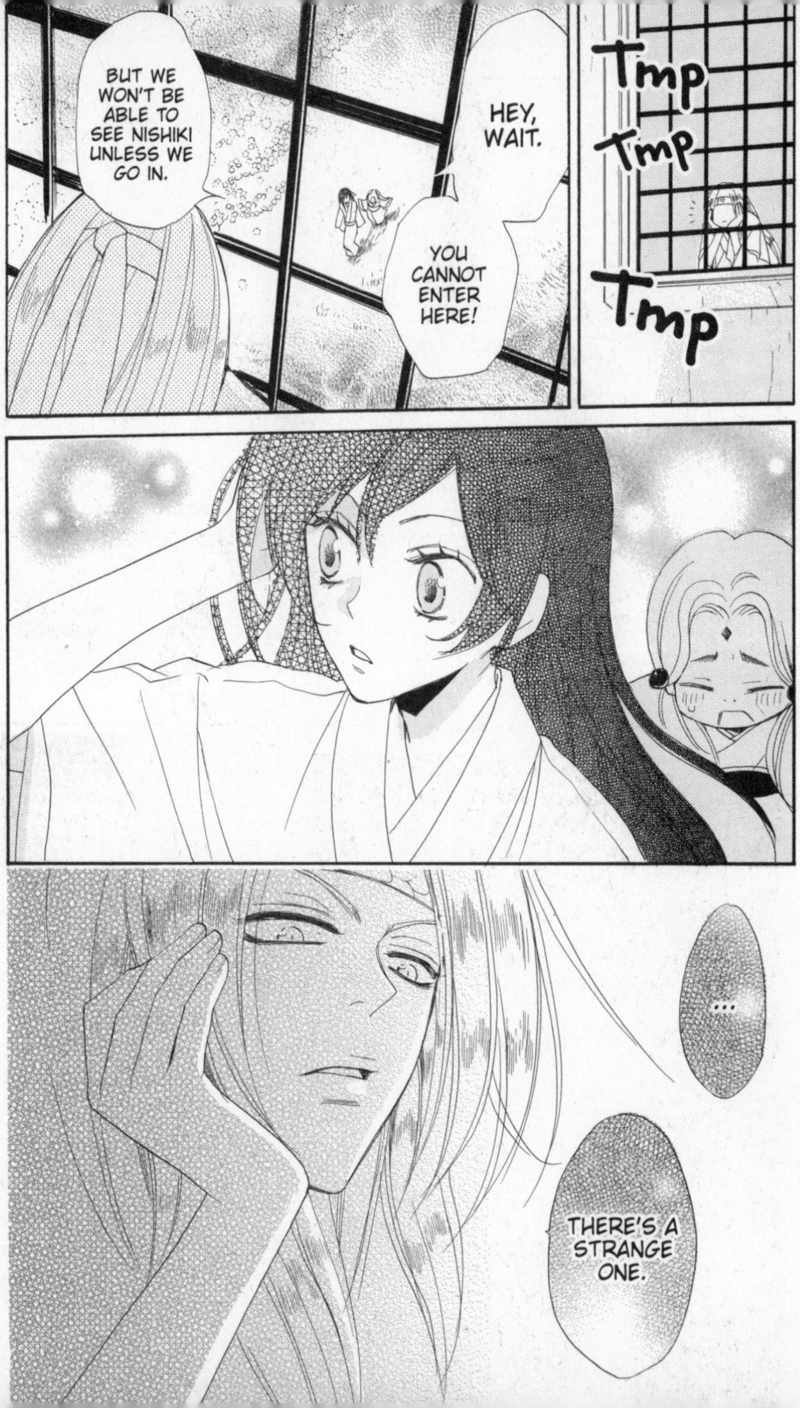
Tmp
Tmp
Tmp
HEY, WAIT.
YOU CANNOT ENTER HERE!
BUT WE WON'T BE ABLE TO SEE NISHIKI UNLESS WE GO IN.
...
THERE'S A STRANGE ONE.

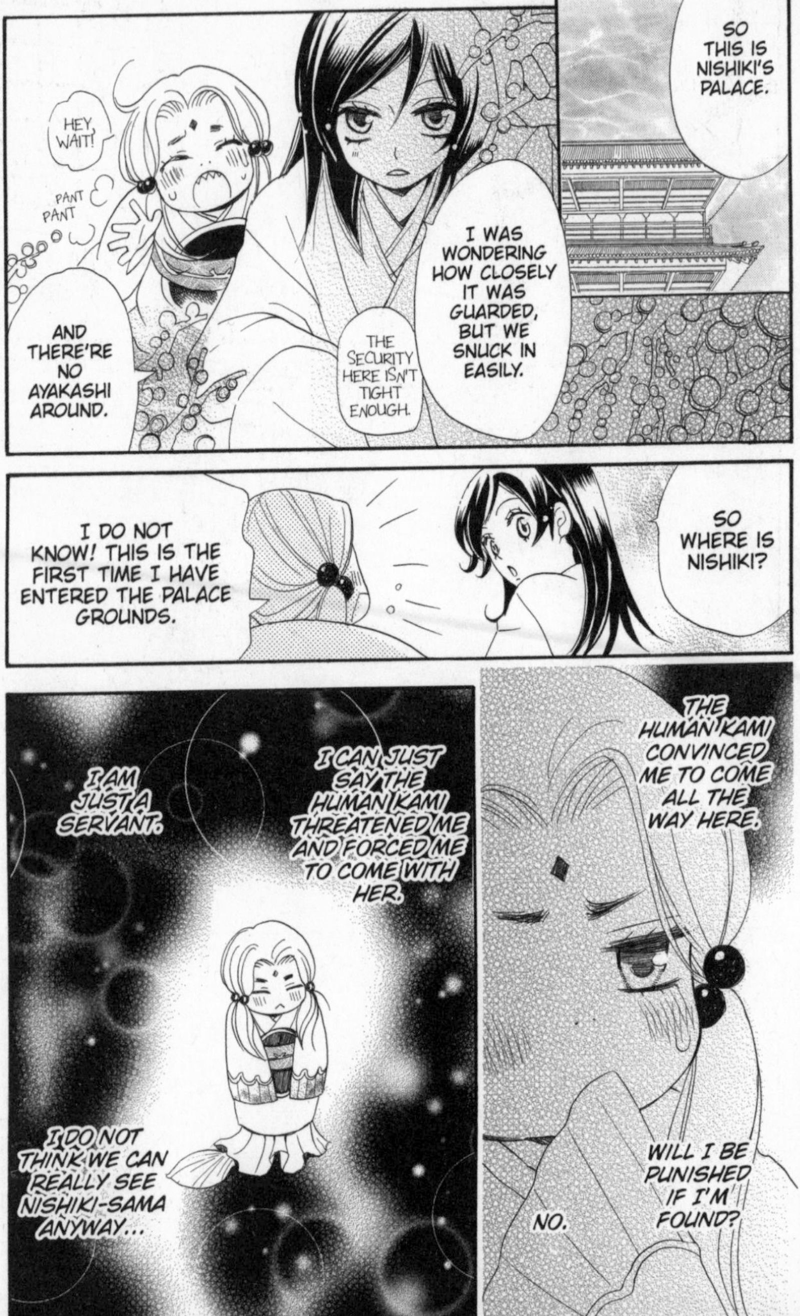
SO THIS IS NISHIKI'S PALACE.
I WAS WONDERING HOW CLOSELY IT WAS GUARDED, BUT WE SNUCK IN EASILY.
THE SECURITY HERE ISN'T TIGHT ENOUGH.
HEY, WAIT!
PANT PANT
AND THERE'RE NO AYAKASHI AROUND.
SO WHERE IS NISHIKI?
I DO NOT KNOW! THIS IS THE FIRST TIME I HAVE ENTERED THE PALACE GROUNDS.
THE HUMAN KAMI CONVINCED ME TO COME ALL THE WAY HERE.
WILL I BE PUNISHED IF I'M FOUND?
NO.
I CAN JUST SAY THE HUMAN KAMI THREATENED ME AND FORCED ME TO COME WITH HER.
I AM JUST A SERVANT.
I DO NOT THINK WE CAN REALLY SEE NISHIKI-SAMA ANYWAY...

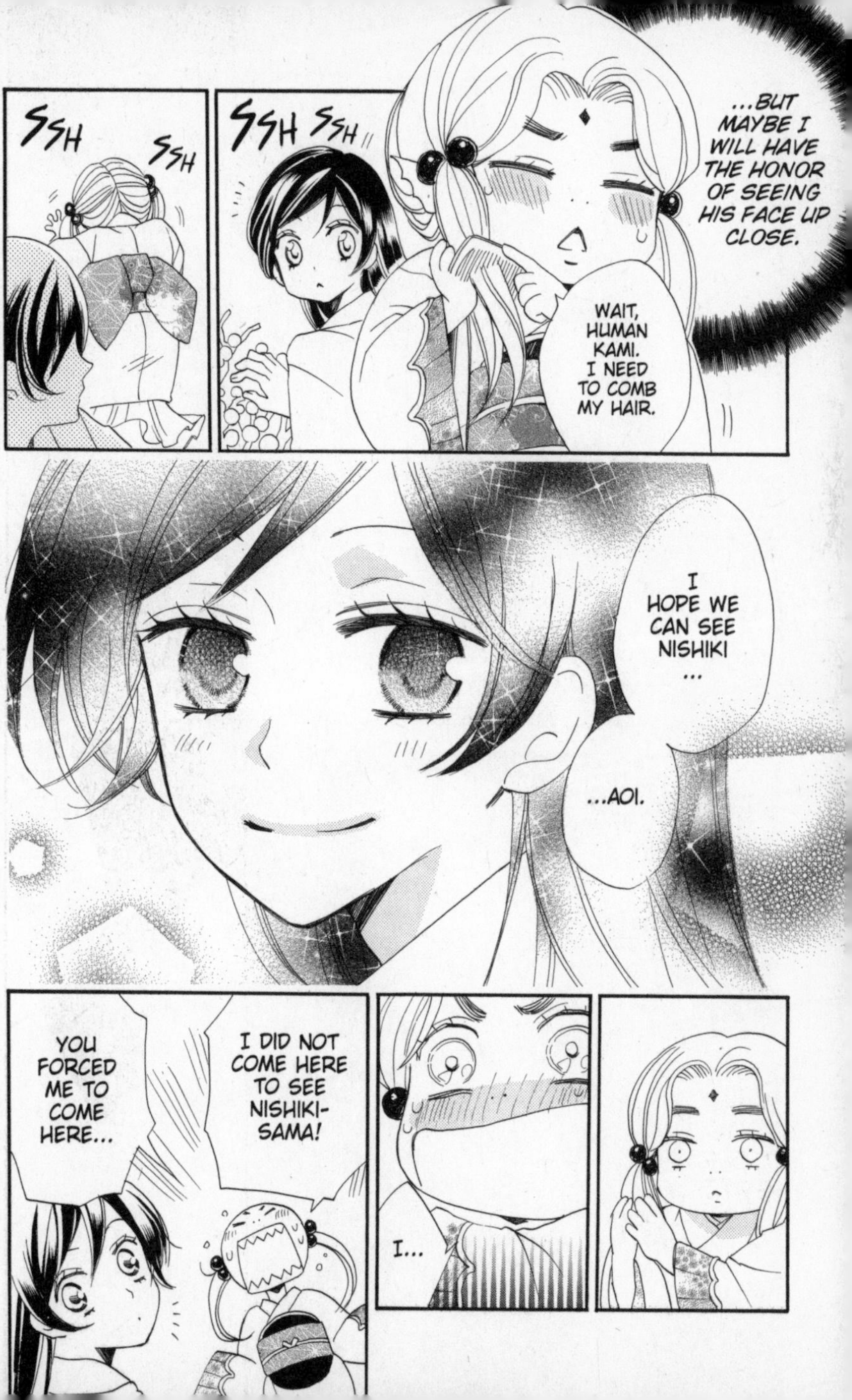
...BUT MAYBE I WILL HAVE THE HONOR OF SEEING HIS FACE UP CLOSE.
SSH SSH
WAIT, HUMAN KAMI. I NEED TO COMB MY HAIR.
SSH SSH
I HOPE WE CAN SEE NISHIKI ...
...AOI.
I...
I DID NOT COME HERE TO SEE NISHIKI-SAMA!
YOU FORCED ME TO COME HERE...

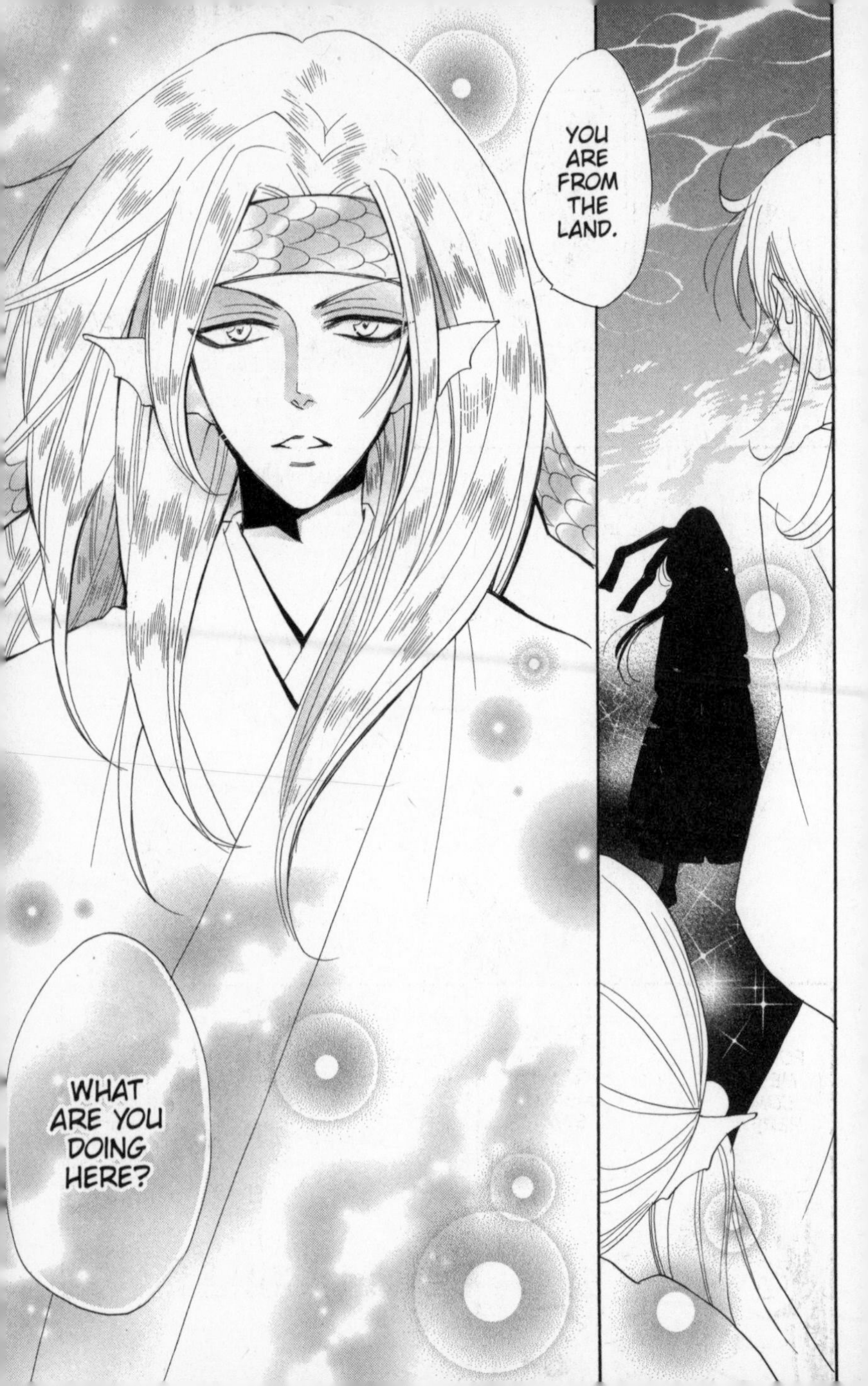
YOU ARE FROM THE LAND.
WHAT ARE YOU DOING HERE?

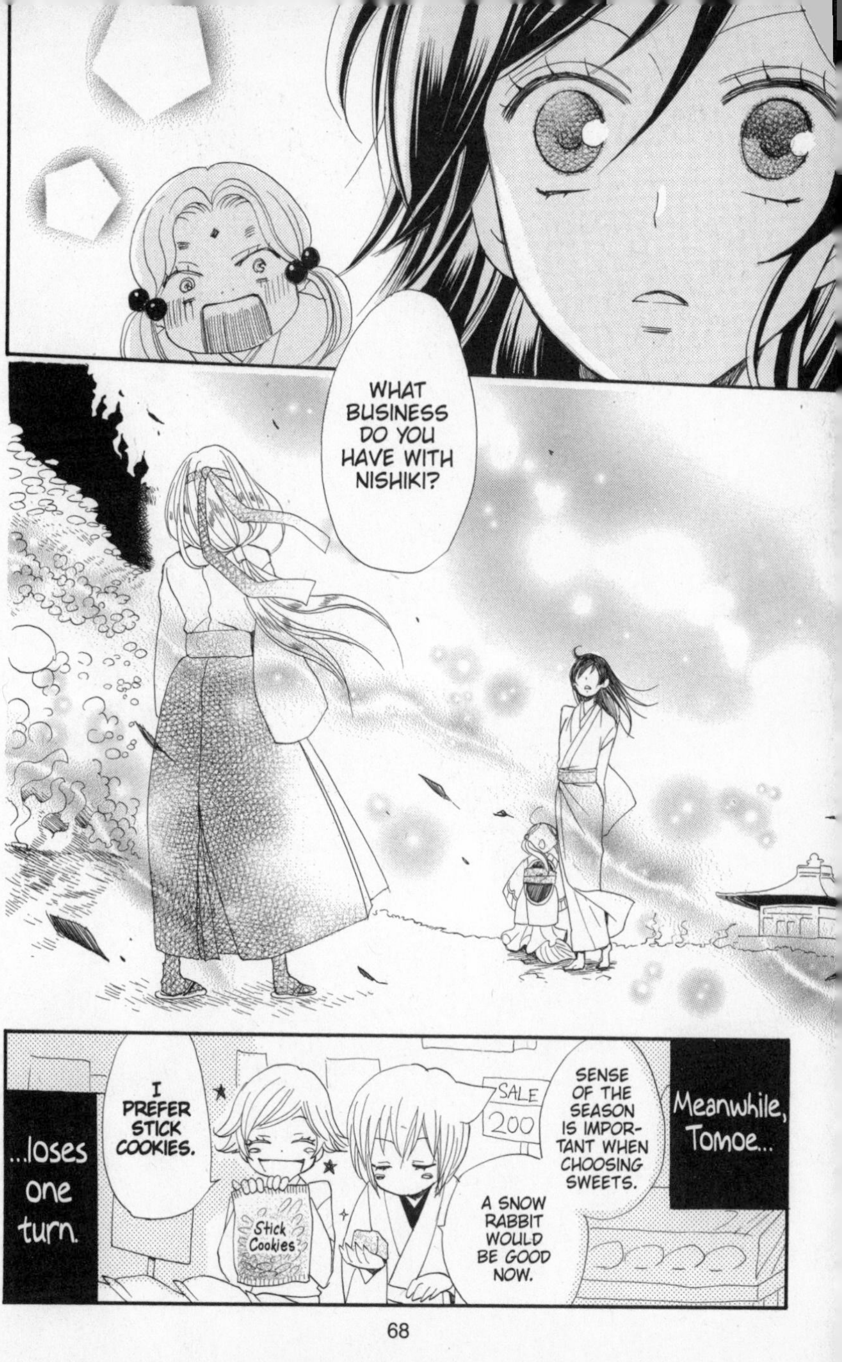
WHAT BUSINESS DO YOU HAVE WITH NISHIKI?
Meanwhile, Tomoe...
SENSE OF THE SEASON IS IMPORTANT WHEN CHOOSING SWEETS.
A SNOW RABBIT WOULD BE GOOD NOW.
SALE
200
I PREFER STICK COOKIES.
Stick Cookies
...loses one turn.

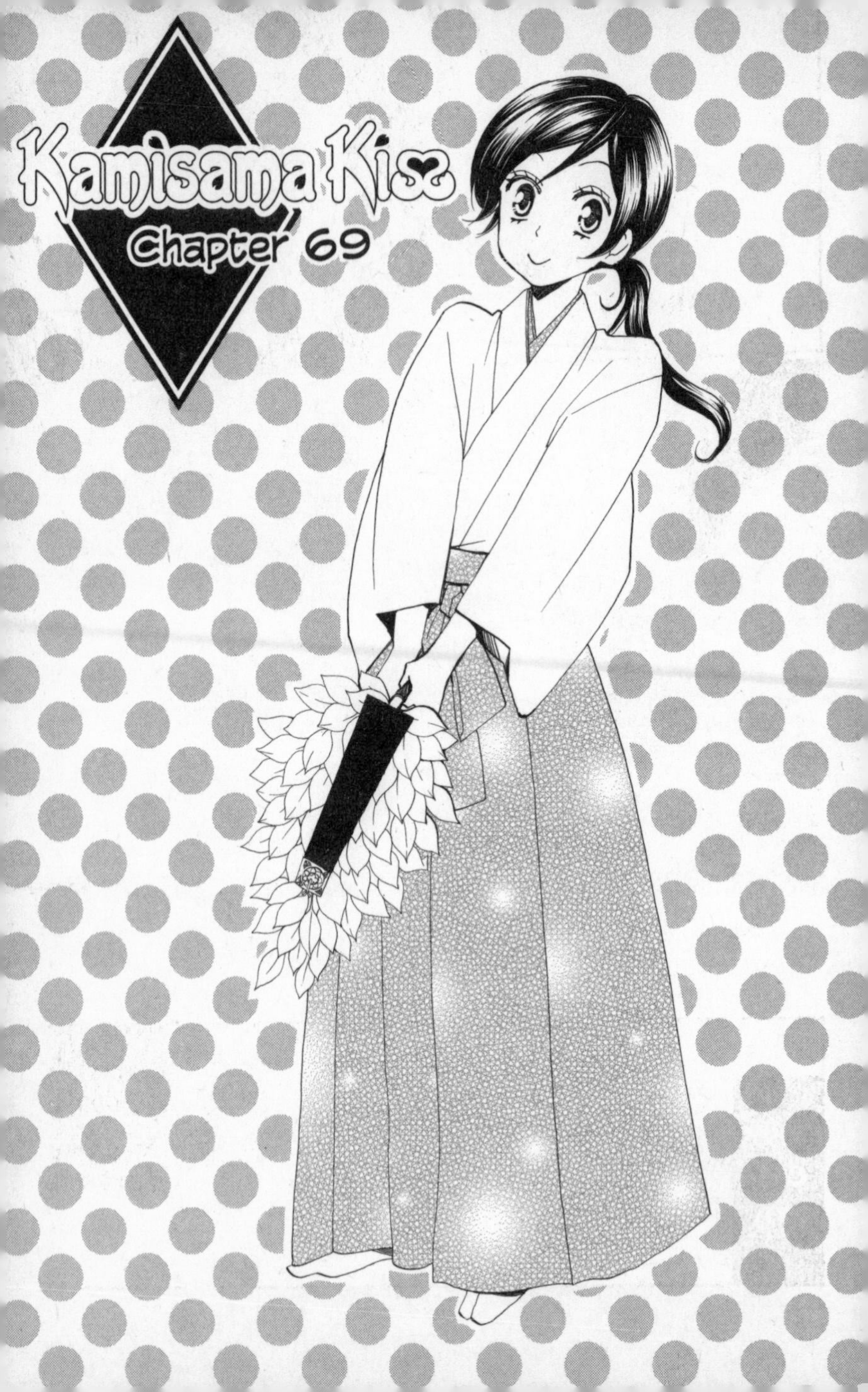
Kamisama Kiss
Chapter 69

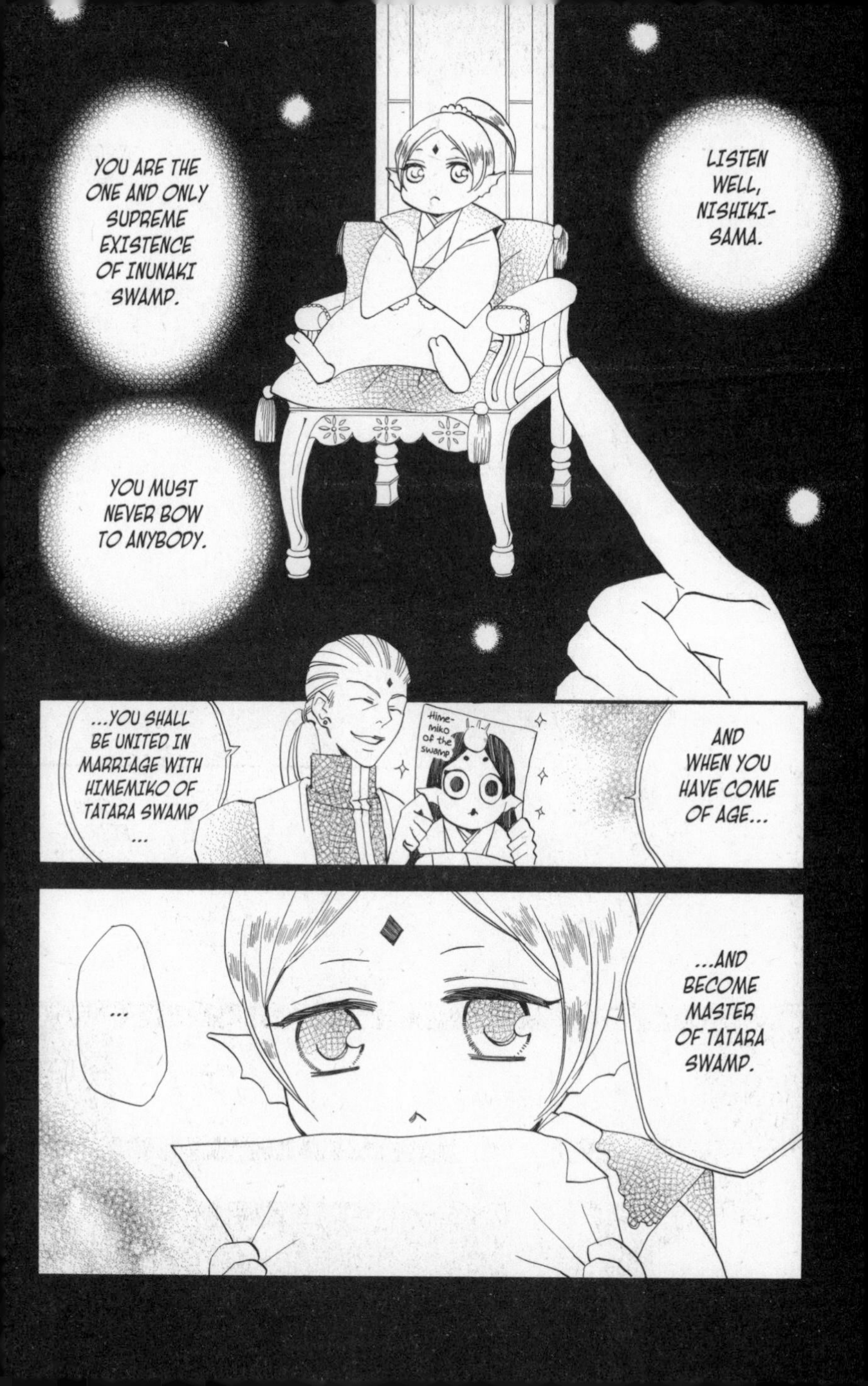
LISTEN WELL, NISHIKI-SAMA.
YOU ARE THE ONE AND ONLY SUPREME EXISTENCE OF INUNAKI SWAMP.
YOU MUST NEVER BOW TO ANYBODY.
AND WHEN YOU HAVE COME OF AGE...
...YOU SHALL BE UNITED IN MARRIAGE WITH HIMEMIKO OF TATARA SWAMP ...
Hime-miko of the swamp
...AND BECOME MASTER OF TATARA SWAMP.
...

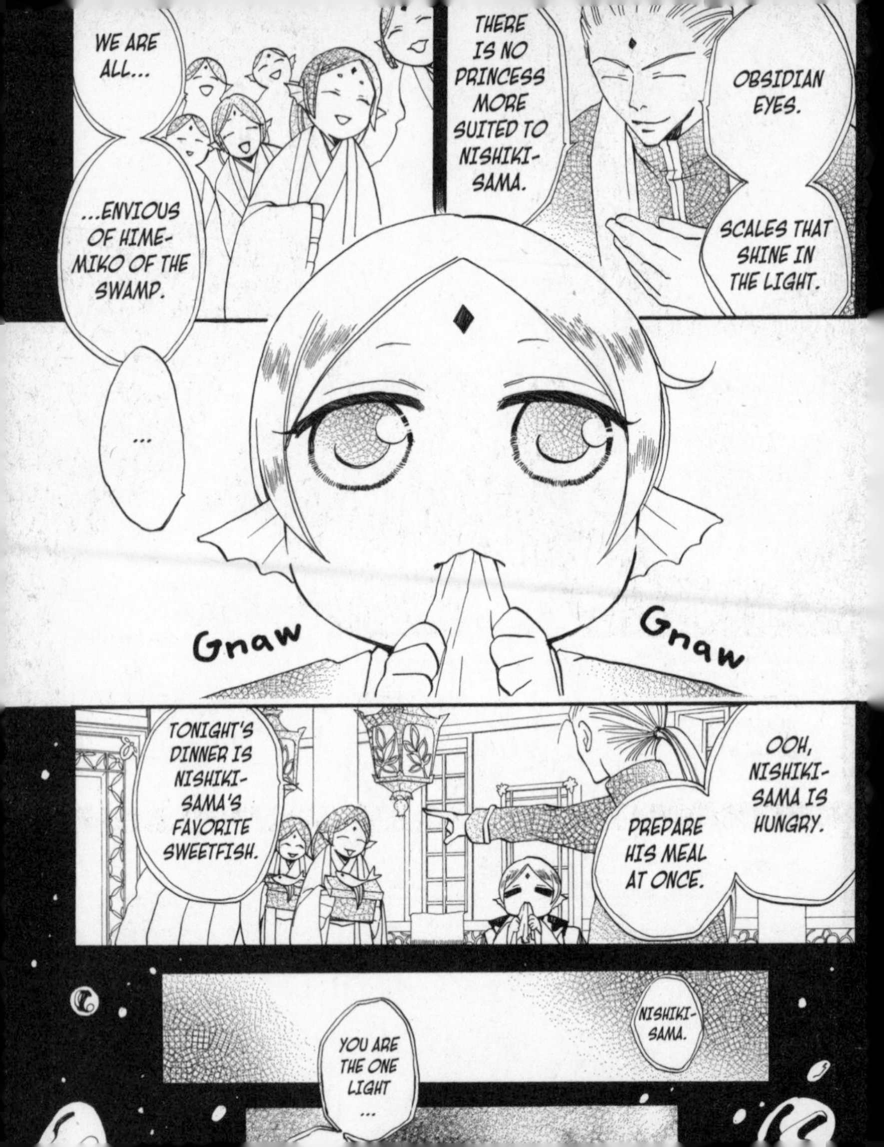
OBSIDIAN EYES.
SCALES THAT SHINE IN THE LIGHT.
THERE IS NO PRINCESS MORE SUITED TO NISHIKI-SAMA.
WE ARE ALL...
...ENVIOUS OF HIME-MIKO OF THE SWAMP.
...
Gnaw
Gnaw
OOH, NISHIKI-SAMA IS HUNGRY.
PREPARE HIS MEAL AT ONCE.
TONIGHT'S DINNER IS NISHIKI-SAMA'S FAVORITE SWEETFISH.
NISHIKI-SAMA.
YOU ARE THE ONE LIGHT ...

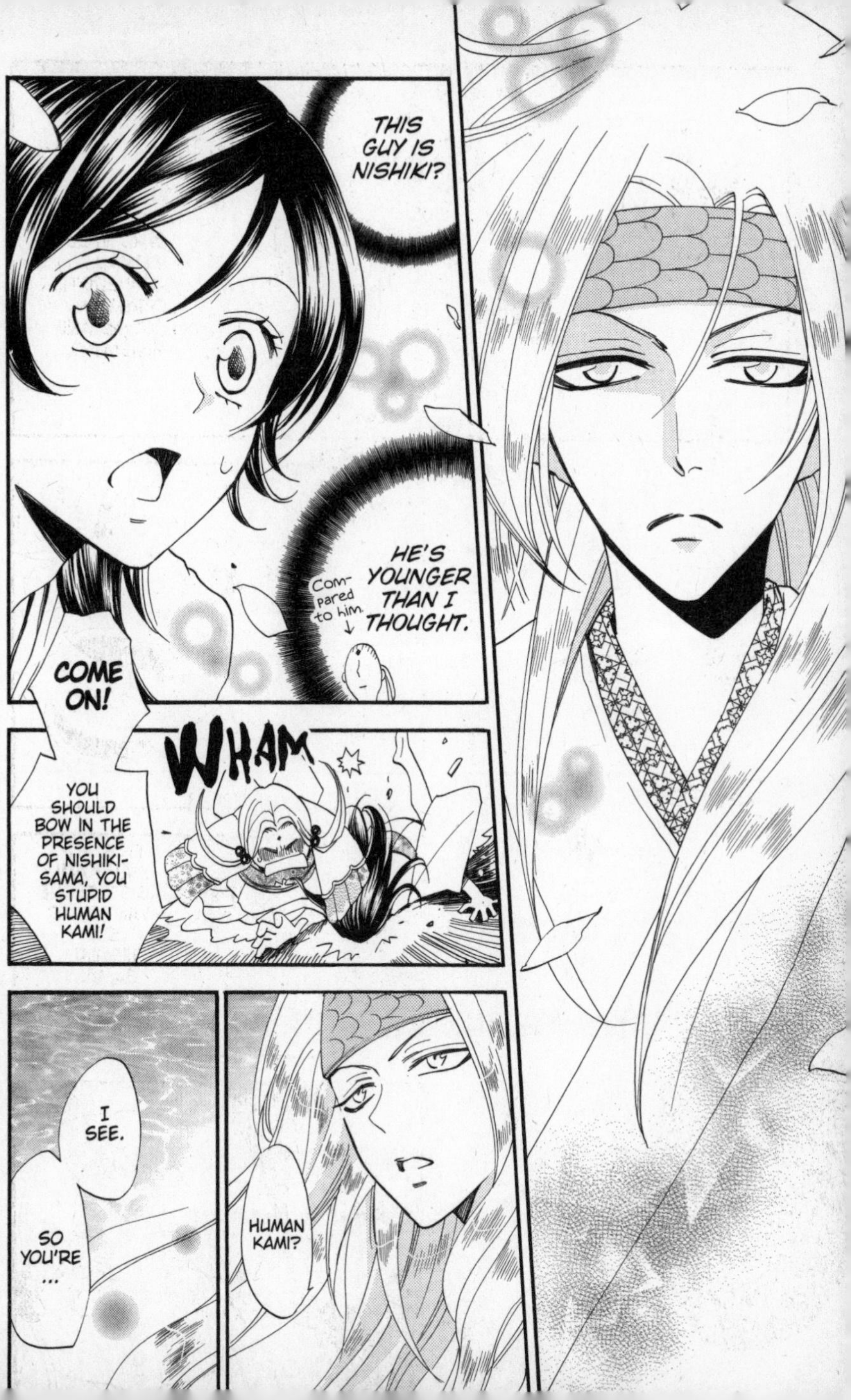

THIS GUY IS NISHIKI?
HE'S YOUNGER THAN I THOUGHT.
Compared to him. ↓
COME ON!
WHAM
YOU SHOULD BOW IN THE PRESENCE OF NISHIKI-SAMA, YOU STUPID HUMAN KAMI!
HUMAN KAMI?
I SEE.
SO YOU'RE ...

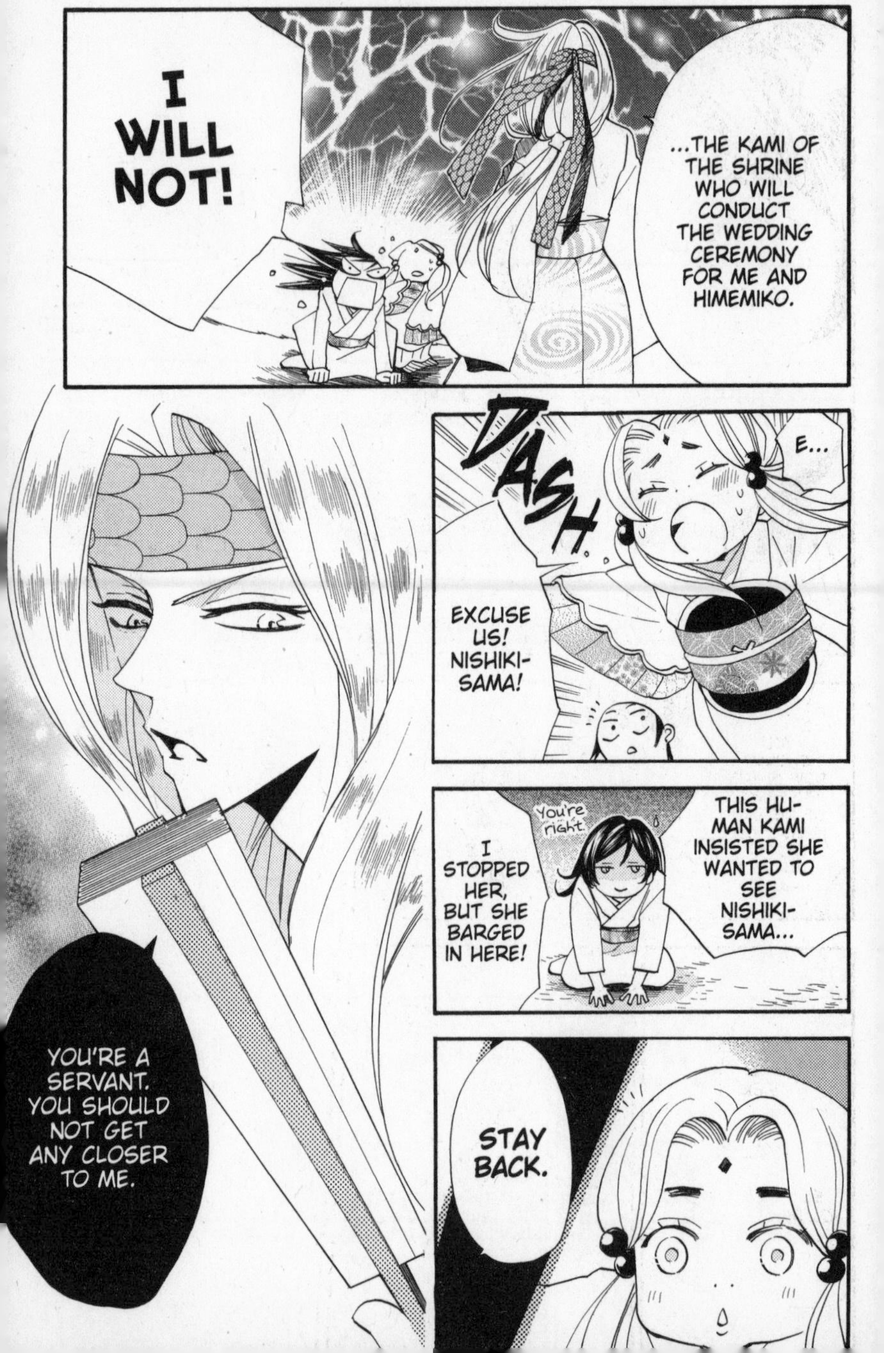
...THE KAMI OF THE SHRINE WHO WILL CONDUCT THE WEDDING CEREMONY FOR ME AND HIMEMIKO.
I WILL NOT!
E...
DASH
EXCUSE US! NISHIKI-SAMA!
THIS HU-MAN KAMI INSISTED SHE WANTED TO SEE NISHIKI-SAMA...
You're right.
I STOPPED HER, BUT SHE BARGED IN HERE!
STAY BACK.
YOU'RE A SERVANT. YOU SHOULD NOT GET ANY CLOSER TO ME.

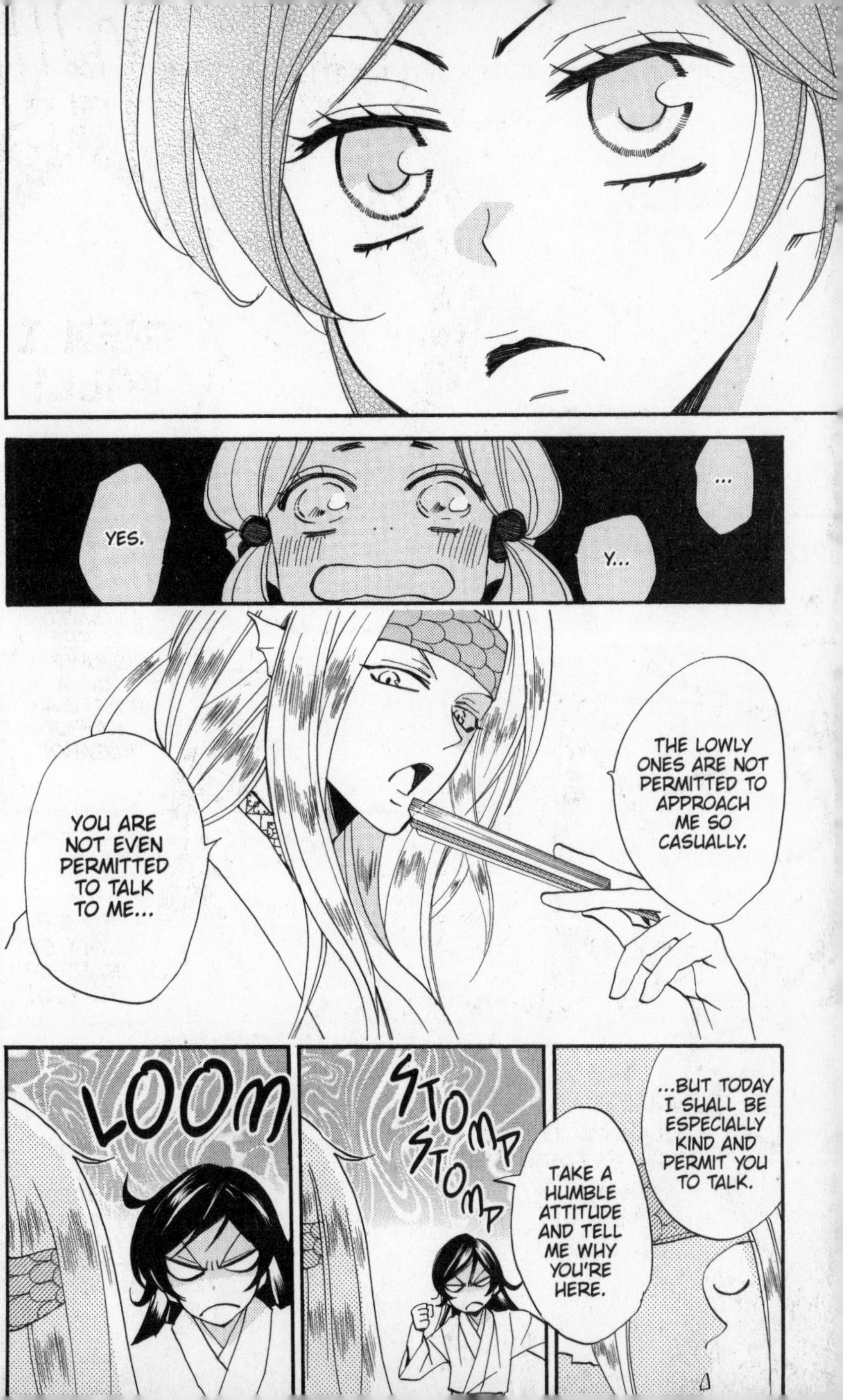
...
Y...
YES.
THE LOWLY ONES ARE NOT PERMITTED TO APPROACH ME SO CASUALLY.
YOU ARE NOT EVEN PERMITTED TO TALK TO ME...
...BUT TODAY I SHALL BE ESPECIALLY KIND AND PERMIT YOU TO TALK.
TAKE A HUMBLE ATTITUDE AND TELL ME WHY YOU'RE HERE.
STOMP STOMP
LOOM

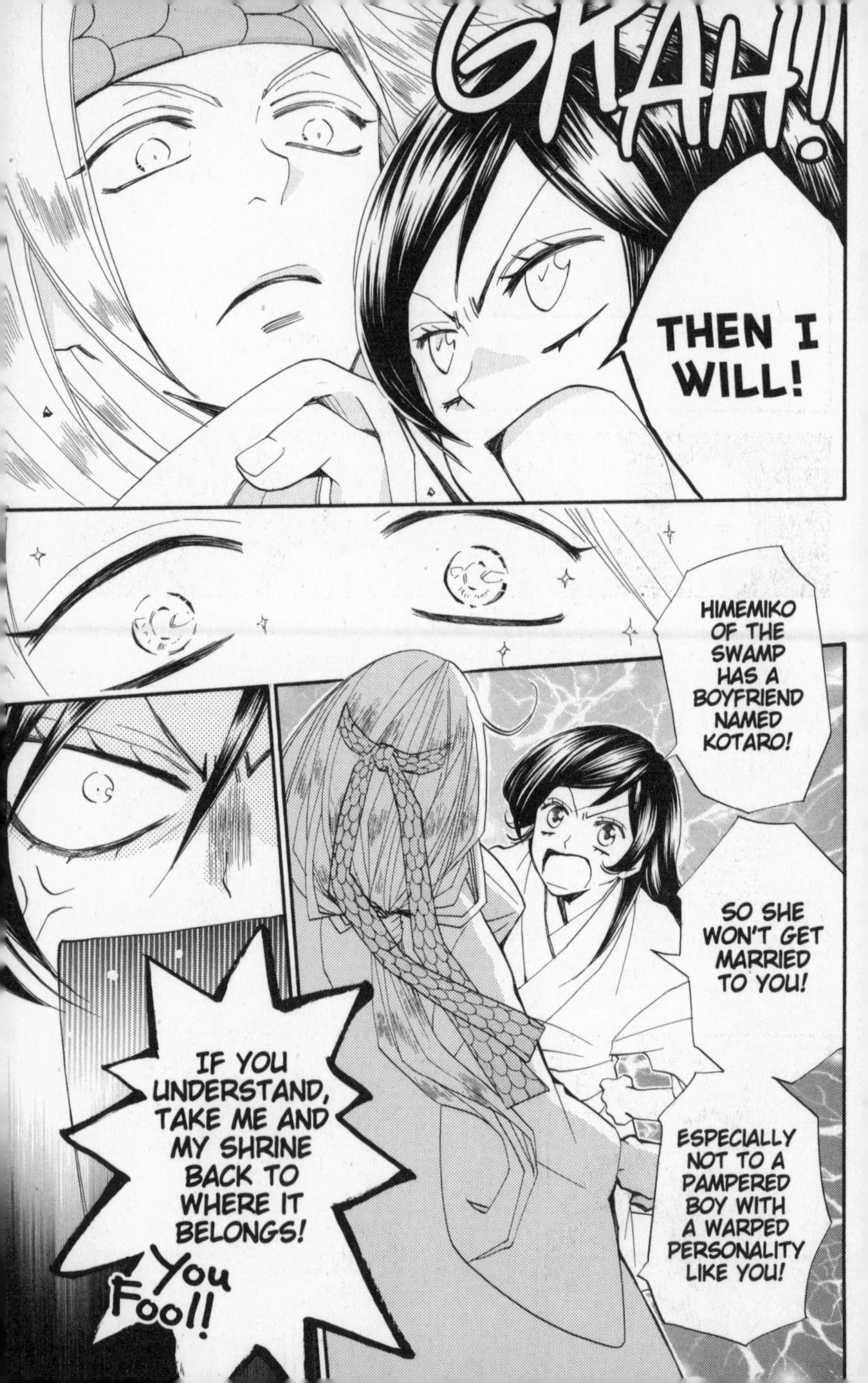
GRAH!!
THEN I WILL!
HIMEMIKO OF THE SWAMP HAS A BOYFRIEND NAMED KOTARO!
SO SHE WON'T GET MARRIED TO YOU!
ESPECIALLY NOT TO A PAMPERED BOY WITH A WARPED PERSONALITY LIKE YOU!
IF YOU UNDERSTAND, TAKE ME AND MY SHRINE BACK TO WHERE IT BELONGS!
You Fool!!

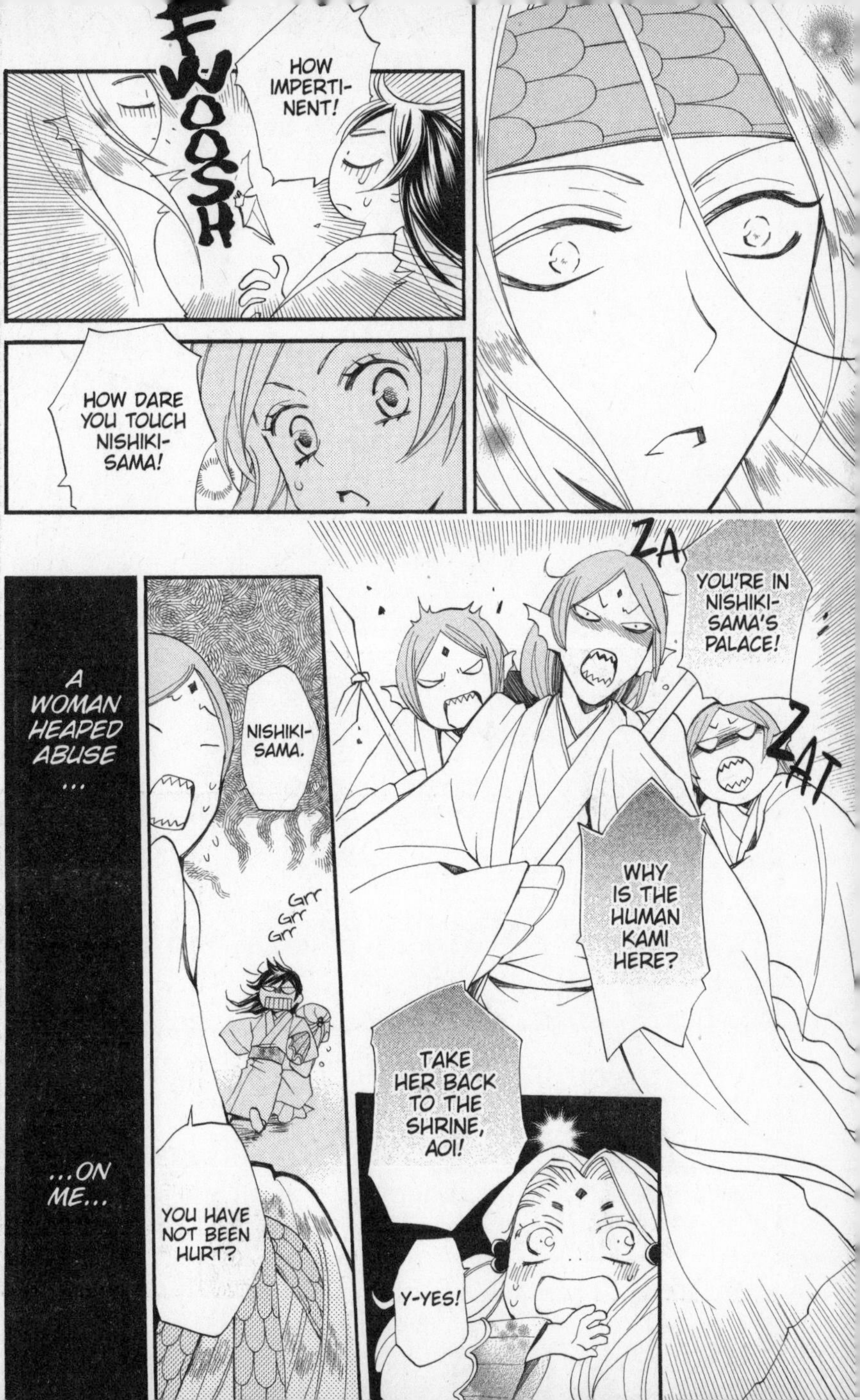
FWOOSH
HOW IMPERTI-NENT!
HOW DARE YOU TOUCH NISHIKI-SAMA!
ZA
YOU'RE IN NISHIKI-SAMA'S PALACE!
ZAT
WHY IS THE HUMAN KAMI HERE?
TAKE HER BACK TO THE SHRINE, AOI!
Y-YES!
NISHIKI-SAMA.
Grr Grr Grr
YOU HAVE NOT BEEN HURT?
A WOMAN HEAPED ABUSE ...
...ON ME...

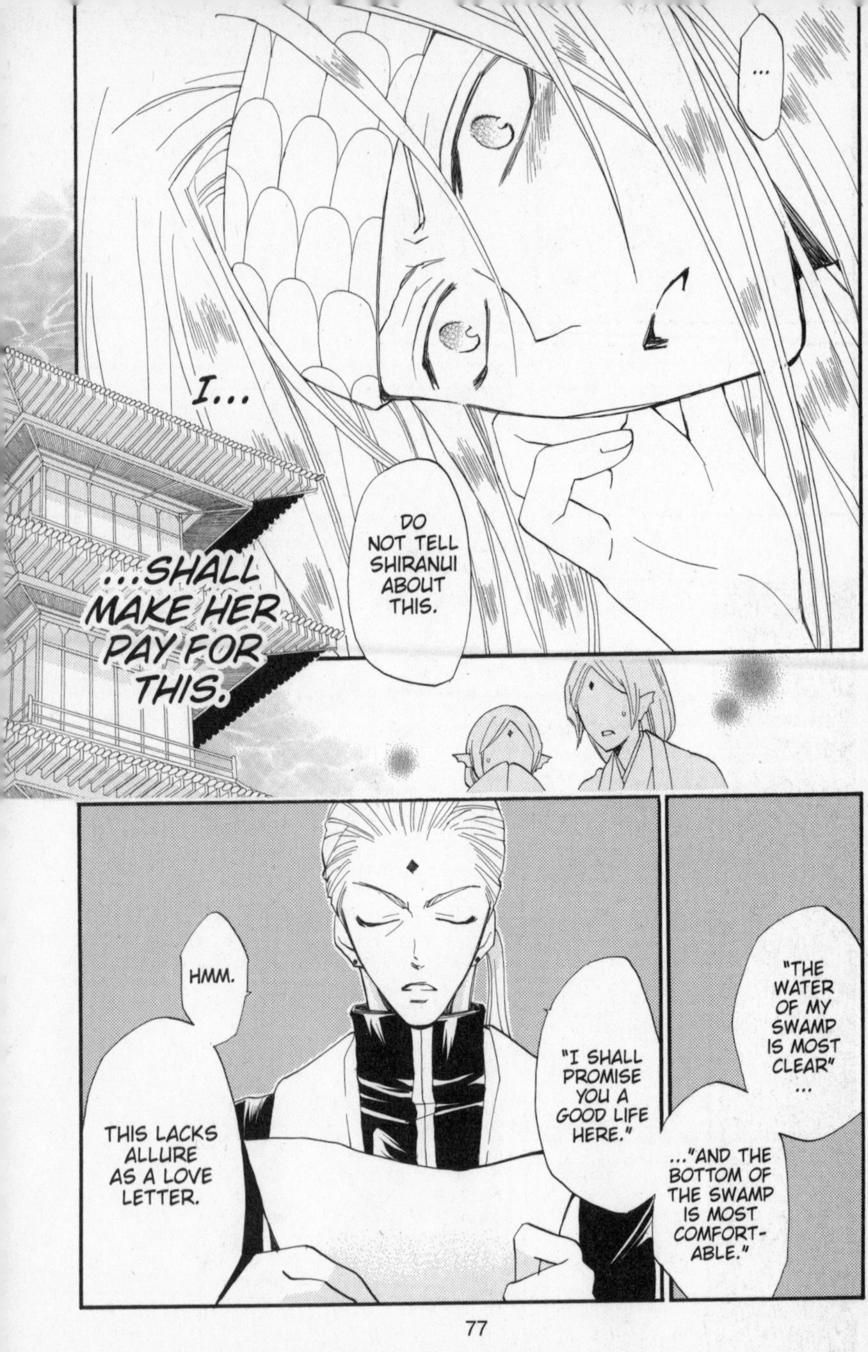
...
I...
...SHALL MAKE HER PAY FOR THIS.
DO NOT TELL SHIRANUI ABOUT THIS.
"THE WATER OF MY SWAMP IS MOST CLEAR" ...
..."AND THE BOTTOM OF THE SWAMP IS MOST COMFORT-ABLE."
"I SHALL PROMISE YOU A GOOD LIFE HERE."
HMM.
THIS LACKS ALLURE AS A LOVE LETTER.

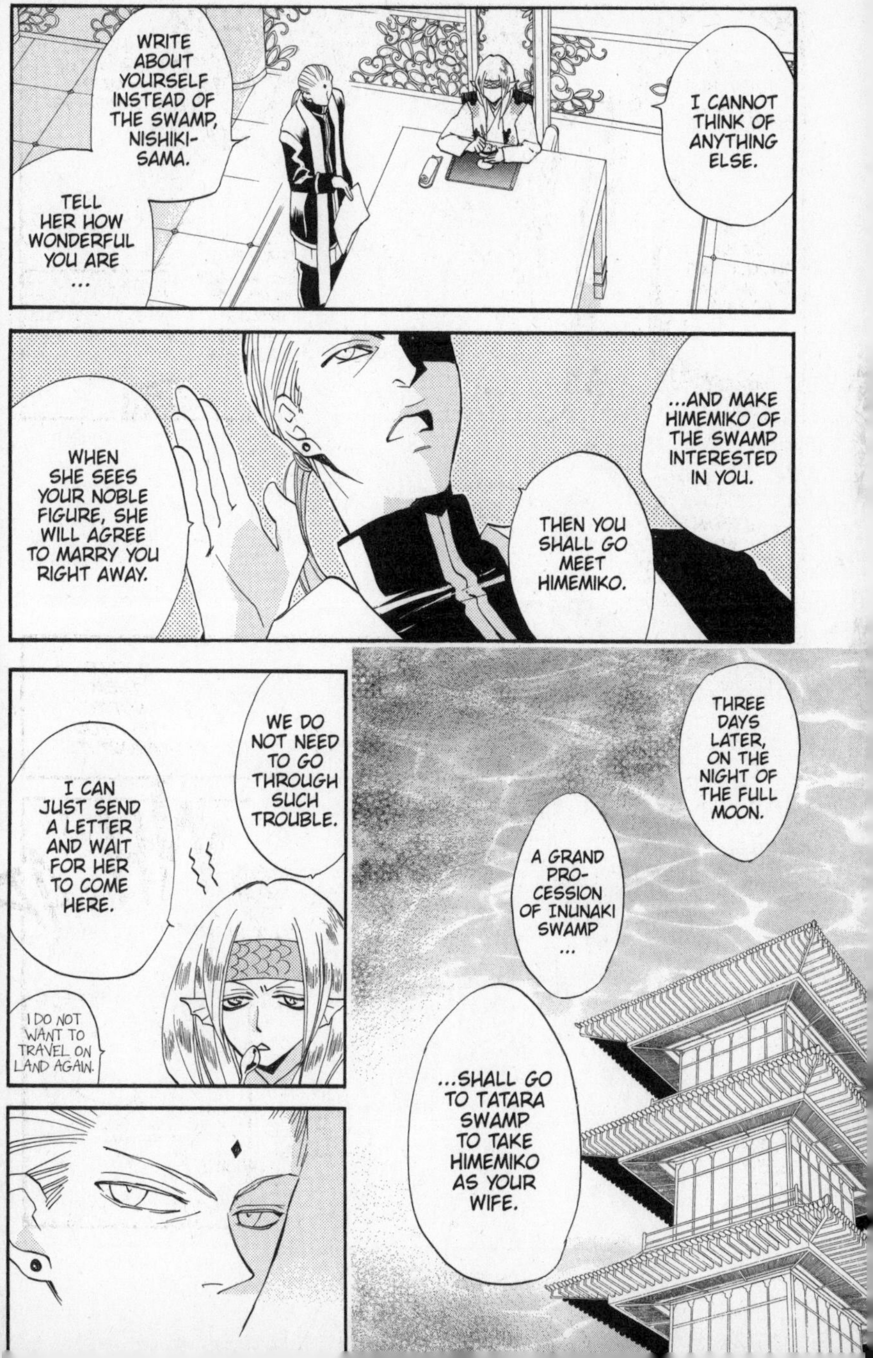
I CANNOT THINK OF ANYTHING ELSE.
WRITE ABOUT YOURSELF INSTEAD OF THE SWAMP, NISHIKI-SAMA.
TELL HER HOW WONDERFUL YOU ARE ...
...AND MAKE HIMEMIKO OF THE SWAMP INTERESTED IN YOU.
THEN YOU SHALL GO MEET HIMEMIKO.
WHEN SHE SEES YOUR NOBLE FIGURE, SHE WILL AGREE TO MARRY YOU RIGHT AWAY.
THREE DAYS LATER, ON THE NIGHT OF THE FULL MOON.
A GRAND PRO-CESSION OF INUNAKI SWAMP ...
...SHALL GO TO TATARA SWAMP TO TAKE HIMEMIKO AS YOUR WIFE.
WE DO NOT NEED TO GO THROUGH SUCH TROUBLE.
I CAN JUST SEND A LETTER AND WAIT FOR HER TO COME HERE.
I DO NOT WANT TO TRAVEL ON LAND AGAIN.

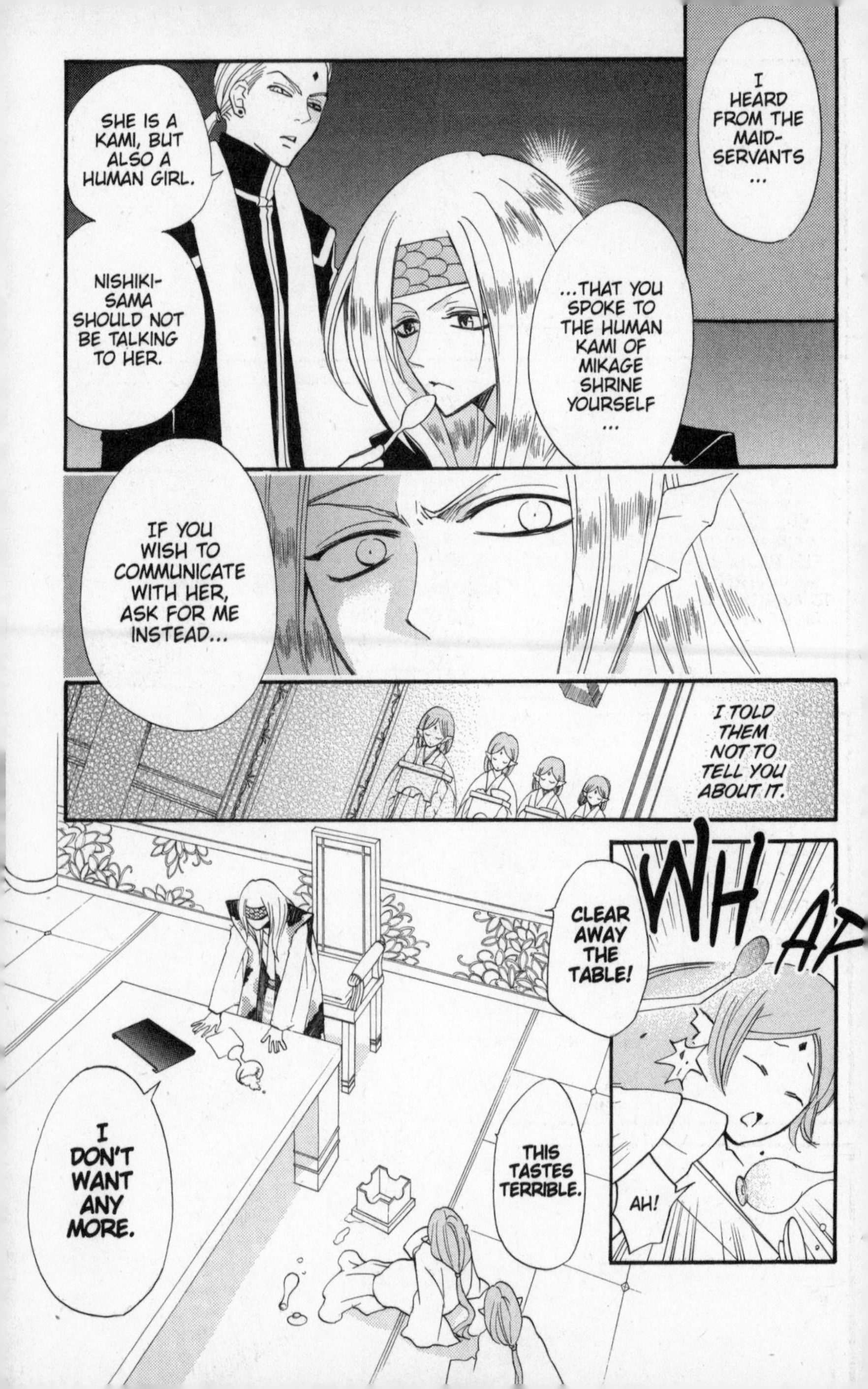

I HEARD FROM THE MAID-SERVANTS ...
...THAT YOU SPOKE TO THE HUMAN KAMI OF MIKAGE SHRINE YOURSELF ...
SHE IS A KAMI, BUT ALSO A HUMAN GIRL.
NISHIKI-SAMA SHOULD NOT BE TALKING TO HER.
IF YOU WISH TO COMMUNICATE WITH HER, ASK FOR ME INSTEAD...
I TOLD THEM NOT TO TELL YOU ABOUT IT.
CLEAR AWAY THE TABLE!
WHAP
AH!
THIS TASTES TERRIBLE.
I DON'T WANT ANY MORE.

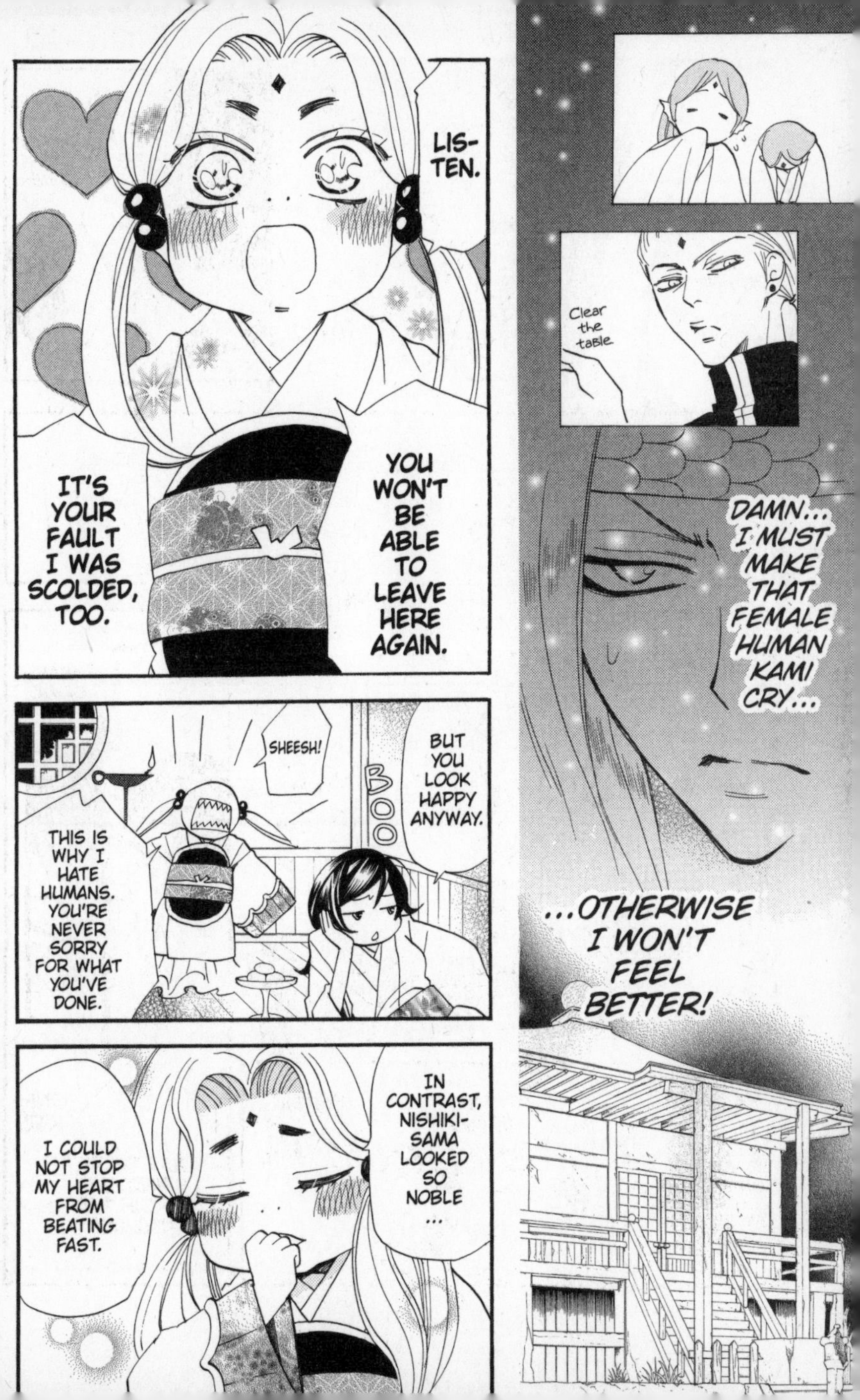
Clear the table.
DAMN... I MUST MAKE THAT FEMALE HUMAN KAMI CRY...
...OTHERWISE I WON'T FEEL BETTER!
LIS-TEN.
YOU WON'T BE ABLE TO LEAVE HERE AGAIN.
IT'S YOUR FAULT I WAS SCOLDED, TOO.
BUT YOU LOOK HAPPY ANYWAY.
SHEESH!
BOO
THIS IS WHY I HATE HUMANS. YOU'RE NEVER SORRY FOR WHAT YOU'VE DONE.
IN CONTRAST, NISHIKI-SAMA LOOKED SO NOBLE ...
I COULD NOT STOP MY HEART FROM BEATING FAST.

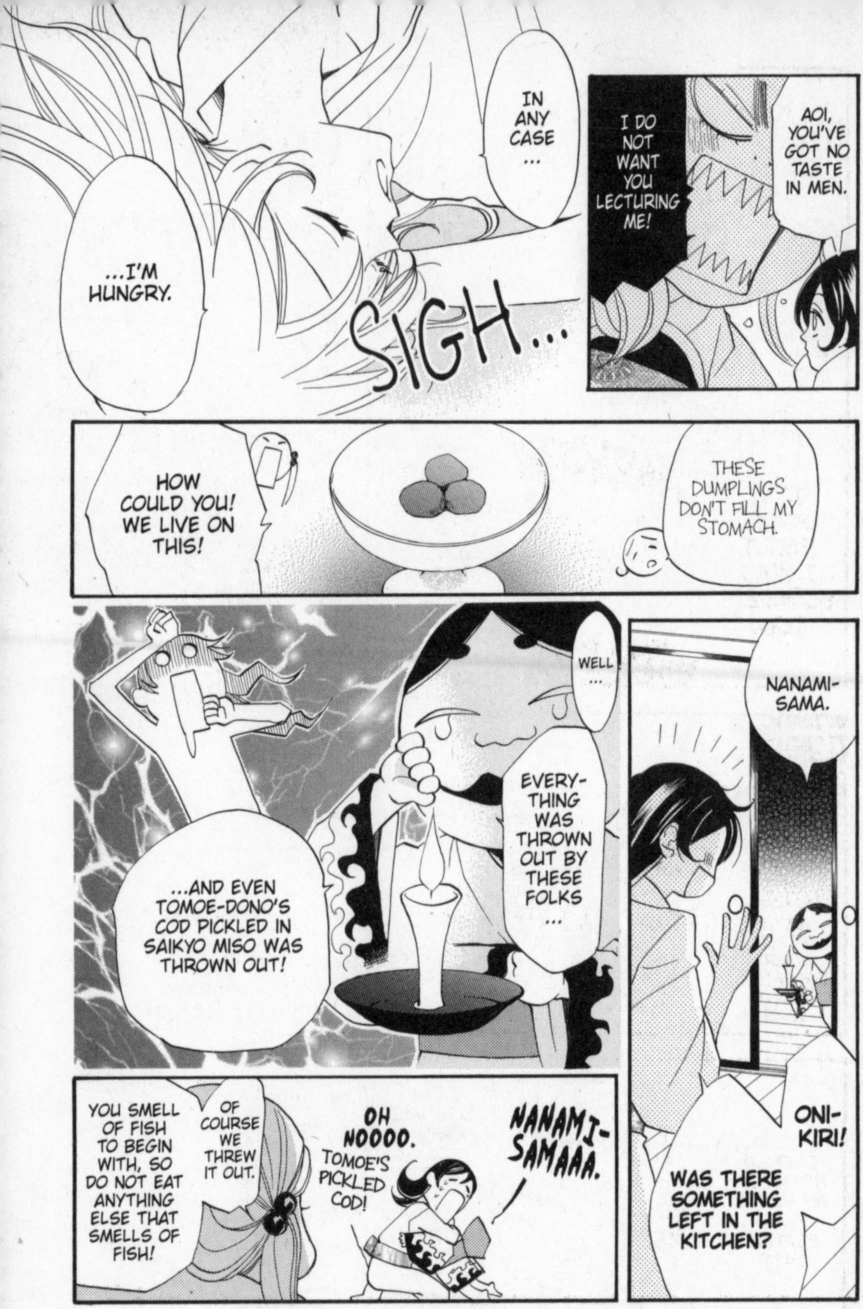
AOI, YOU'VE GOT NO TASTE IN MEN.
I DO NOT WANT YOU LECTURING ME!
IN ANY CASE ...
SIGH...
...I'M HUNGRY.
THESE DUMPLINGS DON'T FILL MY STOMACH.
HOW COULD YOU! WE LIVE ON THIS!
NANAMI-SAMA.
ONI-KIRI!
WAS THERE SOMETHING LEFT IN THE KITCHEN?
WELL ...
EVERYTHING WAS THROWN OUT BY THESE FOLKS ...
...AND EVEN TOMOE-DONO'S COD PICKLED IN SAIKYO MISO WAS THROWN OUT!
NANAMI-SAMAAA.
OH NOOOO. TOMOE'S PICKLED COD!
OF COURSE WE THREW IT OUT.
YOU SMELL OF FISH TO BEGIN WITH, SO DO NOT EAT ANYTHING ELSE THAT SMELLS OF FISH!

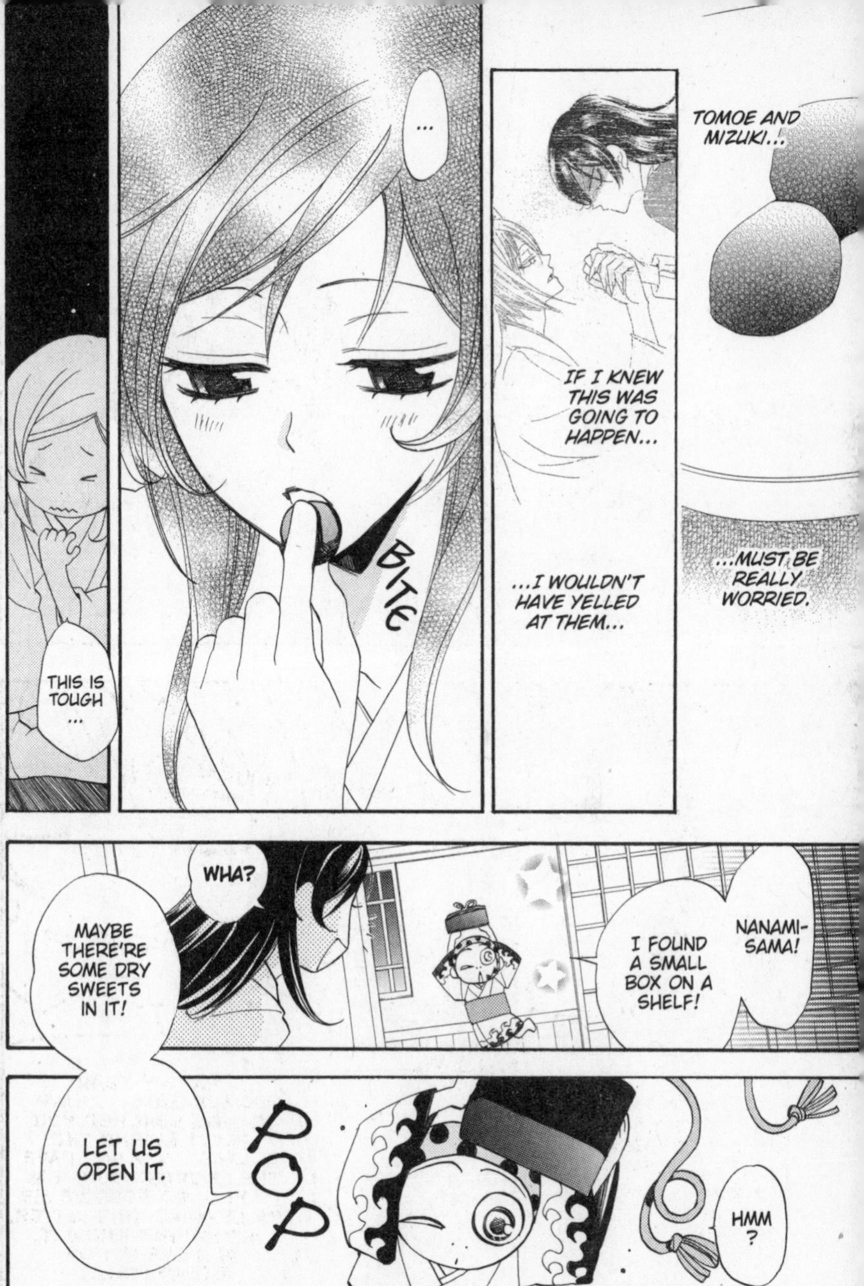
TOMOE AND MIZUKI...
...MUST BE REALLY WORRIED.
IF I KNEW THIS WAS GOING TO HAPPEN...
...I WOULDN'T HAVE YELLED AT THEM...
...
BITE
THIS IS TOUGH...
NANAMI-SAMA!
I FOUND A SMALL BOX ON A SHELF!
WHA?
MAYBE THERE'RE SOME DRY SWEETS IN IT!
HMM?
POP
LET US OPEN IT.

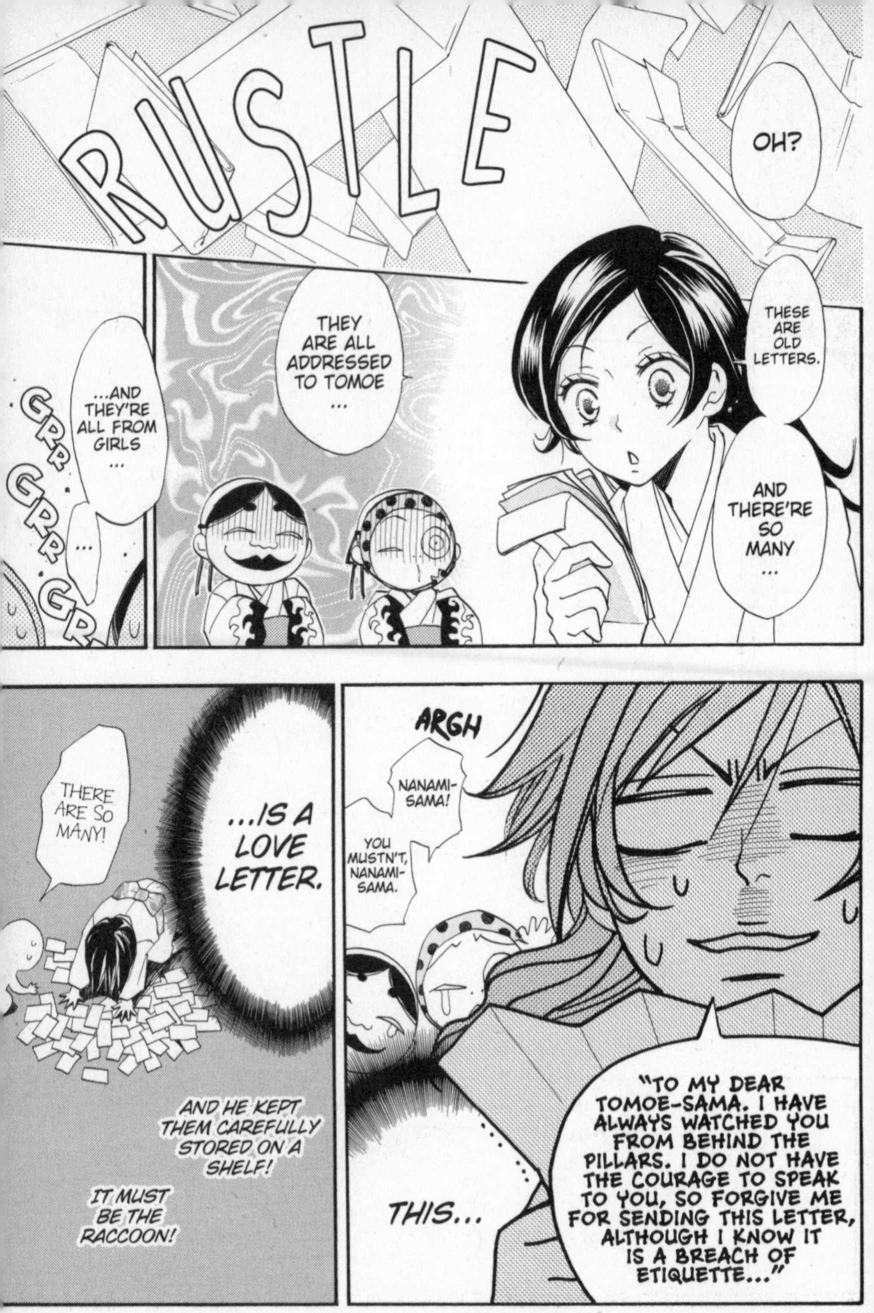
OH?
RUSTLE
THESE ARE OLD LETTERS.
AND THERE'RE SO MANY ...
THEY ARE ALL ADDRESSED TO TOMOE ...
...AND THEY'RE ALL FROM GIRLS ...
...
GRR GRR GR
ARGH
NANAMI-SAMA!
YOU MUSTN'T, NANAMI-SAMA.
"TO MY DEAR TOMOE-SAMA. I HAVE ALWAYS WATCHED YOU FROM BEHIND THE PILLARS. I DO NOT HAVE THE COURAGE TO SPEAK TO YOU, SO FORGIVE ME FOR SENDING THIS LETTER, ALTHOUGH I KNOW IT IS A BREACH OF ETIQUETTE..."
THIS...
...IS A LOVE LETTER.
THERE ARE SO MANY!
AND HE KEPT THEM CAREFULLY STORED ON A SHELF!
IT MUST BE THE RACCOON!

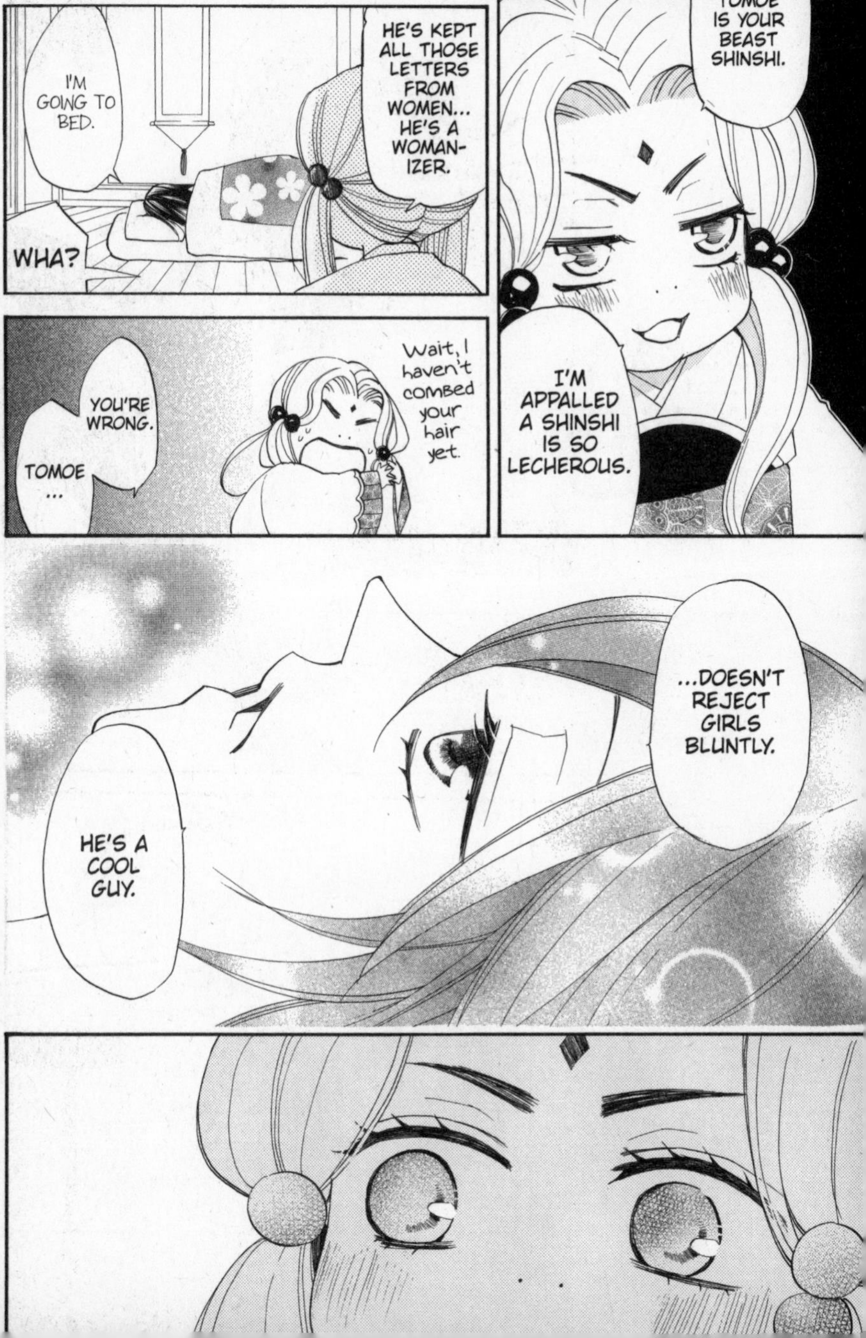
TOMOE IS YOUR BEAST SHINSHI.
I'M APPALLED A SHINSHI IS SO LECHEROUS.
HE'S KEPT ALL THOSE LETTERS FROM WOMEN... HE'S A WOMAN-IZER.
I'M GOING TO BED.
WHA?
Wait, I haven't combed your hair yet.
YOU'RE WRONG.
TOMOE ...
...DOESN'T REJECT GIRLS BLUNTLY.
HE'S A COOL GUY.

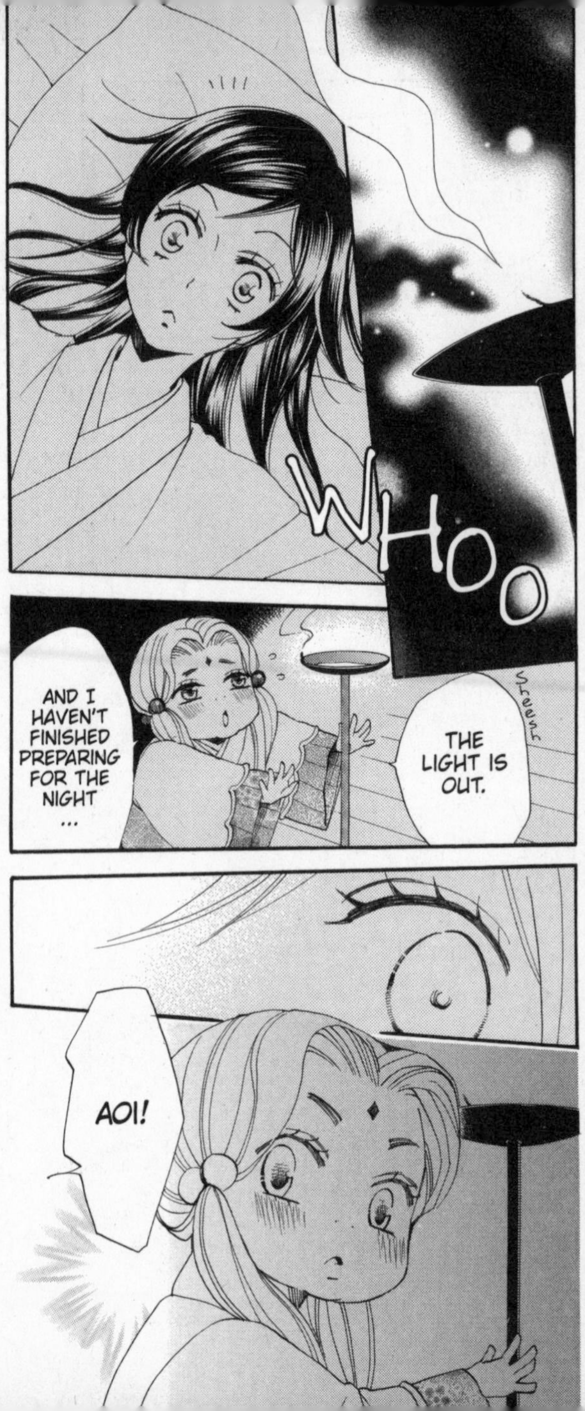
WHOO
THE LIGHT IS OUT.
AND I HAVEN'T FINISHED PREPARING FOR THE NIGHT ...
AOI!

This arc is Himemiko's love story.

Recently, Hana to Yume magazine held a popularity poll for Kamisama Kiss. Thanks to this arc, Himemiko of the swamp ranked very high. ☺♥ Yaay!

Thanks to everybody who participated and voted!!

I hope I'll be able to announce the results in the next volume. ♡

It's starting to get hot. In the manga, it's still winter, though. I must be careful not to draw short-sleeved clothes!

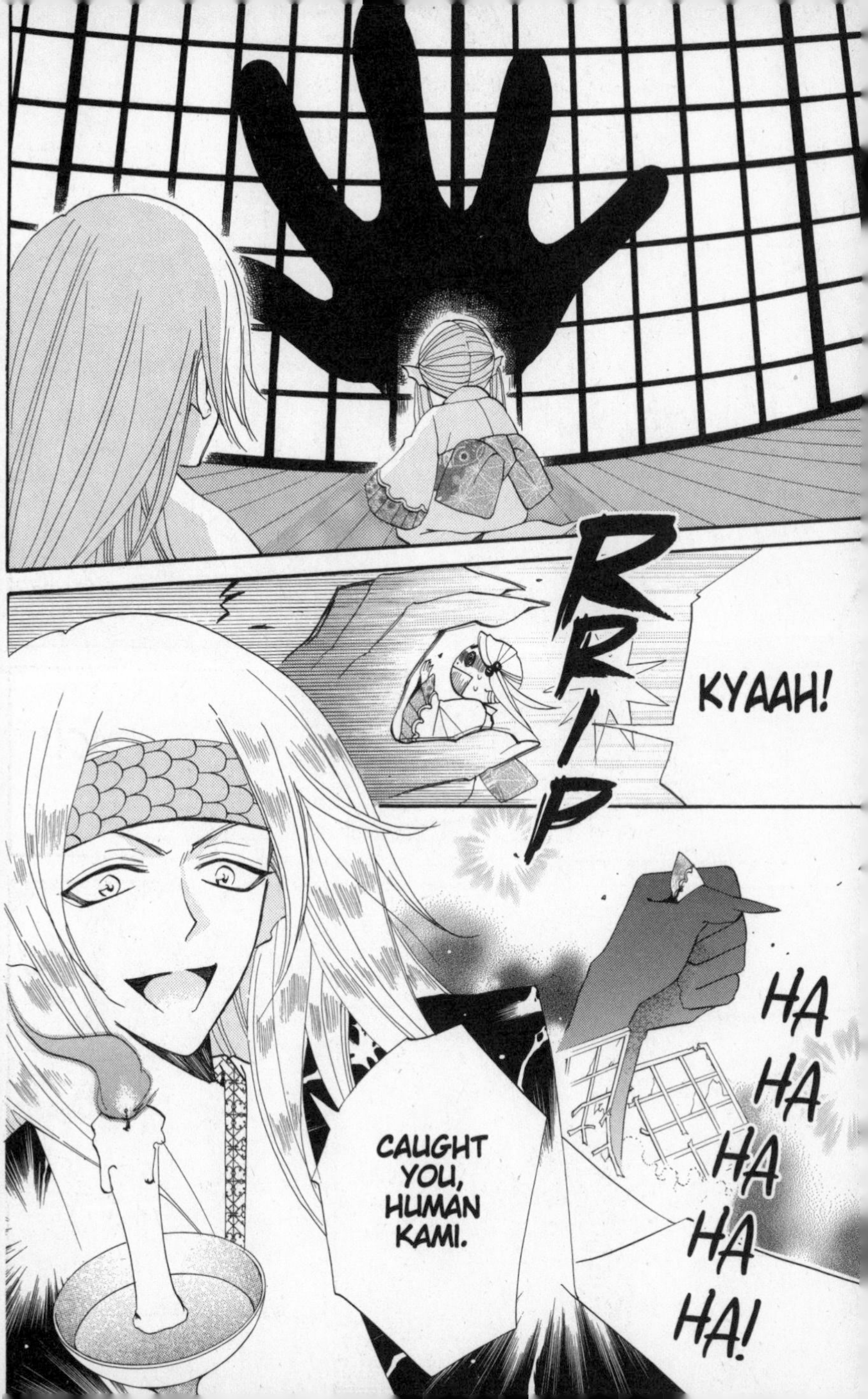
RRIP
KYAAH!
CAUGHT YOU, HUMAN KAMI.
HA HA HA HA HA!

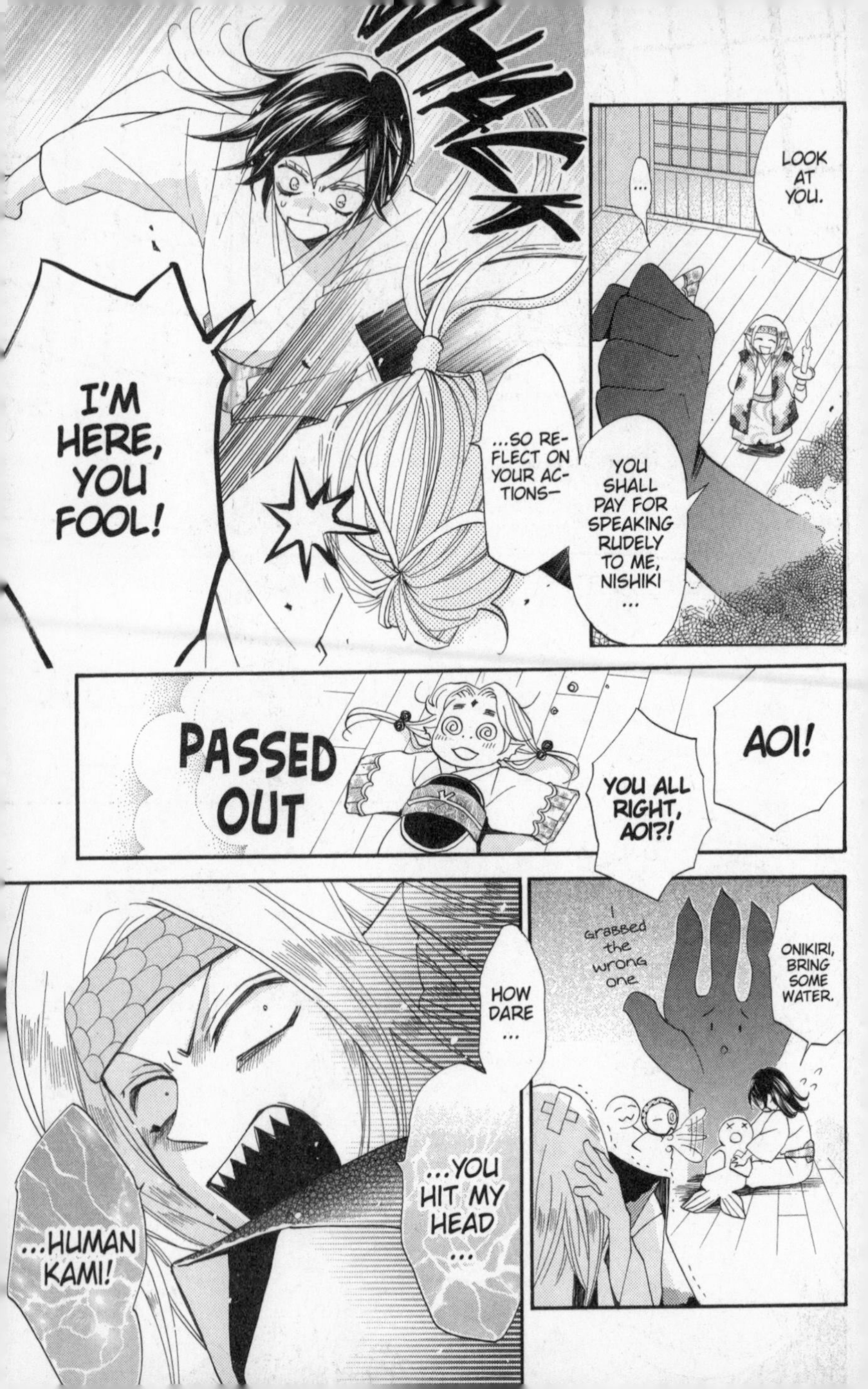
LOOK AT YOU.
...
YOU SHALL PAY FOR SPEAKING RUDELY TO ME, NISHIKI ...
...SO REFLECT ON YOUR ACTIONS—
I'M HERE, YOU FOOL!
AOI!
YOU ALL RIGHT, AOI?!
PASSED OUT
ONIKIRI, BRING SOME WATER.
I grabbed the wrong one
HOW DARE ...
...YOU HIT MY HEAD ...
...HUMAN KAMI!

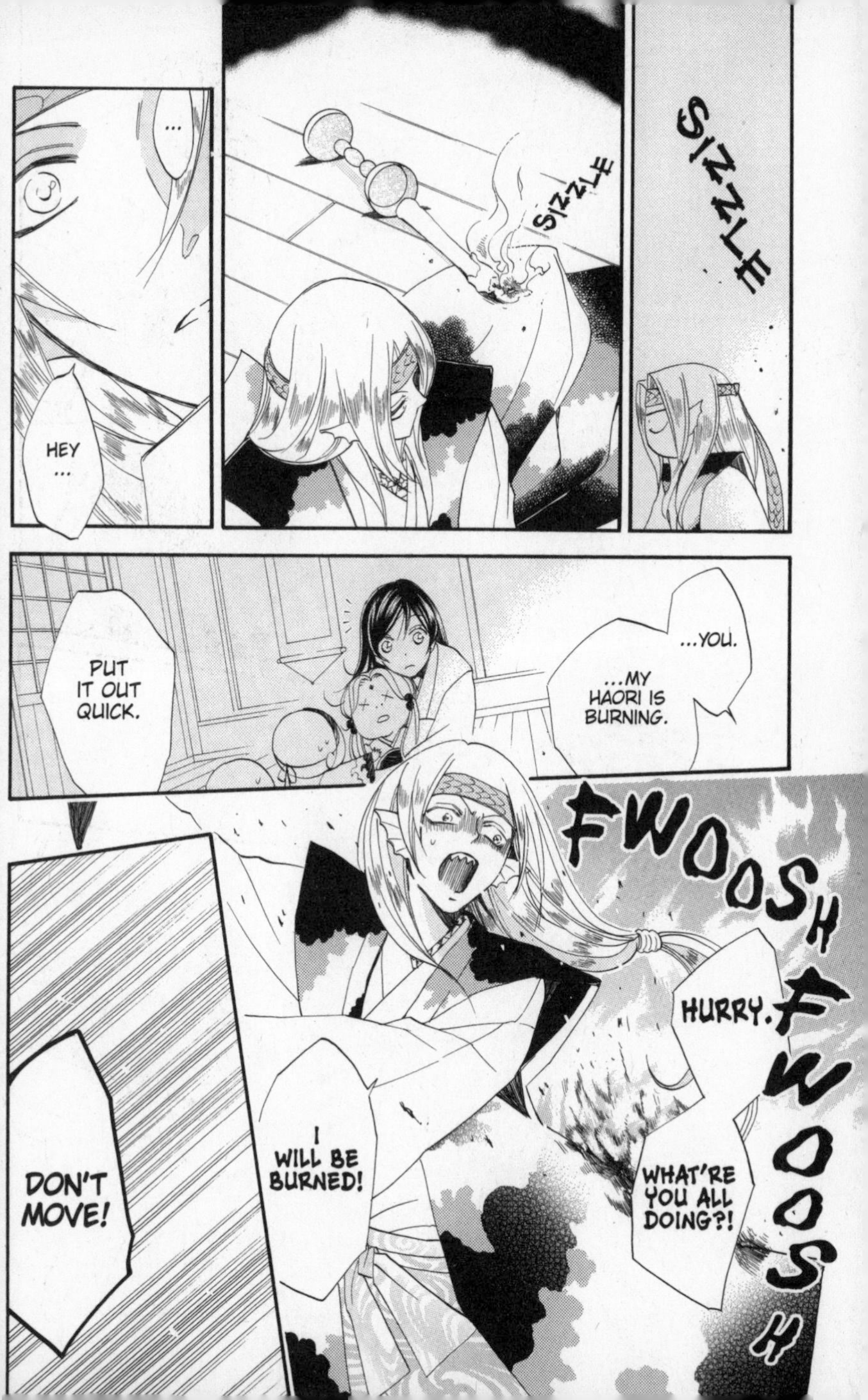
SIZZLE
SIZZLE
...
HEY ...
...YOU.
...MY HAORI IS BURNING.
PUT IT OUT QUICK.
FWOOSH
HURRY.
FWOOSH
WHAT'RE YOU ALL DOING?!
I WILL BE BURNED!
DON'T MOVE!

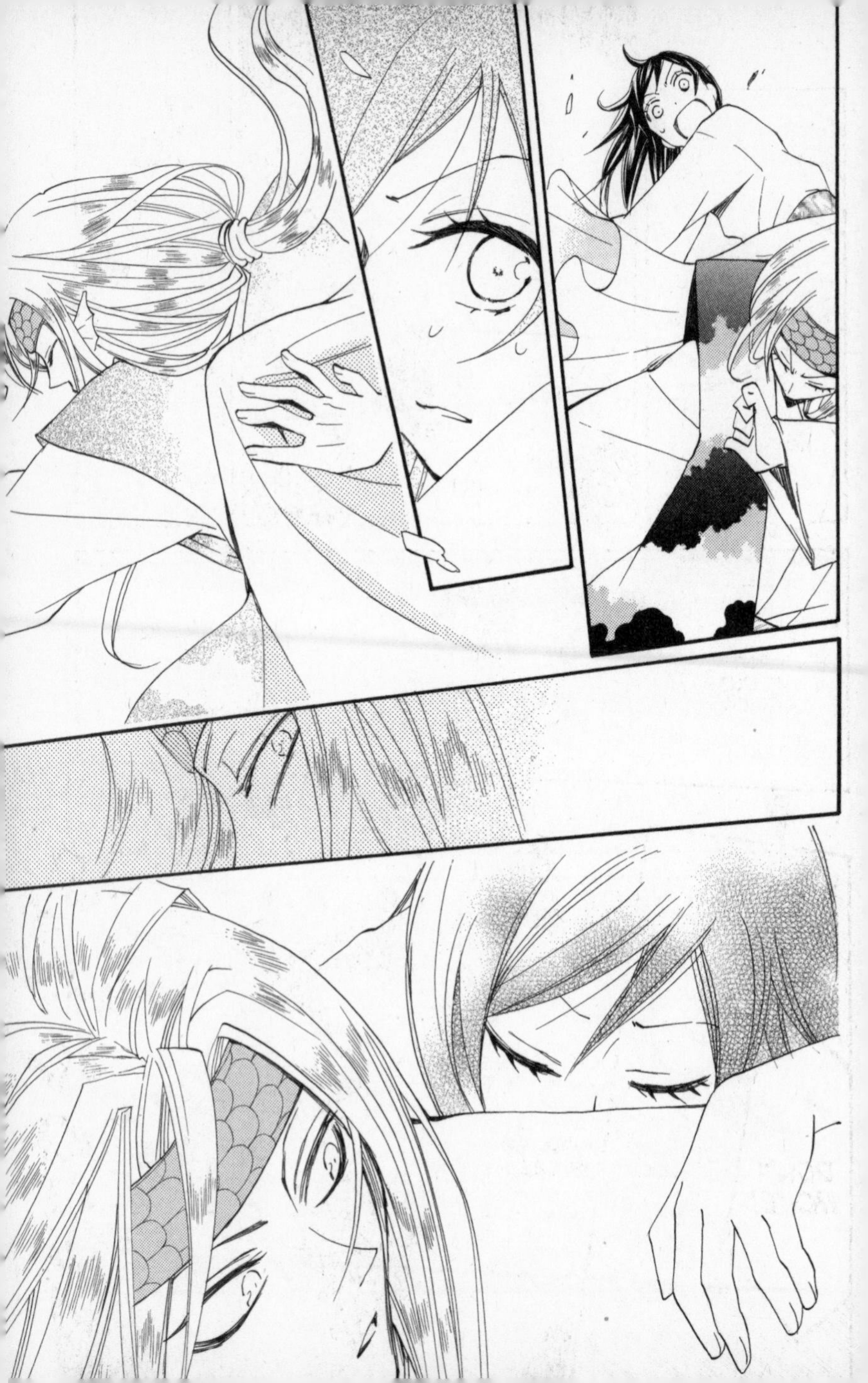

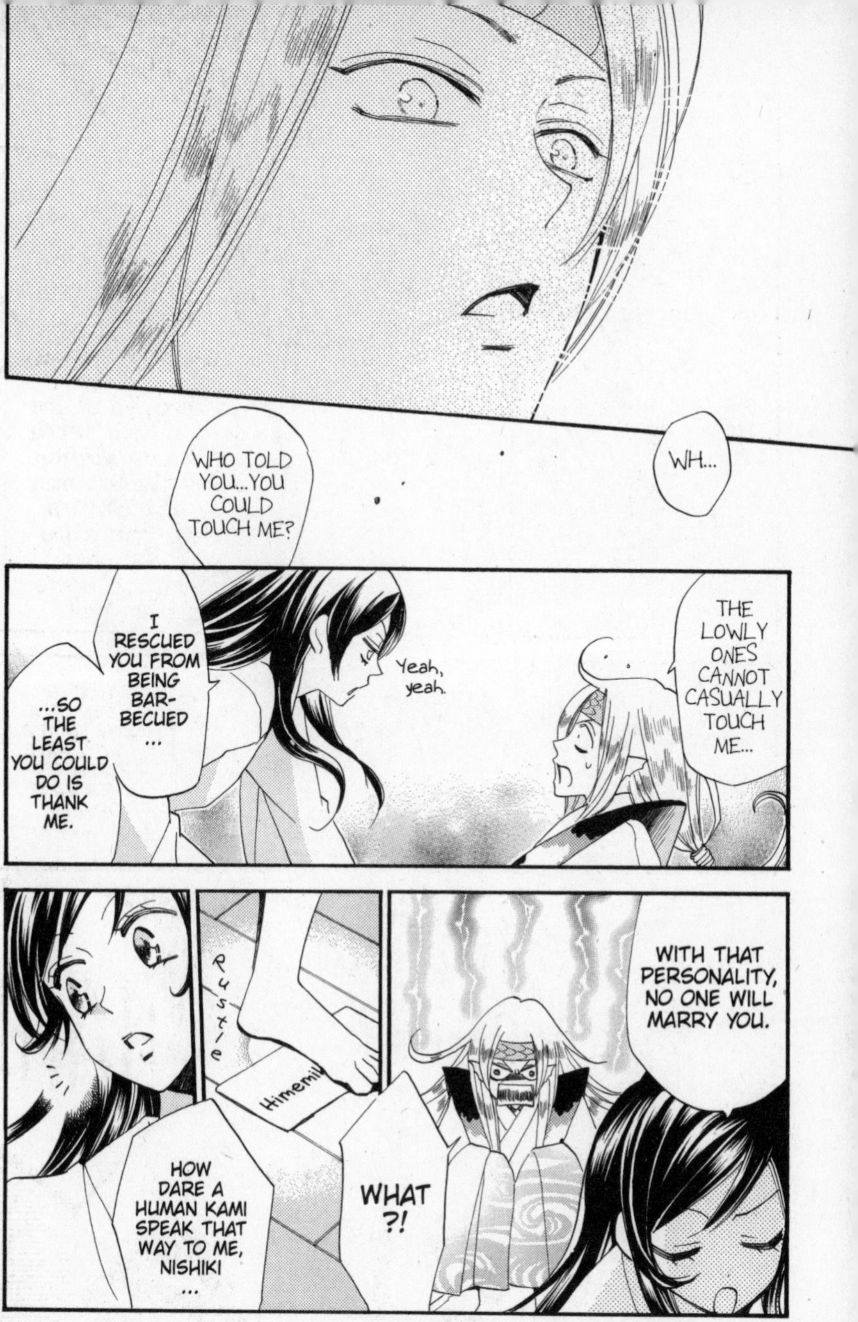

WH...
WHO TOLD YOU...YOU COULD TOUCH ME?
THE LOWLY ONES CANNOT CASUALLY TOUCH ME...
Yeah, yeah.
I RESCUED YOU FROM BEING BAR-BECUED ...
...SO THE LEAST YOU COULD DO IS THANK ME.
WITH THAT PERSONALITY, NO ONE WILL MARRY YOU.
WHAT?!
Rustle
HOW DARE A HUMAN KAMI SPEAK THAT WAY TO ME, NISHIKI ...

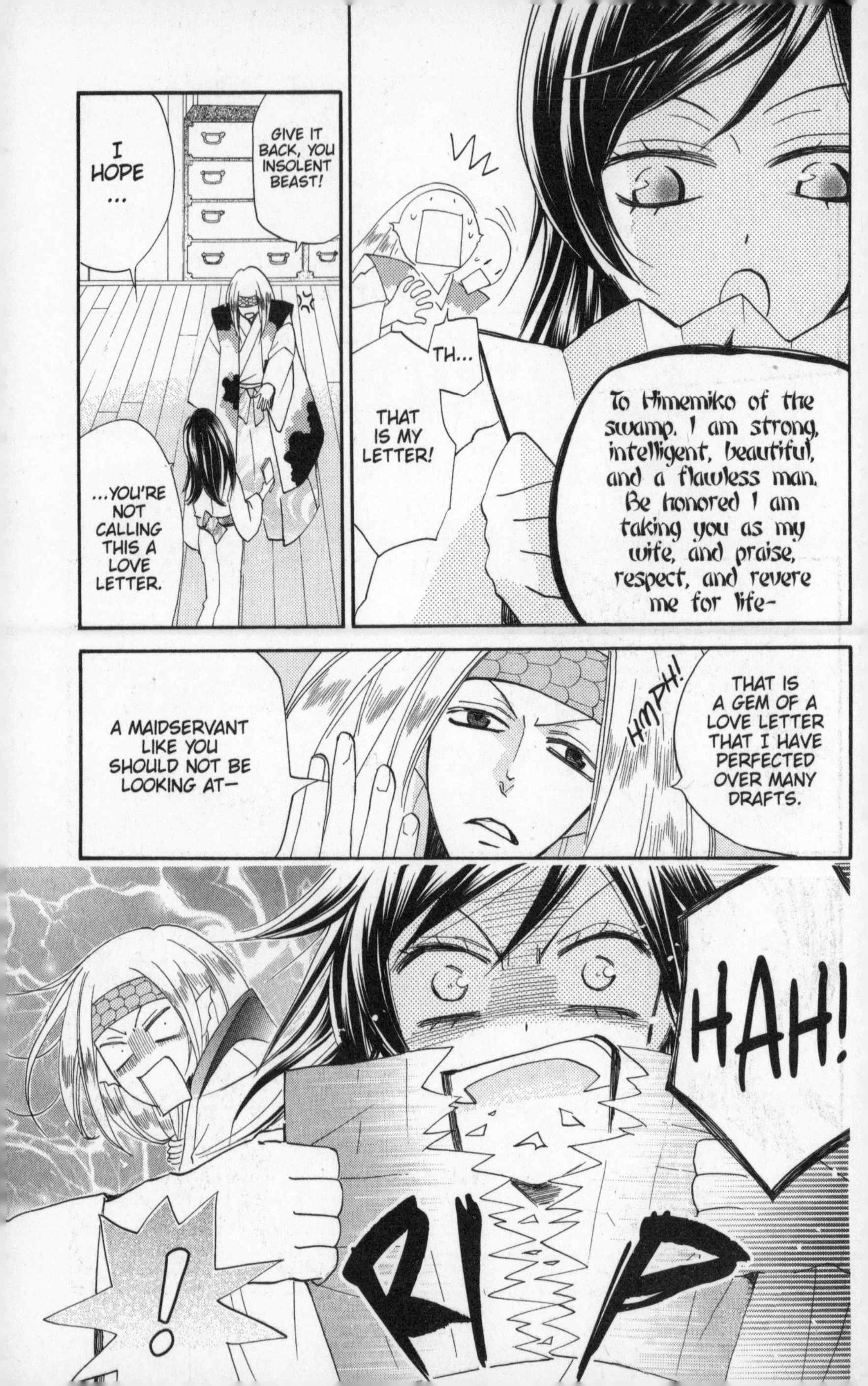
To Himemiko of the swamp. I am strong, intelligent, beautiful, and a flawless man. Be honored I am taking you as my wife, and praise, respect, and revere me for life-
TH...
THAT IS MY LETTER!
GIVE IT BACK, YOU INSOLENT BEAST!
I HOPE ...
...YOU'RE NOT CALLING THIS A LOVE LETTER.
THAT IS A GEM OF A LOVE LETTER THAT I HAVE PERFECTED OVER MANY DRAFTS.
HMPH!
A MAIDSERVANT LIKE YOU SHOULD NOT BE LOOKING AT—
HAH!
RIP
!

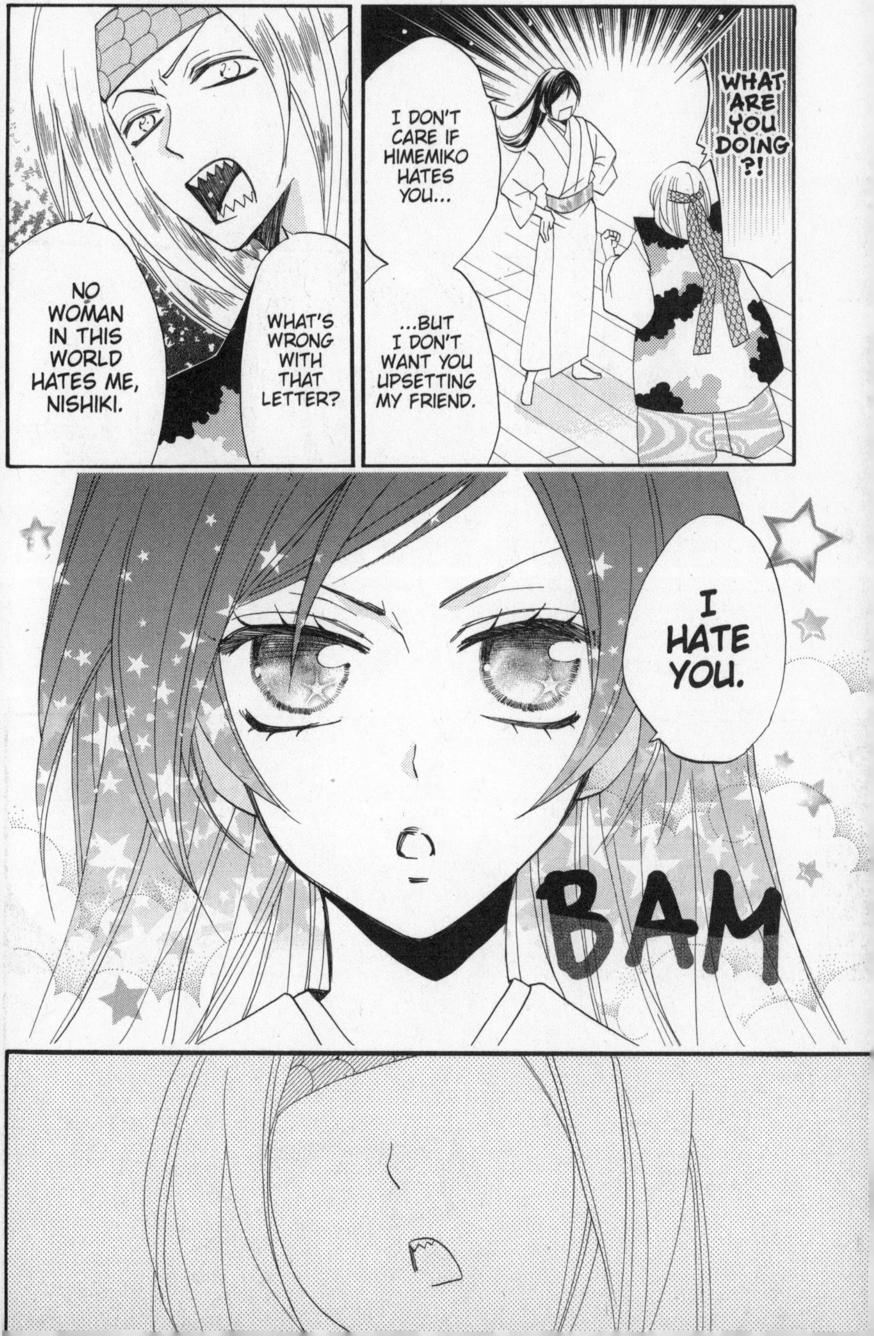
WHAT ARE YOU DOING?!
I DON'T CARE IF HIMEMIKO HATES YOU...
...BUT I DON'T WANT YOU UPSETTING MY FRIEND.
WHAT'S WRONG WITH THAT LETTER?
NO WOMAN IN THIS WORLD HATES ME, NISHIKI.
I HATE YOU.
BAM

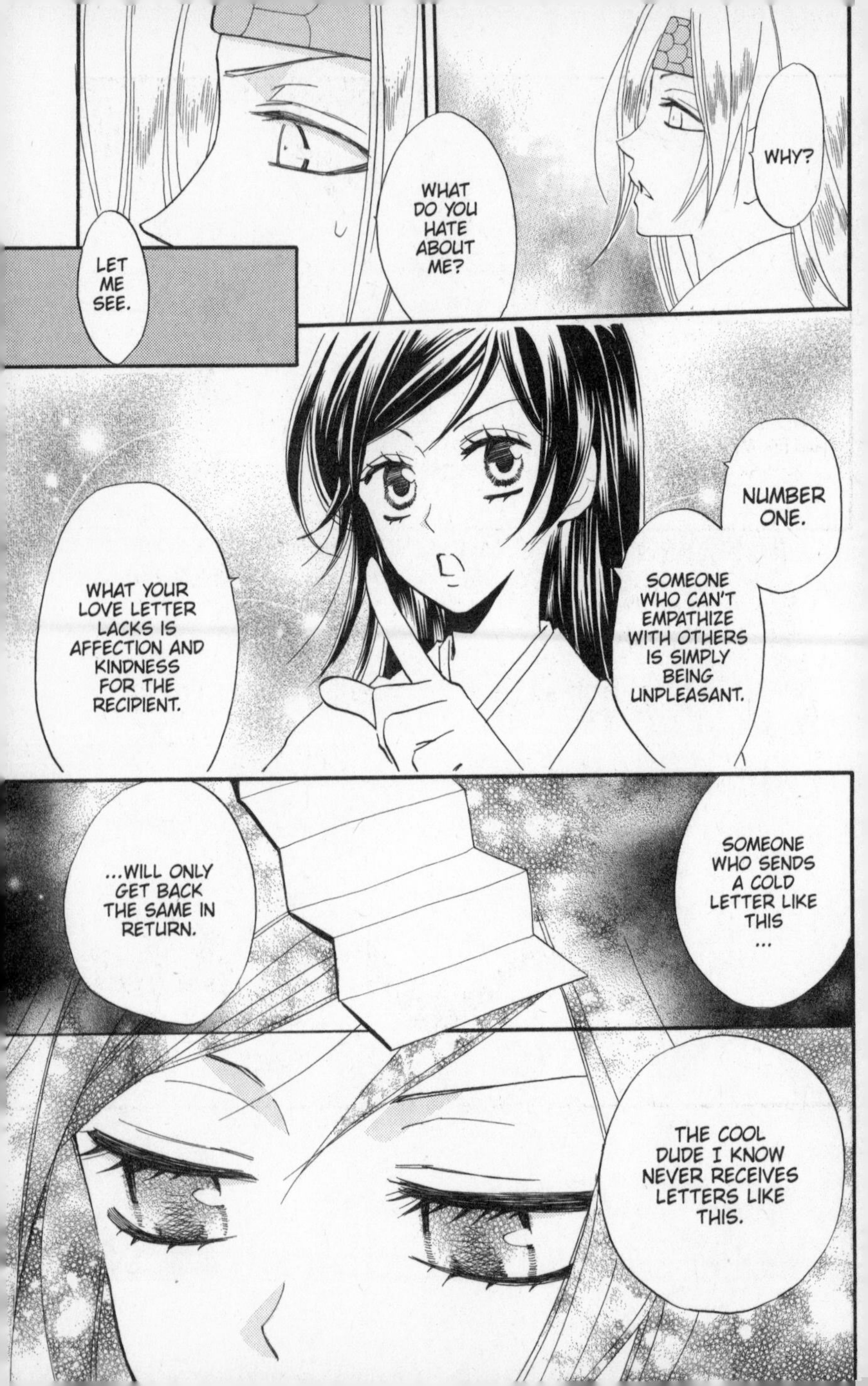
WHY?
WHAT DO YOU HATE ABOUT ME?
LET ME SEE.
NUMBER ONE.
SOMEONE WHO CAN'T EMPATHIZE WITH OTHERS IS SIMPLY BEING UNPLEASANT.
WHAT YOUR LOVE LETTER LACKS IS AFFECTION AND KINDNESS FOR THE RECIPIENT.
SOMEONE WHO SENDS A COLD LETTER LIKE THIS ...
...WILL ONLY GET BACK THE SAME IN RETURN.
THE COOL DUDE I KNOW NEVER RECEIVES LETTERS LIKE THIS.

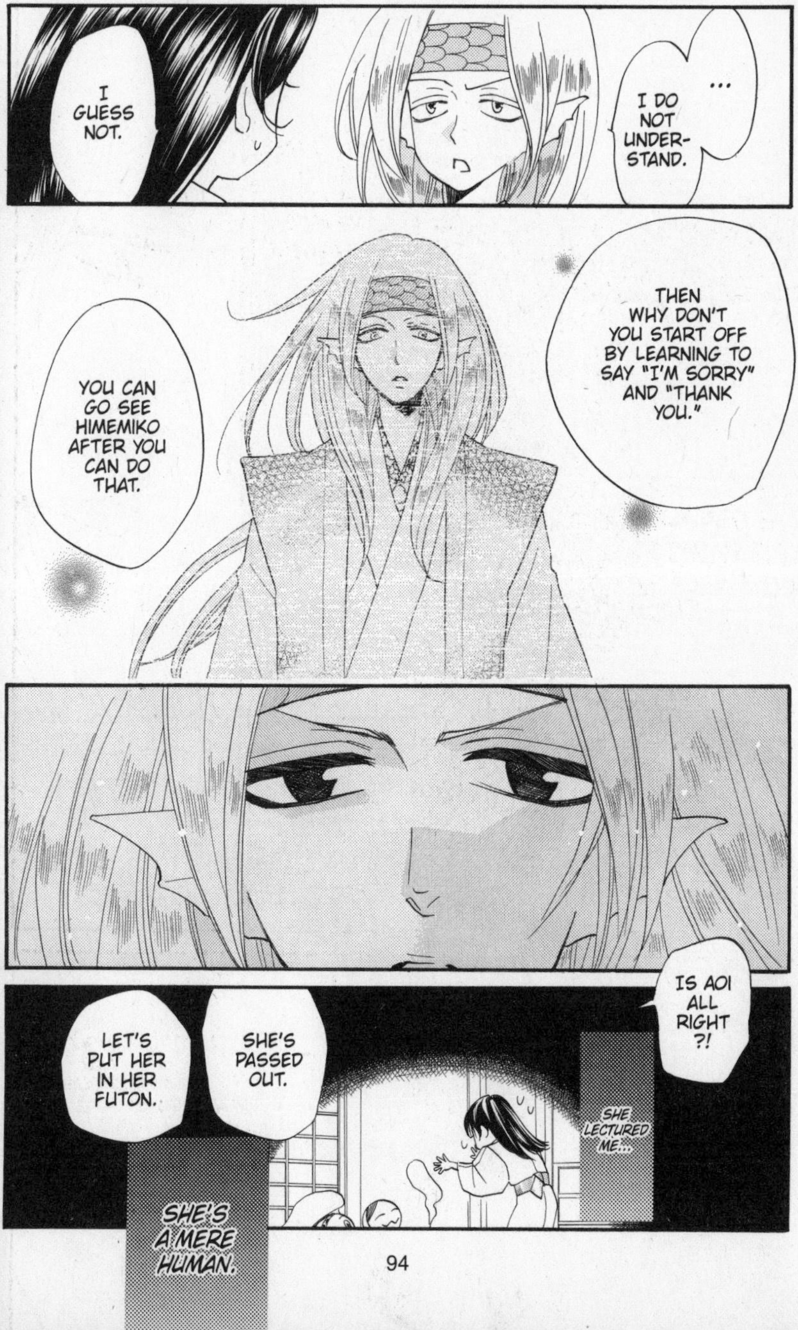
... I DO NOT UNDER-STAND.
I GUESS NOT.
THEN WHY DON'T YOU START OFF BY LEARNING TO SAY "I'M SORRY" AND "THANK YOU."
YOU CAN GO SEE HIMEMIKO AFTER YOU CAN DO THAT.
IS AOI ALL RIGHT?!
SHE LECTURED ME...
SHE'S PASSED OUT.
LET'S PUT HER IN HER FUTON.
SHE'S A MERE HUMAN.

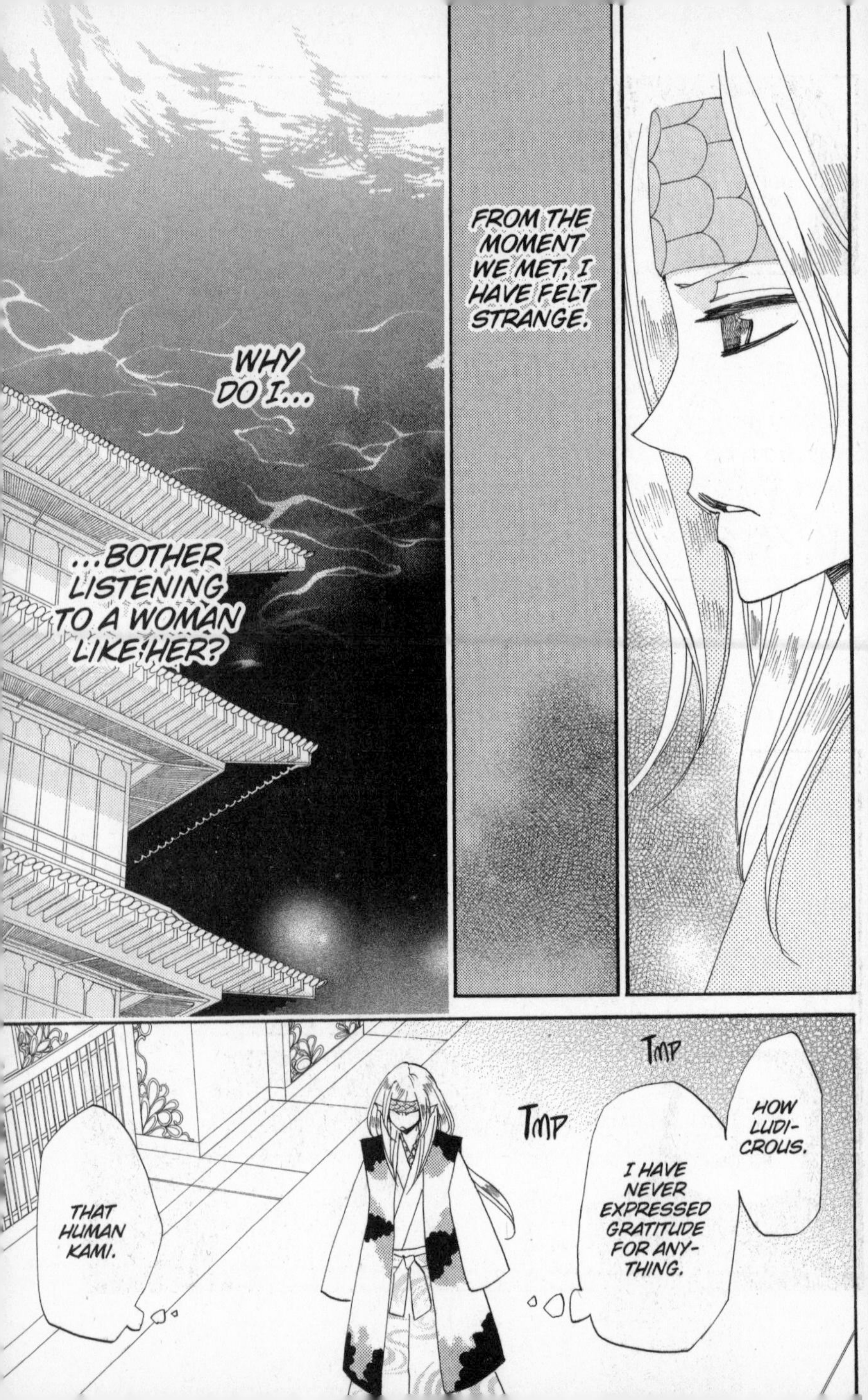
FROM THE MOMENT WE MET, I HAVE FELT STRANGE.
WHY DO I...
...BOTHER LISTENING TO A WOMAN LIKE HER?
TMP
HOW LUDICROUS.
TMP
I HAVE NEVER EXPRESSED GRATITUDE FOR ANYTHING.
THAT HUMAN KAMI.

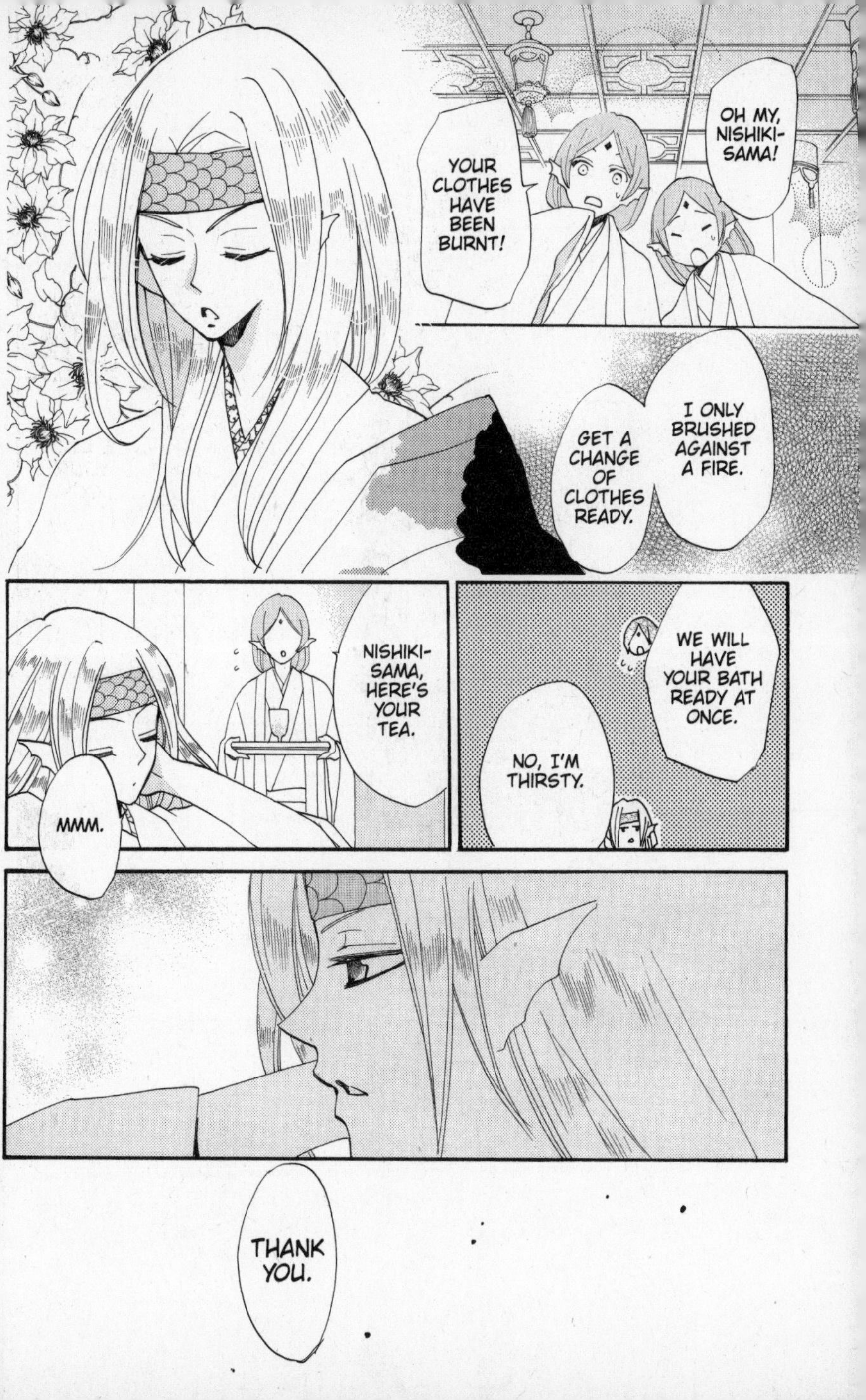
OH MY, NISHIKI-SAMA!
YOUR CLOTHES HAVE BEEN BURNT!
I ONLY BRUSHED AGAINST A FIRE.
GET A CHANGE OF CLOTHES READY.
WE WILL HAVE YOUR BATH READY AT ONCE.
NO, I'M THIRSTY.
NISHIKI-SAMA, HERE'S YOUR TEA.
MMM.
THANK YOU.

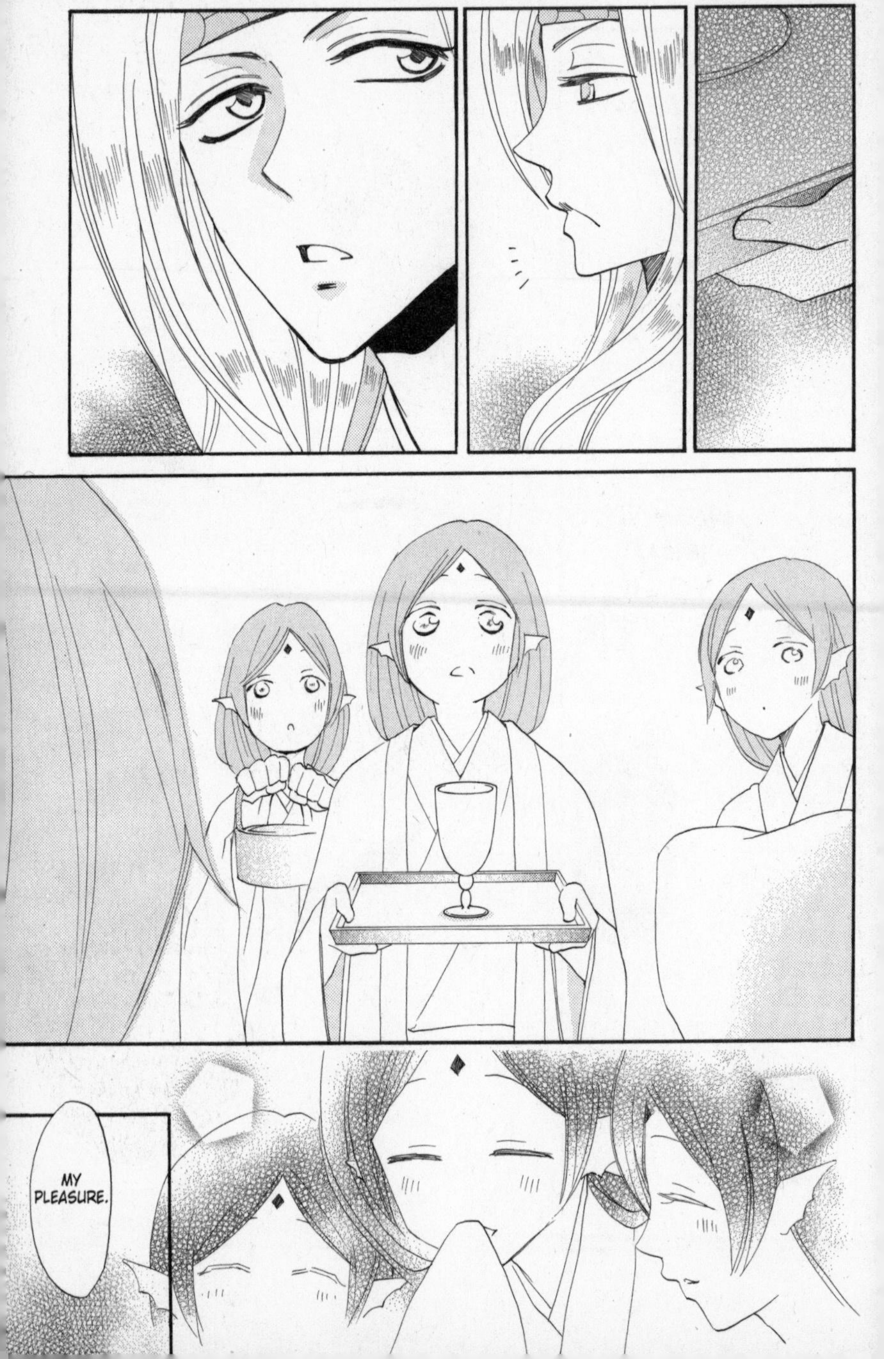
MY PLEASURE.

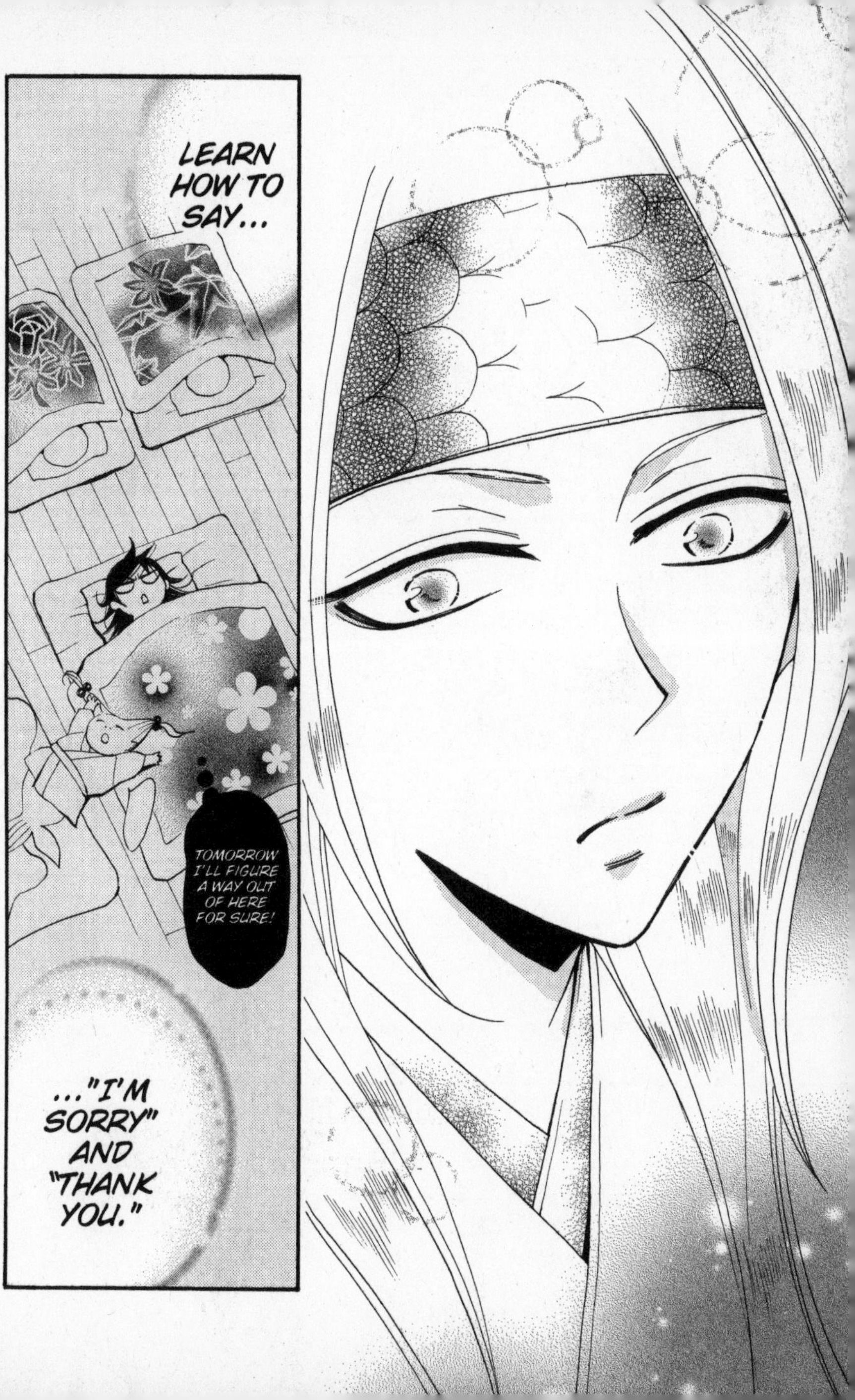
LEARN HOW TO SAY...
TOMORROW I'LL FIGURE A WAY OUT OF HERE FOR SURE!
..."I'M SORRY" AND "THANK YOU."

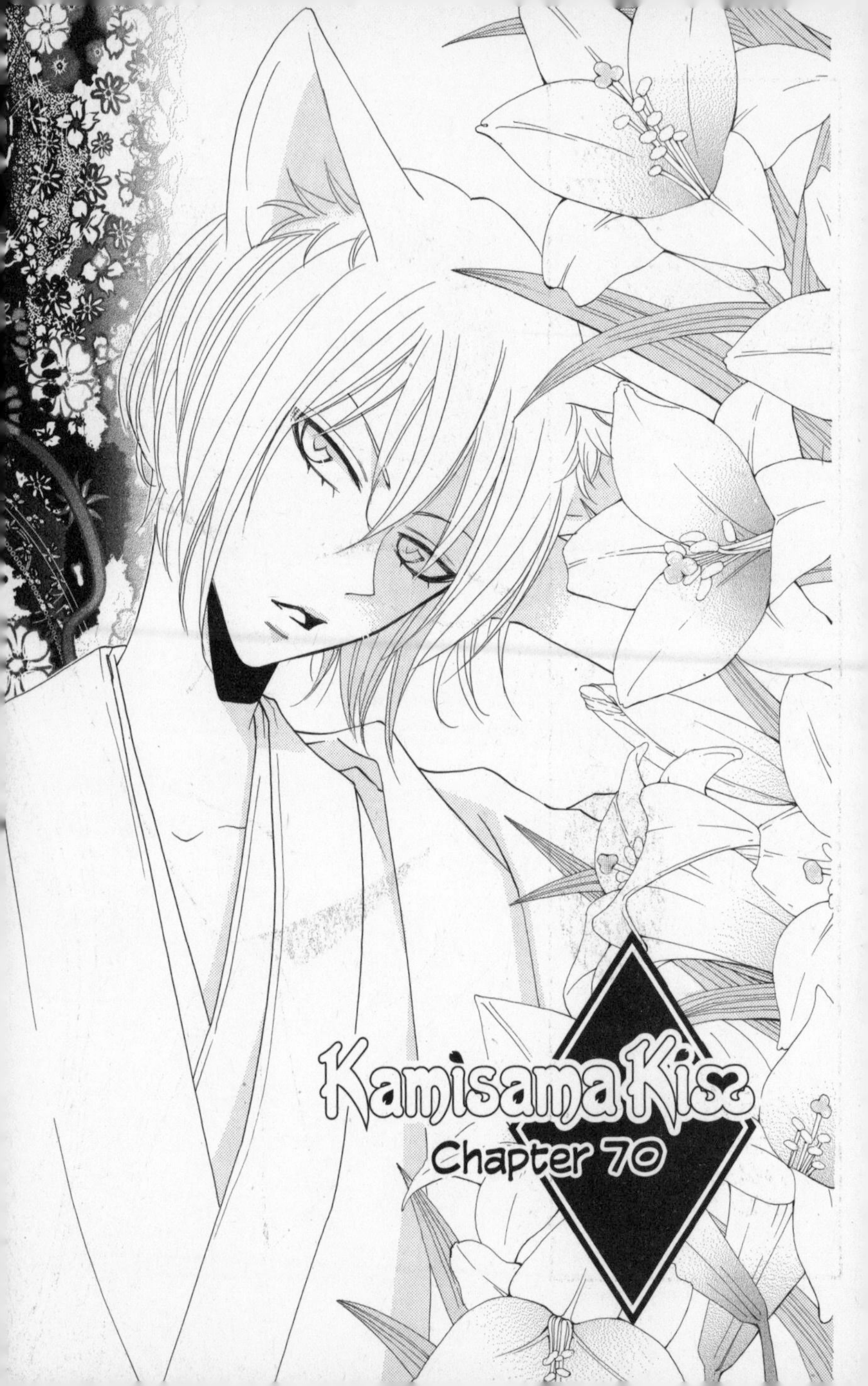
Kamisama Kiss
Chapter 70

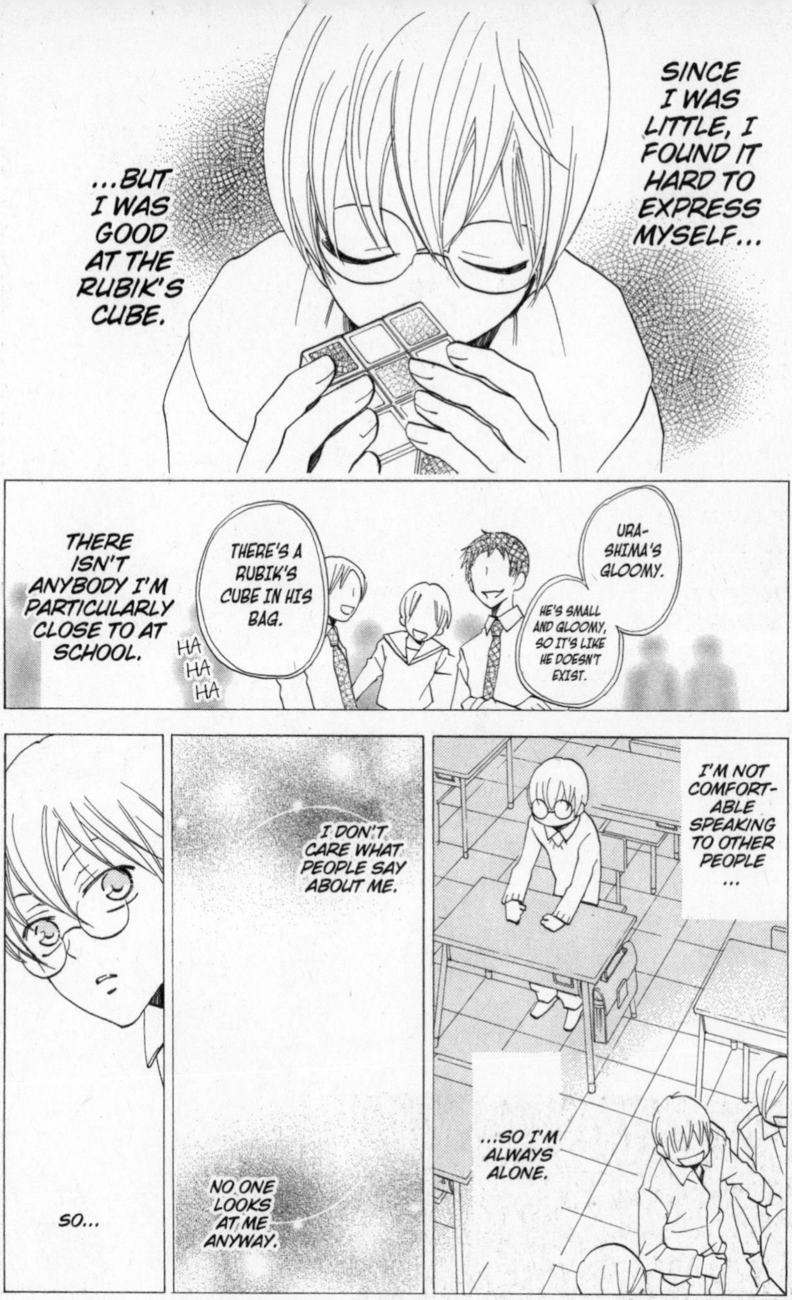
SINCE I WAS LITTLE, I FOUND IT HARD TO EXPRESS MYSELF...
...BUT I WAS GOOD AT THE RUBIK'S CUBE.
URA-SHIMA'S GLOOMY.
HE'S SMALL AND GLOOMY, SO IT'S LIKE HE DOESN'T EXIST.
THERE'S A RUBIK'S CUBE IN HIS BAG.
HA HA HA
THERE ISN'T ANYBODY I'M PARTICULARLY CLOSE TO AT SCHOOL.
I'M NOT COMFORT-ABLE SPEAKING TO OTHER PEOPLE ...
...SO I'M ALWAYS ALONE.
I DON'T CARE WHAT PEOPLE SAY ABOUT ME.
NO ONE LOOKS AT ME ANYWAY.
SO...

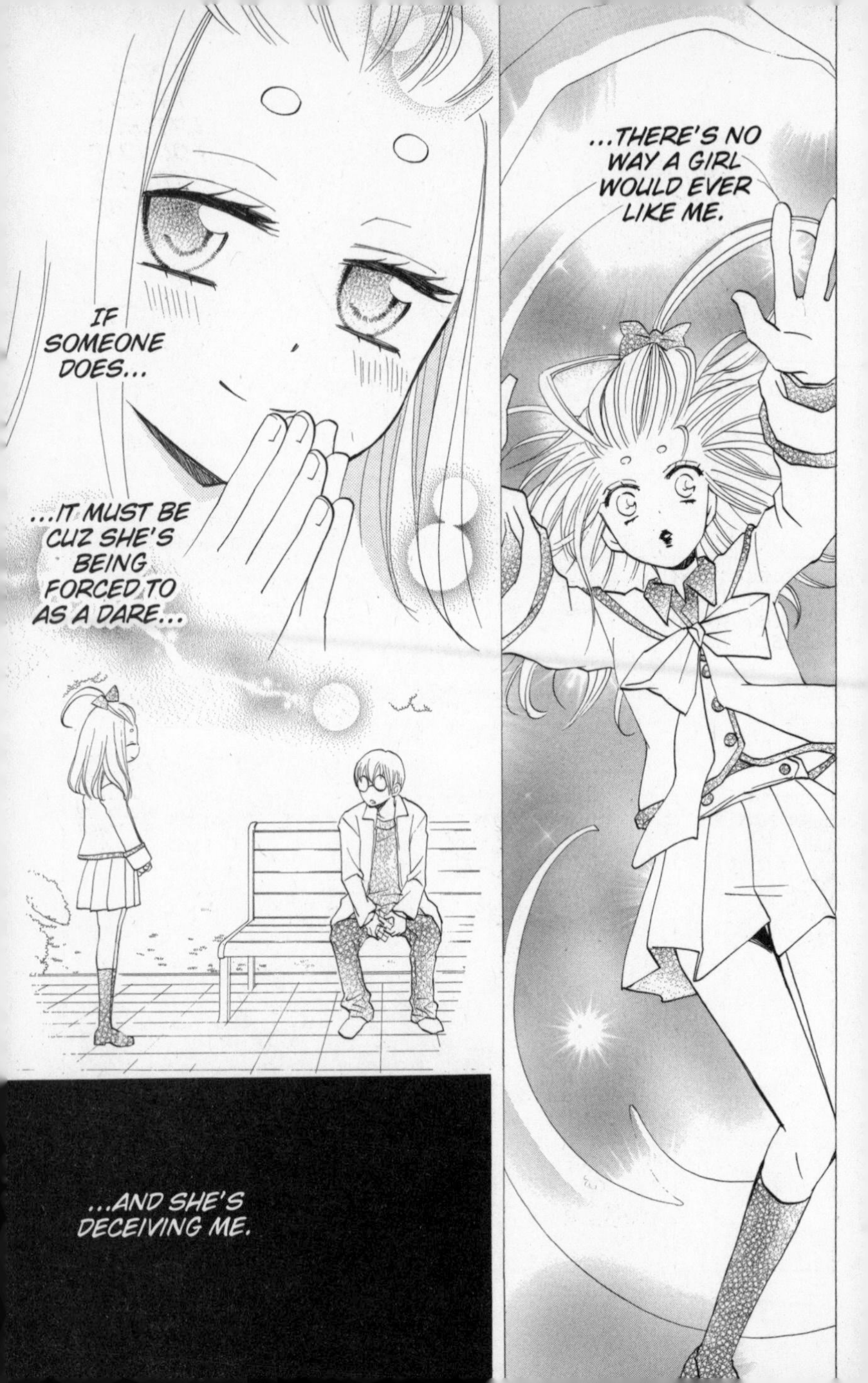
...THERE'S NO WAY A GIRL WOULD EVER LIKE ME.
IF SOMEONE DOES...
...IT MUST BE CUZ SHE'S BEING FORCED TO AS A DARE...
...AND SHE'S DECEIVING ME.

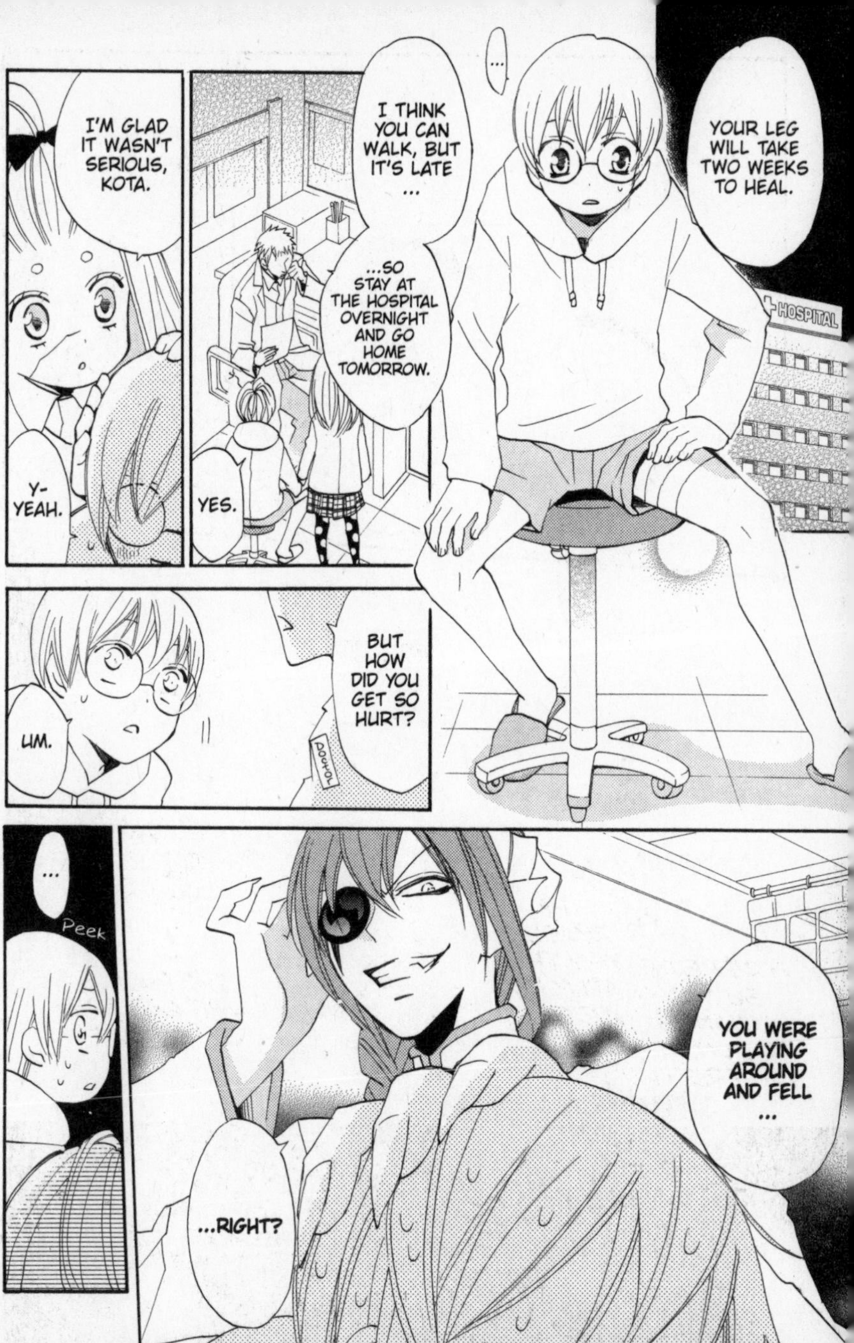
YOUR LEG WILL TAKE TWO WEEKS TO HEAL.
HOSPITAL
...
I THINK YOU CAN WALK, BUT IT'S LATE ...
...SO STAY AT THE HOSPITAL OVERNIGHT AND GO HOME TOMORROW.
YES.
I'M GLAD IT WASN'T SERIOUS, KOTA.
Y-YEAH.
BUT HOW DID YOU GET SO HURT?
DOCTOR
UM.
YOU WERE PLAYING AROUND AND FELL ...
...RIGHT?
...
Peek

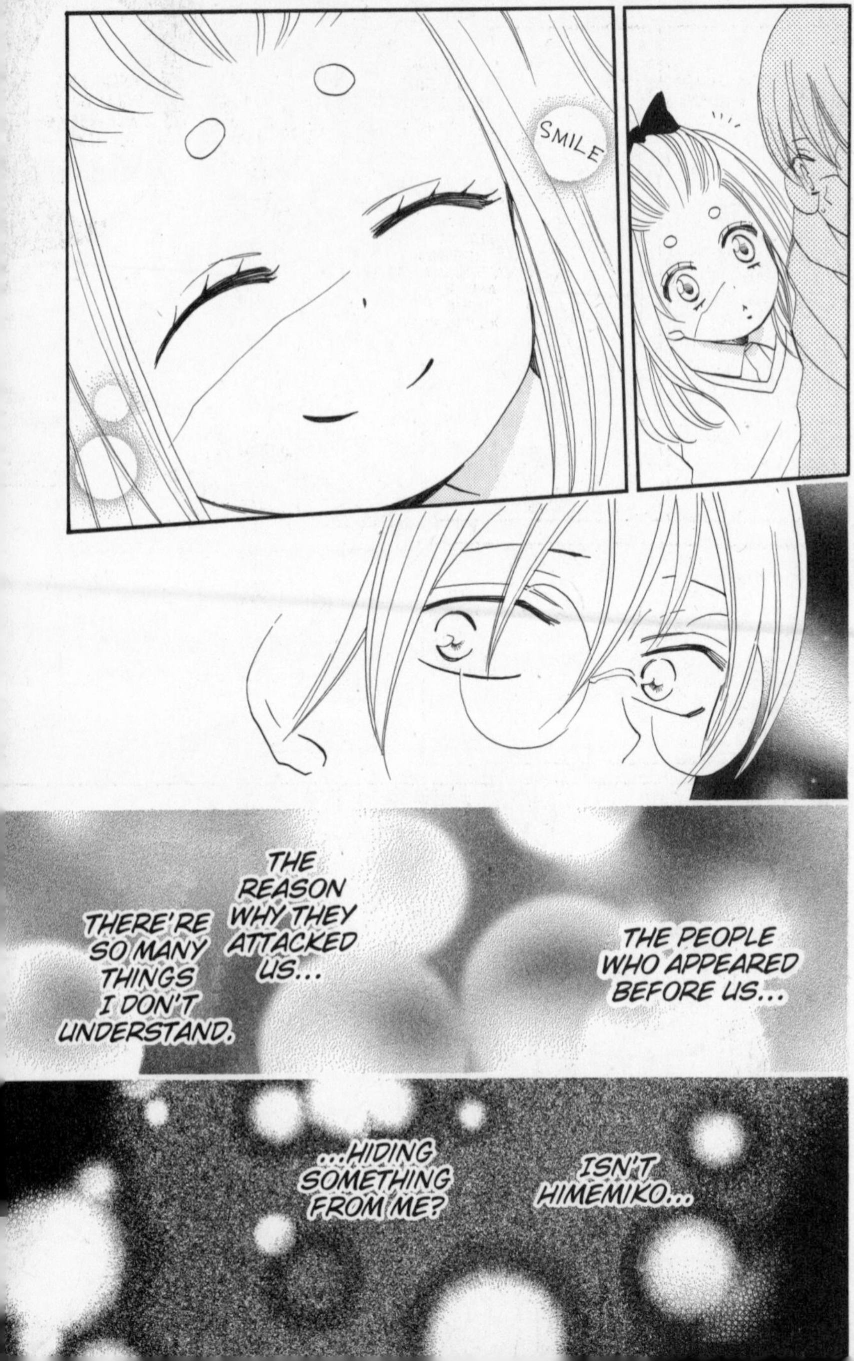
SMILE
THE PEOPLE WHO APPEARED BEFORE US...
THE REASON WHY THEY ATTACKED US...
THERE'RE SO MANY THINGS I DON'T UNDERSTAND.
ISN'T HIMEMIKO...
...HIDING SOMETHING FROM ME?

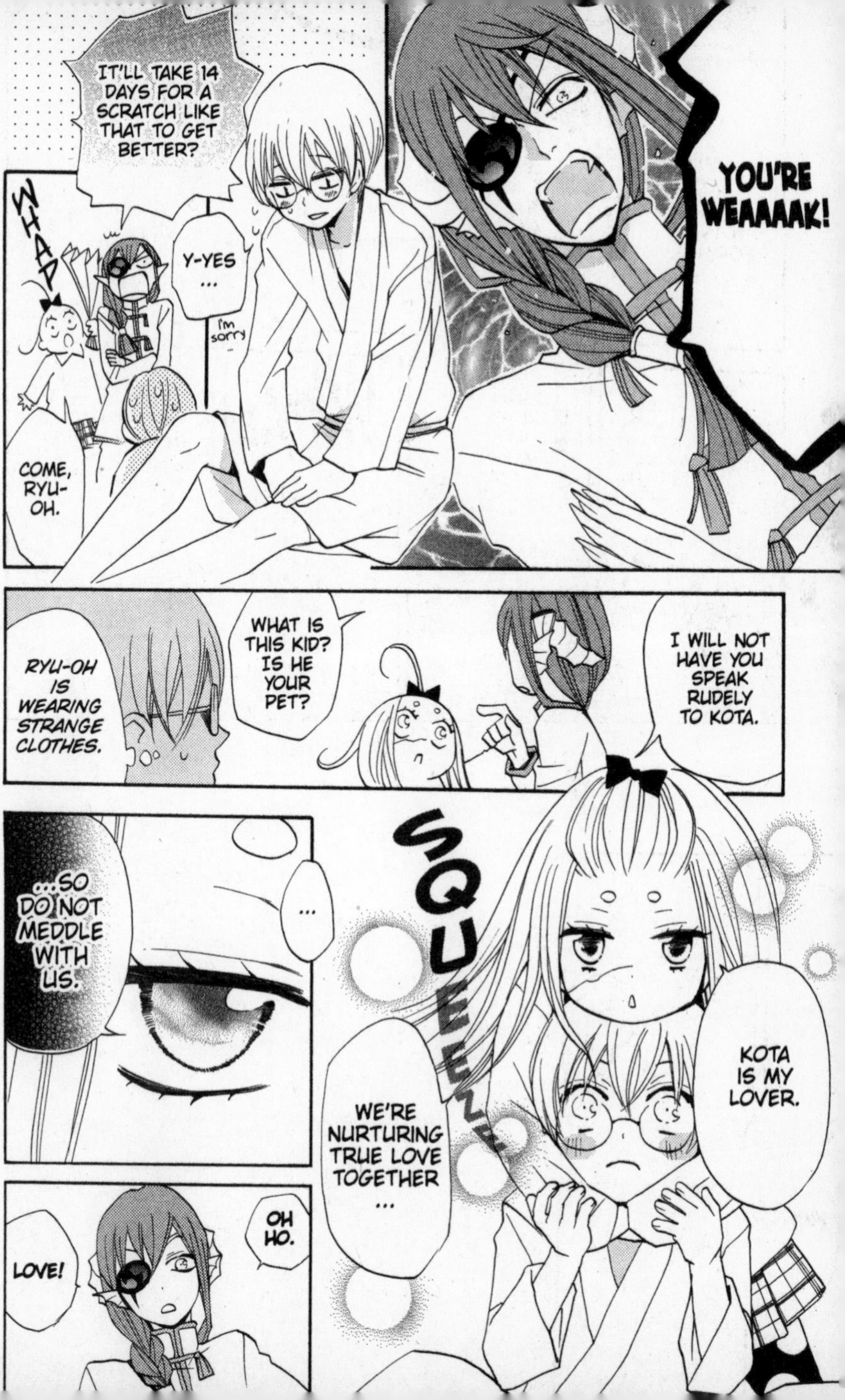
YOU'RE WEAAAAK!
IT'LL TAKE 14 DAYS FOR A SCRATCH LIKE THAT TO GET BETTER?
Y-YES ...
I'm sorry ...
WHAP
COME, RYU-OH.
I WILL NOT HAVE YOU SPEAK RUDELY TO KOTA.
WHAT IS THIS KID? IS HE YOUR PET?
RYU-OH IS WEARING STRANGE CLOTHES.
SQUEEZE
KOTA IS MY LOVER.
WE'RE NURTURING TRUE LOVE TOGETHER ...
...
...SO DO NOT MEDDLE WITH US.
OH HO.
LOVE!

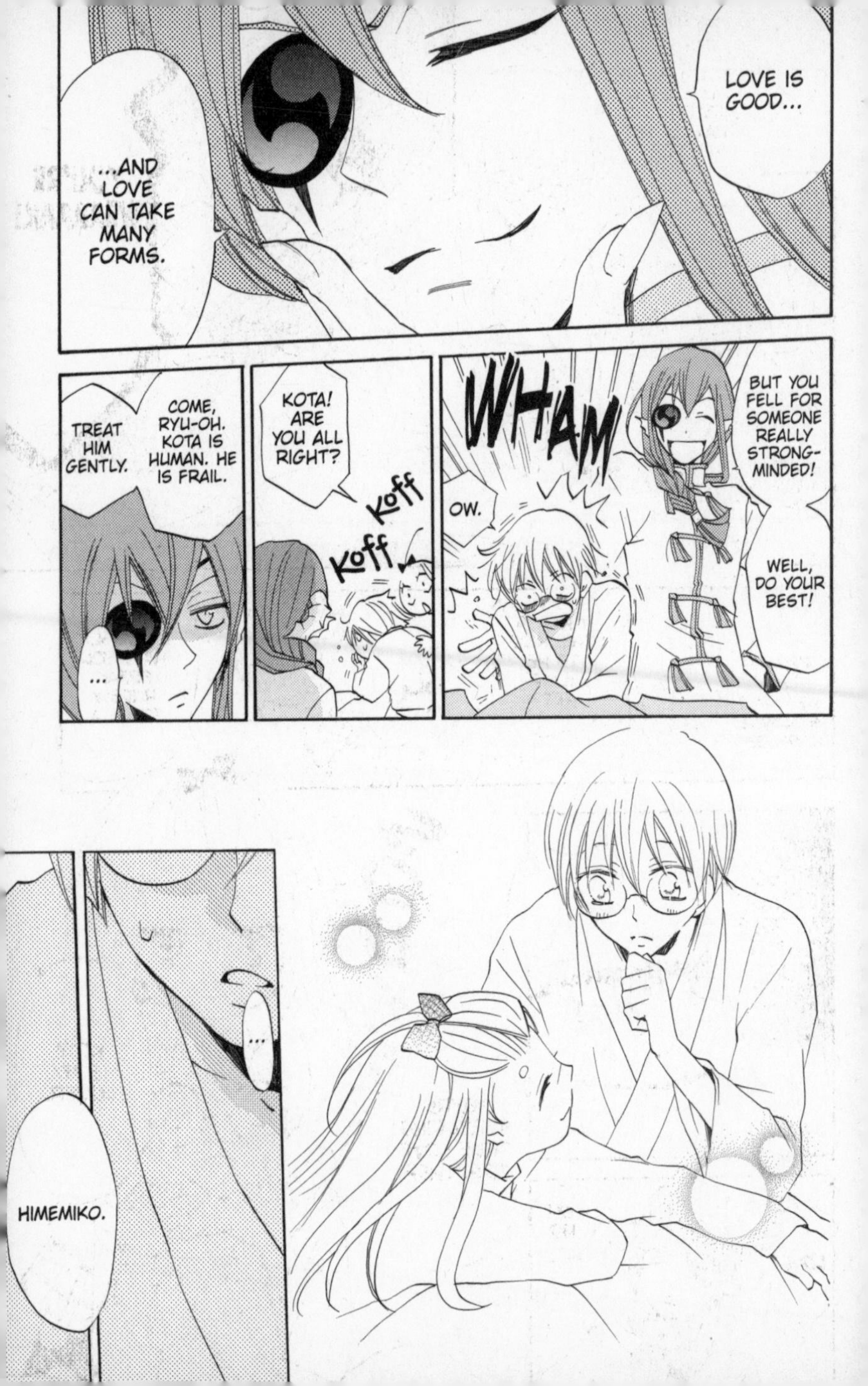
LOVE IS GOOD...
...AND LOVE CAN TAKE MANY FORMS.
BUT YOU FELL FOR SOMEONE REALLY STRONG-MINDED!
WHAM
WELL, DO YOUR BEST!
OW.
KOTA! ARE YOU ALL RIGHT?
KOFF
KOFF
COME, RYU-OH. KOTA IS HUMAN. HE IS FRAIL.
TREAT HIM GENTLY.
...
...
HIMEMIKO.

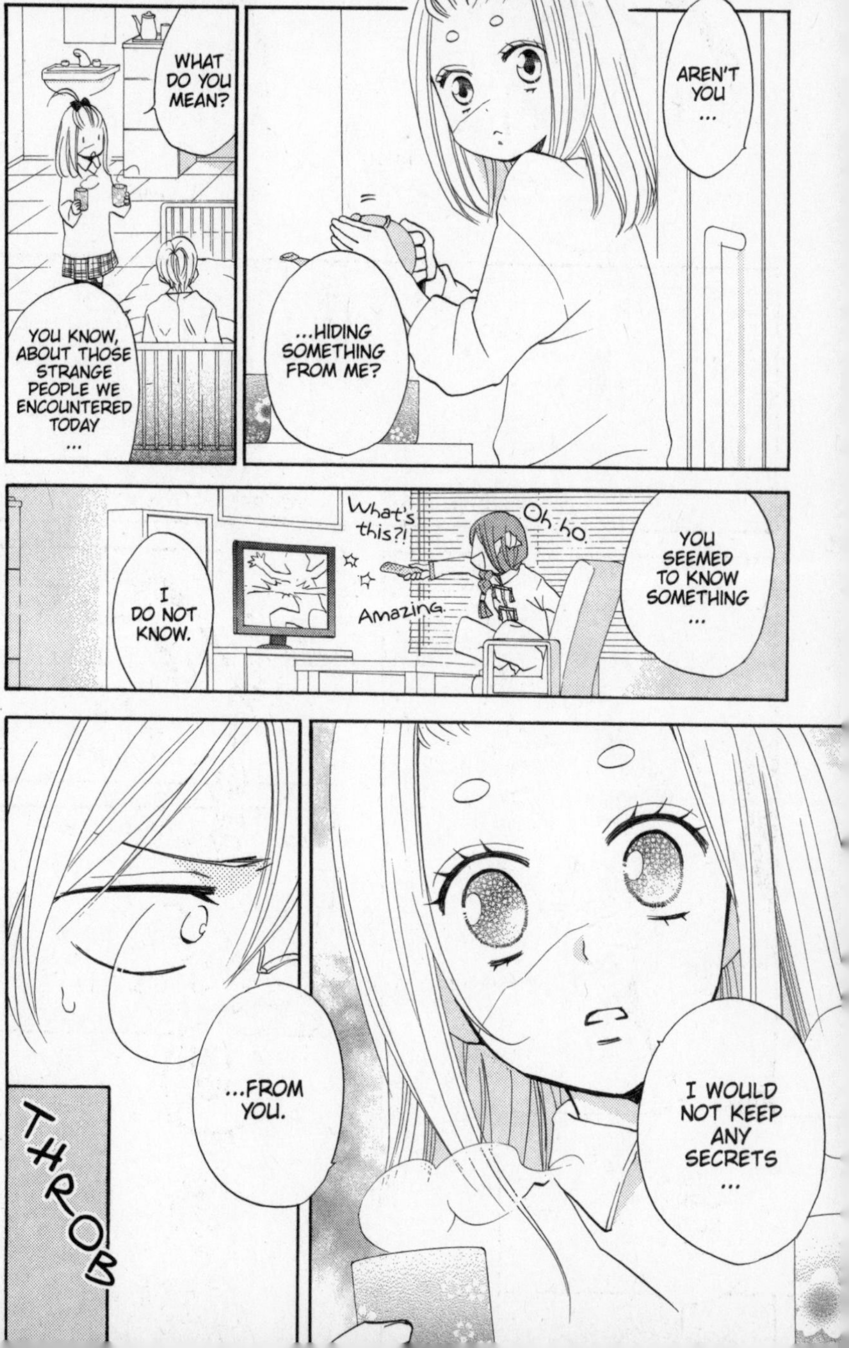
AREN'T YOU ...
...HIDING SOMETHING FROM ME?
WHAT DO YOU MEAN?
YOU KNOW, ABOUT THOSE STRANGE PEOPLE WE ENCOUNTERED TODAY ...
YOU SEEMED TO KNOW SOMETHING ...
Oh ho.
What's this?!
Amazing.
I DO NOT KNOW.
I WOULD NOT KEEP ANY SECRETS ...
...FROM YOU.
THROB

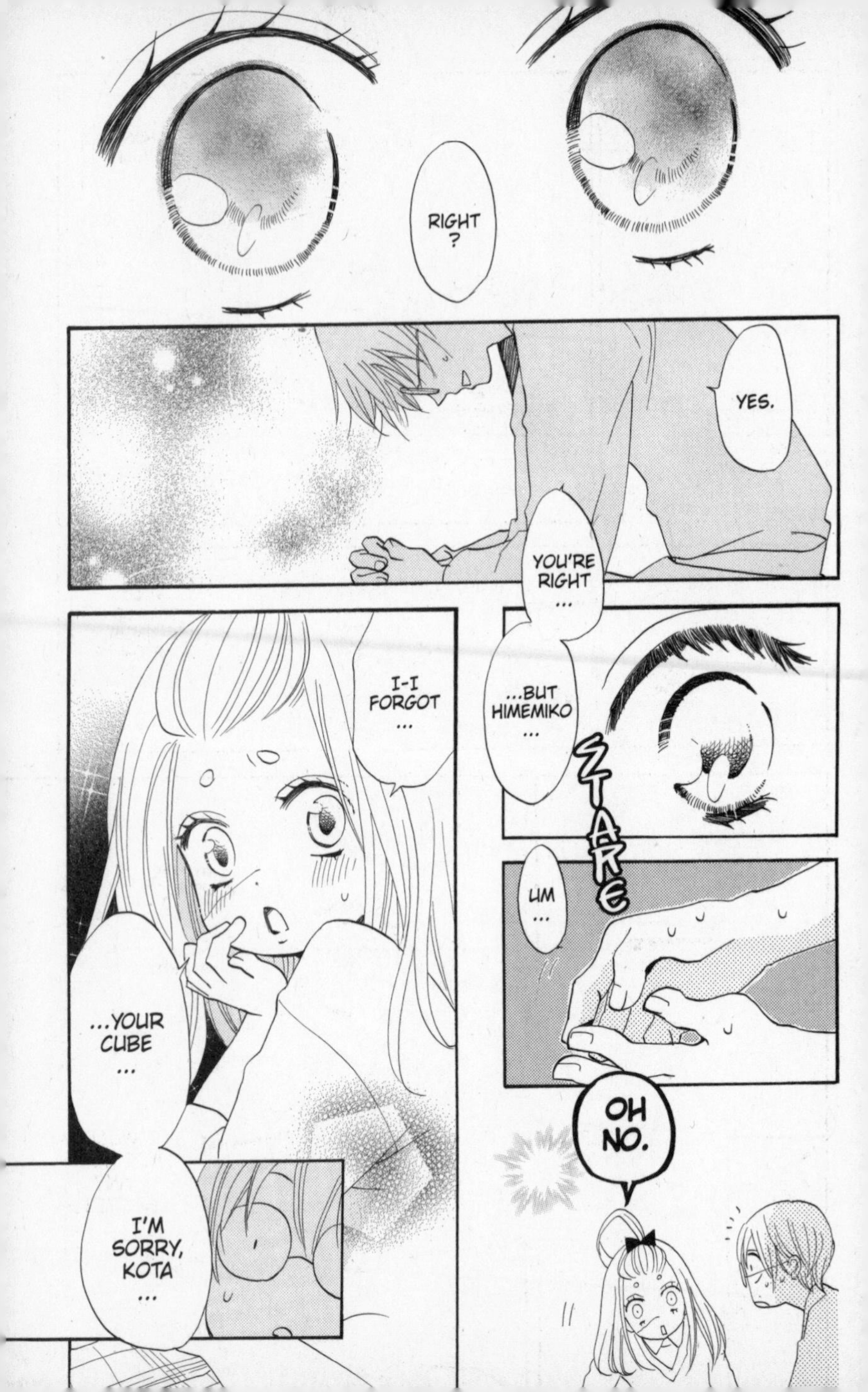
RIGHT?
YES.
YOU'RE RIGHT...
...BUT HIMEMIKO...
STARE
UM...
OH NO.
I-I FORGOT...
...YOUR CUBE...
I'M SORRY, KOTA...

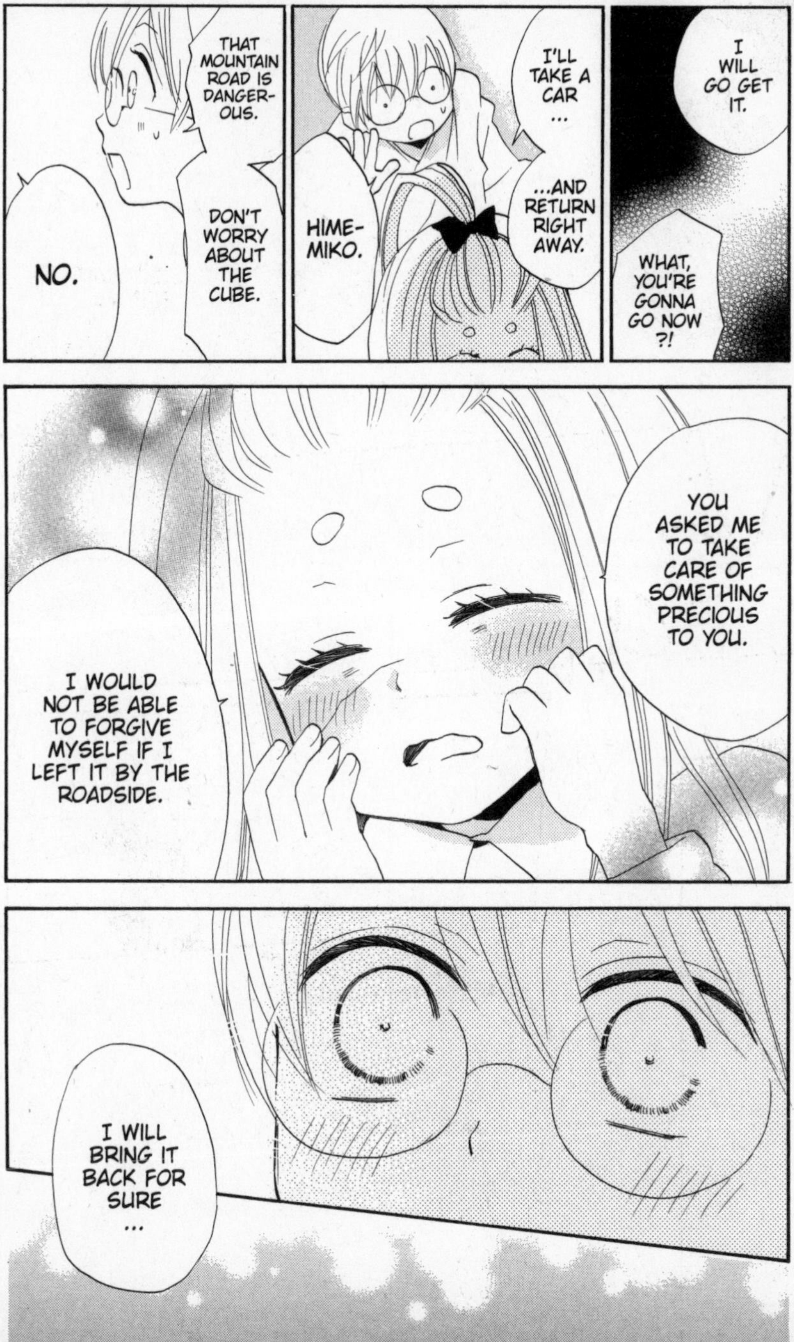
I WILL GO GET IT.
WHAT, YOU'RE GONNA GO NOW ?!
I'LL TAKE A CAR ...
...AND RETURN RIGHT AWAY.
HIME-MIKO.
THAT MOUNTAIN ROAD IS DANGER-OUS.
DON'T WORRY ABOUT THE CUBE.
NO.
YOU ASKED ME TO TAKE CARE OF SOMETHING PRECIOUS TO YOU.
I WOULD NOT BE ABLE TO FORGIVE MYSELF IF I LEFT IT BY THE ROADSIDE.
I WILL BRING IT BACK FOR SURE ...

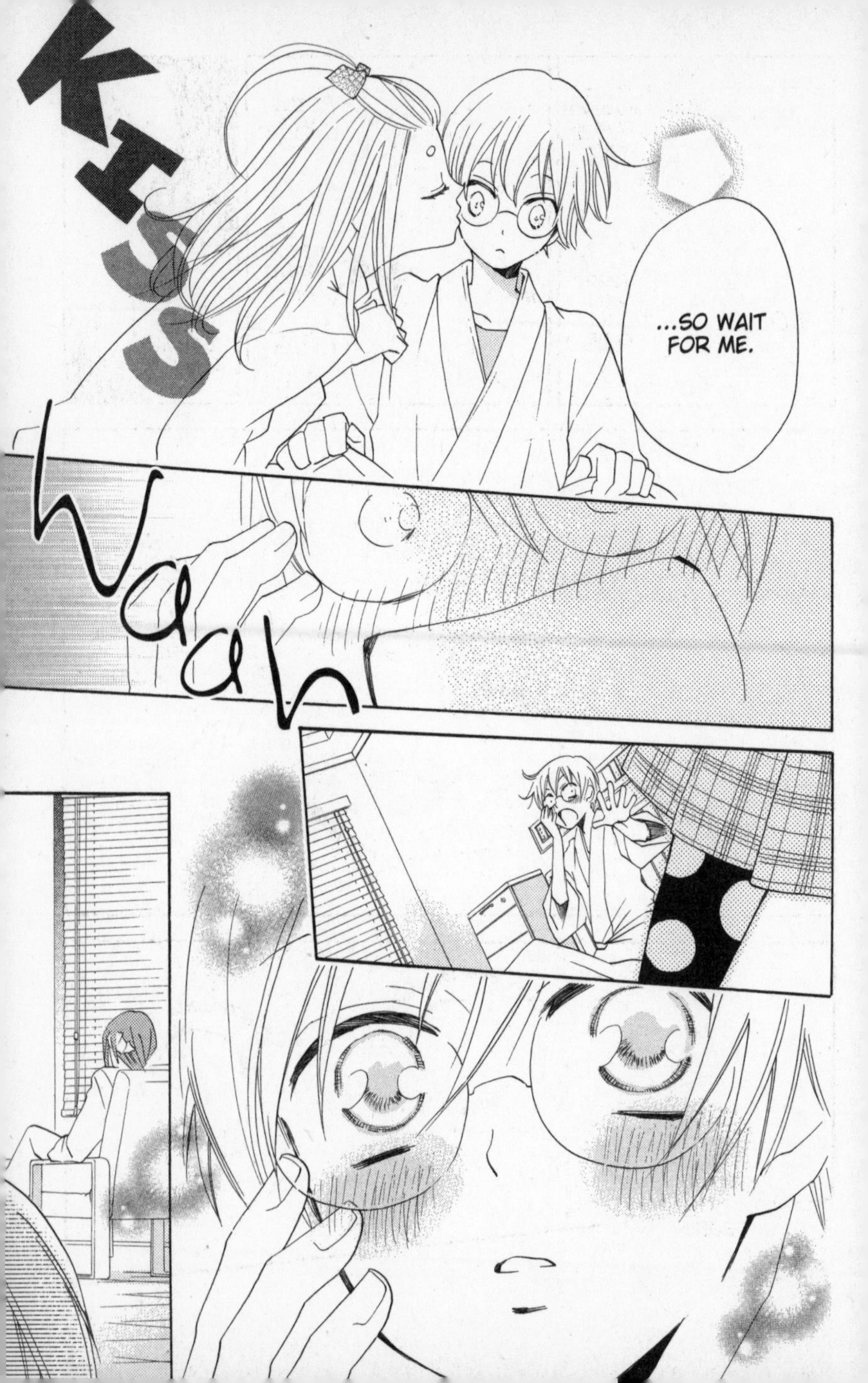
KISS
...SO WAIT FOR ME.
Waah

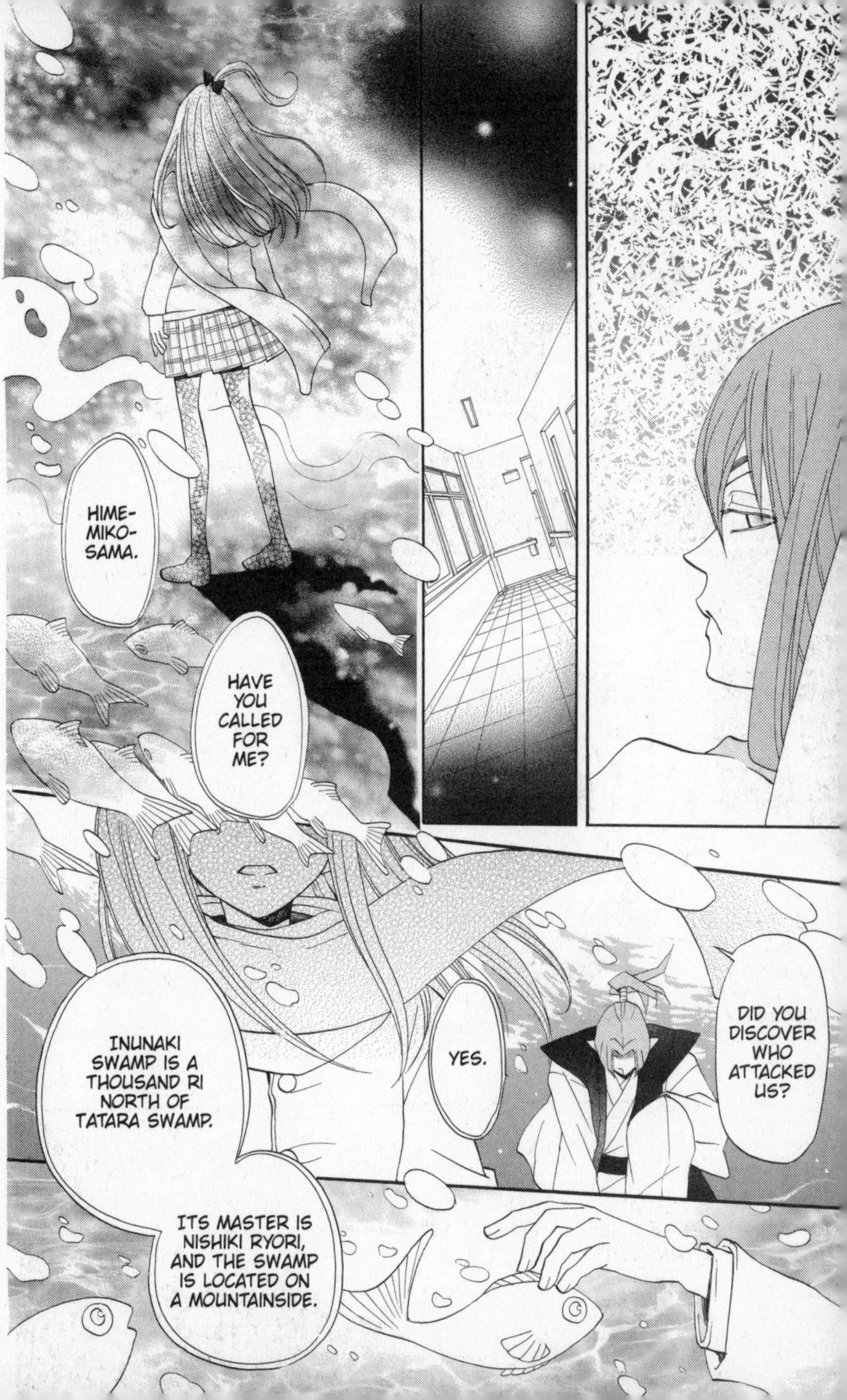
HIME-MIKO-SAMA.
HAVE YOU CALLED FOR ME?
DID YOU DISCOVER WHO ATTACKED US?
YES.
INUNAKI SWAMP IS A THOUSAND RI NORTH OF TATARA SWAMP.
ITS MASTER IS NISHIKI RYORI, AND THE SWAMP IS LOCATED ON A MOUNTAINSIDE.

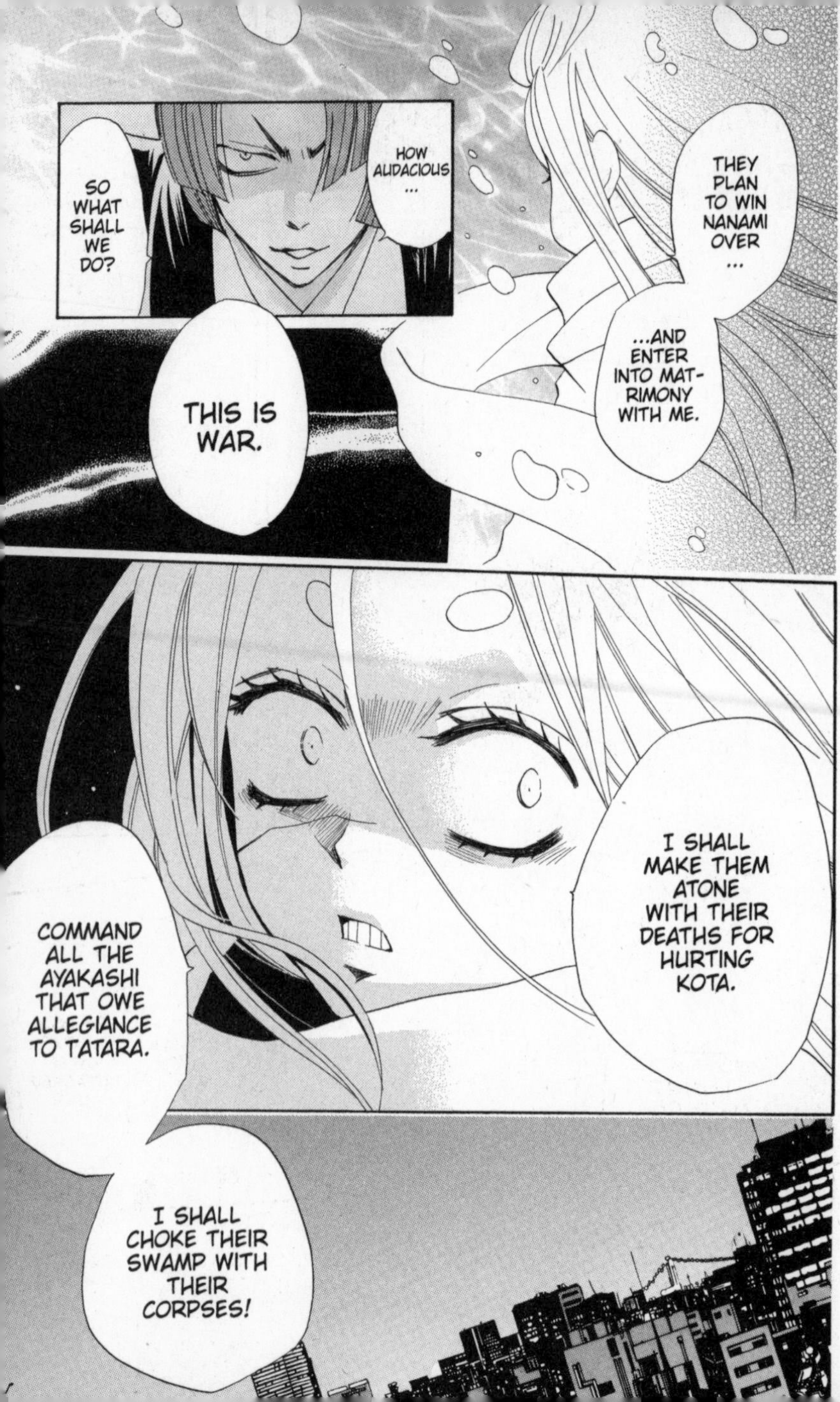
THEY PLAN TO WIN NANAMI OVER...
...AND ENTER INTO MAT-RIMONY WITH ME.
HOW AUDACIOUS...
SO WHAT SHALL WE DO?
THIS IS WAR.
I SHALL MAKE THEM ATONE WITH THEIR DEATHS FOR HURTING KOTA.
COMMAND ALL THE AYAKASHI THAT OWE ALLEGIANCE TO TATARA.
I SHALL CHOKE THEIR SWAMP WITH THEIR CORPSES!

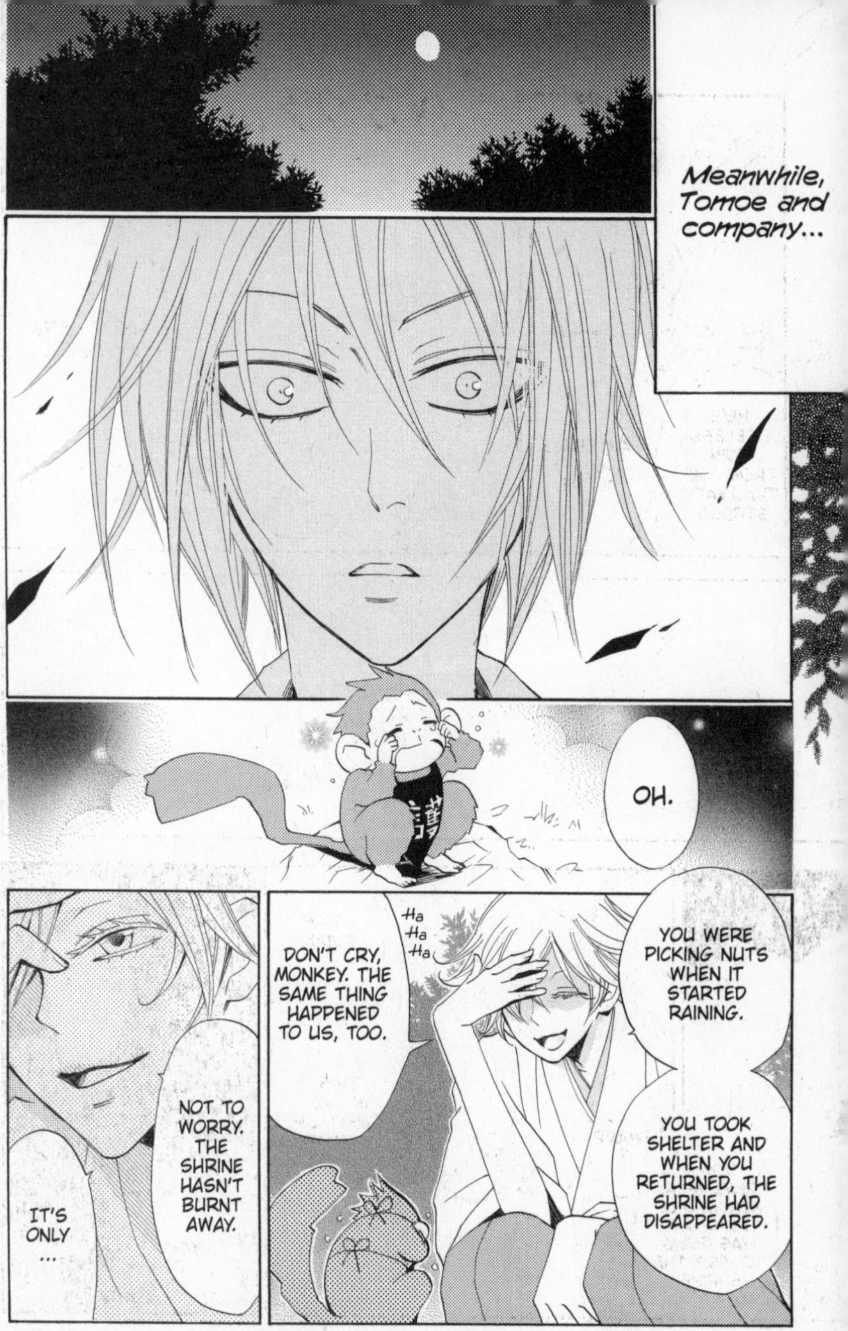

Meanwhile, Tomoe and company...
OH.
YOU WERE PICKING NUTS WHEN IT STARTED RAINING.
YOU TOOK SHELTER AND WHEN YOU RETURNED, THE SHRINE HAD DISAPPEARED.
Ha Ha Ha
DON'T CRY, MONKEY. THE SAME THING HAPPENED TO US, TOO.
NOT TO WORRY. THE SHRINE HASN'T BURNT AWAY.
IT'S ONLY ...

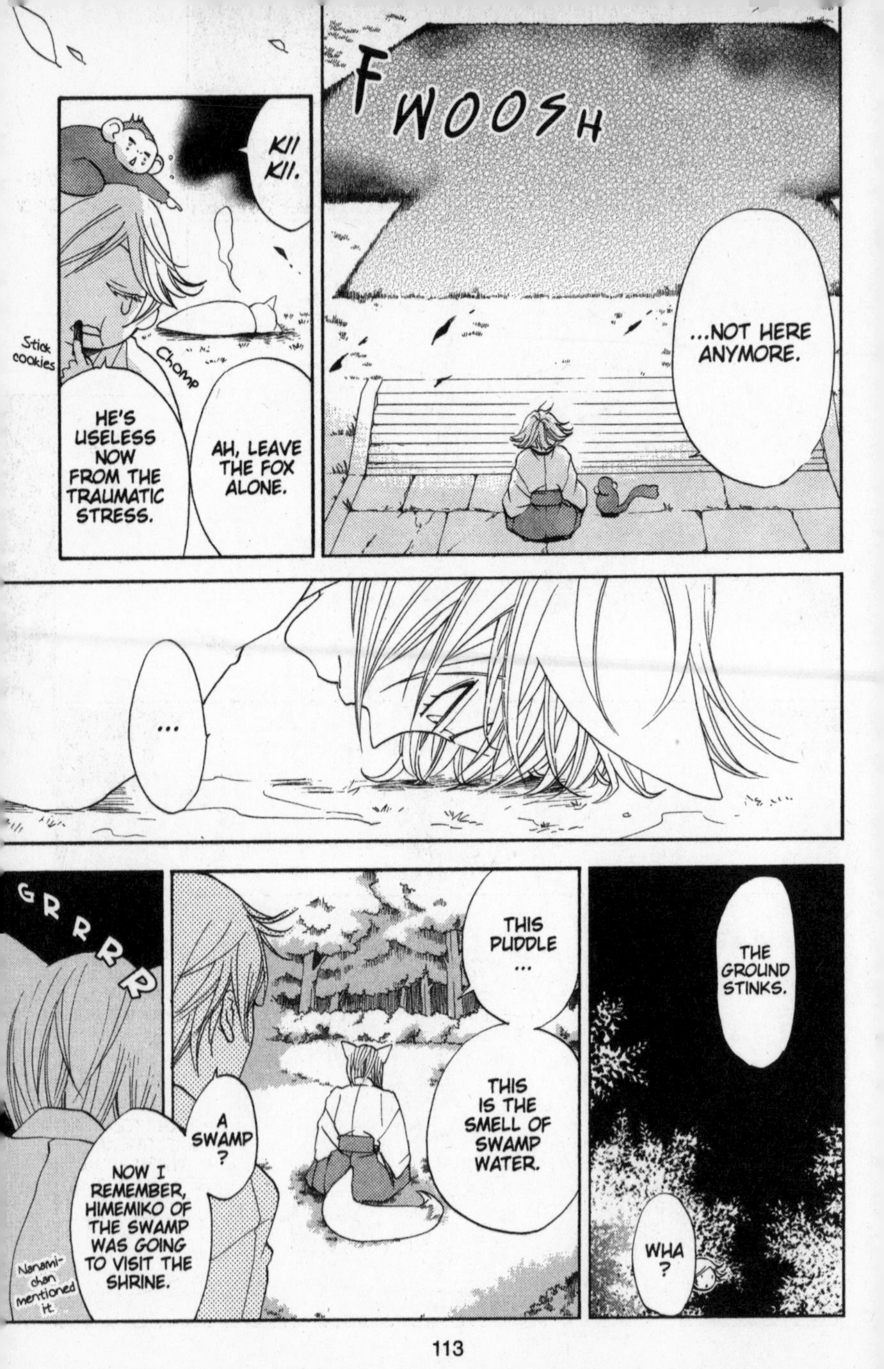
FWOOSH
...NOT HERE ANYMORE.
KII KII.
Stick cookies
Chomp
AH, LEAVE THE FOX ALONE.
HE'S USELESS NOW FROM THE TRAUMATIC STRESS.
...
THE GROUND STINKS.
WHA?
THIS PUDDLE...
THIS IS THE SMELL OF SWAMP WATER.
GRRRR
A SWAMP?
NOW I REMEMBER, HIMEMIKO OF THE SWAMP WAS GOING TO VISIT THE SHRINE.
Nanami-chan mentioned it

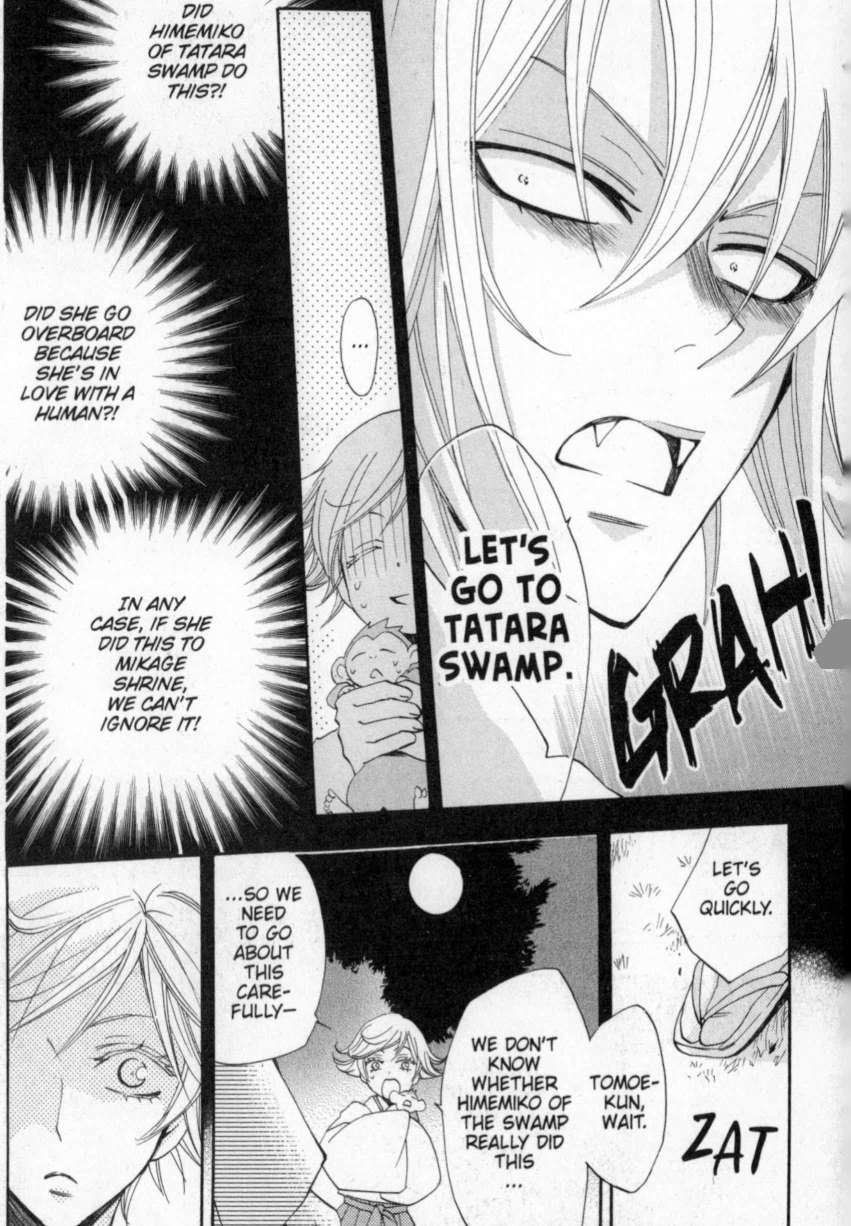
LET'S GO TO TATARA SWAMP.
GRAH!
...
DID HIMEMIKO OF TATARA SWAMP DO THIS?!
DID SHE GO OVERBOARD BECAUSE SHE'S IN LOVE WITH A HUMAN?!
IN ANY CASE, IF SHE DID THIS TO MIKAGE SHRINE, WE CAN'T IGNORE IT!
LET'S GO QUICKLY.
ZAT
TOMOE-KUN, WAIT.
WE DON'T KNOW WHETHER HIMEMIKO OF THE SWAMP REALLY DID THIS ...
...SO WE NEED TO GO ABOUT THIS CARE-FULLY—

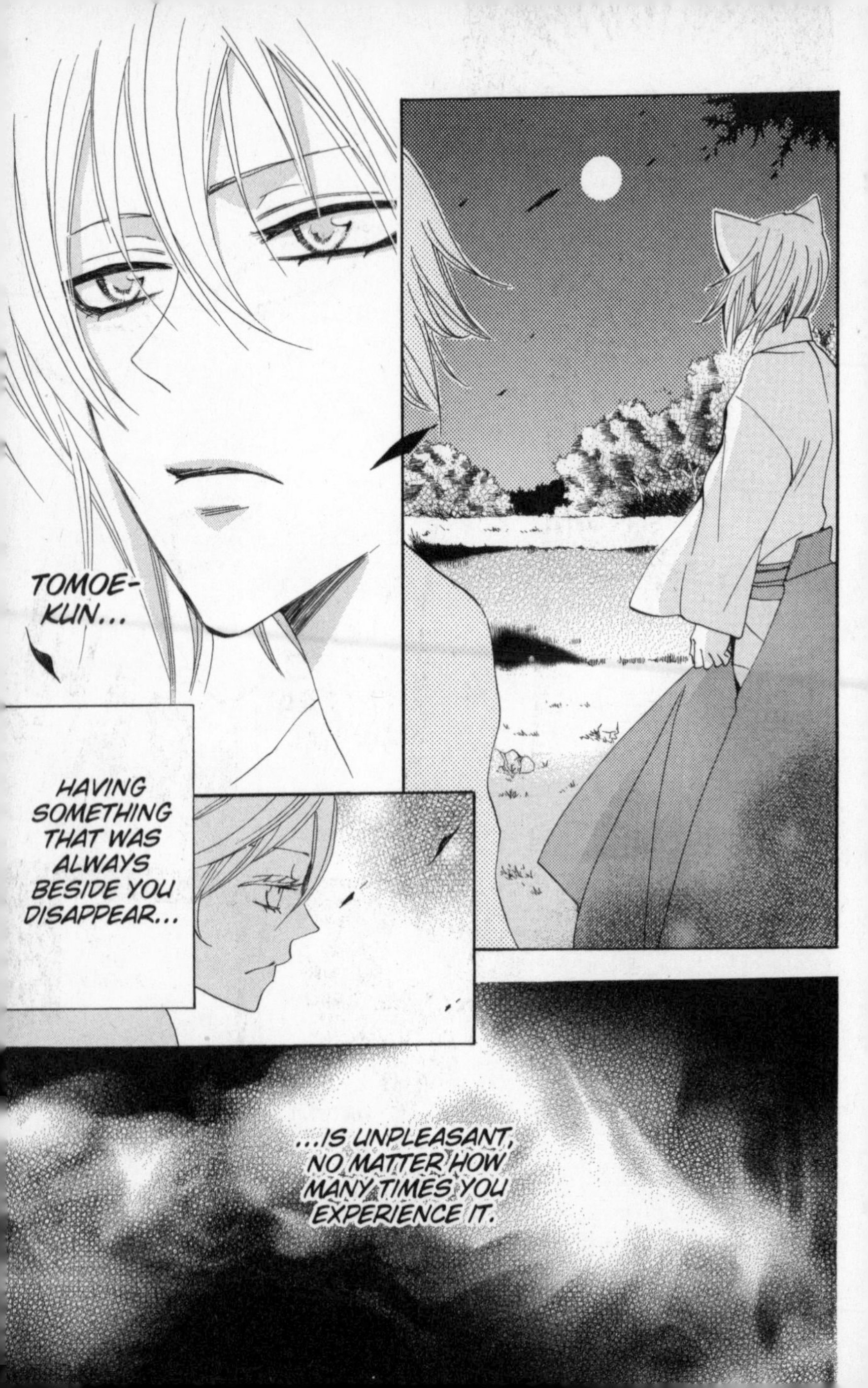
TOMOE-KUN...
HAVING SOMETHING THAT WAS ALWAYS BESIDE YOU DISAPPEAR...
...IS UNPLEASANT, NO MATTER HOW MANY TIMES YOU EXPERIENCE IT.

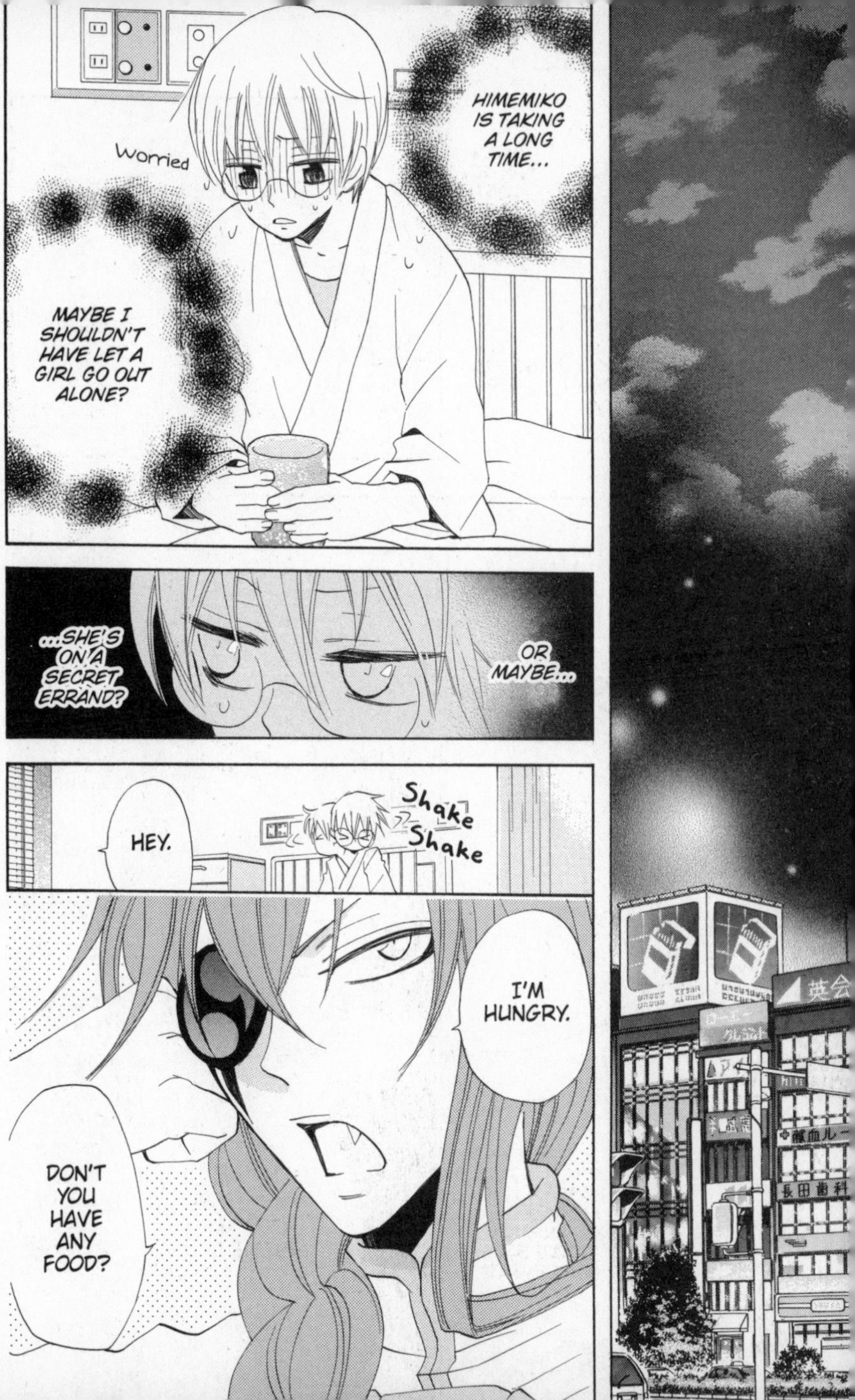
HIMEMIKO IS TAKING A LONG TIME...
Worried
MAYBE I SHOULDN'T HAVE LET A GIRL GO OUT ALONE?
OR MAYBE...
...SHE'S ON A SECRET ERRAND?
Shake Shake
HEY.
I'M HUNGRY.
DON'T YOU HAVE ANY FOOD?

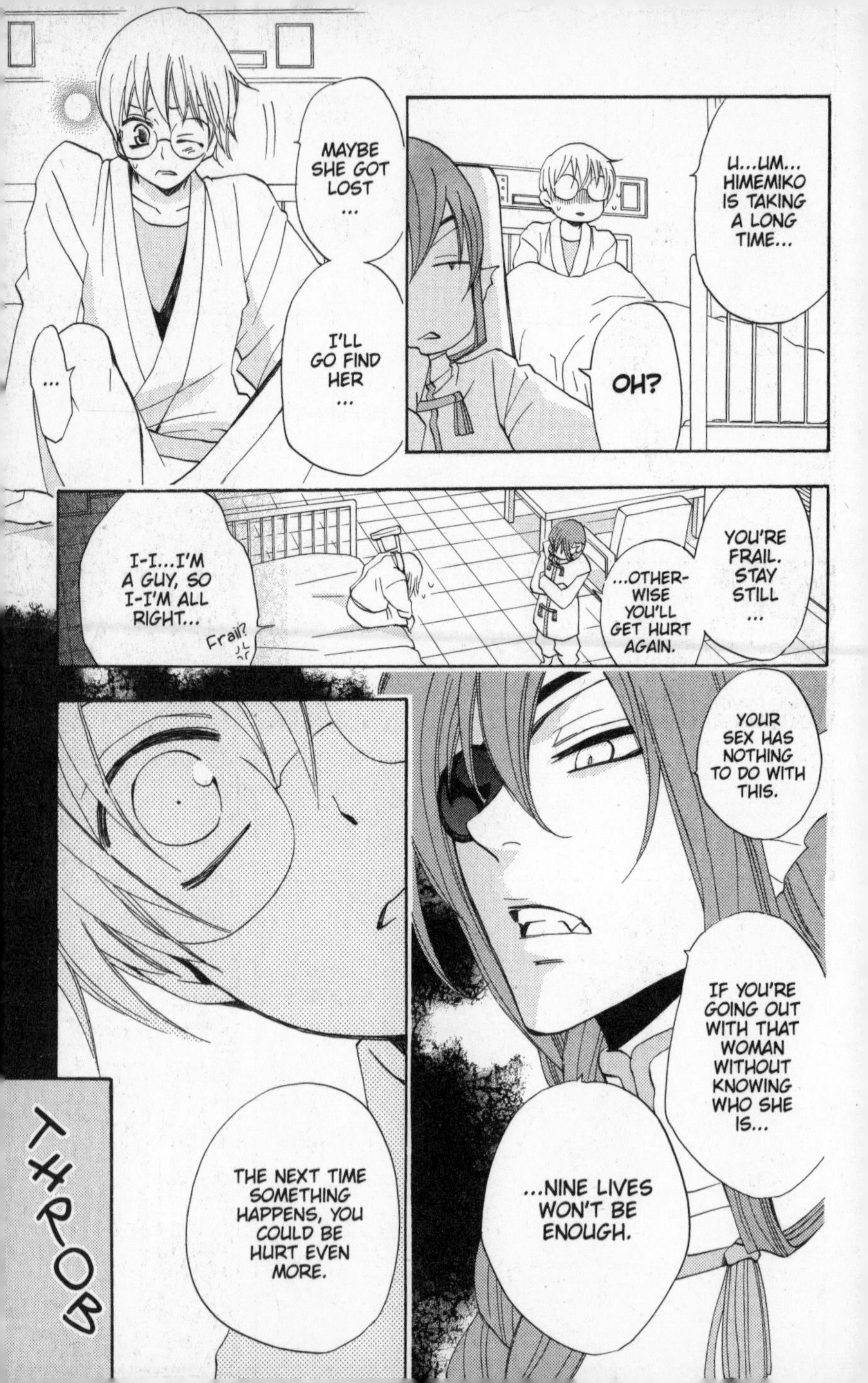
U...UM... HIMEMIKO IS TAKING A LONG TIME...
OH?
MAYBE SHE GOT LOST ...
I'LL GO FIND HER ...
...
YOU'RE FRAIL. STAY STILL ...
...OTHER-WISE YOU'LL GET HURT AGAIN.
I-I...I'M A GUY, SO I-I'M ALL RIGHT...
Frail?
YOUR SEX HAS NOTHING TO DO WITH THIS.
IF YOU'RE GOING OUT WITH THAT WOMAN WITHOUT KNOWING WHO SHE IS...
...NINE LIVES WON'T BE ENOUGH.
THE NEXT TIME SOMETHING HAPPENS, YOU COULD BE HURT EVEN MORE.
THROB

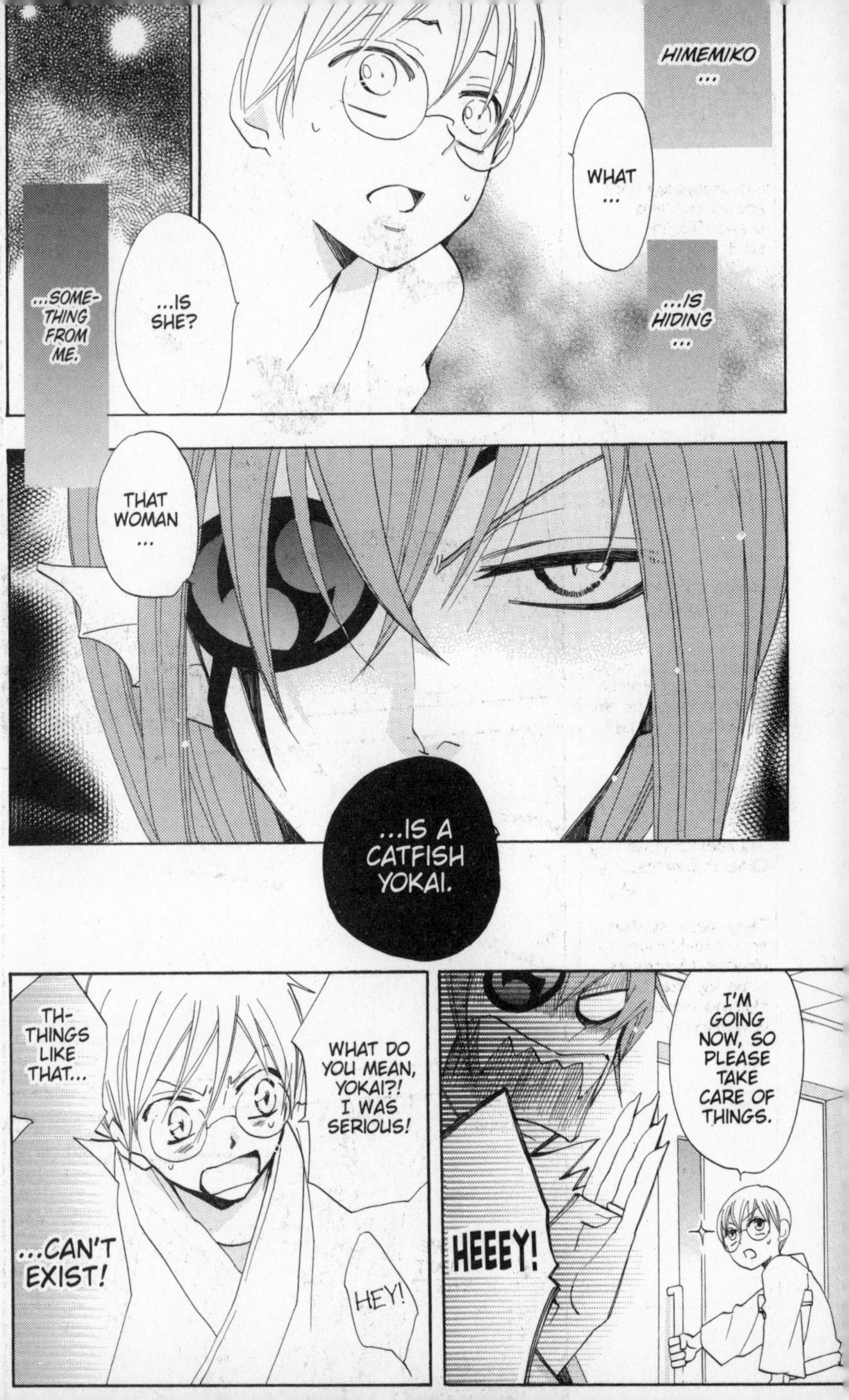
HIMEMIKO ...
WHAT ...
...IS HIDING ...
...IS SHE?
...SOME-THING FROM ME.
THAT WOMAN ...
...IS A CATFISH YOKAI.
I'M GOING NOW, SO PLEASE TAKE CARE OF THINGS.
HEEEY!
WHAT DO YOU MEAN, YOKAI?! I WAS SERIOUS!
HEY!
TH-THINGS LIKE THAT...
...CAN'T EXIST!

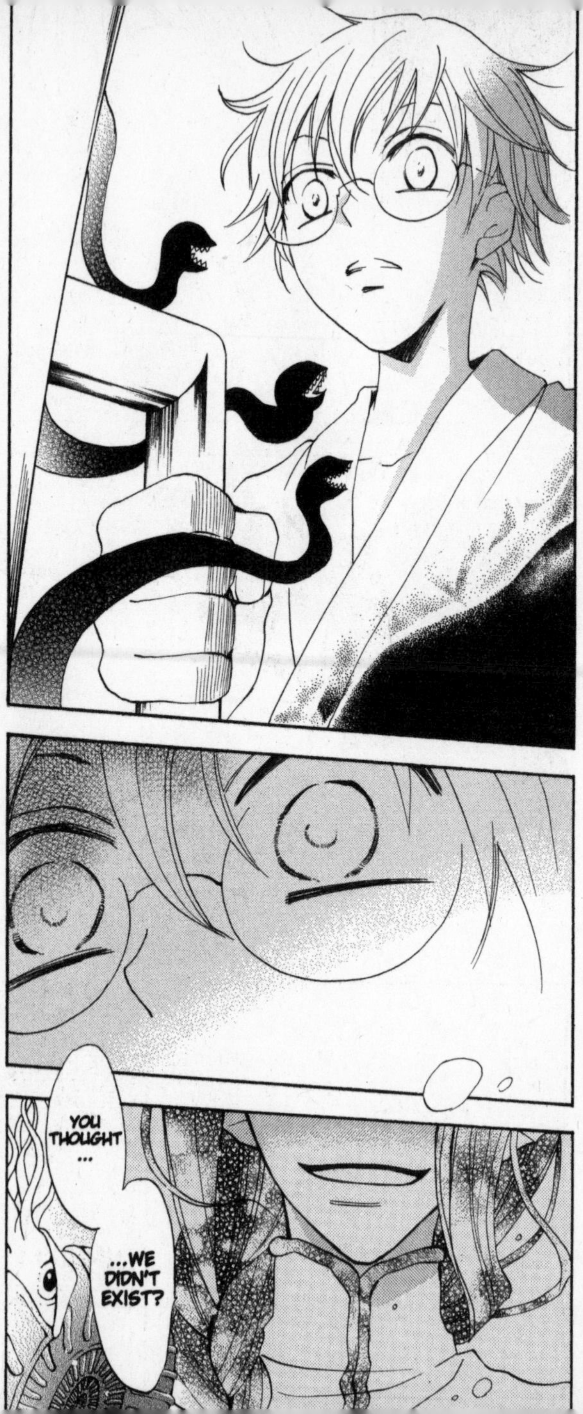
YOU THOUGHT ...
...WE DIDN'T EXIST?

Nowadays my nails are in terrible shape. They're so dry.

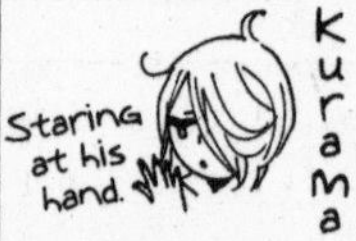
Kurama
Staring at his hand.

I find it strange. My hands don't get too dry...

The other day, new episodes of Poirot were broadcast on satellite, so I was glued to my TV. "Three Act Tragedy," "The Clocks," "Hallowe'en Party," and "Murder on the Orient Express."

They were so fun to watch! I love Poirot. Mysteries grab my heart when the murderer is charming.

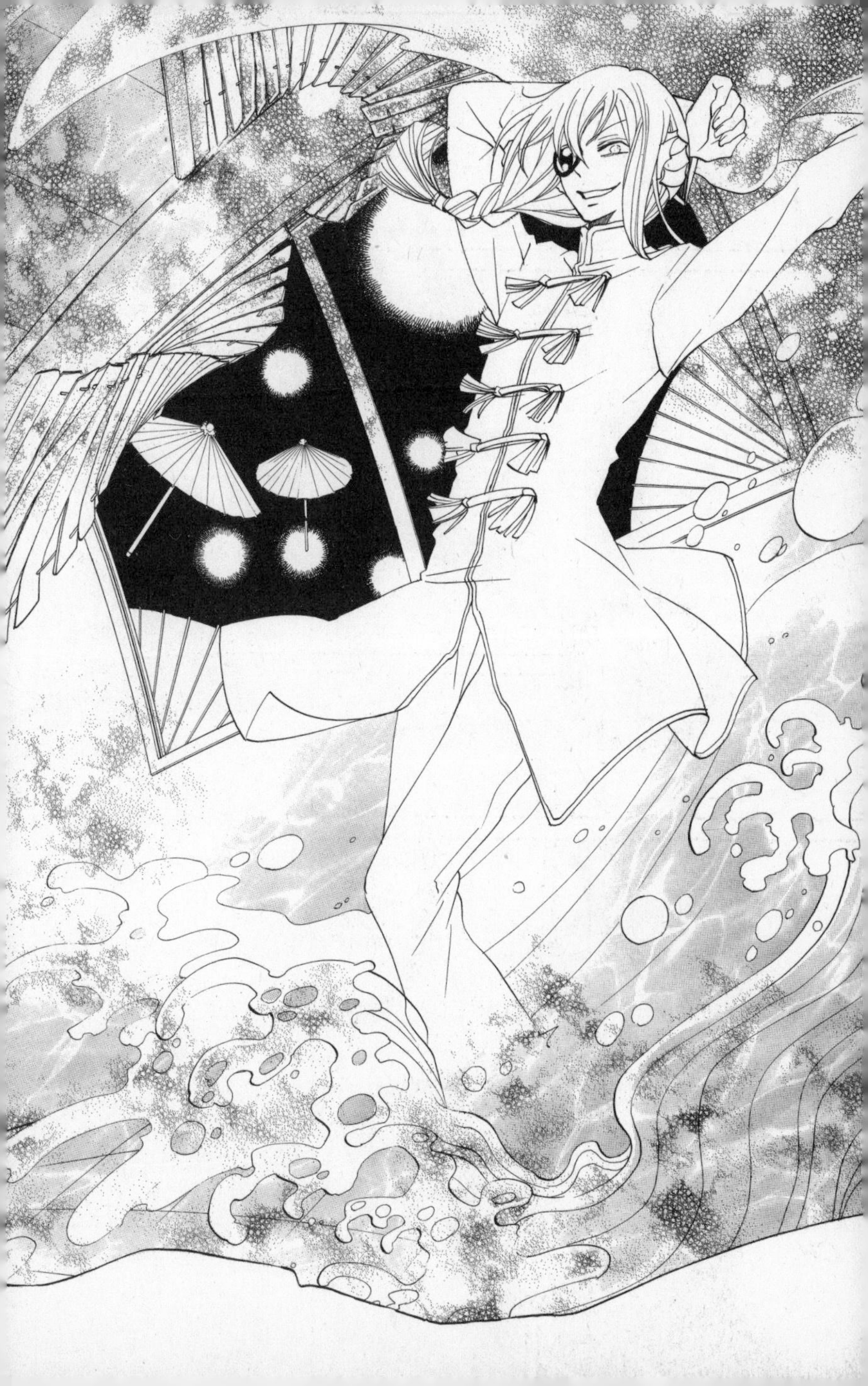

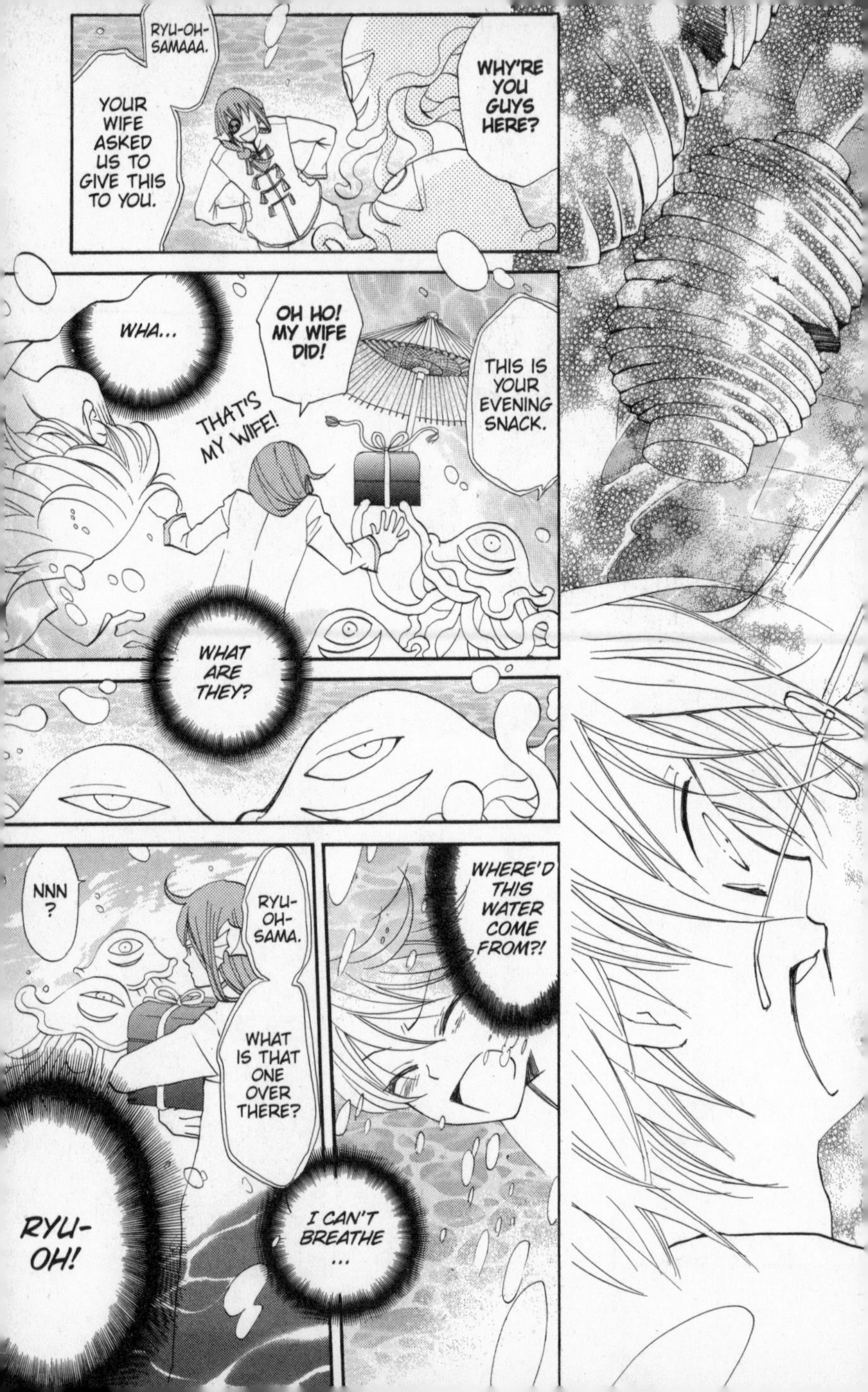
WHY'RE YOU GUYS HERE?
RYU-OH-SAMAAA.
YOUR WIFE ASKED US TO GIVE THIS TO YOU.
THIS IS YOUR EVENING SNACK.
OH HO! MY WIFE DID!
WHA...
THAT'S MY WIFE!
WHAT ARE THEY?
WHERE'D THIS WATER COME FROM?!
I CAN'T BREATHE ...
RYU-OH-SAMA.
NNN ?
WHAT IS THAT ONE OVER THERE?
RYU-OH!

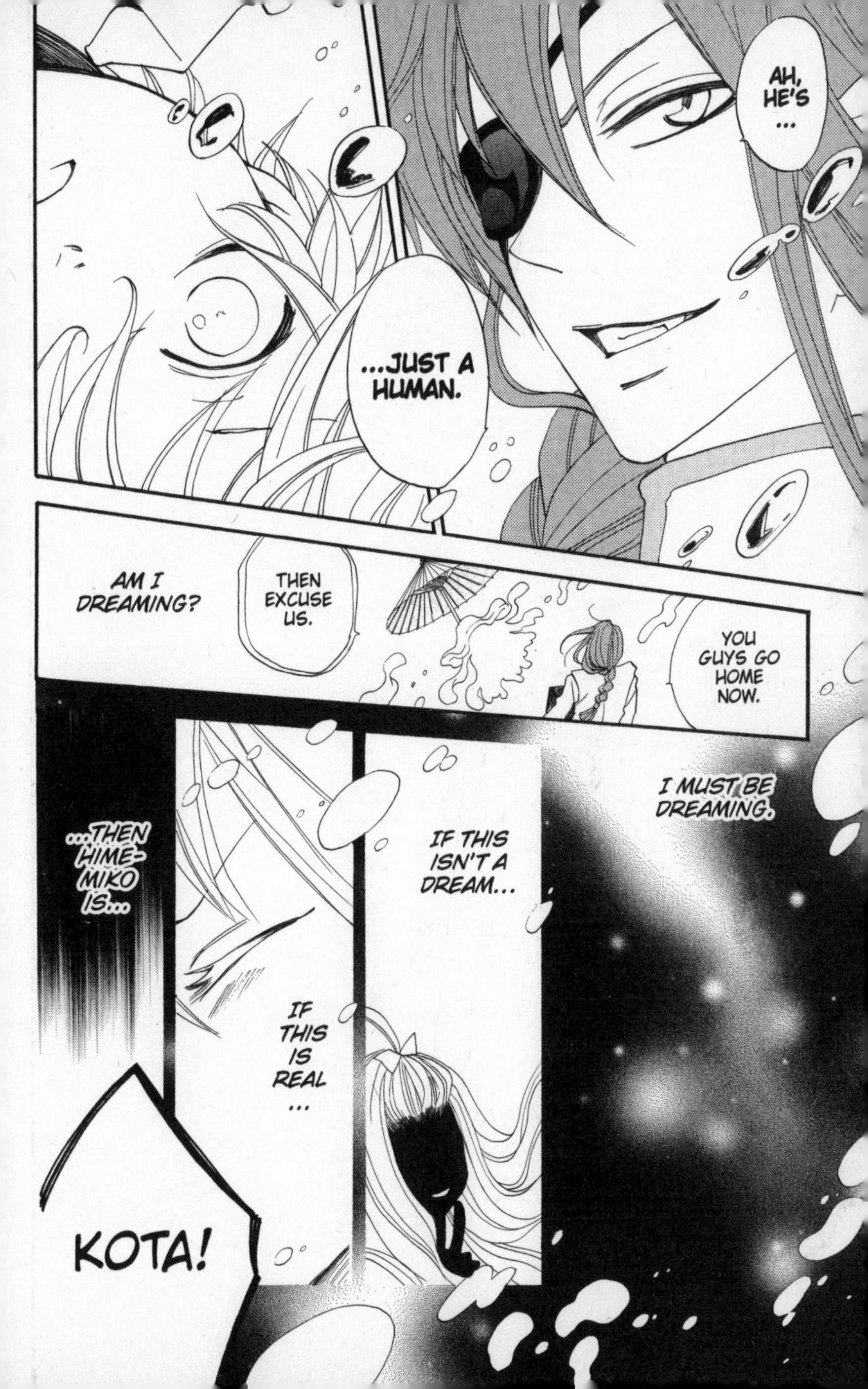
AH, HE'S ...
...JUST A HUMAN.
YOU GUYS GO HOME NOW.
THEN EXCUSE US.
AM I DREAMING?
I MUST BE DREAMING.
IF THIS ISN'T A DREAM...
IF THIS IS REAL ...
...THEN HIME-MIKO IS...
KOTA!

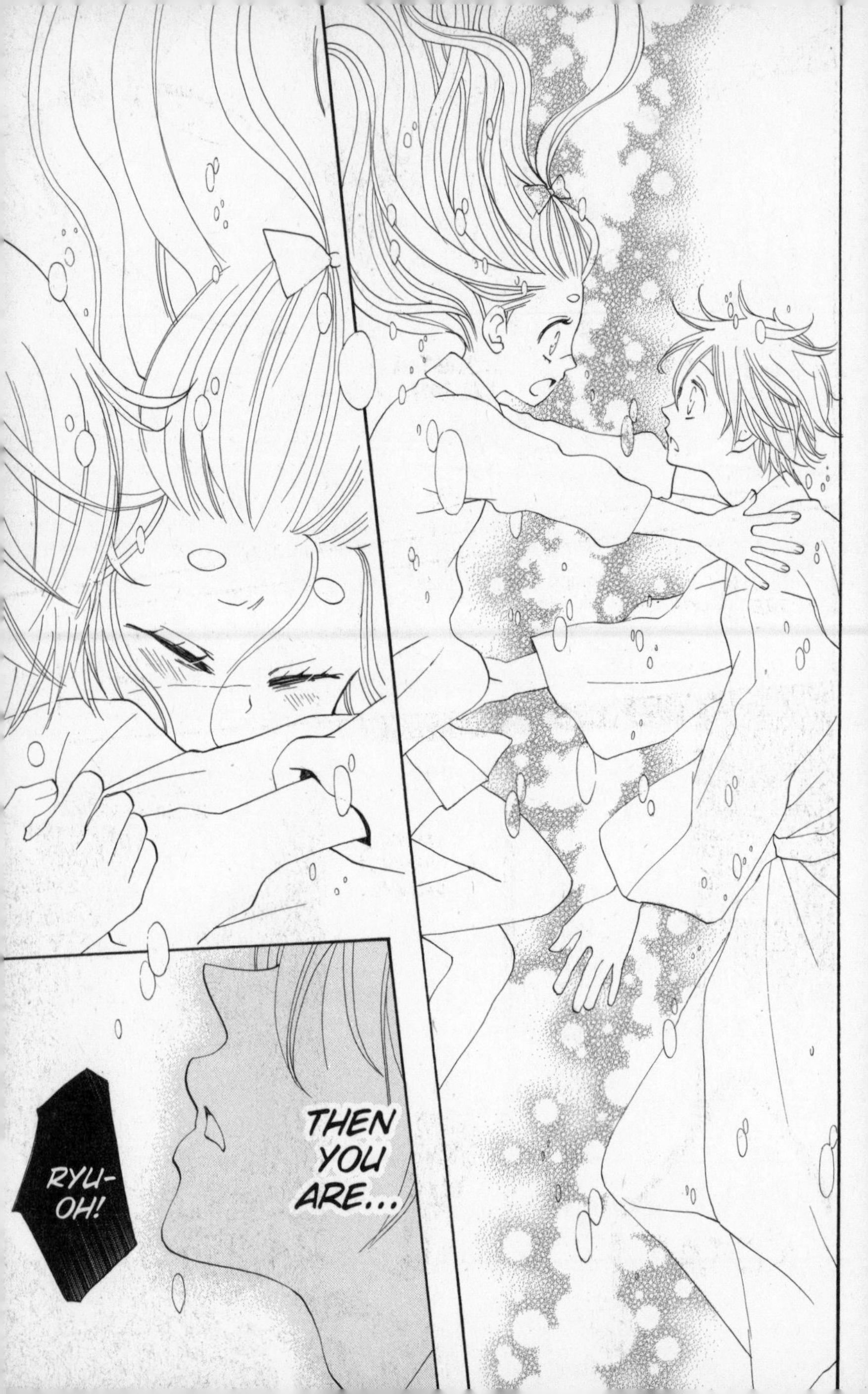
THEN YOU ARE...
RYU-OH!

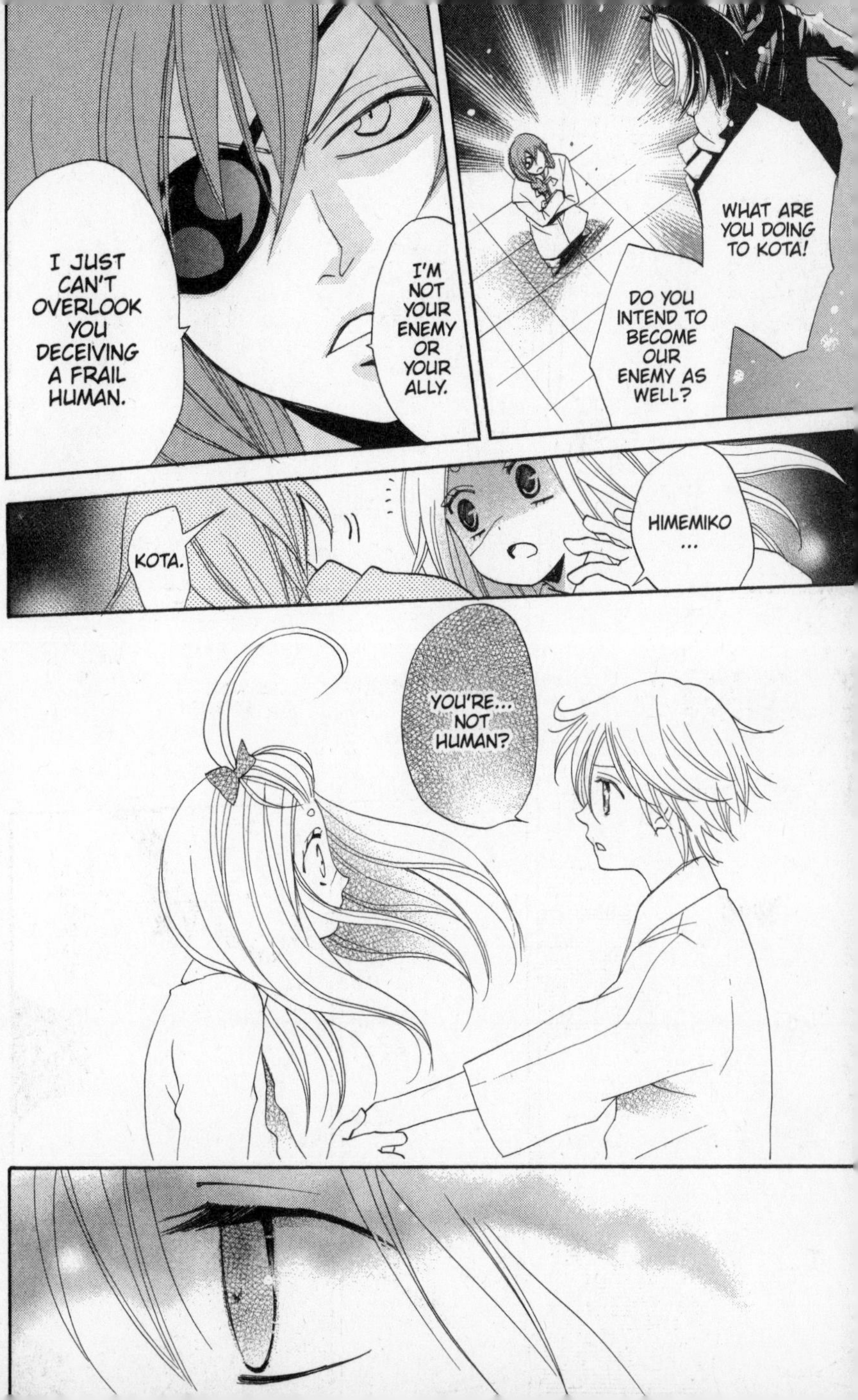
WHAT ARE YOU DOING TO KOTA!
DO YOU INTEND TO BECOME OUR ENEMY AS WELL?
I'M NOT YOUR ENEMY OR YOUR ALLY.
I JUST CAN'T OVERLOOK YOU DECEIVING A FRAIL HUMAN.
HIMEMIKO...
KOTA.
YOU'RE... NOT HUMAN?

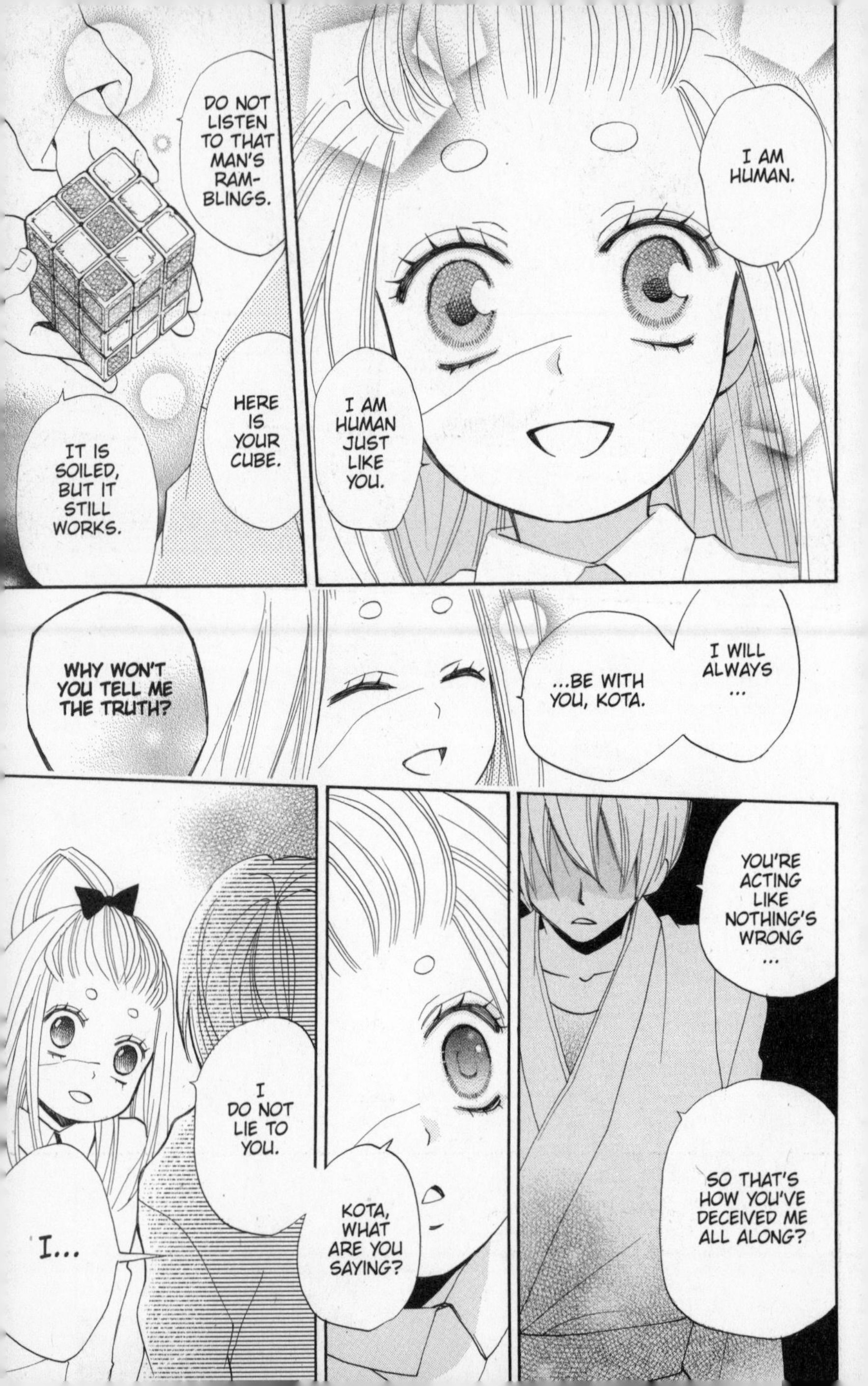
I AM HUMAN.
I AM HUMAN JUST LIKE YOU.
DO NOT LISTEN TO THAT MAN'S RAMBLINGS.
HERE IS YOUR CUBE.
IT IS SOILED, BUT IT STILL WORKS.
I WILL ALWAYS ...
...BE WITH YOU, KOTA.
WHY WON'T YOU TELL ME THE TRUTH?
YOU'RE ACTING LIKE NOTHING'S WRONG ...
SO THAT'S HOW YOU'VE DECEIVED ME ALL ALONG?
KOTA, WHAT ARE YOU SAYING?
I DO NOT LIE TO YOU.
I...

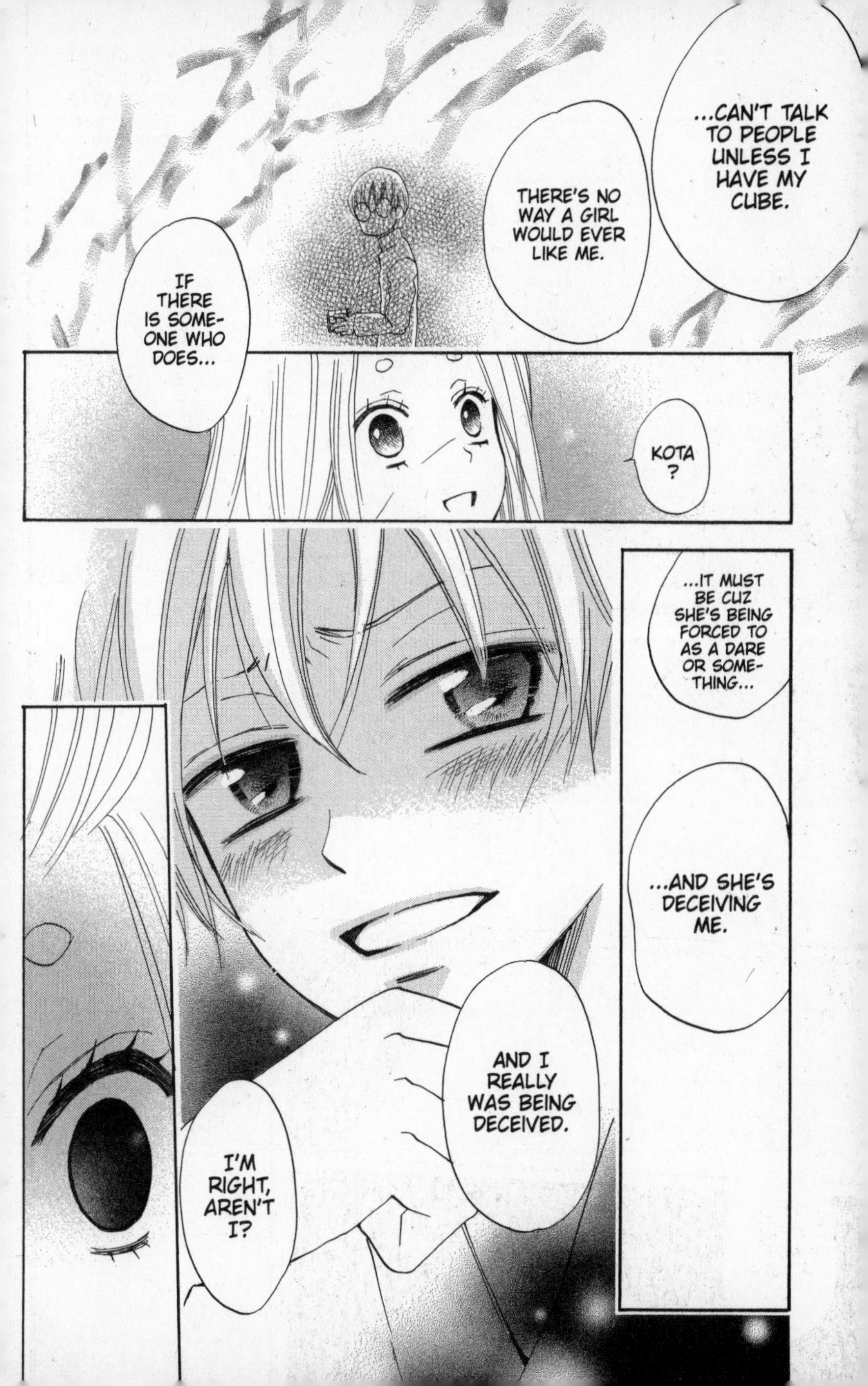
...CAN'T TALK TO PEOPLE UNLESS I HAVE MY CUBE.
THERE'S NO WAY A GIRL WOULD EVER LIKE ME.
IF THERE IS SOME-ONE WHO DOES...
KOTA?
...IT MUST BE CUZ SHE'S BEING FORCED TO AS A DARE OR SOME-THING...
...AND SHE'S DECEIVING ME.
AND I REALLY WAS BEING DECEIVED.
I'M RIGHT, AREN'T I?

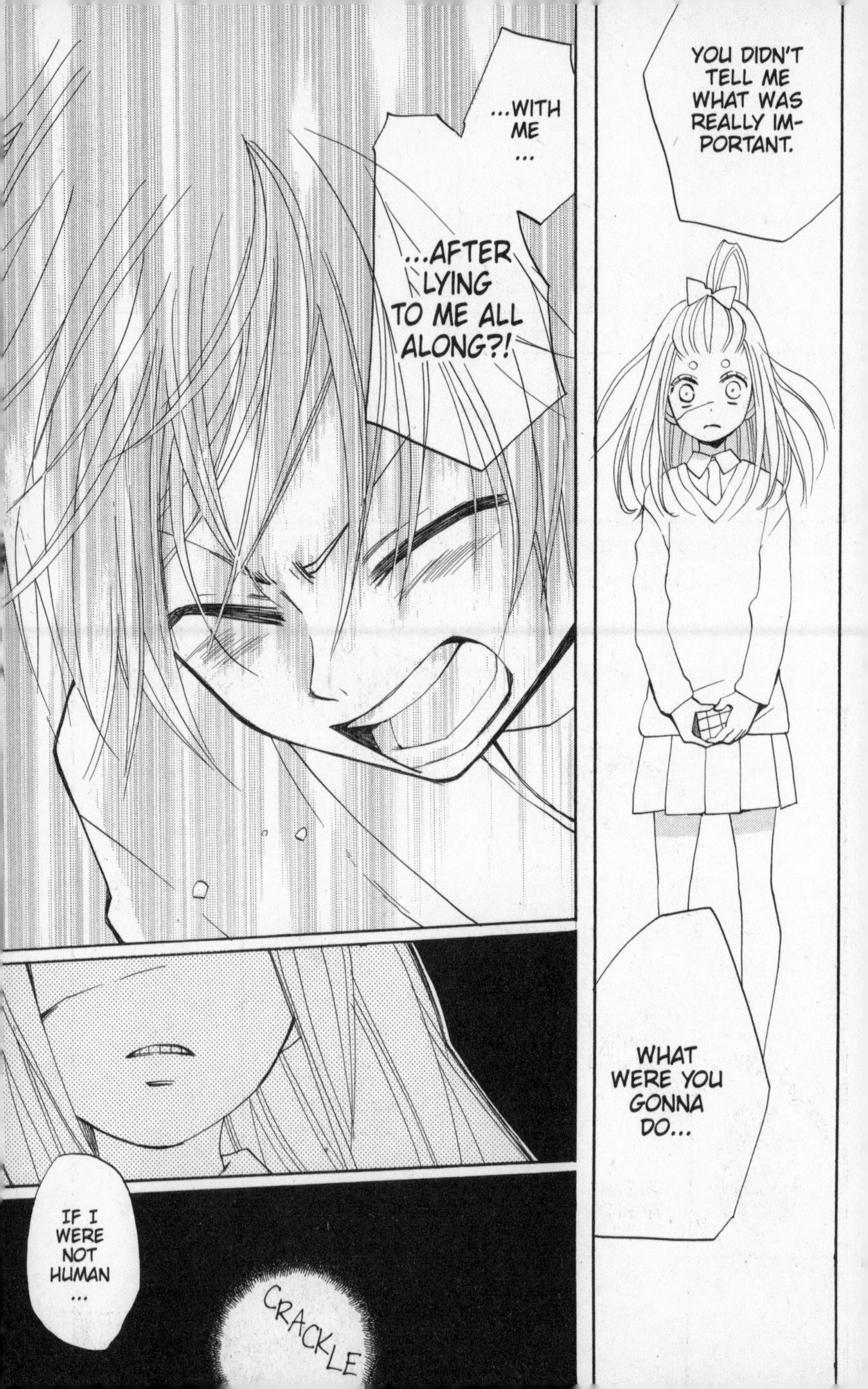
YOU DIDN'T TELL ME WHAT WAS REALLY IM-PORTANT.
WHAT WERE YOU GONNA DO...
...WITH ME...
...AFTER LYING TO ME ALL ALONG?!
IF I WERE NOT HUMAN...
CRACKLE

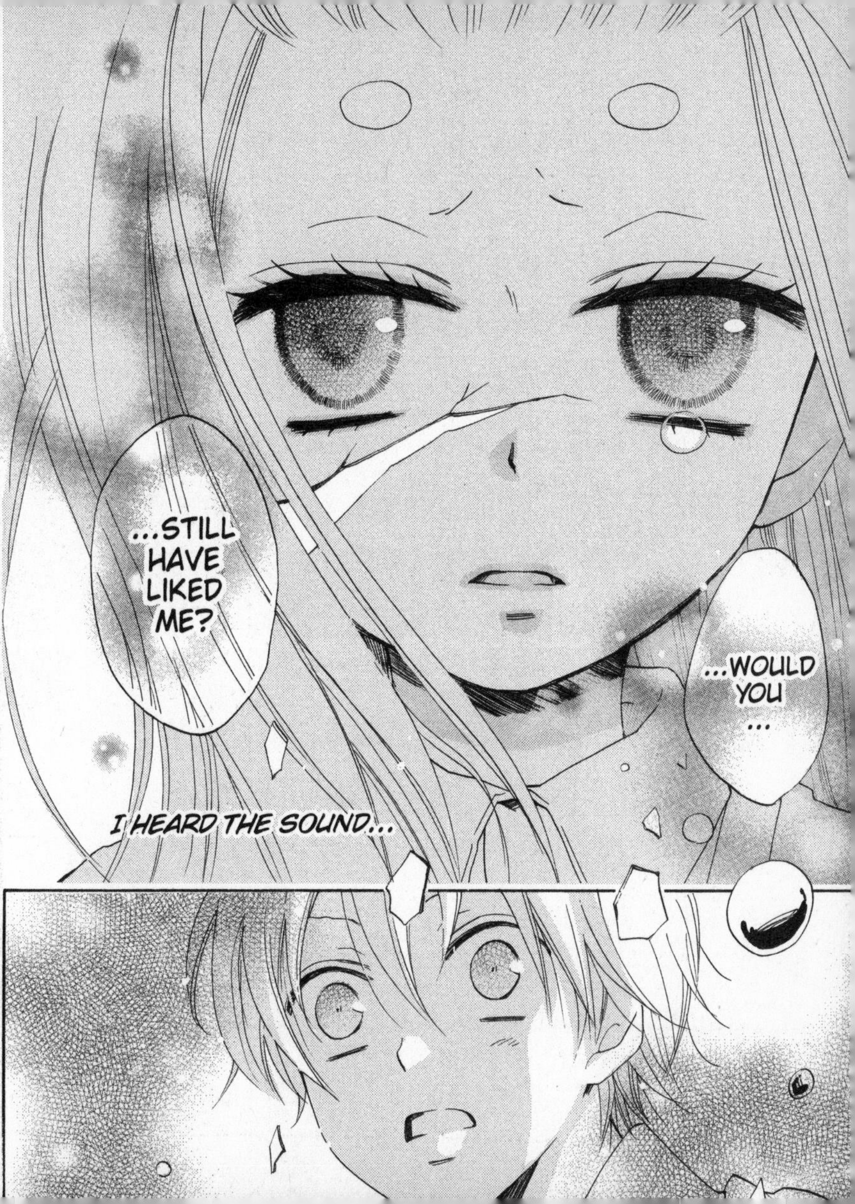
...WOULD YOU ...
...STILL HAVE LIKED ME?
I HEARD THE SOUND...

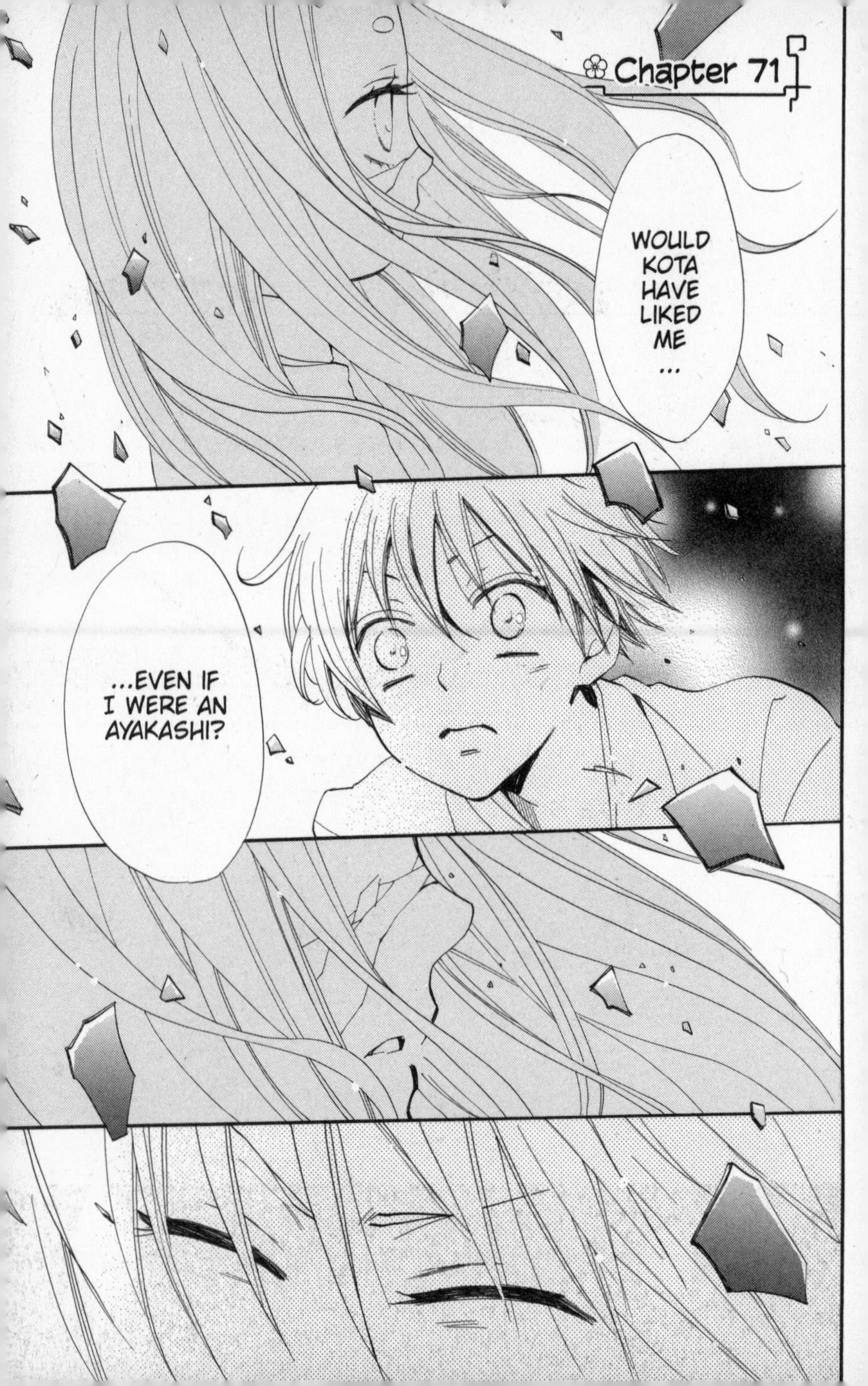
Chapter 71
WOULD KOTA HAVE LIKED ME ...
...EVEN IF I WERE AN AYAKASHI?

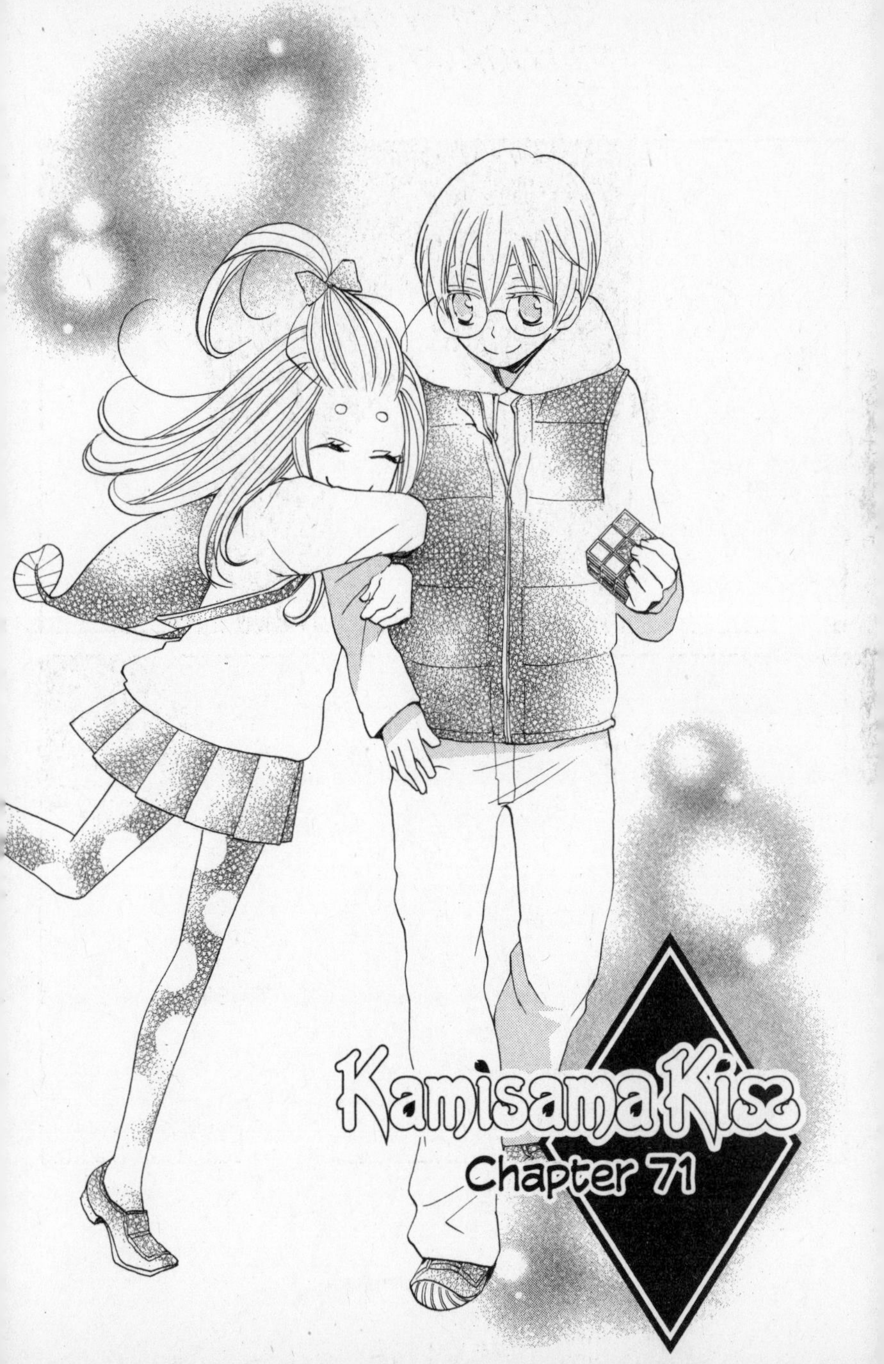
Kamisama Kiss
Chapter 71

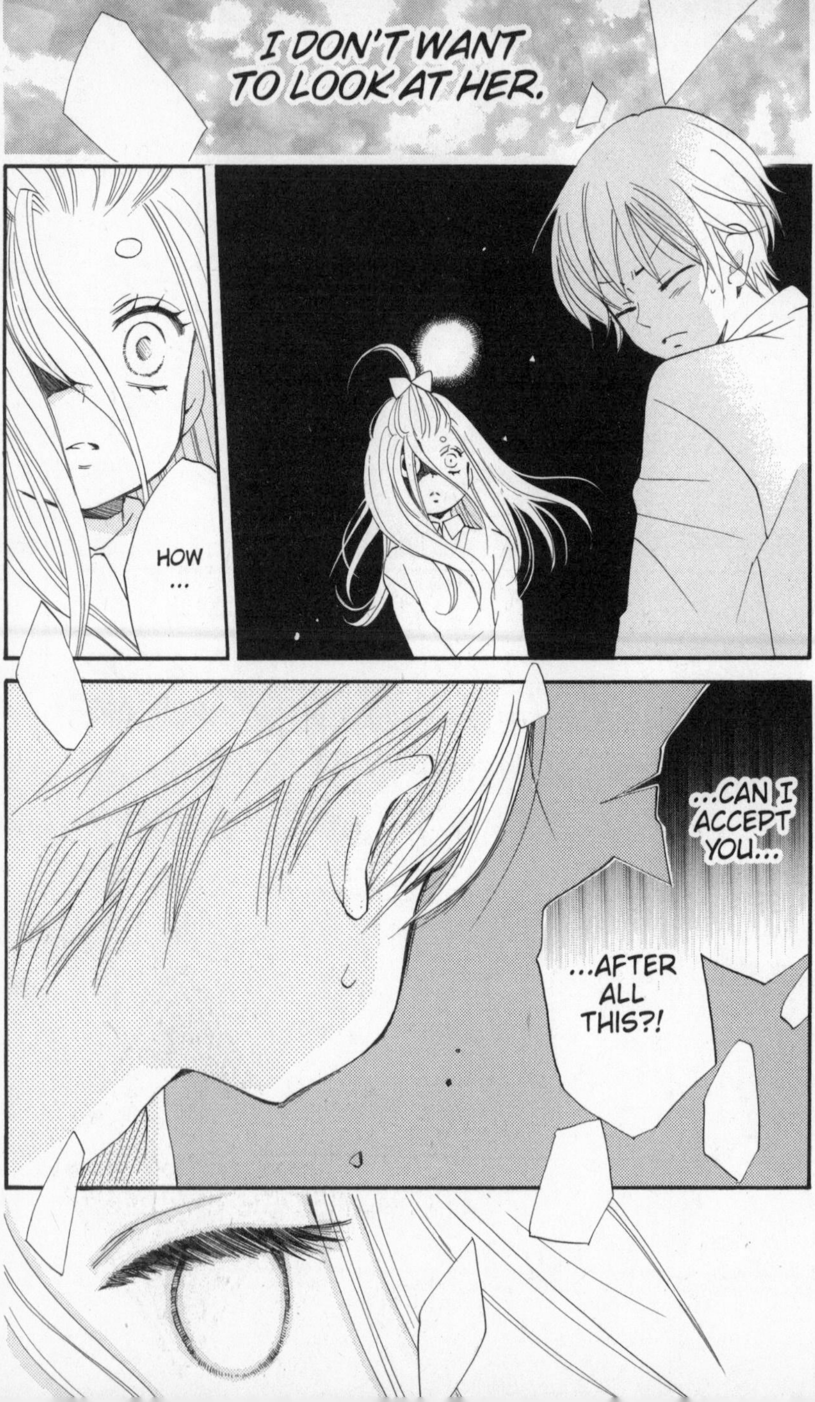
I DON'T WANT TO LOOK AT HER.
HOW ...
...CAN I ACCEPT YOU...
...AFTER ALL THIS?!

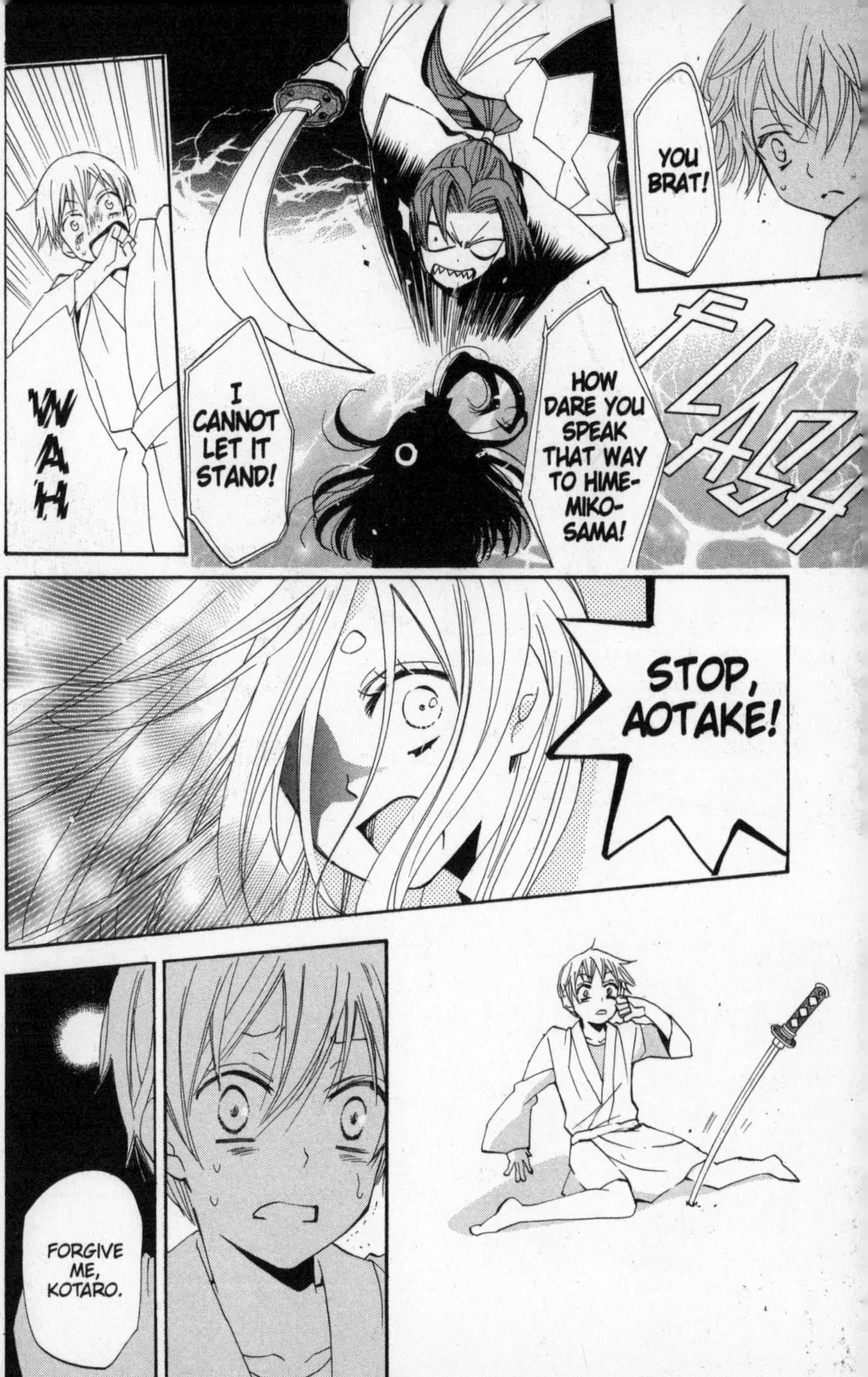
YOU BRAT!
FLASH
HOW DARE YOU SPEAK THAT WAY TO HIME-MIKO-SAMA!
I CANNOT LET IT STAND!
WAH
STOP, AOTAKE!
FORGIVE ME, KOTARO.

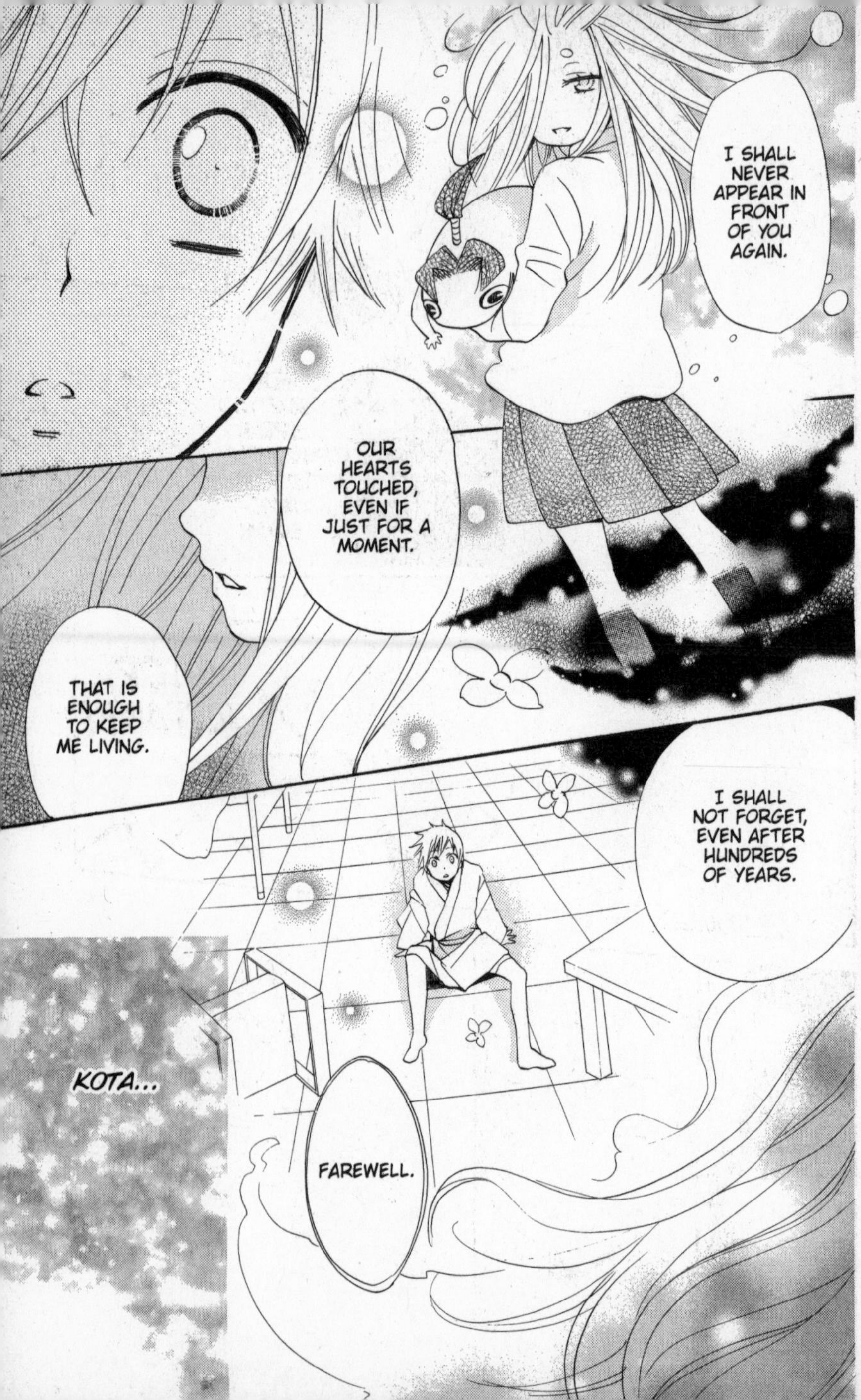
I SHALL NEVER APPEAR IN FRONT OF YOU AGAIN.
OUR HEARTS TOUCHED, EVEN IF JUST FOR A MOMENT.
THAT IS ENOUGH TO KEEP ME LIVING.
I SHALL NOT FORGET, EVEN AFTER HUNDREDS OF YEARS.
FAREWELL.
KOTA...

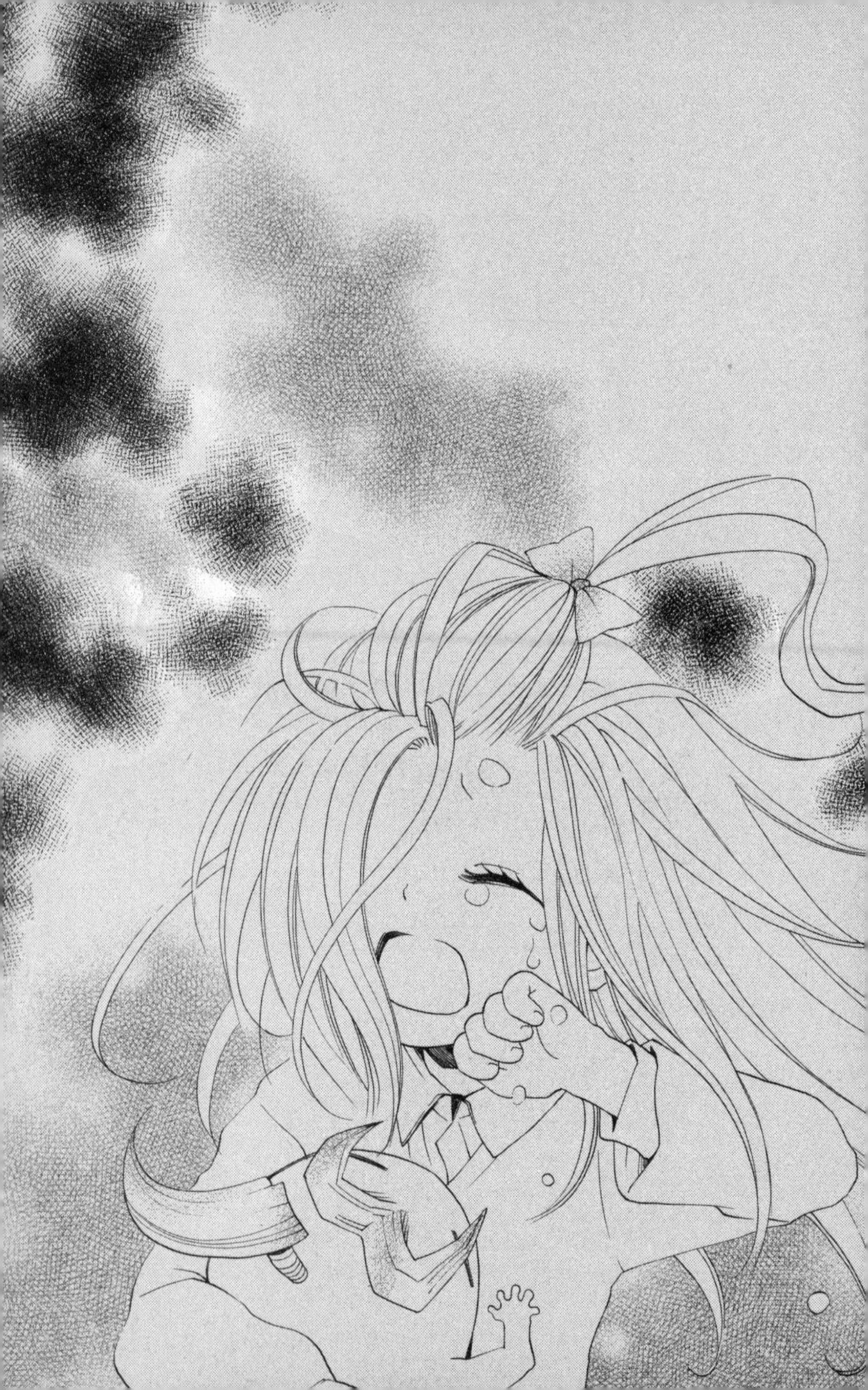

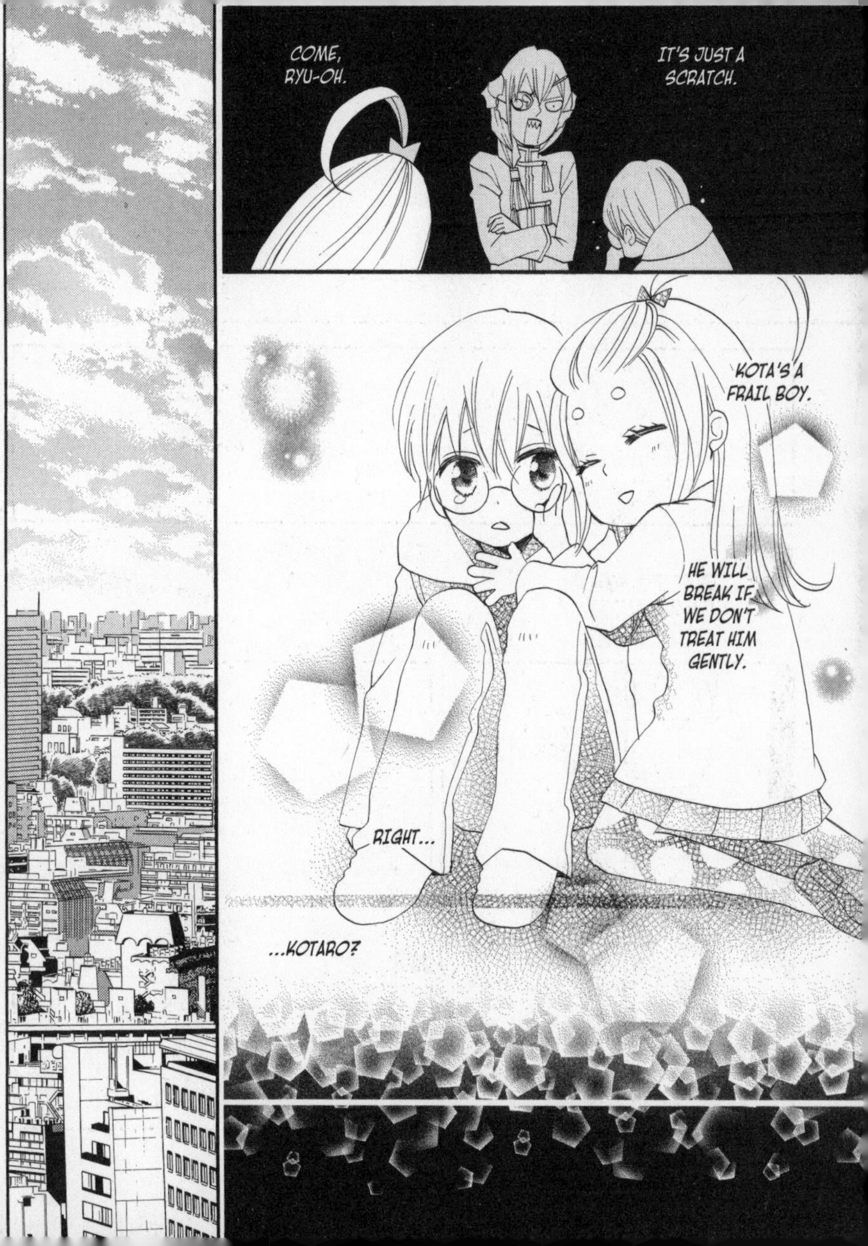
IT'S JUST A SCRATCH.
COME, RYU-OH.
KOTA'S A FRAIL BOY.
HE WILL BREAK IF WE DON'T TREAT HIM GENTLY.
RIGHT...
...KOTARO?

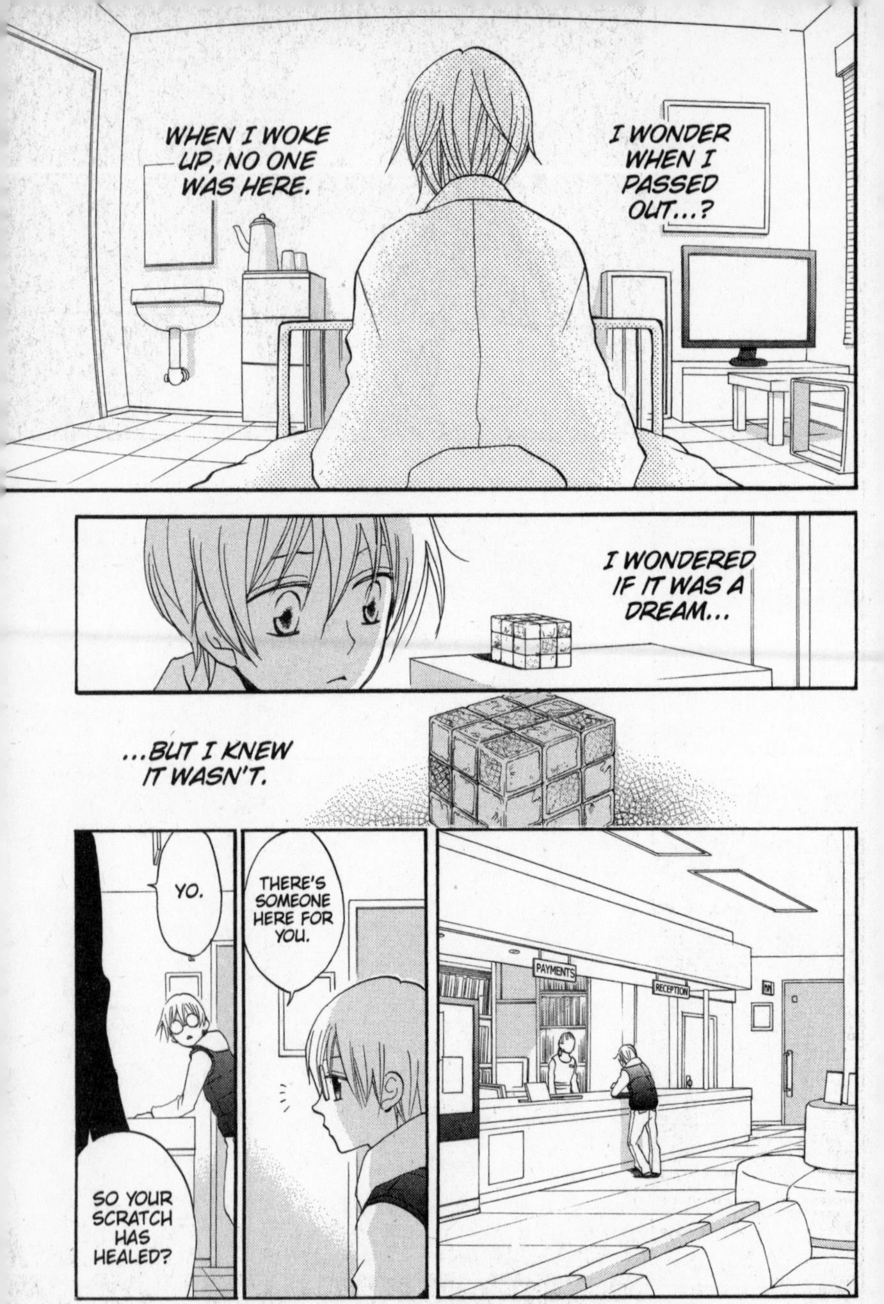
I WONDER WHEN I PASSED OUT...?
WHEN I WOKE UP, NO ONE WAS HERE.
I WONDERED IF IT WAS A DREAM...
...BUT I KNEW IT WASN'T.
PAYMENTS
RECEPTION
THERE'S SOMEONE HERE FOR YOU.
YO.
SO YOUR SCRATCH HAS HEALED?

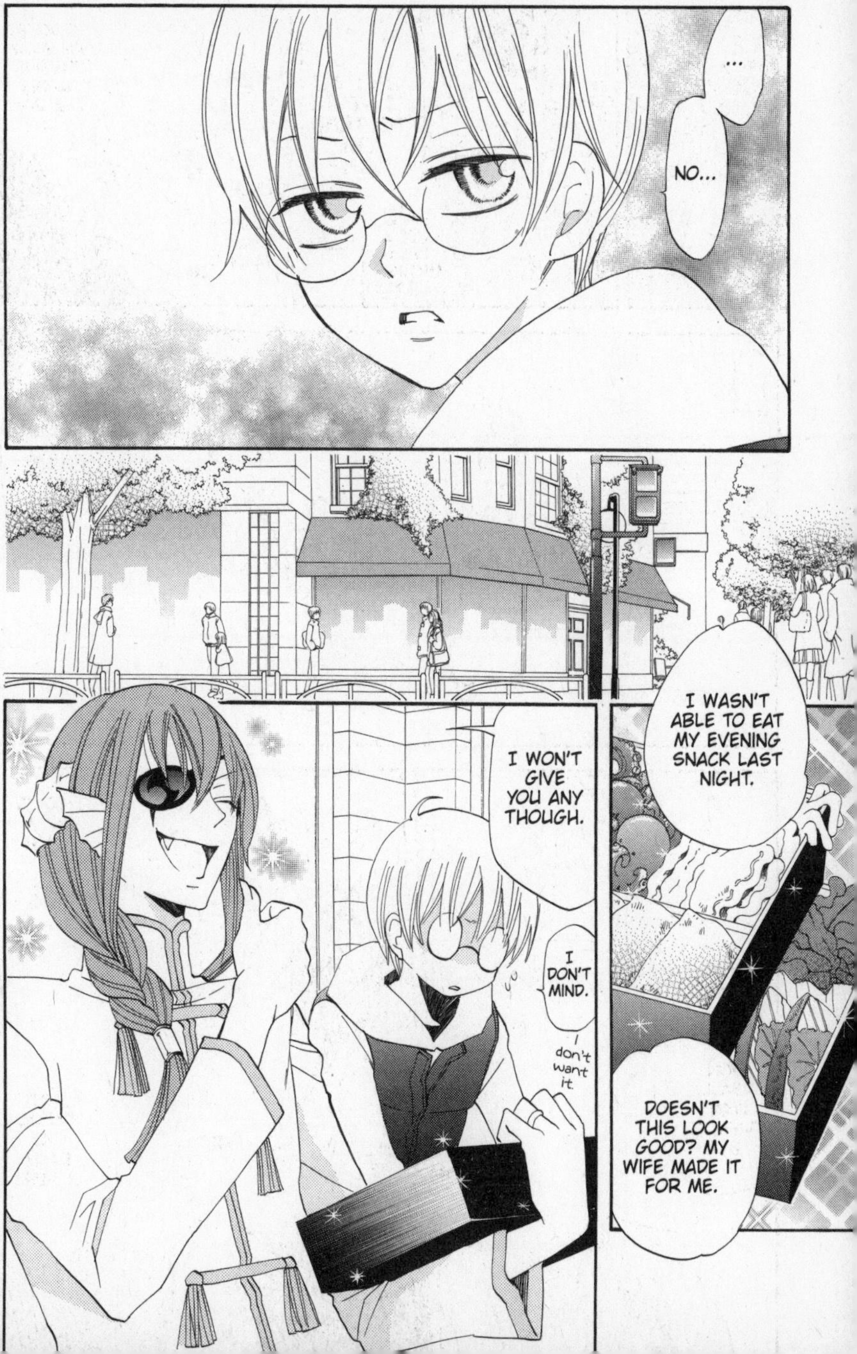
...
NO...
I WASN'T ABLE TO EAT MY EVENING SNACK LAST NIGHT.
DOESN'T THIS LOOK GOOD? MY WIFE MADE IT FOR ME.
I WON'T GIVE YOU ANY THOUGH.
I DON'T MIND.
I don't want it.

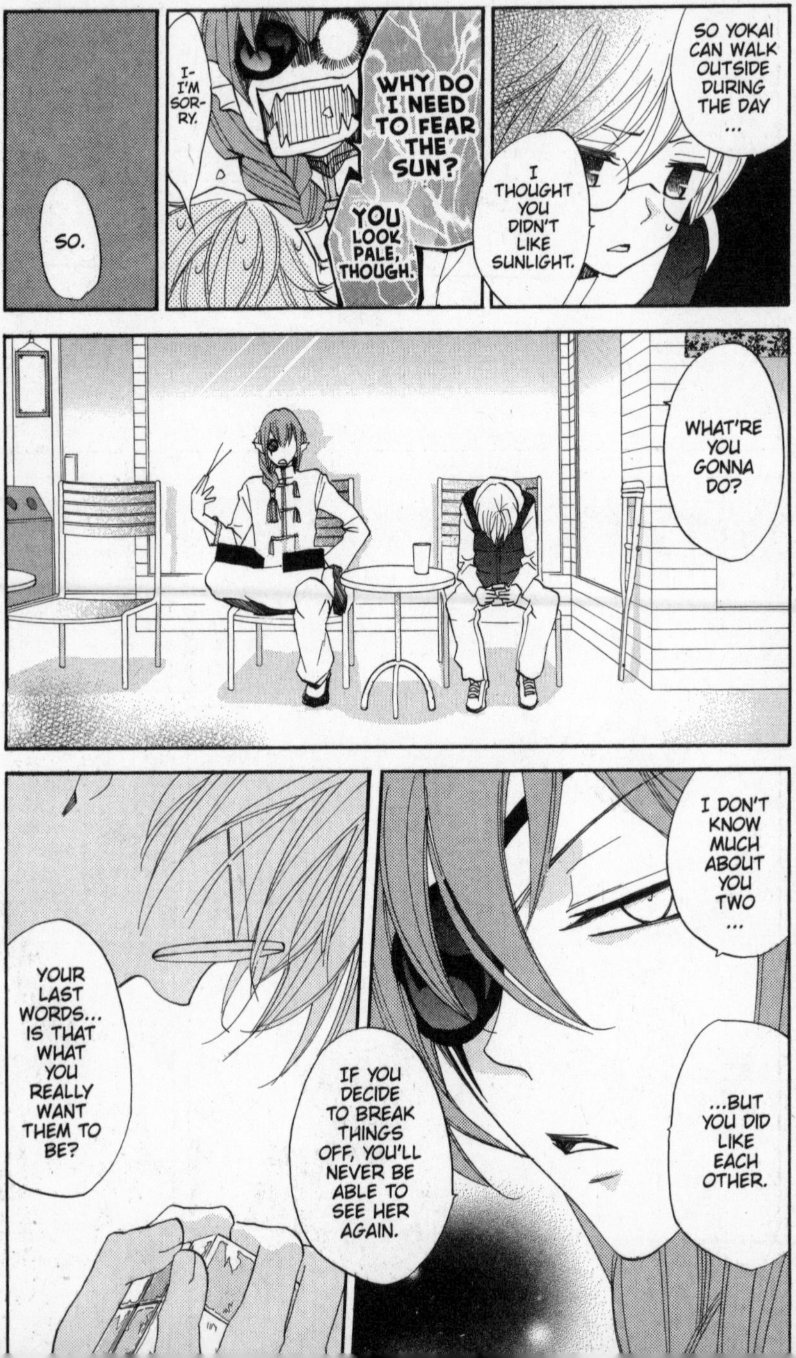
SO YOKAI CAN WALK OUTSIDE DURING THE DAY ...
I THOUGHT YOU DIDN'T LIKE SUNLIGHT.
WHY DO I NEED TO FEAR THE SUN?
YOU LOOK PALE, THOUGH.
I- I'M SOR-RY.
SO.
WHAT'RE YOU GONNA DO?
I DON'T KNOW MUCH ABOUT YOU TWO ...
...BUT YOU DID LIKE EACH OTHER.
IF YOU DECIDE TO BREAK THINGS OFF, YOU'LL NEVER BE ABLE TO SEE HER AGAIN.
YOUR LAST WORDS... IS THAT WHAT YOU REALLY WANT THEM TO BE?

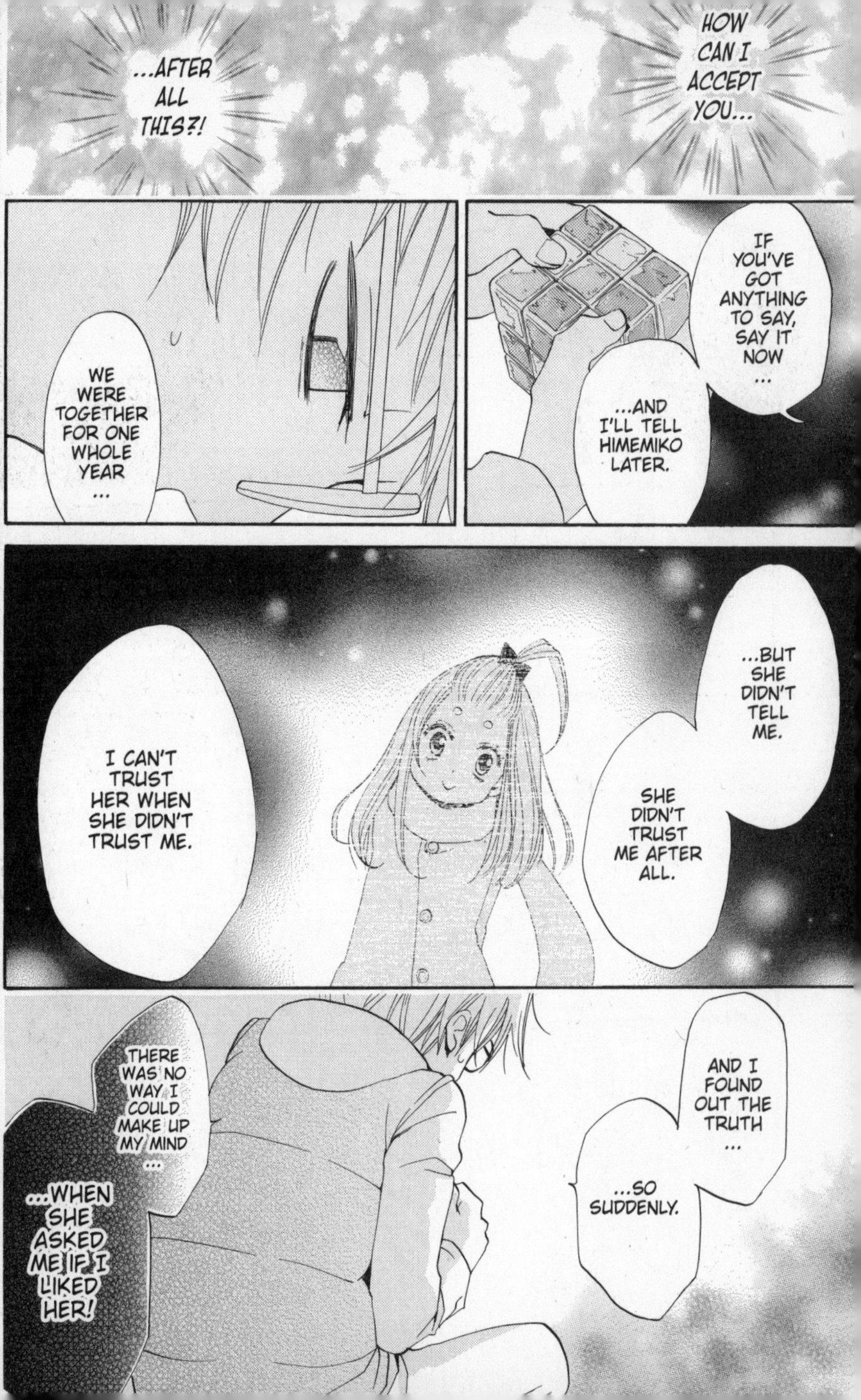
HOW CAN I ACCEPT YOU...
...AFTER ALL THIS?!
IF YOU'VE GOT ANYTHING TO SAY, SAY IT NOW...
...AND I'LL TELL HIMEMIKO LATER.
WE WERE TOGETHER FOR ONE WHOLE YEAR...
...BUT SHE DIDN'T TELL ME.
SHE DIDN'T TRUST ME AFTER ALL.
I CAN'T TRUST HER WHEN SHE DIDN'T TRUST ME.
AND I FOUND OUT THE TRUTH...
...SO SUDDENLY.
THERE WAS NO WAY I COULD MAKE UP MY MIND...
...WHEN SHE ASKED ME IF I LIKED HER!

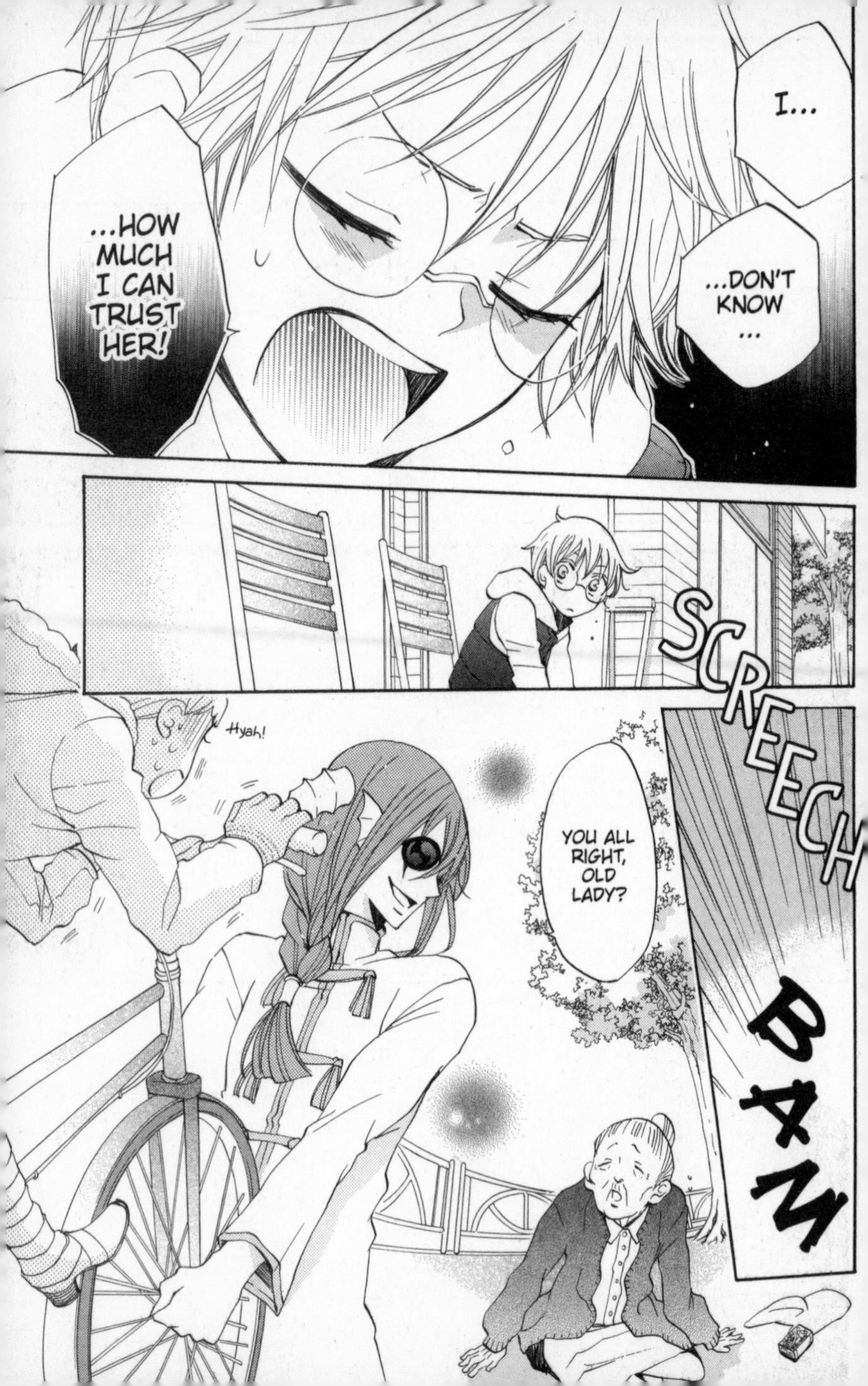
I...
...DON'T KNOW ...
...HOW MUCH I CAN TRUST HER!
SCREECH
BAM
Hyah!
YOU ALL RIGHT, OLD LADY?

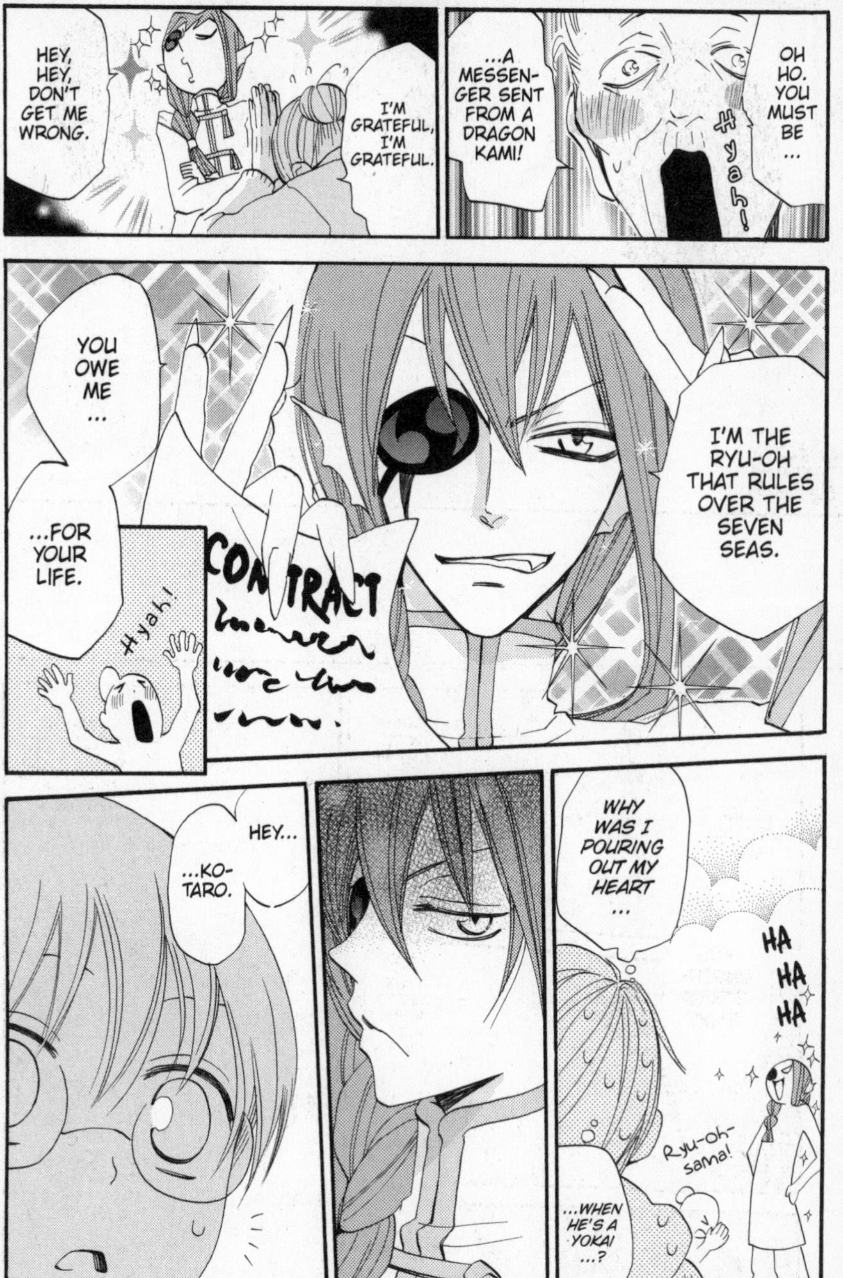
OH HO. YOU MUST BE ...
Hyah!
...A MESSENGER SENT FROM A DRAGON KAMI!
I'M GRATEFUL, I'M GRATEFUL.
HEY, HEY, DON'T GET ME WRONG.
I'M THE RYU-OH THAT RULES OVER THE SEVEN SEAS.
YOU OWE ME ...
...FOR YOUR LIFE.
CONTRACT
Hyah!
WHY WAS I POURING OUT MY HEART ...
HA HA HA
Ryu-oh-sama!
...WHEN HE'S A YOKAI ...?
HEY...
...KO-TARO.

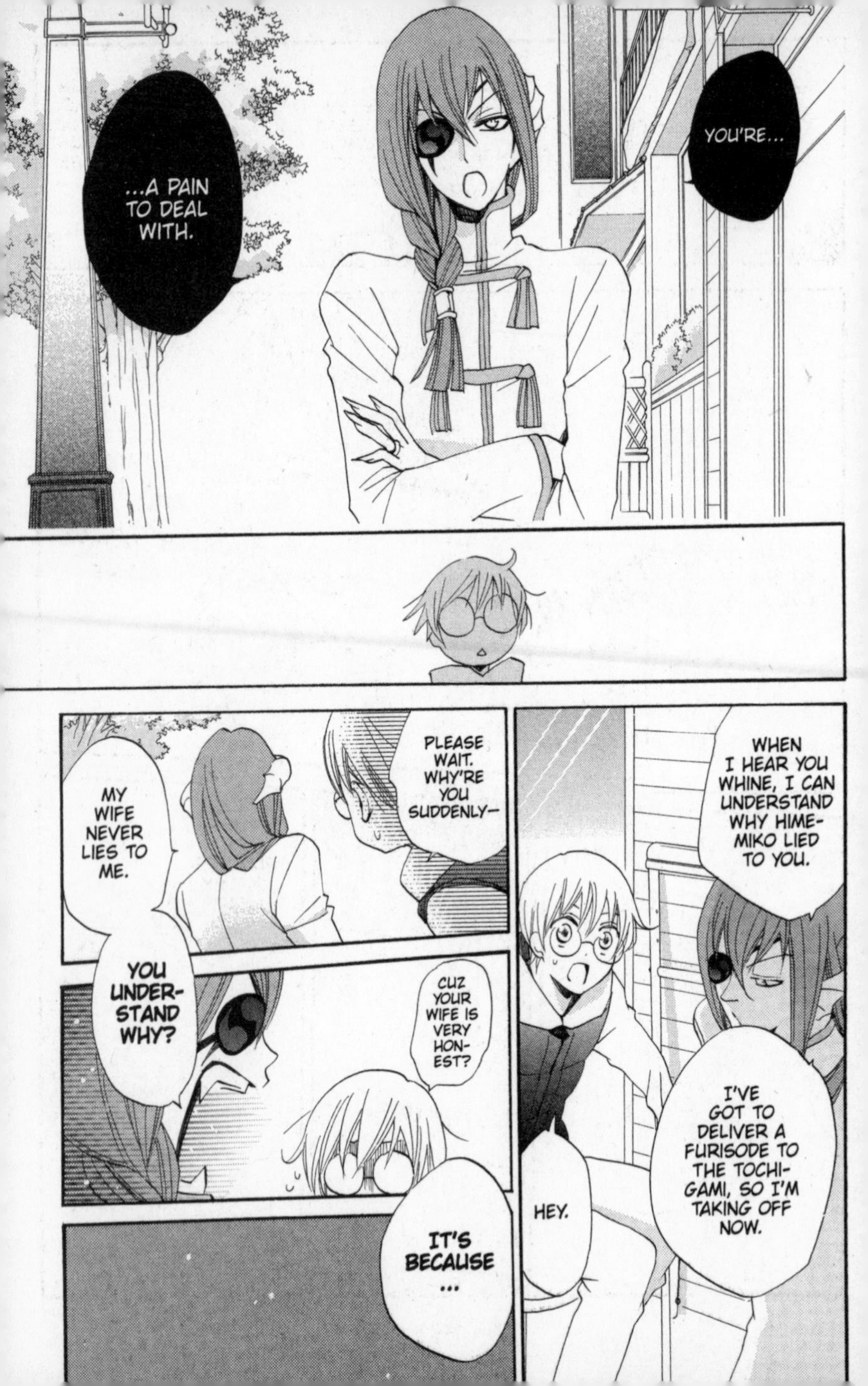
YOU'RE...
...A PAIN TO DEAL WITH.
WHEN I HEAR YOU WHINE, I CAN UNDERSTAND WHY HIME-MIKO LIED TO YOU.
I'VE GOT TO DELIVER A FURISODE TO THE TOCHI-GAMI, SO I'M TAKING OFF NOW.
HEY.
PLEASE WAIT. WHY'RE YOU SUDDENLY—
MY WIFE NEVER LIES TO ME.
CUZ YOUR WIFE IS VERY HON-EST?
YOU UNDER-STAND WHY?
IT'S BECAUSE...

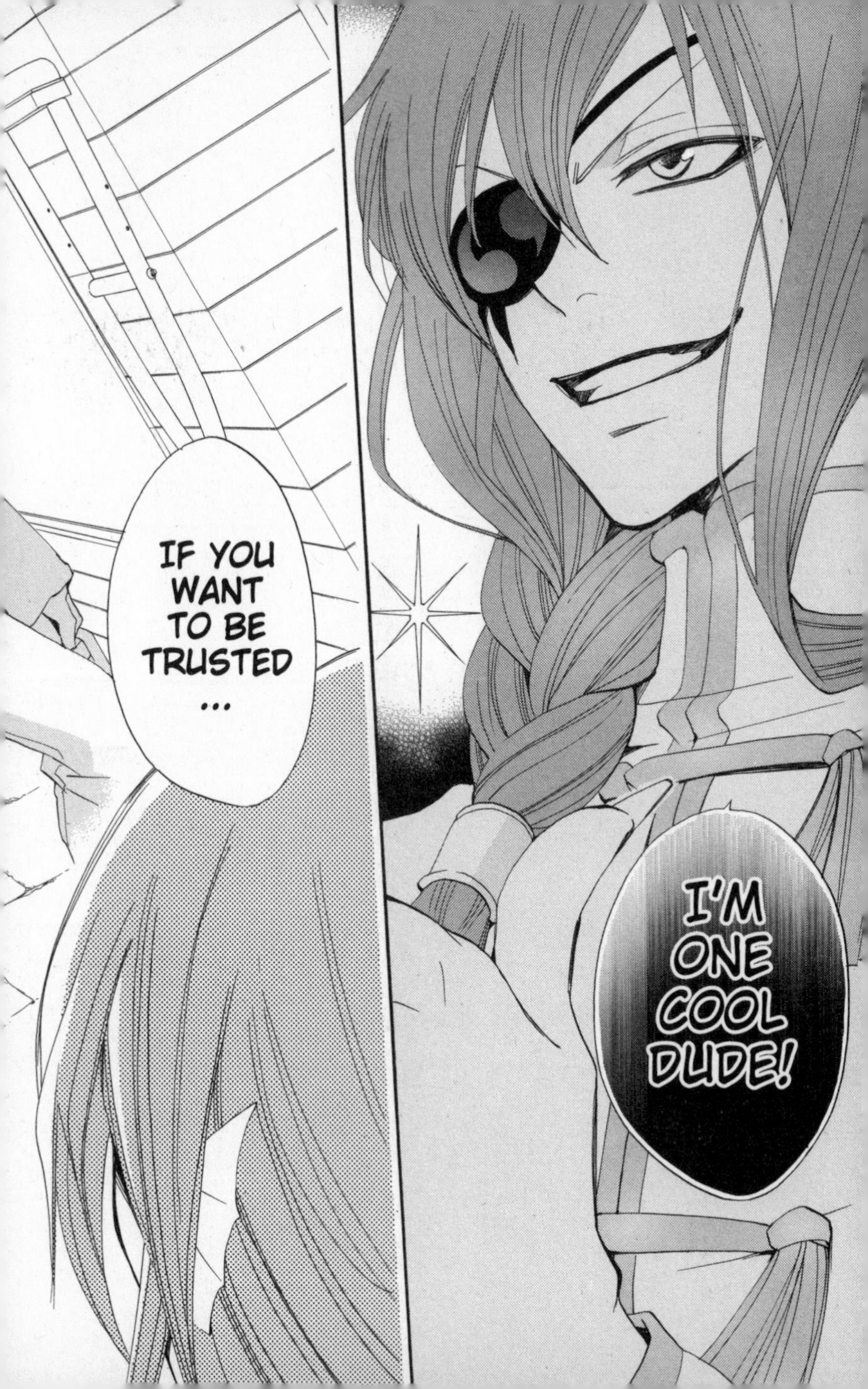
I'M ONE COOL DUDE!
IF YOU WANT TO BE TRUSTED ...

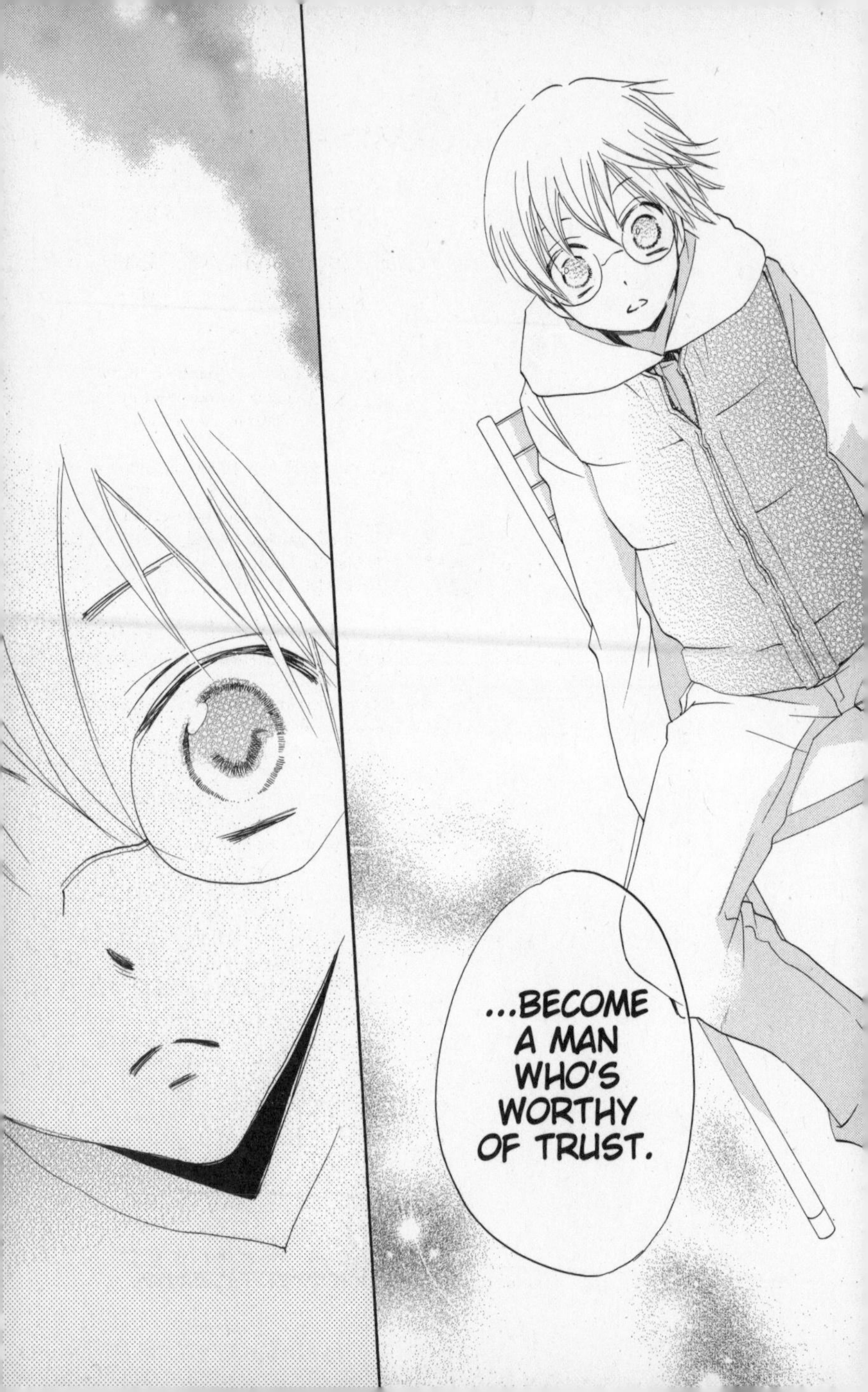
...BECOME A MAN WHO'S WORTHY OF TRUST.

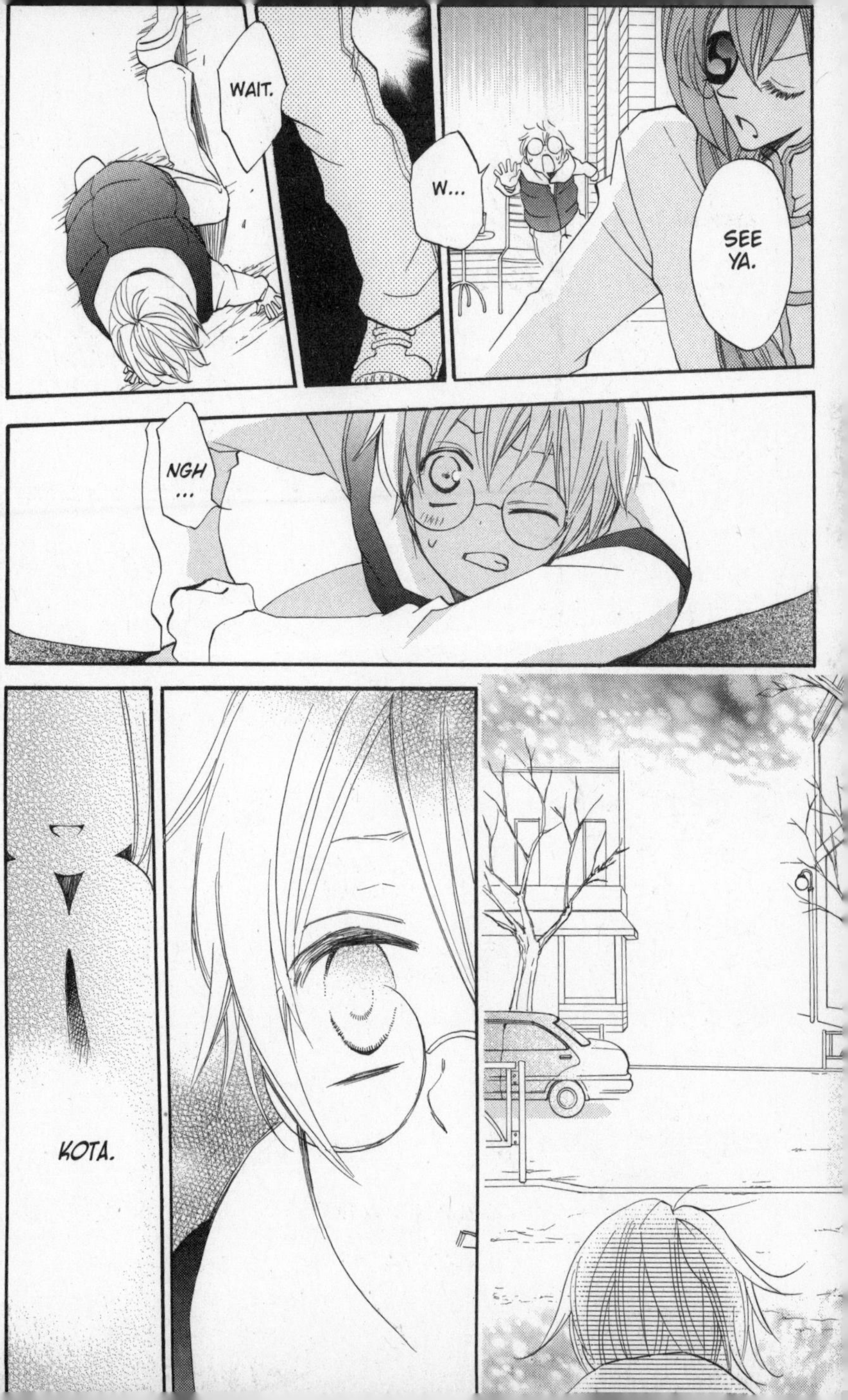
SEE YA.
W...
WAIT.
NGH ...
KOTA.

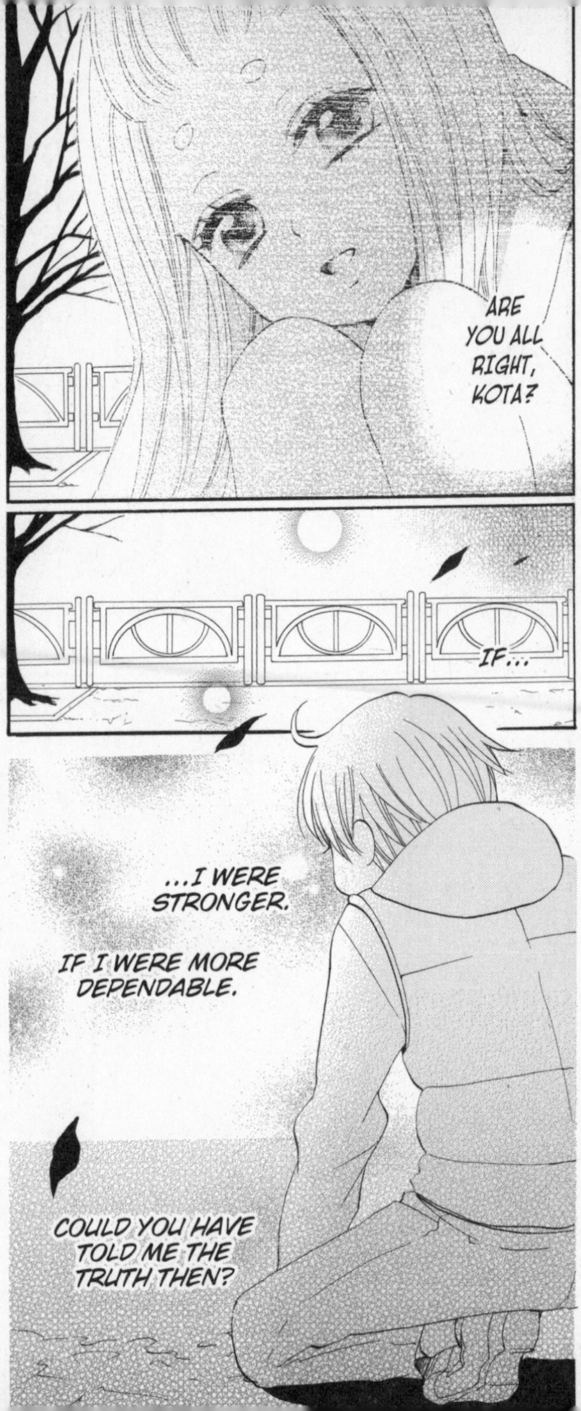
ARE YOU ALL RIGHT, KOTA?
IF...
...I WERE STRONGER.
IF I WERE MORE DEPENDABLE.
COULD YOU HAVE TOLD ME THE TRUTH THEN?

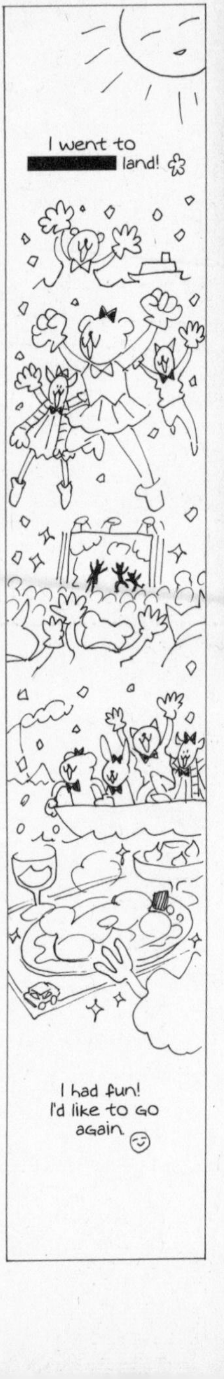
I went to [redacted] land!
I had fun! I'd like to GO again.

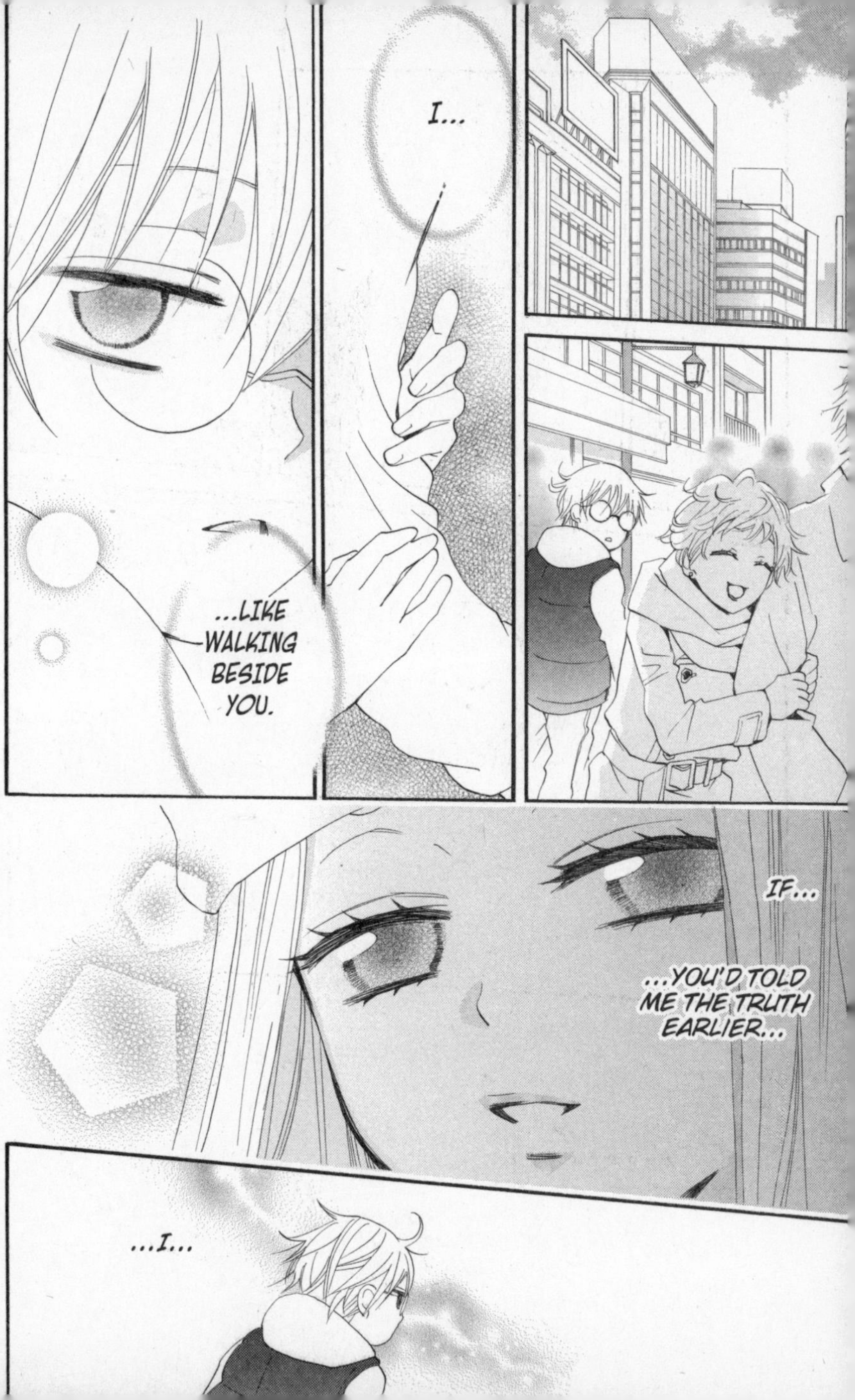
I...
...LIKE WALKING BESIDE YOU.
IF...
...YOU'D TOLD ME THE TRUTH EARLIER...
...I...

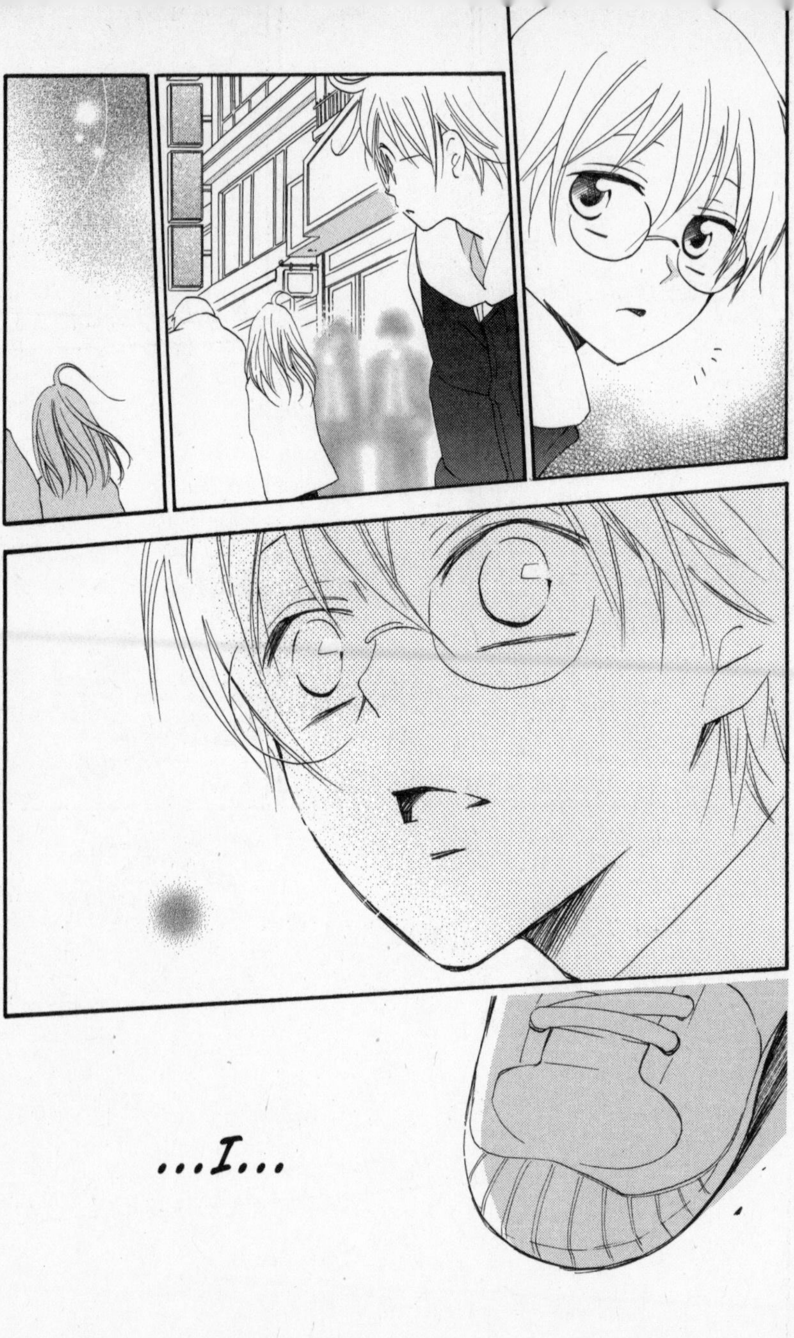
...I...

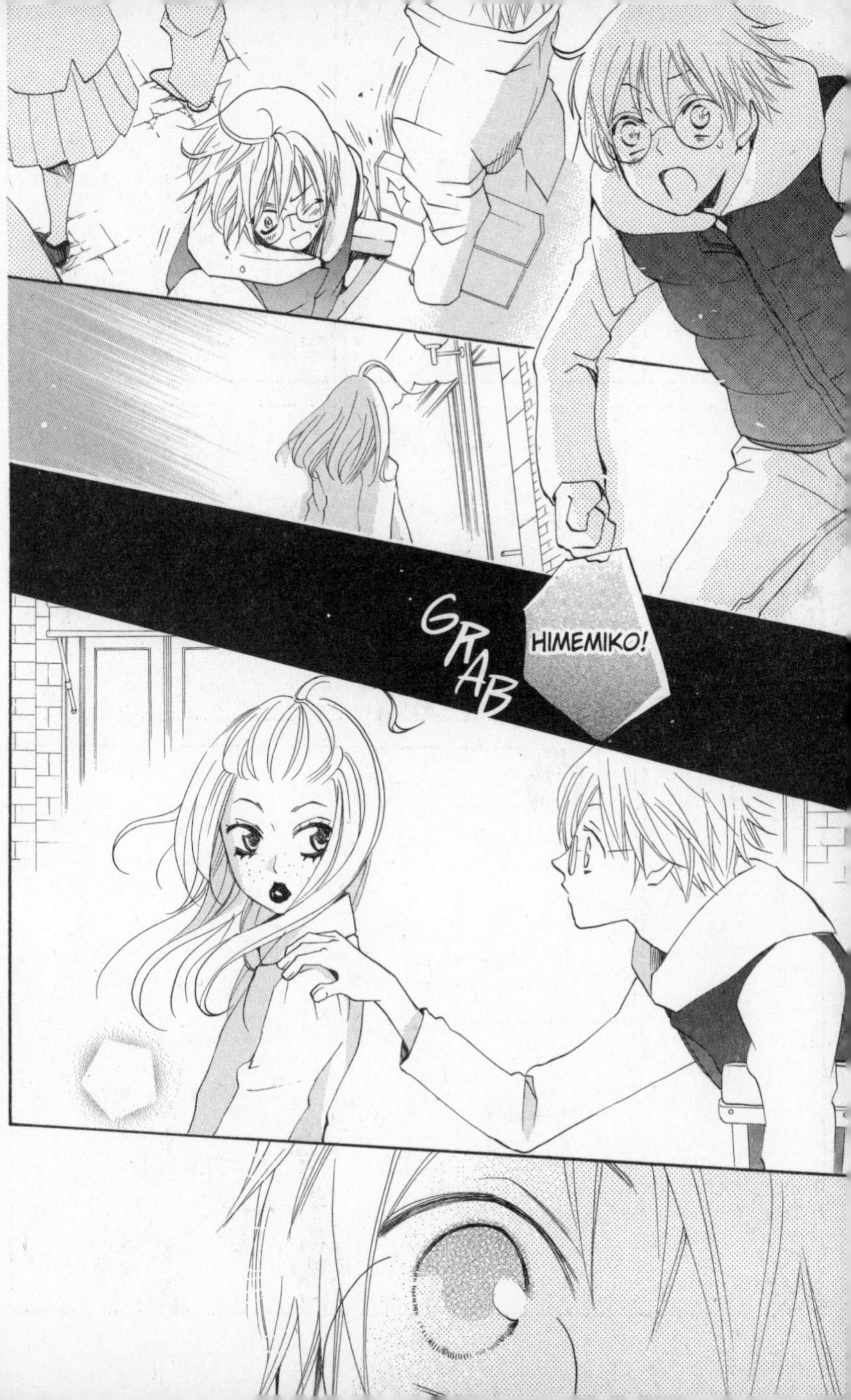
HIMEMIKO!
GRAB

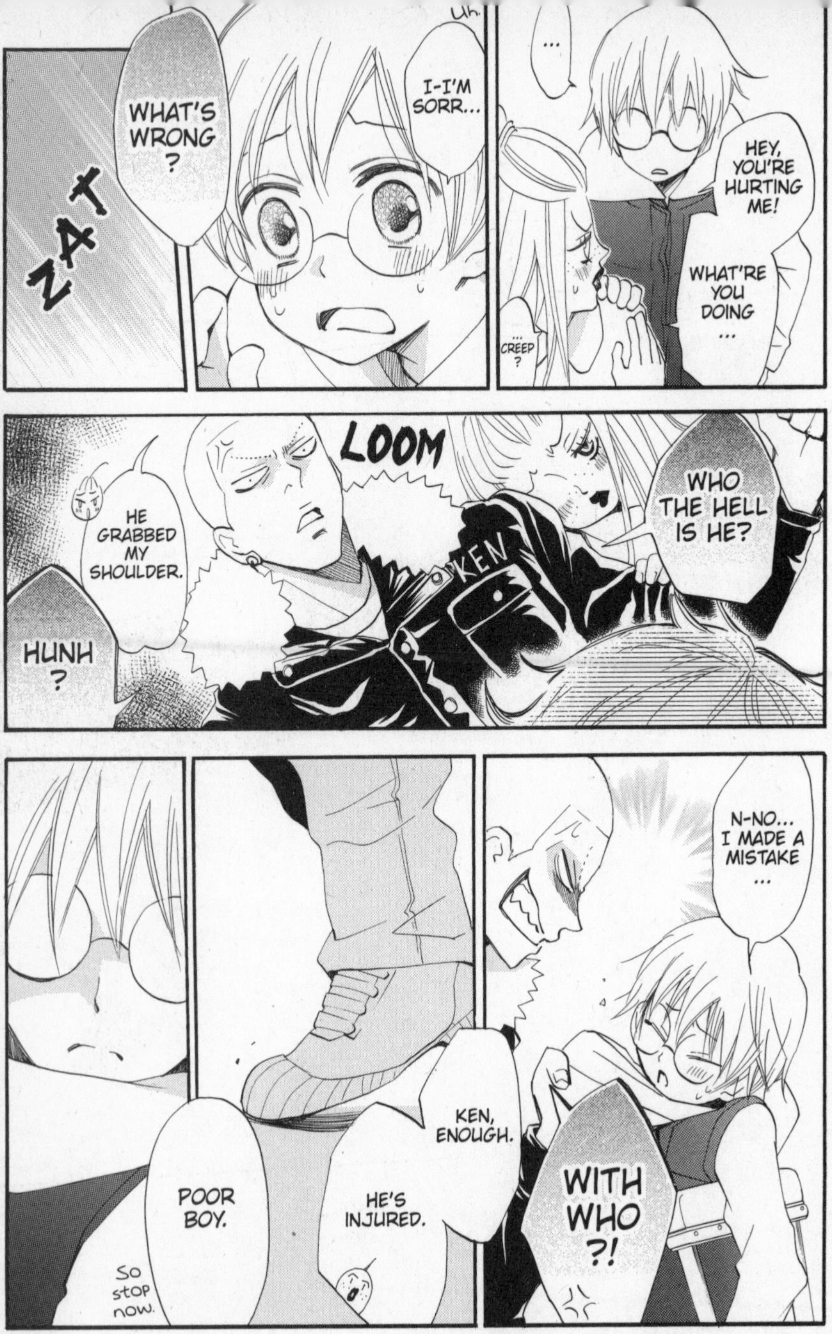
...
HEY, YOU'RE HURTING ME!
WHAT'RE YOU DOING ...
... CREEP ?
Uh.
I-I'M SORR...
WHAT'S WRONG ?
ZAT
WHO THE HELL IS HE?
LOOM
KEN
HE GRABBED MY SHOULDER.
HUNH ?
N-NO... I MADE A MISTAKE ...
WITH WHO ?!
KEN, ENOUGH.
HE'S INJURED.
POOR BOY.
So stop now.

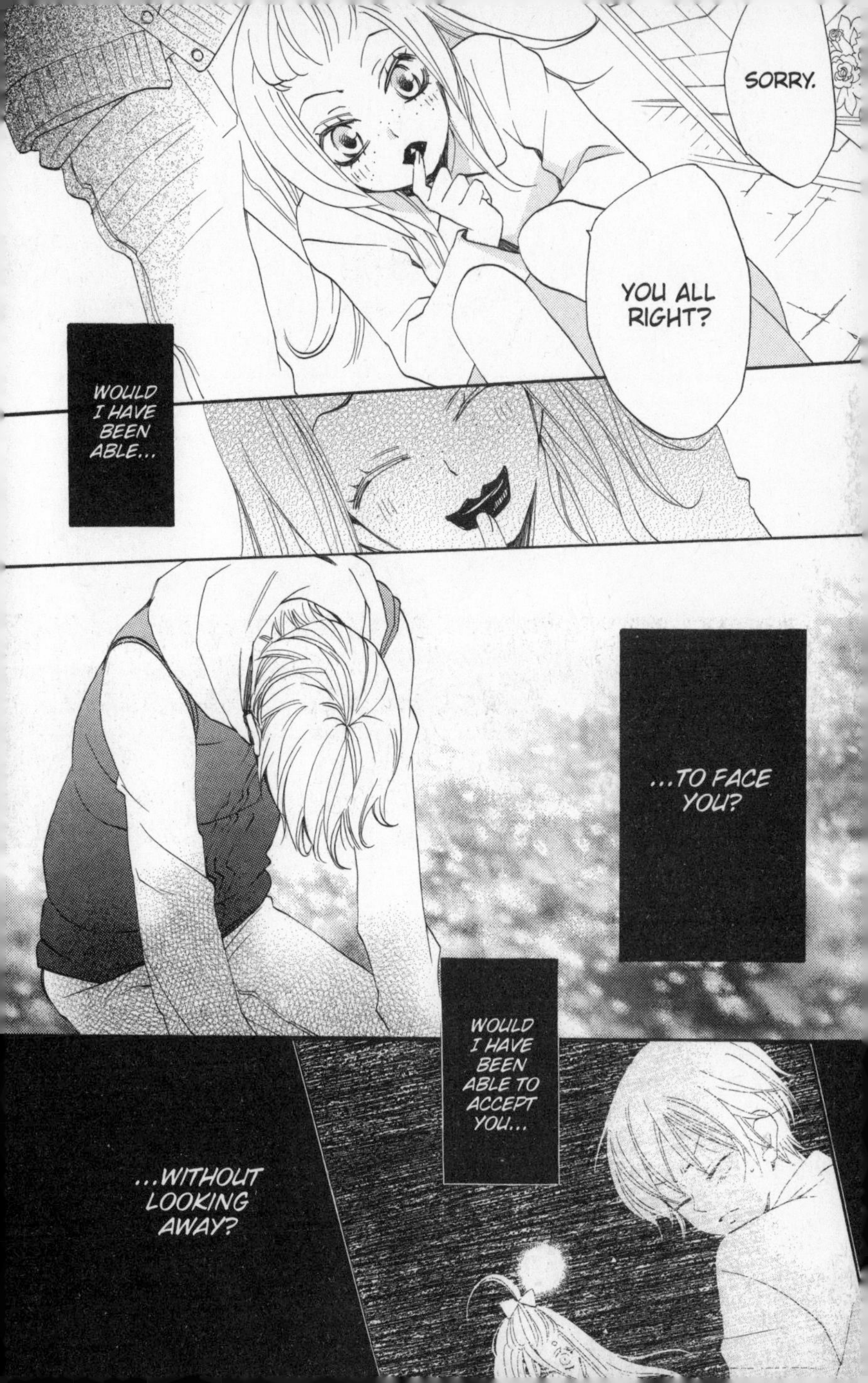
SORRY.
YOU ALL RIGHT?
WOULD I HAVE BEEN ABLE...
...TO FACE YOU?
WOULD I HAVE BEEN ABLE TO ACCEPT YOU...
...WITHOUT LOOKING AWAY?

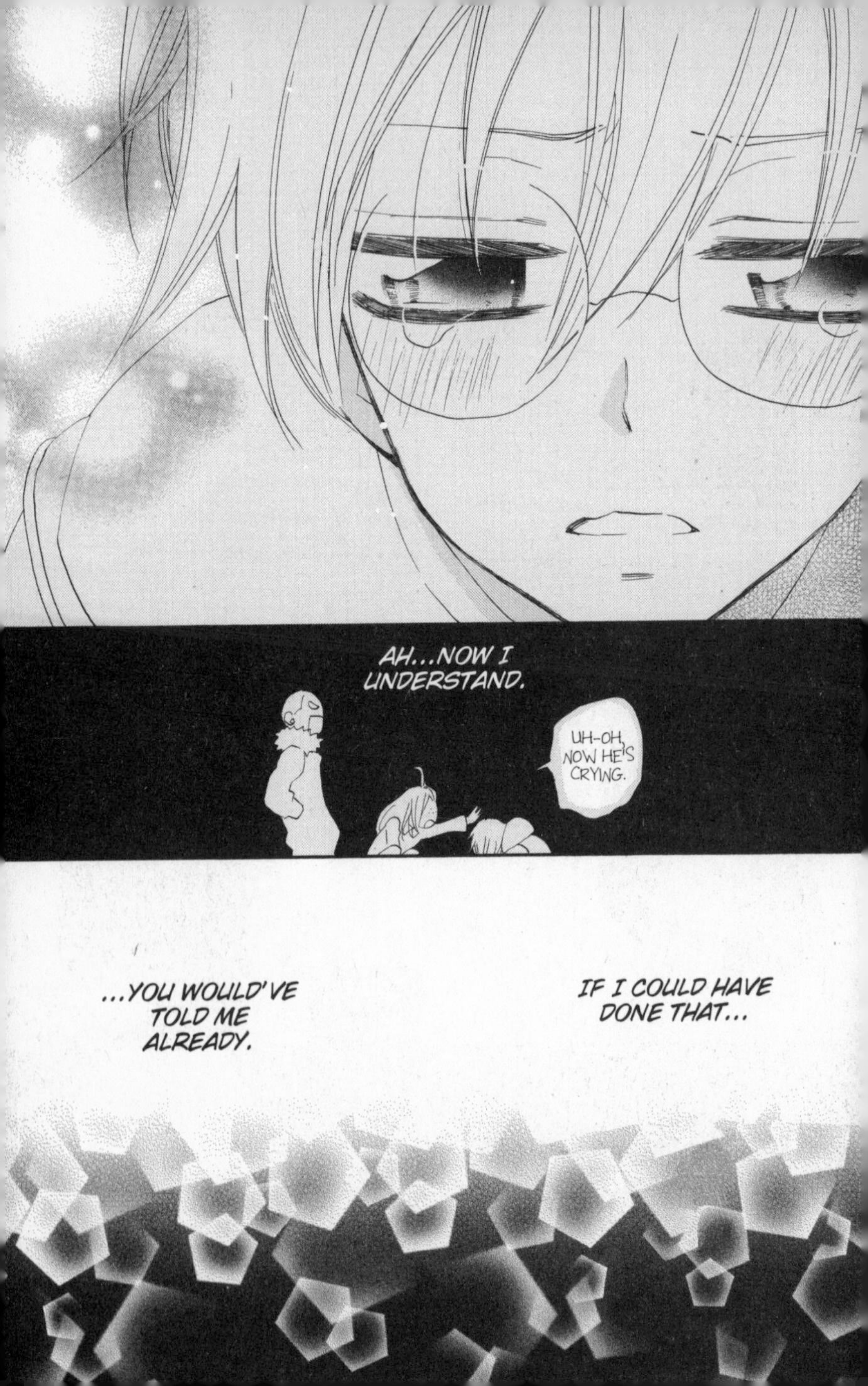
AH...NOW I UNDERSTAND.
UH-OH, NOW HE'S CRYING.
IF I COULD HAVE DONE THAT...
...YOU WOULD'VE TOLD ME ALREADY.

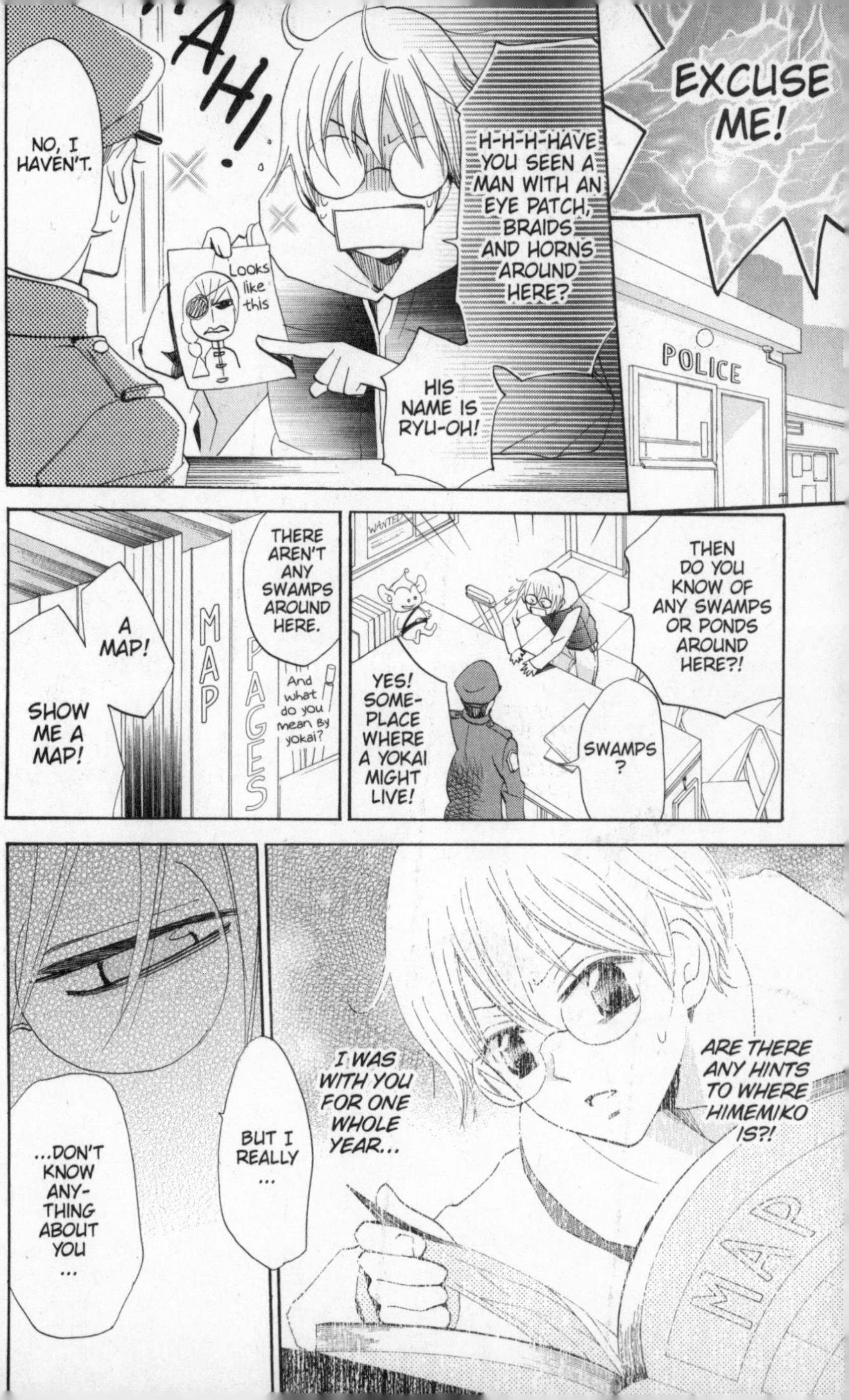
EXCUSE ME!
POLICE
H-H-H-HAVE YOU SEEN A MAN WITH AN EYE PATCH, BRAIDS AND HORNS AROUND HERE?
HIS NAME IS RYU-OH!
Looks like this
'AH!
NO, I HAVEN'T.
THEN DO YOU KNOW OF ANY SWAMPS OR PONDS AROUND HERE?!
SWAMPS?
YES! SOME-PLACE WHERE A YOKAI MIGHT LIVE!
THERE AREN'T ANY SWAMPS AROUND HERE.
And what do you mean by yokai?
PAGES
MAP
A MAP!
SHOW ME A MAP!
ARE THERE ANY HINTS TO WHERE HIMEMIKO IS?!
MAP
I WAS WITH YOU FOR ONE WHOLE YEAR...
BUT I REALLY...
...DON'T KNOW ANY-THING ABOUT YOU...

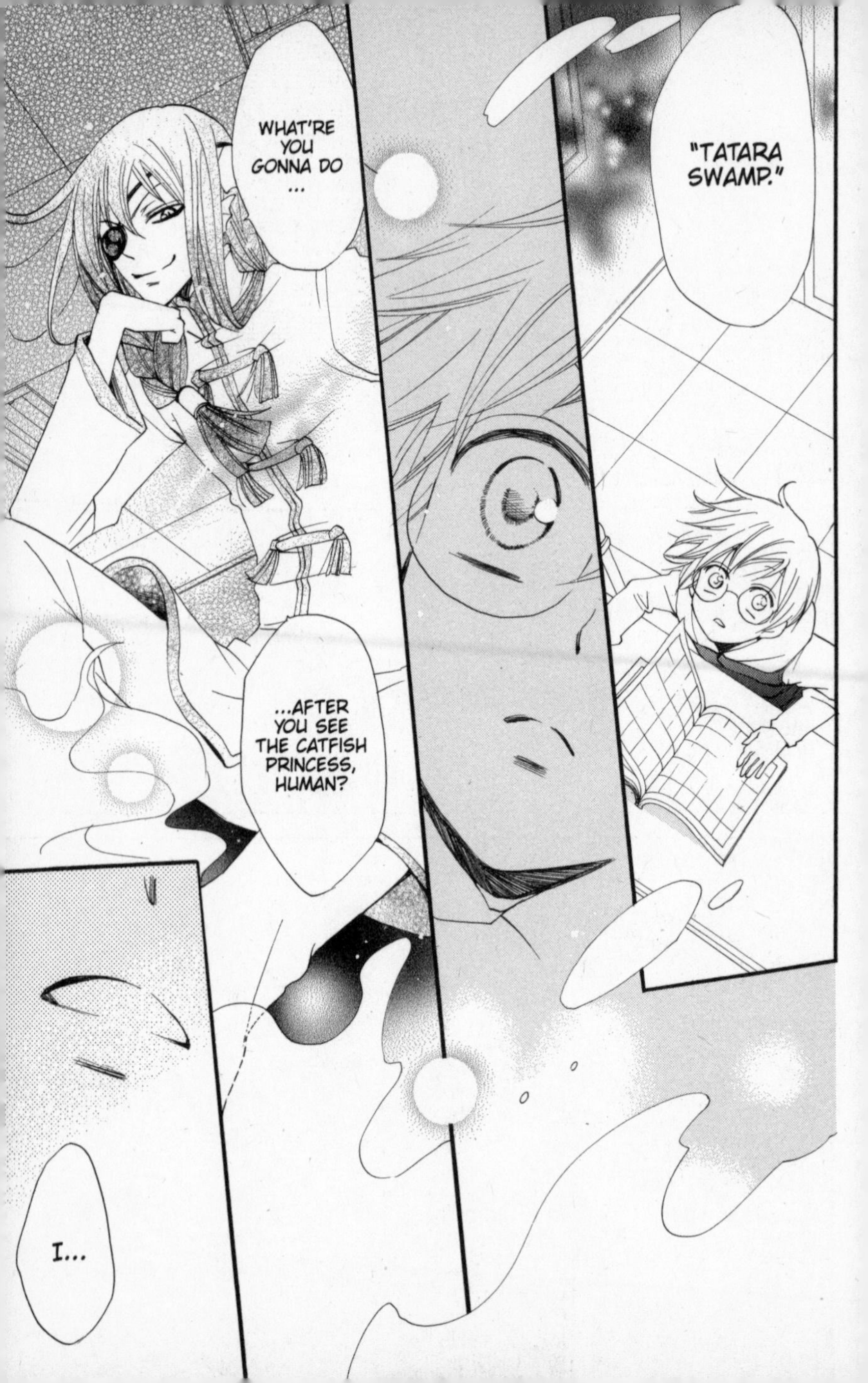
"TATARA SWAMP."
WHAT'RE YOU GONNA DO ...
...AFTER YOU SEE THE CATFISH PRINCESS, HUMAN?
I...

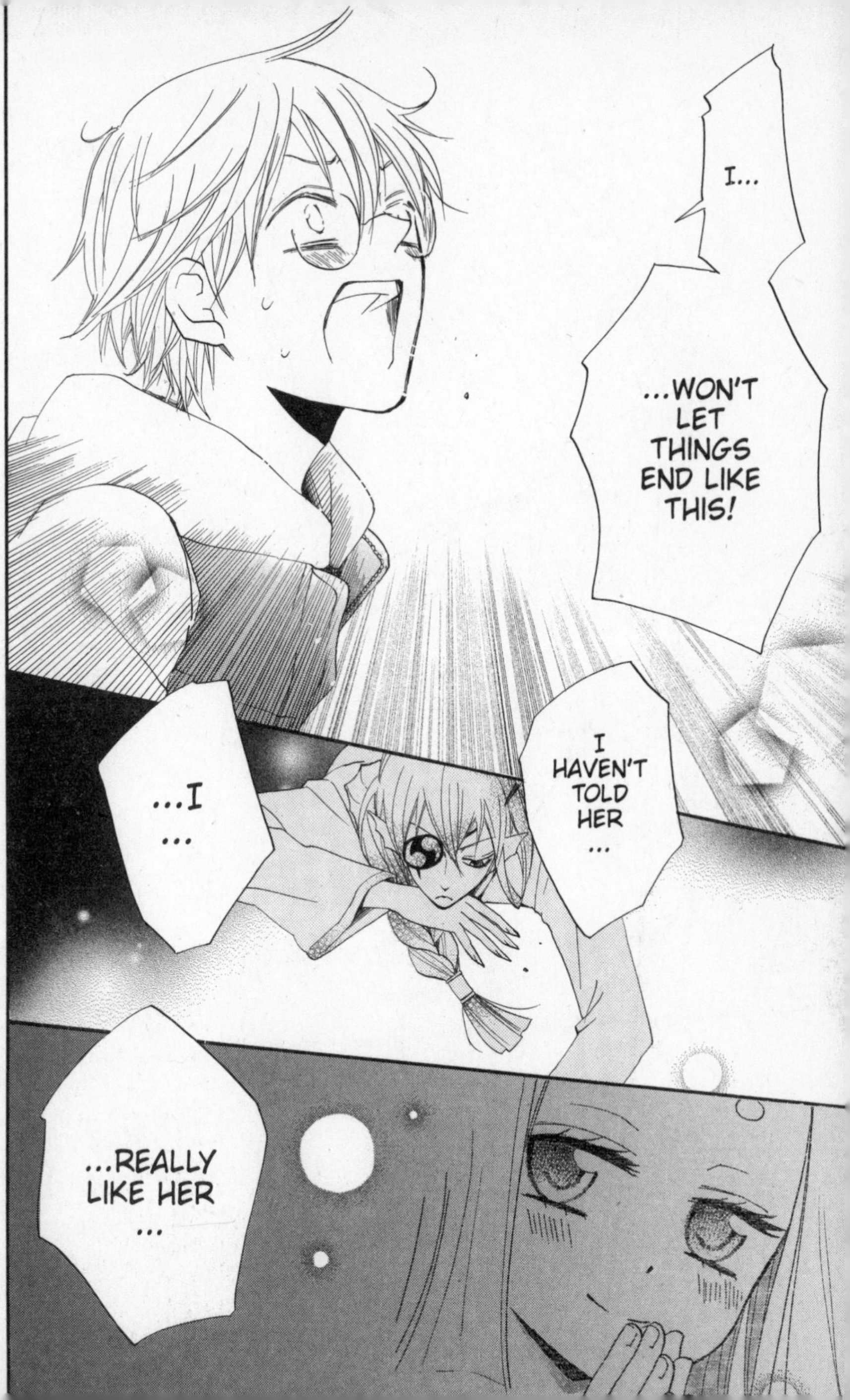
I...
...WON'T LET THINGS END LIKE THIS!
I HAVEN'T TOLD HER ...
...I ...
...REALLY LIKE HER ...

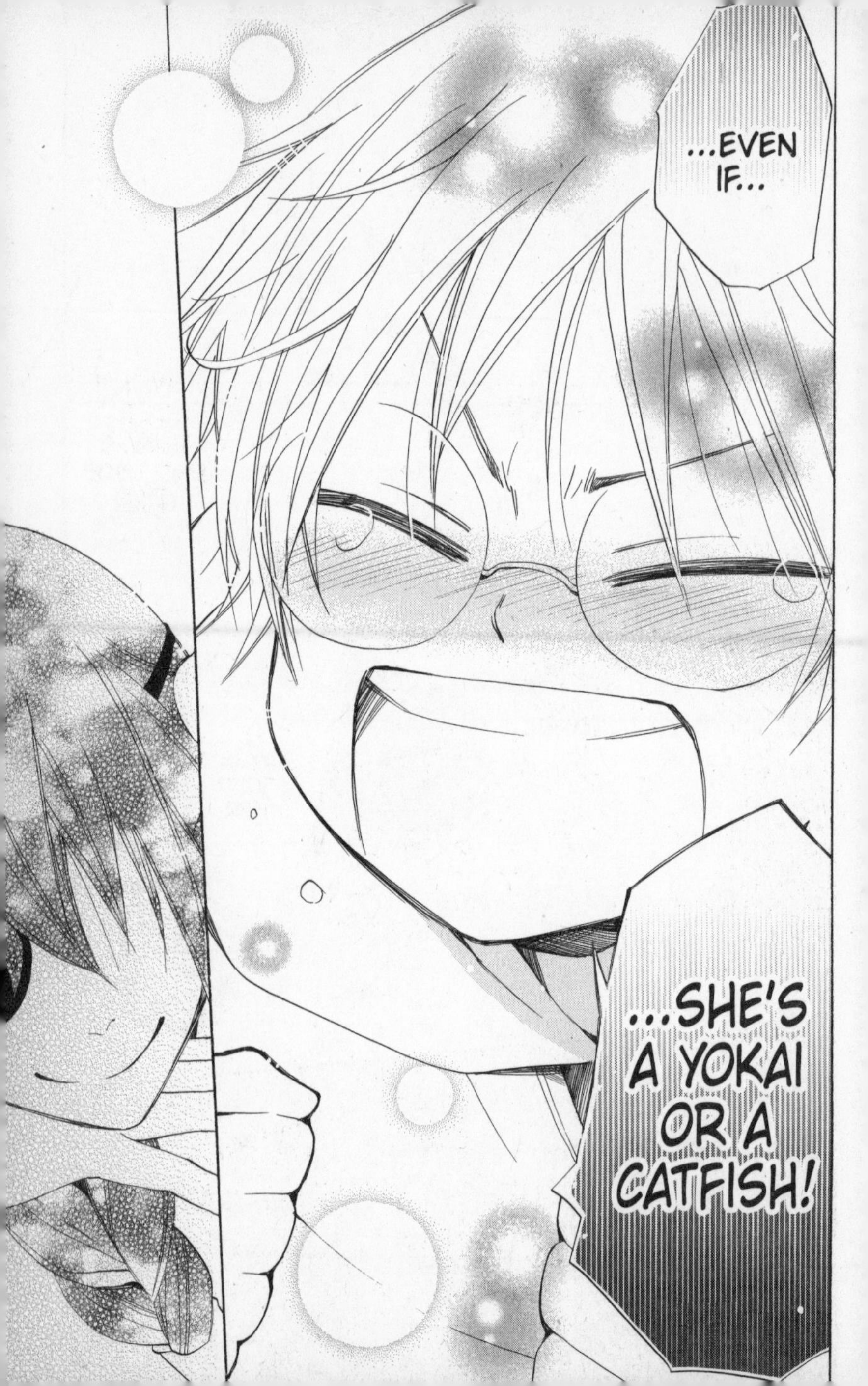
...EVEN IF...
...SHE'S A YOKAI OR A CATFISH!

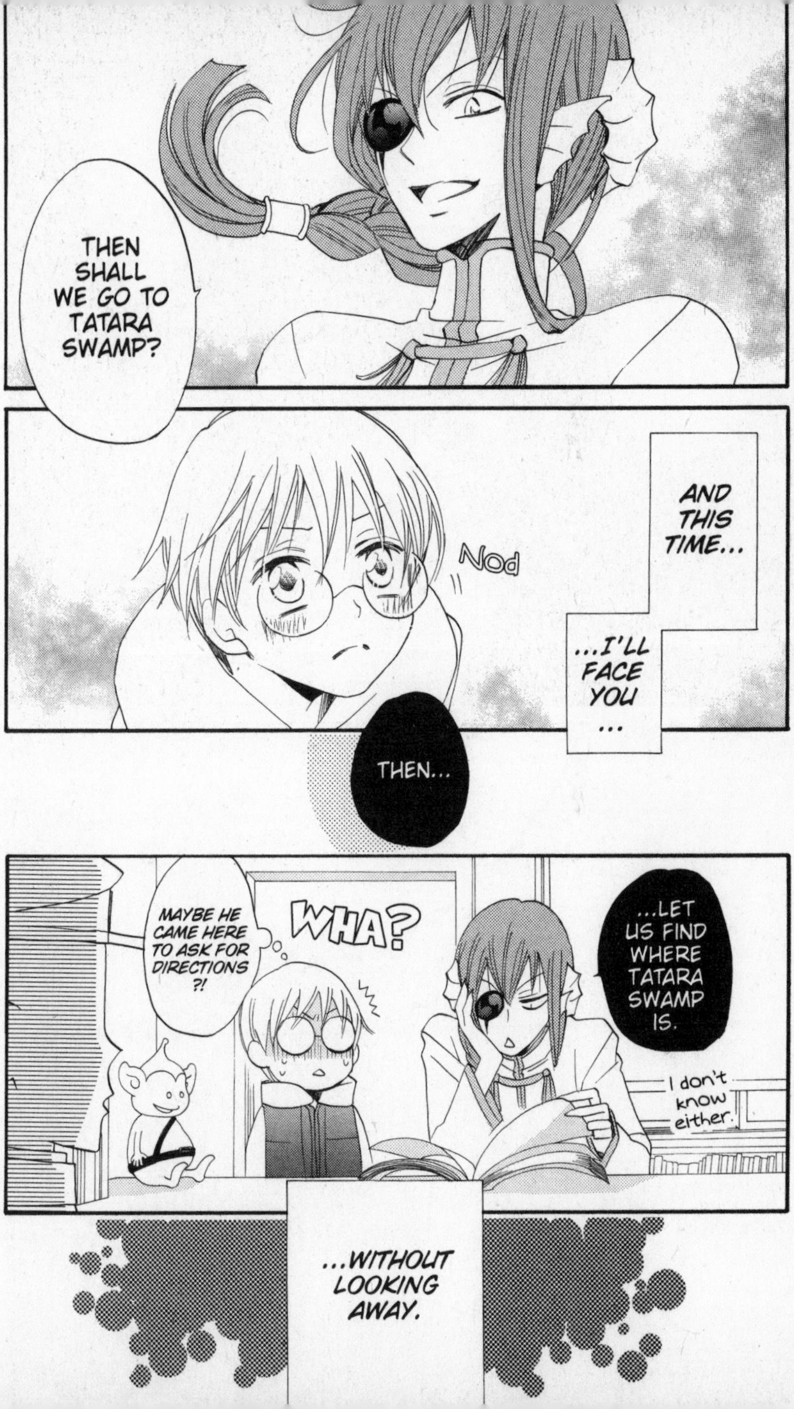
THEN SHALL WE GO TO TATARA SWAMP?
AND THIS TIME...
...I'LL FACE YOU ...
Nod
THEN...
...LET US FIND WHERE TATARA SWAMP IS.
I don't know either.
WHA?
MAYBE HE CAME HERE TO ASK FOR DIRECTIONS ?!
...WITHOUT LOOKING AWAY.

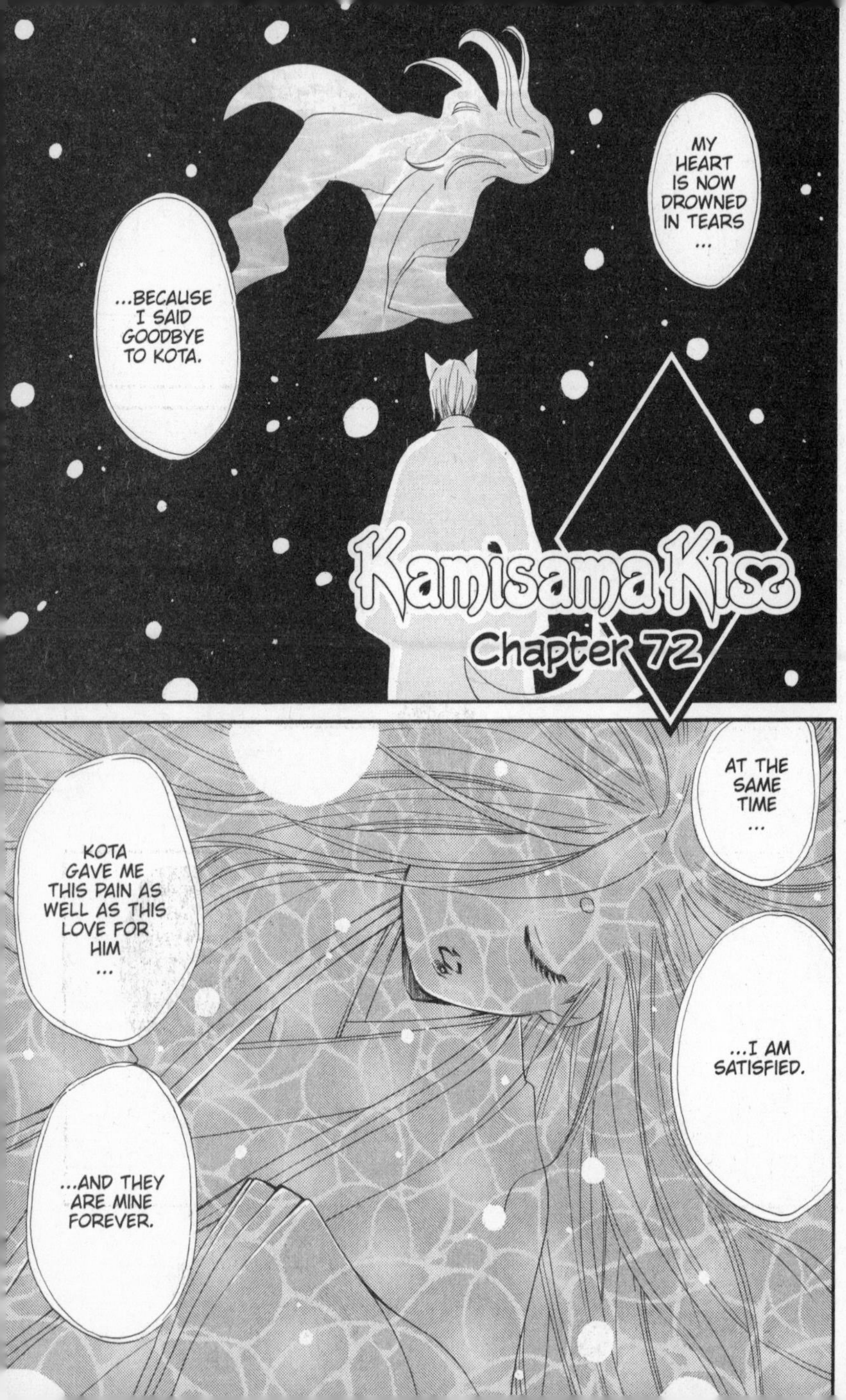
MY HEART IS NOW DROWNED IN TEARS...
...BECAUSE I SAID GOODBYE TO KOTA.
Kamisama Kiss
Chapter 72
AT THE SAME TIME...
...I AM SATISFIED.
KOTA GAVE ME THIS PAIN AS WELL AS THIS LOVE FOR HIM...
...AND THEY ARE MINE FOREVER.

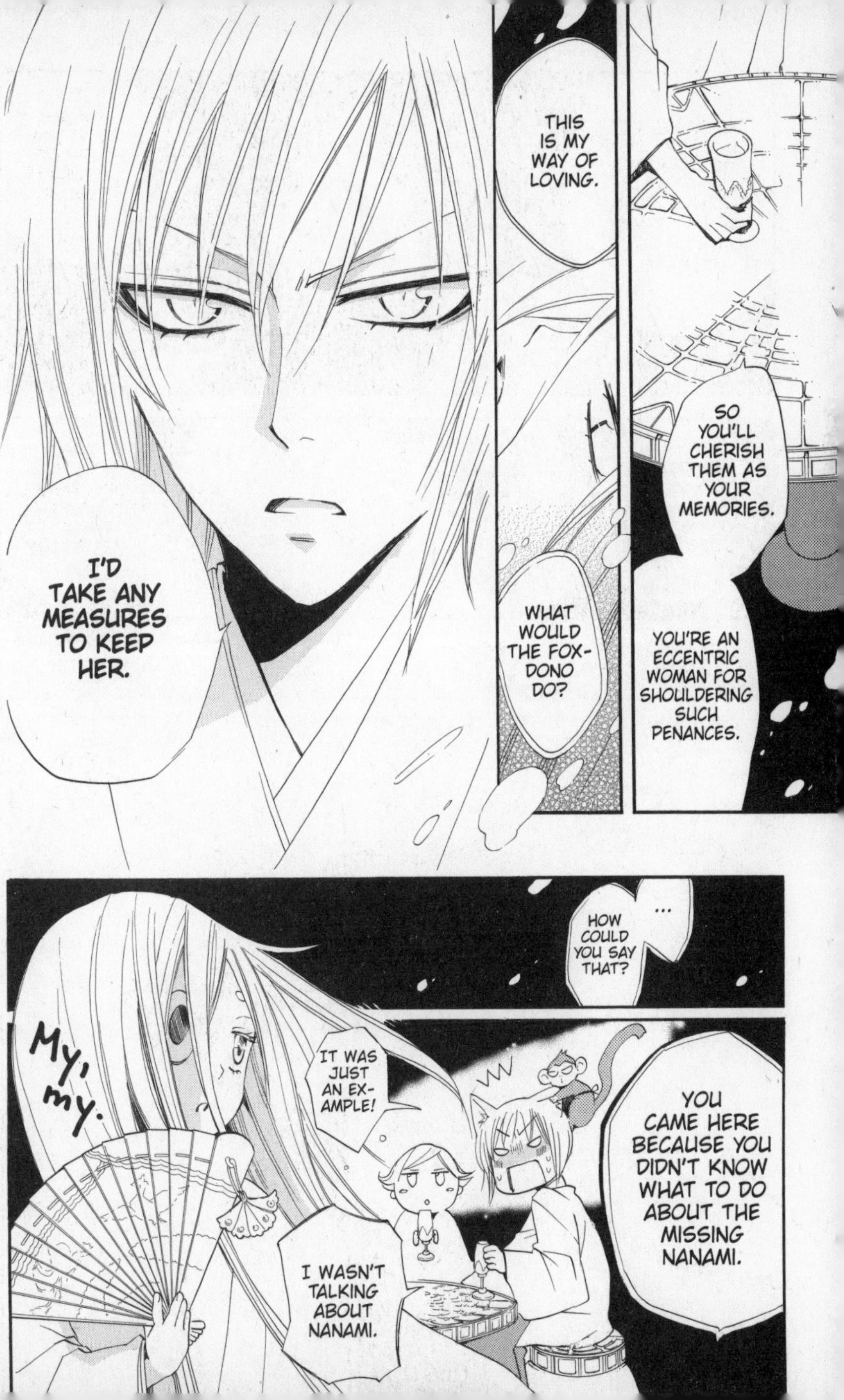
SO YOU'LL CHERISH THEM AS YOUR MEMORIES.
YOU'RE AN ECCENTRIC WOMAN FOR SHOULDERING SUCH PENANCES.
THIS IS MY WAY OF LOVING.
WHAT WOULD THE FOX-DONO DO?
I'D TAKE ANY MEASURES TO KEEP HER.
...
HOW COULD YOU SAY THAT?
YOU CAME HERE BECAUSE YOU DIDN'T KNOW WHAT TO DO ABOUT THE MISSING NANAMI.
IT WAS JUST AN EX-AMPLE!
My, my.
I WASN'T TALKING ABOUT NANAMI.

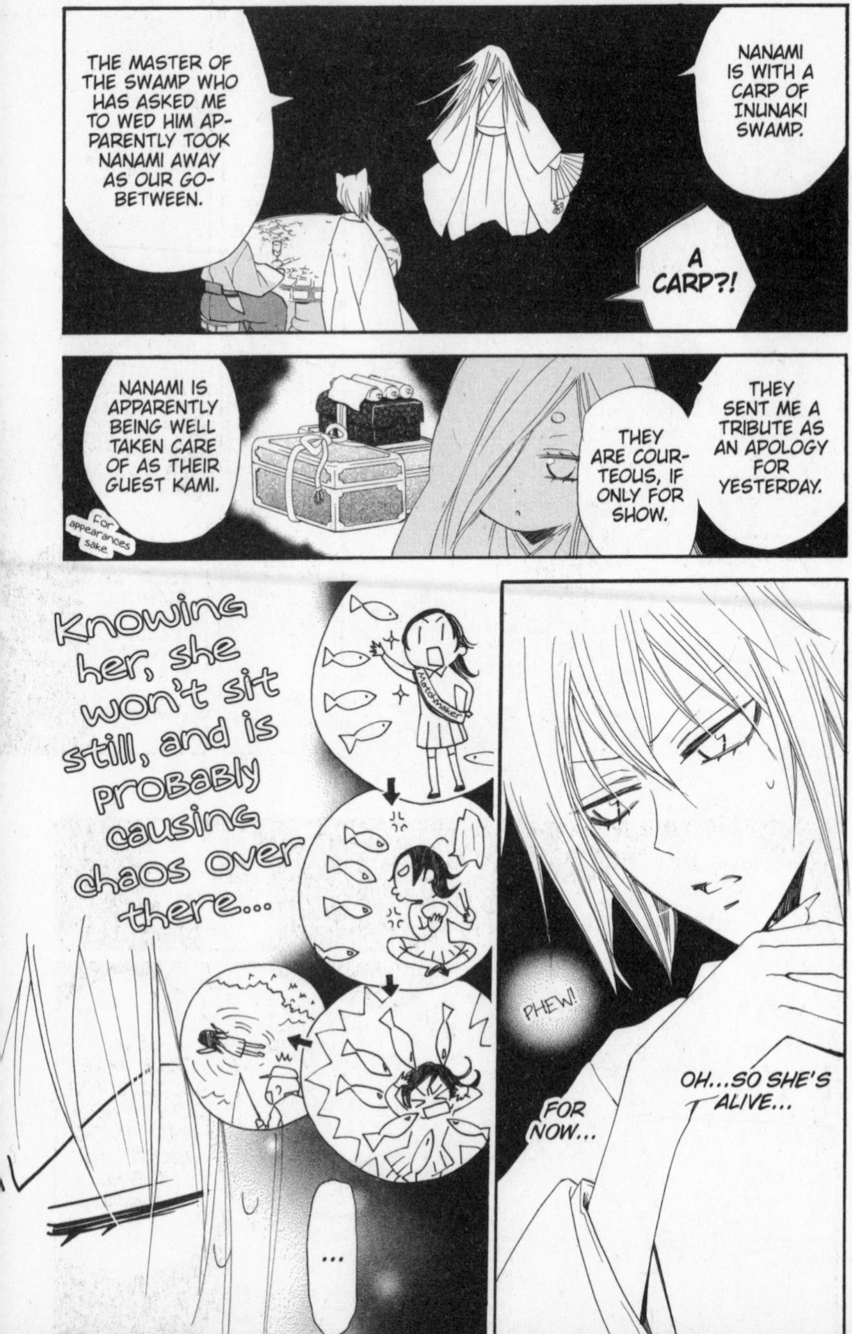
NANAMI IS WITH A CARP OF INUNAKI SWAMP.
A CARP?!
THE MASTER OF THE SWAMP WHO HAS ASKED ME TO WED HIM APPARENTLY TOOK NANAMI AWAY AS OUR GO-BETWEEN.
THEY SENT ME A TRIBUTE AS AN APOLOGY FOR YESTERDAY.
THEY ARE COURTEOUS, IF ONLY FOR SHOW.
NANAMI IS APPARENTLY BEING WELL TAKEN CARE OF AS THEIR GUEST KAMI.
For appearances sake.
PHEW!
OH...SO SHE'S ALIVE...
FOR NOW...
Knowing her, she won't sit still, and is probably causing chaos over there...
Matchmaker
...

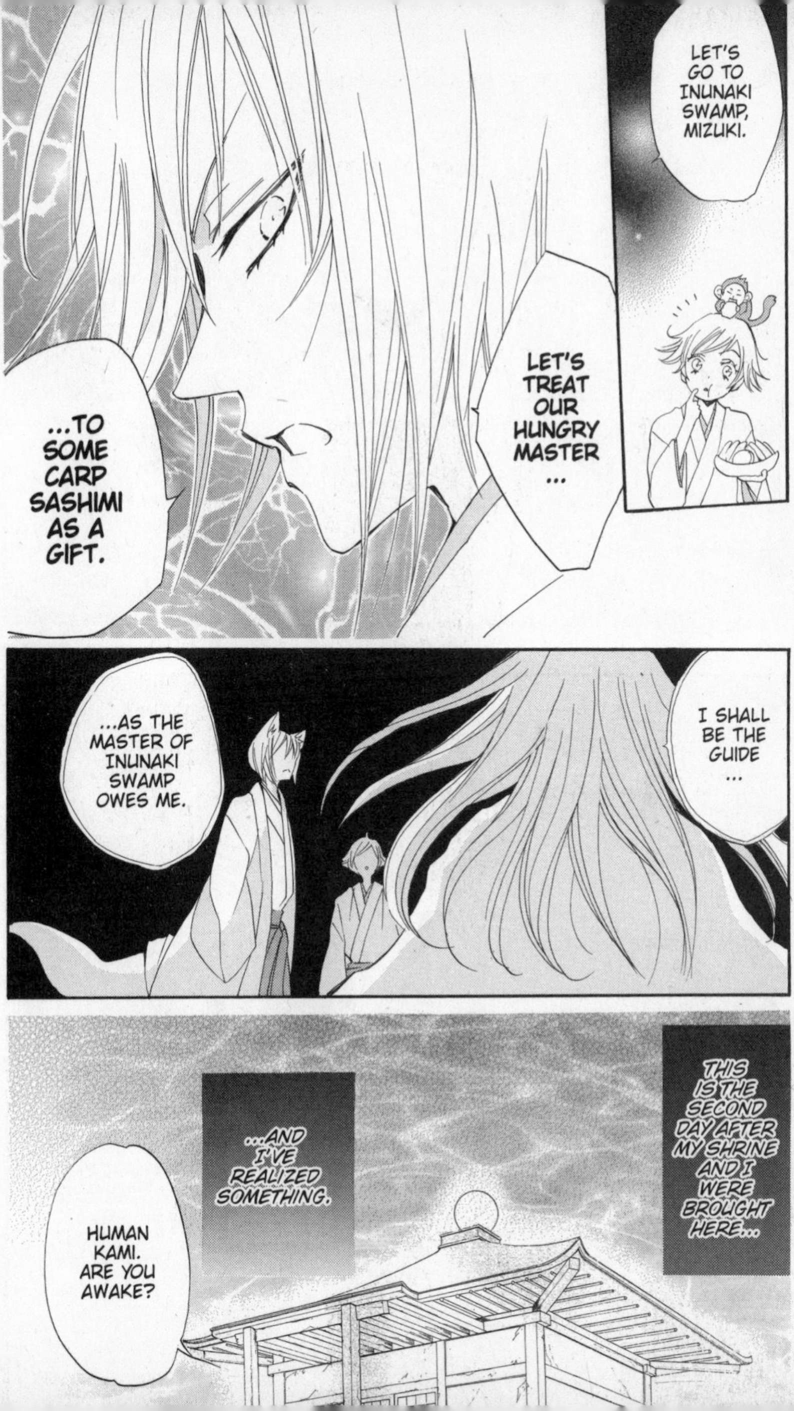
LET'S GO TO INUNAKI SWAMP, MIZUKI.
LET'S TREAT OUR HUNGRY MASTER...
...TO SOME CARP SASHIMI AS A GIFT.
I SHALL BE THE GUIDE...
...AS THE MASTER OF INUNAKI SWAMP OWES ME.
THIS IS THE SECOND DAY AFTER MY SHRINE AND I WERE BROUGHT HERE...
...AND I'VE REALIZED SOMETHING.
HUMAN KAMI. ARE YOU AWAKE?

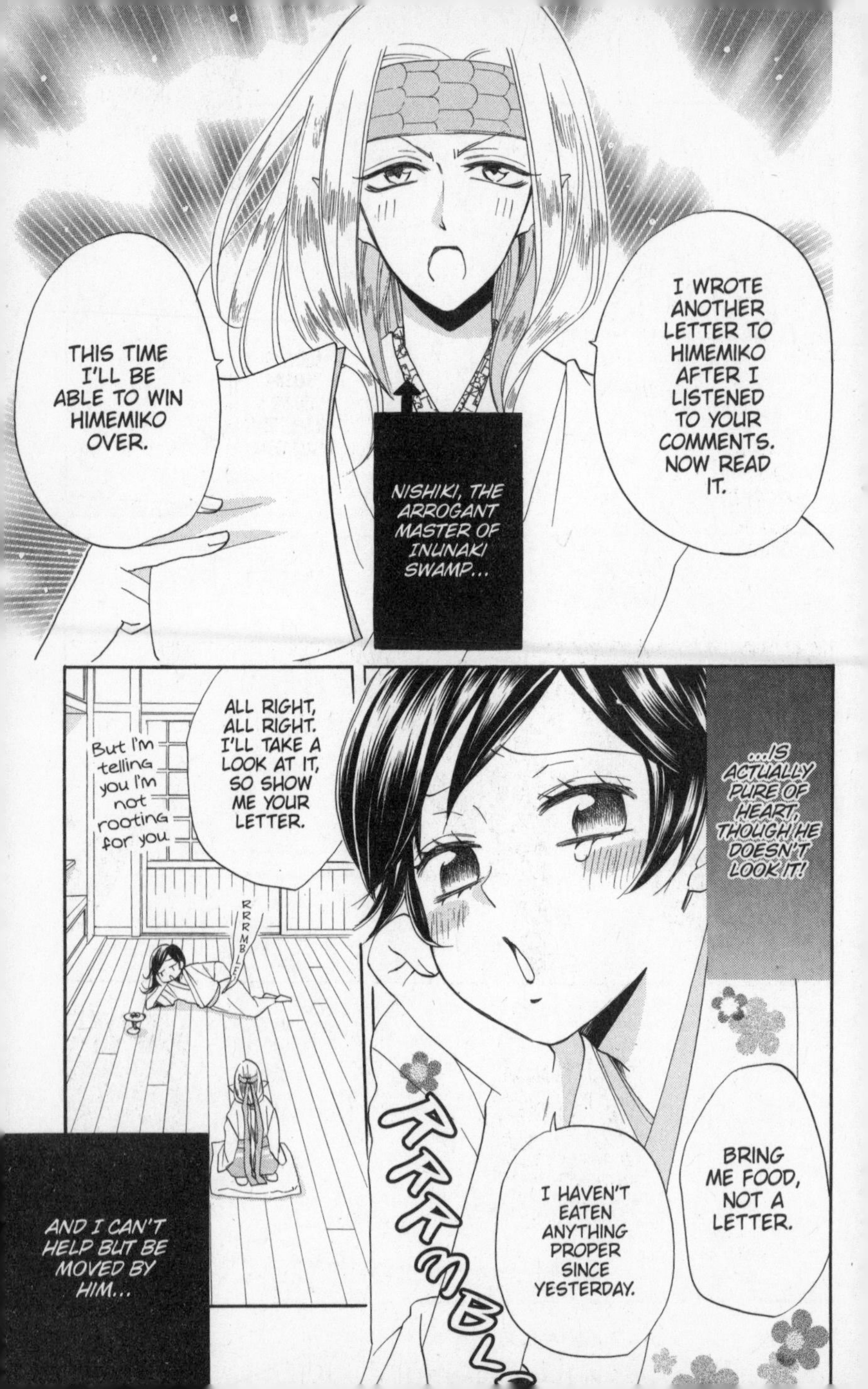
I WROTE ANOTHER LETTER TO HIMEMIKO AFTER I LISTENED TO YOUR COMMENTS. NOW READ IT.
THIS TIME I'LL BE ABLE TO WIN HIMEMIKO OVER.
NISHIKI, THE ARROGANT MASTER OF INUNAKI SWAMP...
...IS ACTUALLY PURE OF HEART, THOUGH HE DOESN'T LOOK IT!
BRING ME FOOD, NOT A LETTER.
I HAVEN'T EATEN ANYTHING PROPER SINCE YESTERDAY.
RRRMBL
ALL RIGHT, ALL RIGHT. I'LL TAKE A LOOK AT IT, SO SHOW ME YOUR LETTER.
But I'm telling you I'm not rooting for you.
RRRMBLE
AND I CAN'T HELP BUT BE MOVED BY HIM...

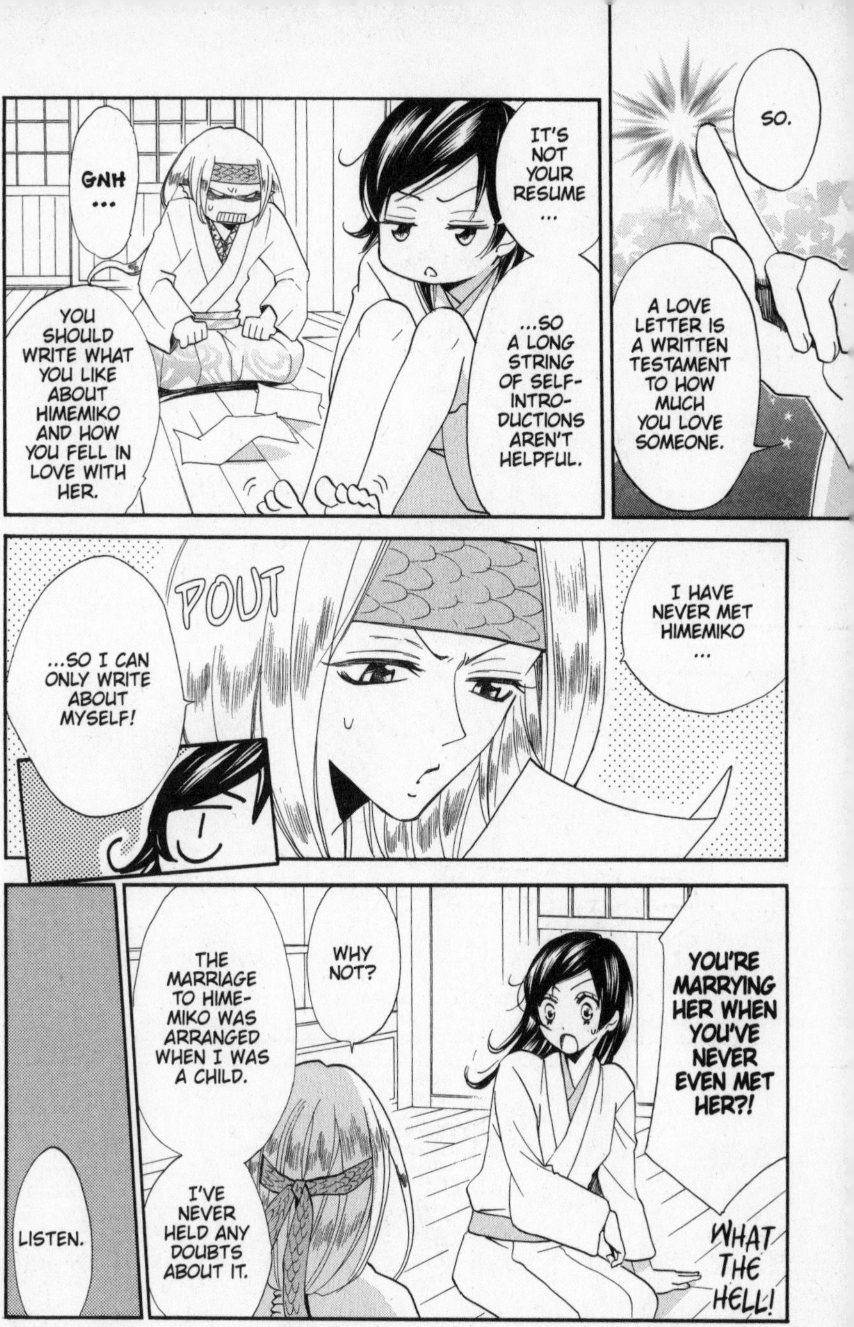
SO.
A LOVE LETTER IS A WRITTEN TESTAMENT TO HOW MUCH YOU LOVE SOMEONE.
IT'S NOT YOUR RESUME...
...SO A LONG STRING OF SELF-INTRODUCTIONS AREN'T HELPFUL.
GNH...
YOU SHOULD WRITE WHAT YOU LIKE ABOUT HIMEMIKO AND HOW YOU FELL IN LOVE WITH HER.
I HAVE NEVER MET HIMEMIKO...
POUT
...SO I CAN ONLY WRITE ABOUT MYSELF!
YOU'RE MARRYING HER WHEN YOU'VE NEVER EVEN MET HER?!
WHAT THE HELL!
WHY NOT?
THE MARRIAGE TO HIMEMIKO WAS ARRANGED WHEN I WAS A CHILD.
I'VE NEVER HELD ANY DOUBTS ABOUT IT.
LISTEN.

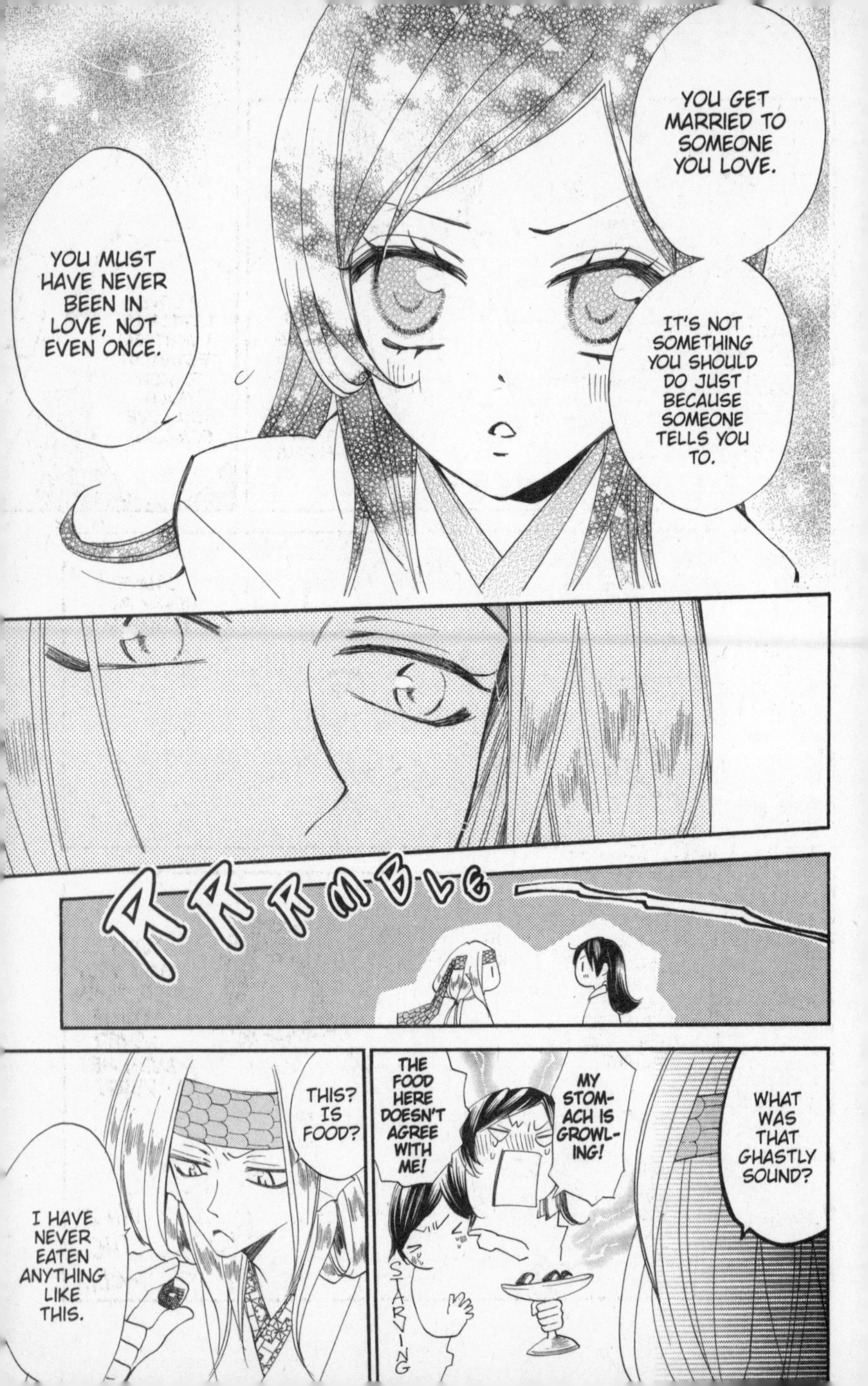
YOU GET MARRIED TO SOMEONE YOU LOVE.
IT'S NOT SOMETHING YOU SHOULD DO JUST BECAUSE SOMEONE TELLS YOU TO.
YOU MUST HAVE NEVER BEEN IN LOVE, NOT EVEN ONCE.
RRRMBLE
WHAT WAS THAT GHASTLY SOUND?
MY STOM-ACH IS GROWL-ING!
THE FOOD HERE DOESN'T AGREE WITH ME!
STARVING
THIS? IS FOOD?
I HAVE NEVER EATEN ANYTHING LIKE THIS.

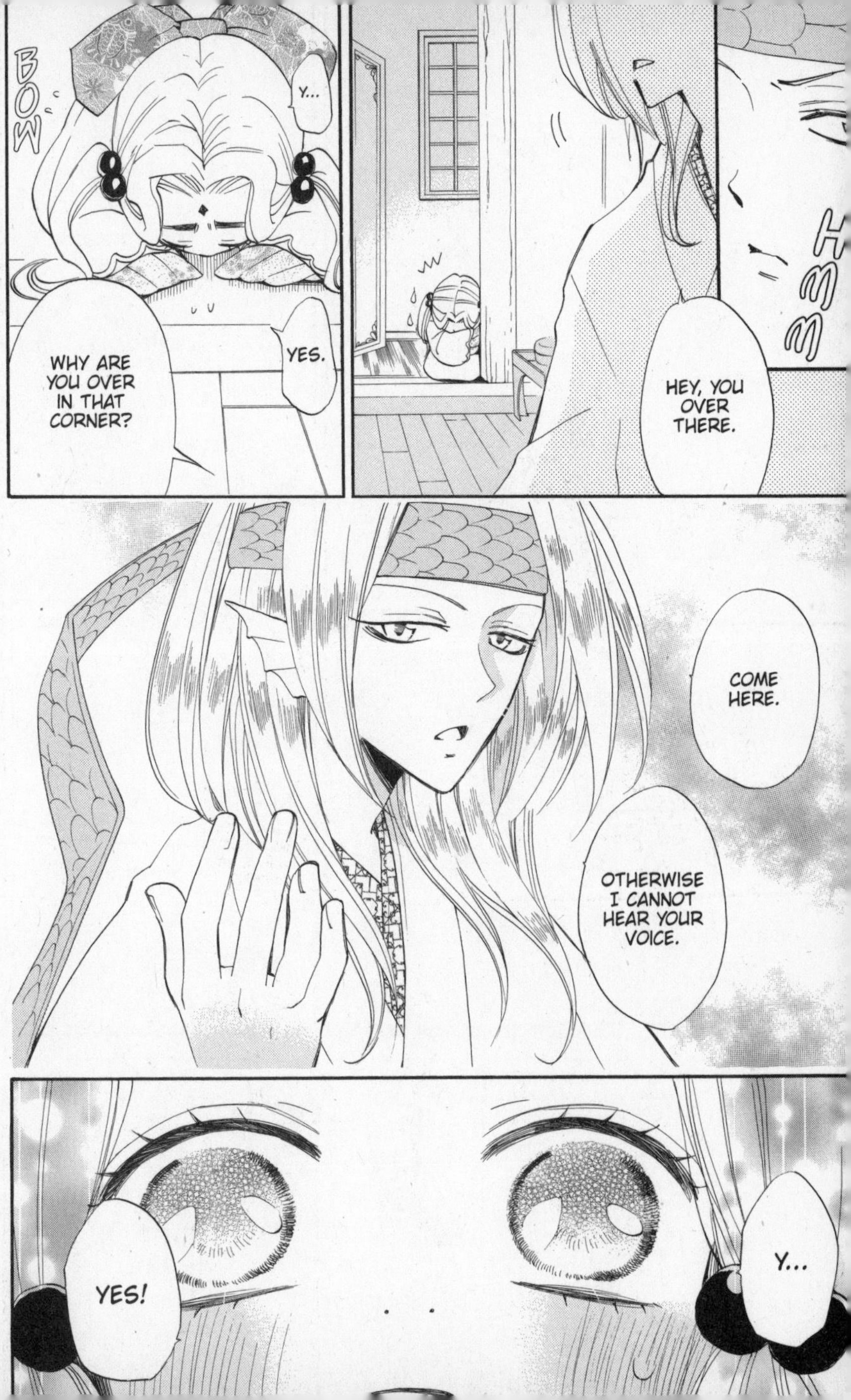
HEY, YOU OVER THERE.
Y...
BOW
YES.
WHY ARE YOU OVER IN THAT CORNER?
COME HERE.
OTHERWISE I CANNOT HEAR YOUR VOICE.
Y...
YES!

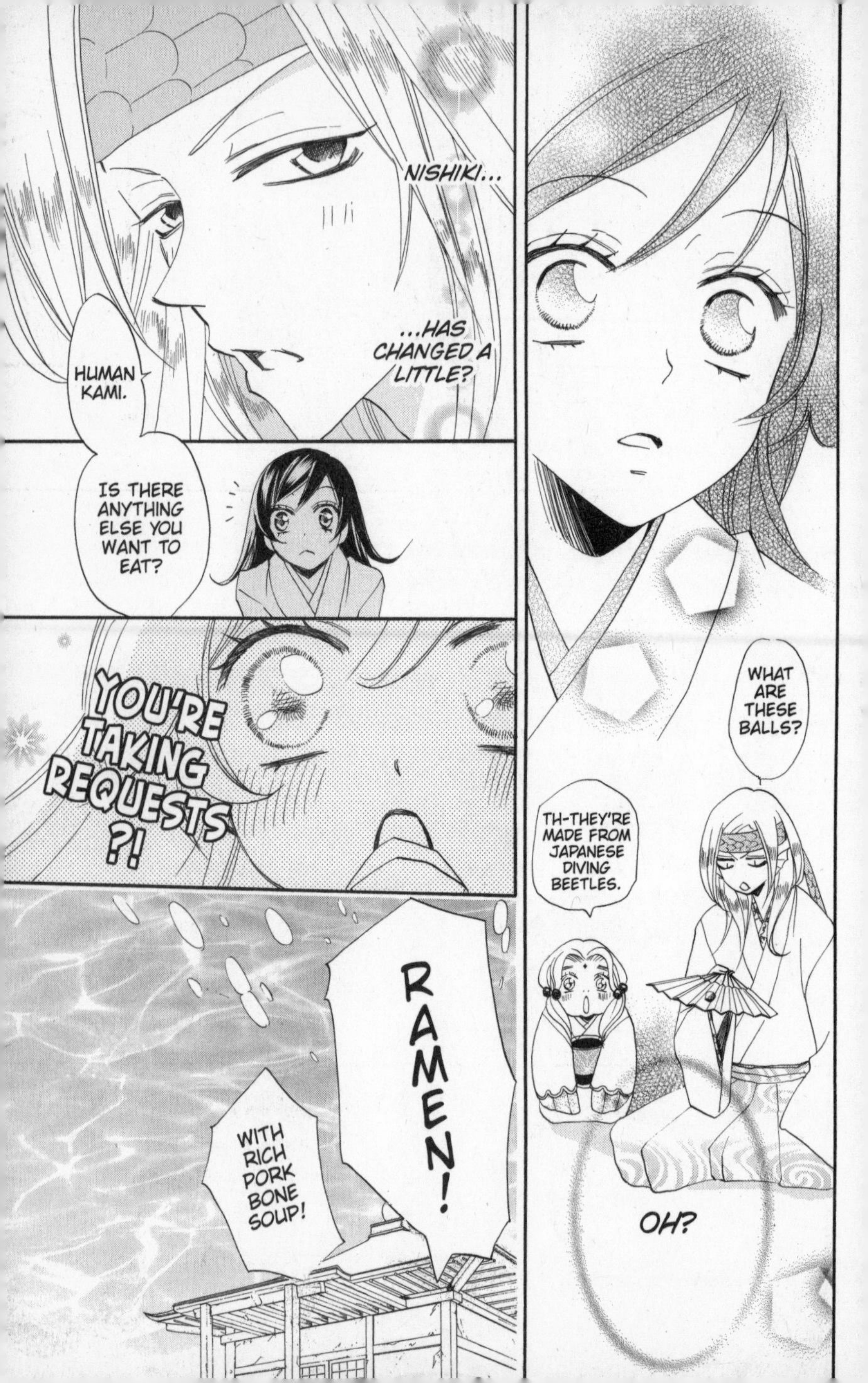
WHAT ARE THESE BALLS?
TH-THEY'RE MADE FROM JAPANESE DIVING BEETLES.
OH?
NISHIKI...
...HAS CHANGED A LITTLE?
HUMAN KAMI.
IS THERE ANYTHING ELSE YOU WANT TO EAT?
YOU'RE TAKING REQUESTS?!
RAMEN!
WITH RICH PORK BONE SOUP!

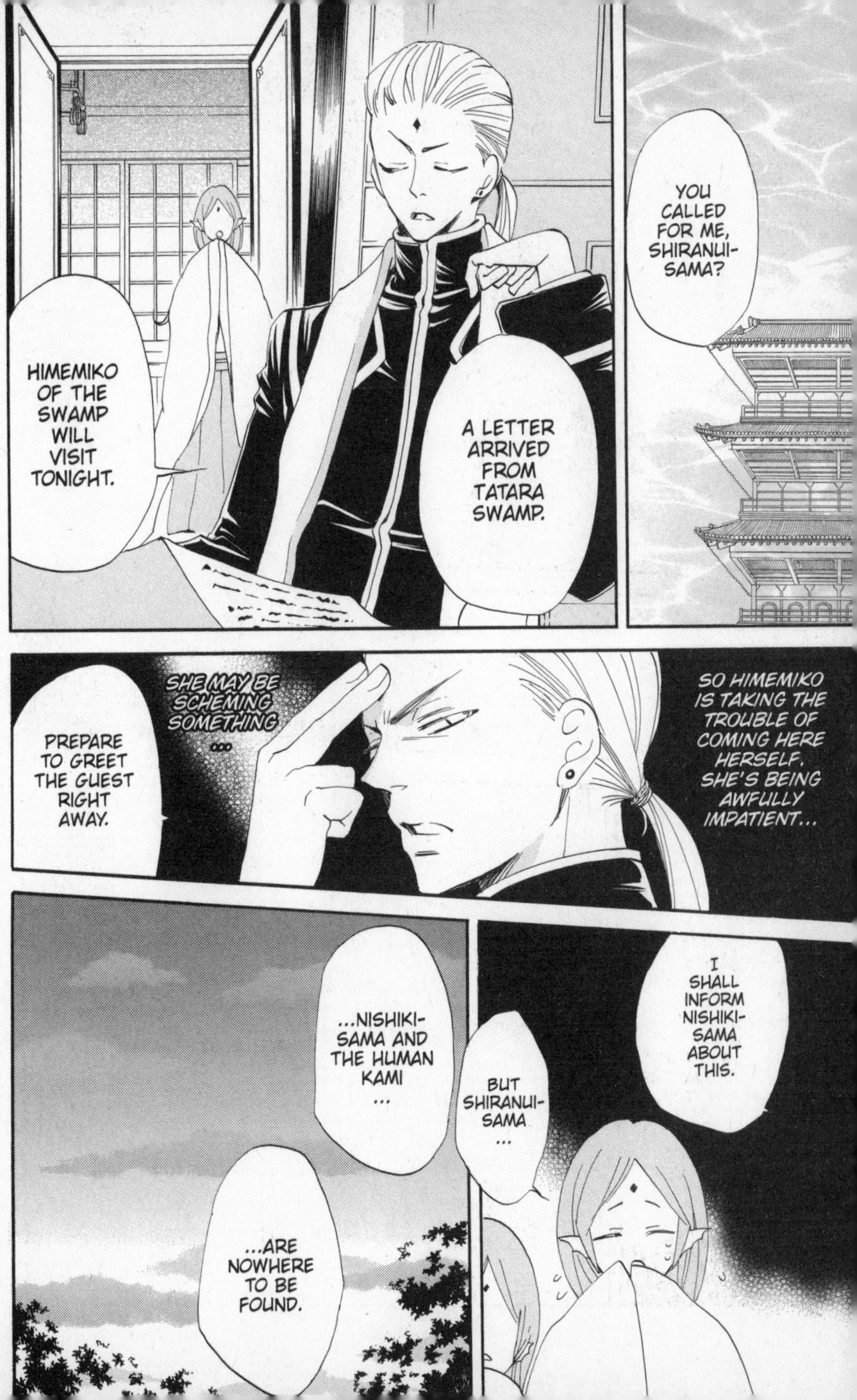
YOU CALLED FOR ME, SHIRANUI-SAMA?
A LETTER ARRIVED FROM TATARA SWAMP.
HIMEMIKO OF THE SWAMP WILL VISIT TONIGHT.
SO HIMEMIKO IS TAKING THE TROUBLE OF COMING HERE HERSELF. SHE'S BEING AWFULLY IMPATIENT...
SHE MAY BE SCHEMING SOMETHING ...
PREPARE TO GREET THE GUEST RIGHT AWAY.
I SHALL INFORM NISHIKI-SAMA ABOUT THIS.
BUT SHIRANUI-SAMA ...
...NISHIKI-SAMA AND THE HUMAN KAMI ...
...ARE NOWHERE TO BE FOUND.

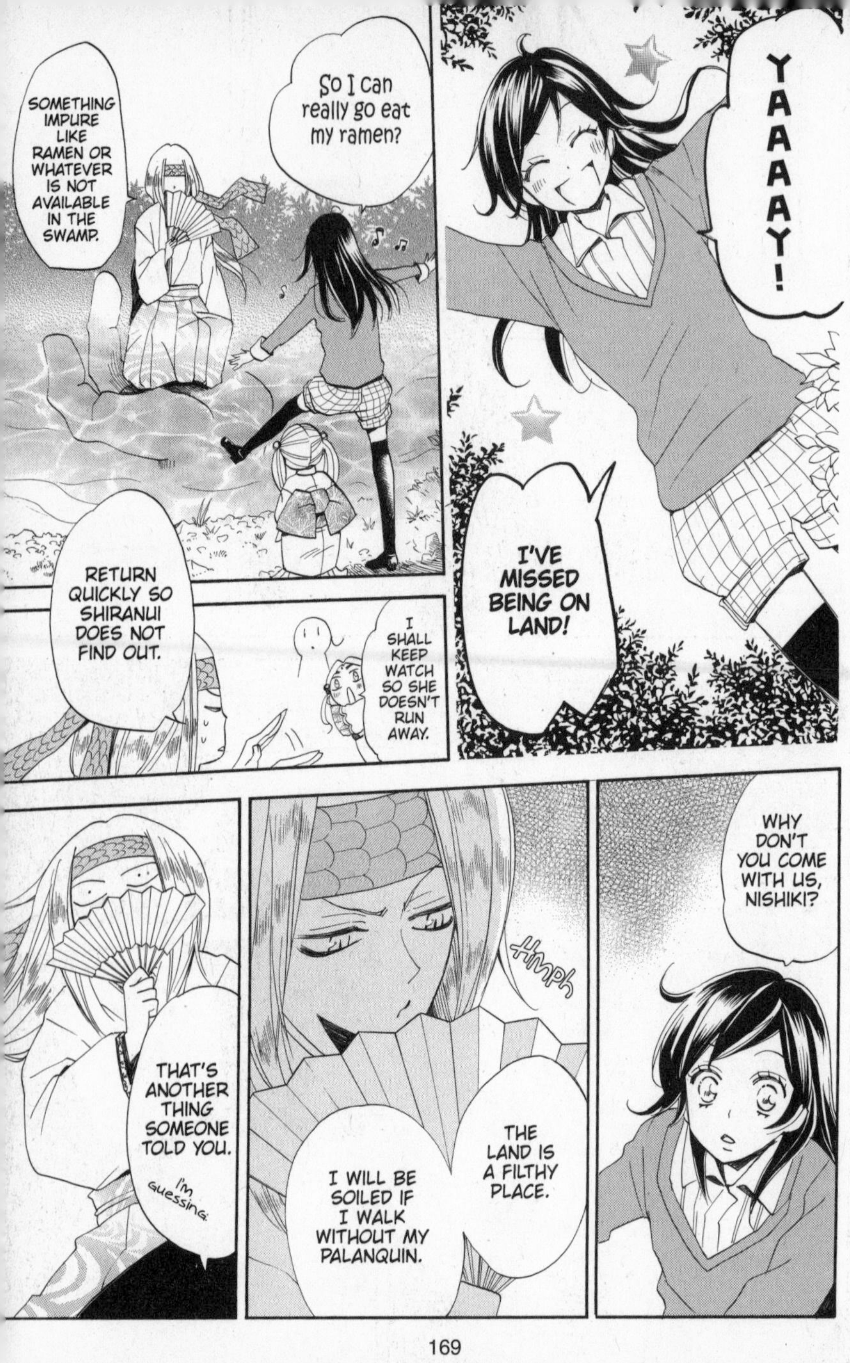
YAAAAY!
I'VE MISSED BEING ON LAND!
So I can really go eat my ramen?
SOMETHING IMPURE LIKE RAMEN OR WHATEVER IS NOT AVAILABLE IN THE SWAMP.
I SHALL KEEP WATCH SO SHE DOESN'T RUN AWAY.
RETURN QUICKLY SO SHIRANUI DOES NOT FIND OUT.
WHY DON'T YOU COME WITH US, NISHIKI?
THE LAND IS A FILTHY PLACE.
Hmph
I WILL BE SOILED IF I WALK WITHOUT MY PALANQUIN.
THAT'S ANOTHER THING SOMEONE TOLD YOU.
I'm guessing.

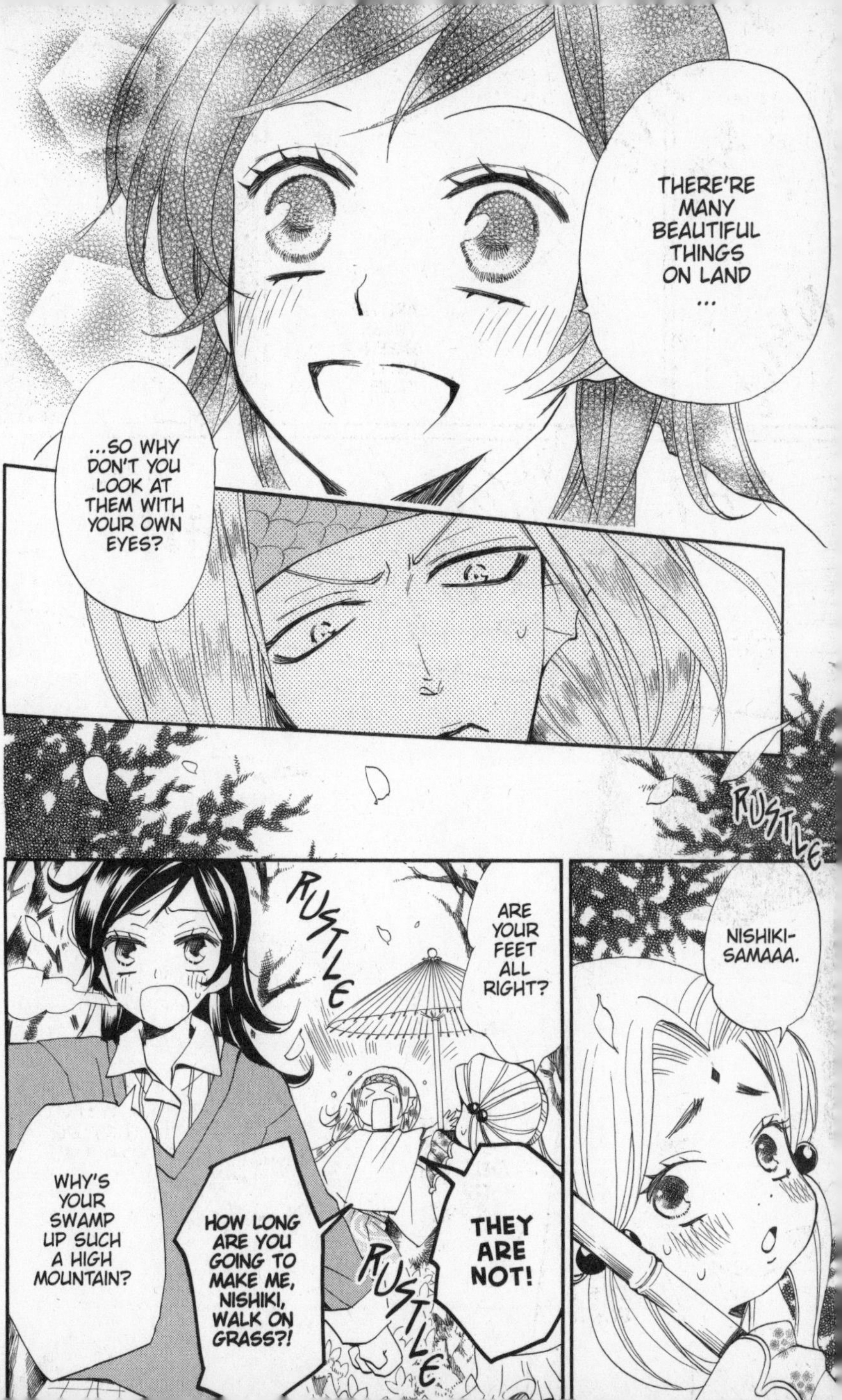
THERE'RE MANY BEAUTIFUL THINGS ON LAND ...
...SO WHY DON'T YOU LOOK AT THEM WITH YOUR OWN EYES?
RUSTLE
NISHIKI-SAMAAA.
ARE YOUR FEET ALL RIGHT?
RUSTLE
THEY ARE NOT!
HOW LONG ARE YOU GOING TO MAKE ME, NISHIKI, WALK ON GRASS?!
RUSTLE
WHY'S YOUR SWAMP UP SUCH A HIGH MOUNTAIN?

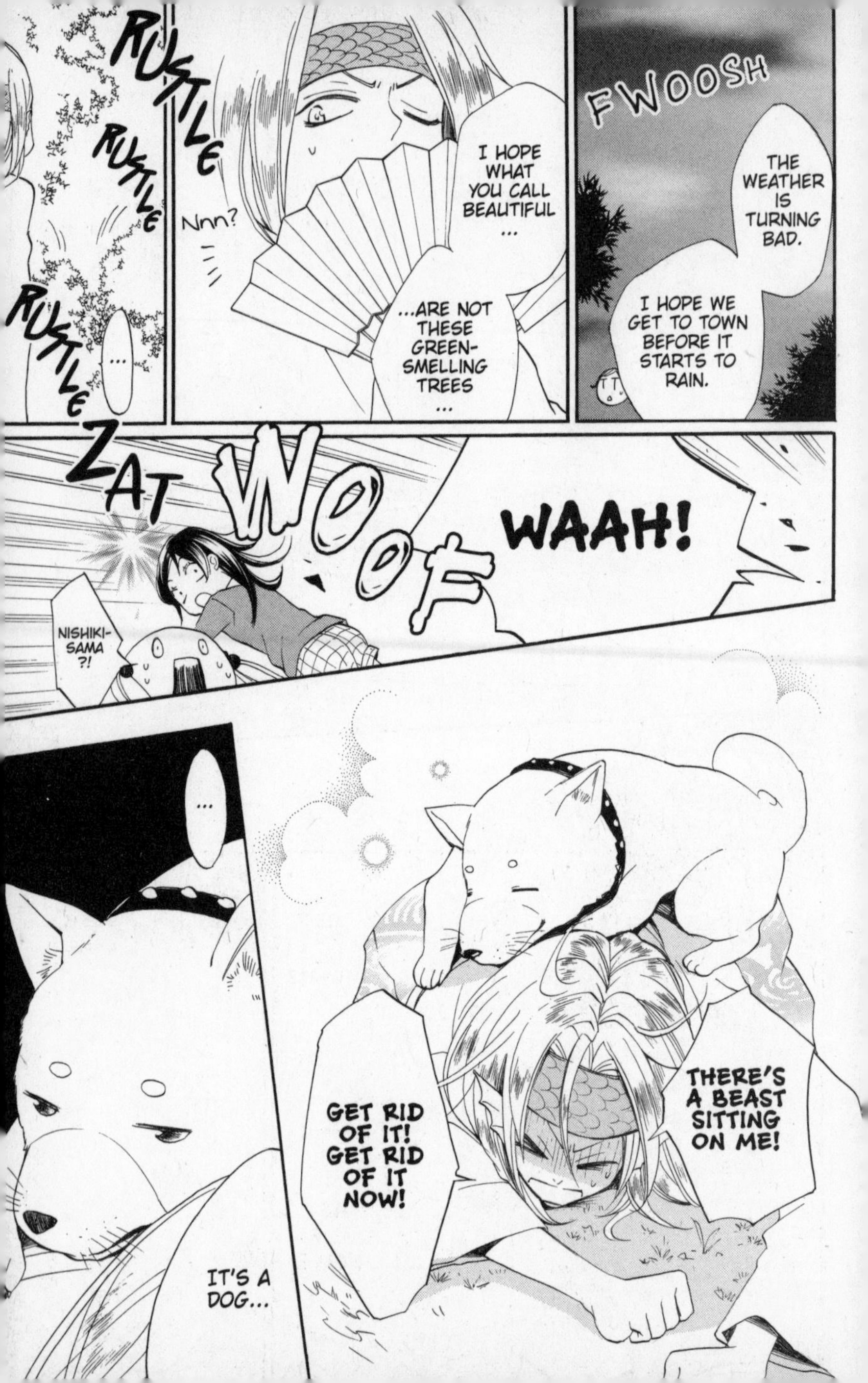
FWOOSH
THE WEATHER IS TURNING BAD.
I HOPE WE GET TO TOWN BEFORE IT STARTS TO RAIN.
I HOPE WHAT YOU CALL BEAUTIFUL ...
...ARE NOT THESE GREEN-SMELLING TREES ...
Nnn?
RUSTLE
RUSTLE
RUSTLE
...
WAAH!
WOOF
ZAT
NISHIKI-SAMA ?!
THERE'S A BEAST SITTING ON ME!
GET RID OF IT! GET RID OF IT NOW!
IT'S A DOG...
...

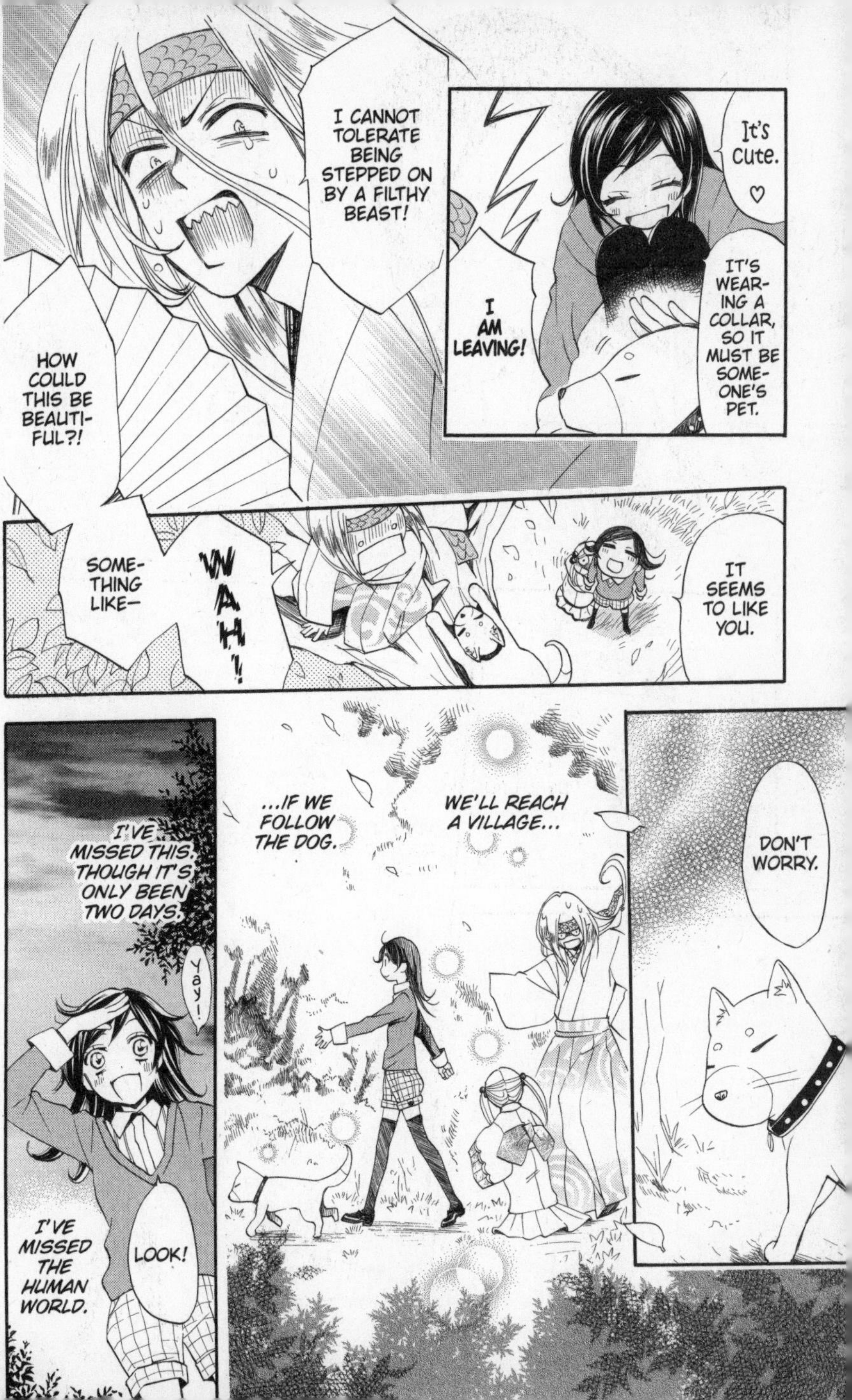

It's Cute. ♡
IT'S WEAR-ING A COLLAR, SO IT MUST BE SOME-ONE'S PET.
I AM LEAVING!
I CANNOT TOLERATE BEING STEPPED ON BY A FILTHY BEAST!
HOW COULD THIS BE BEAUTI-FUL?!
IT SEEMS TO LIKE YOU.
WAH!!
SOME-THING LIKE—
DON'T WORRY.
WE'LL REACH A VILLAGE...
...IF WE FOLLOW THE DOG.
I'VE MISSED THIS. THOUGH IT'S ONLY BEEN TWO DAYS.
Yay!
LOOK!
I'VE MISSED THE HUMAN WORLD.

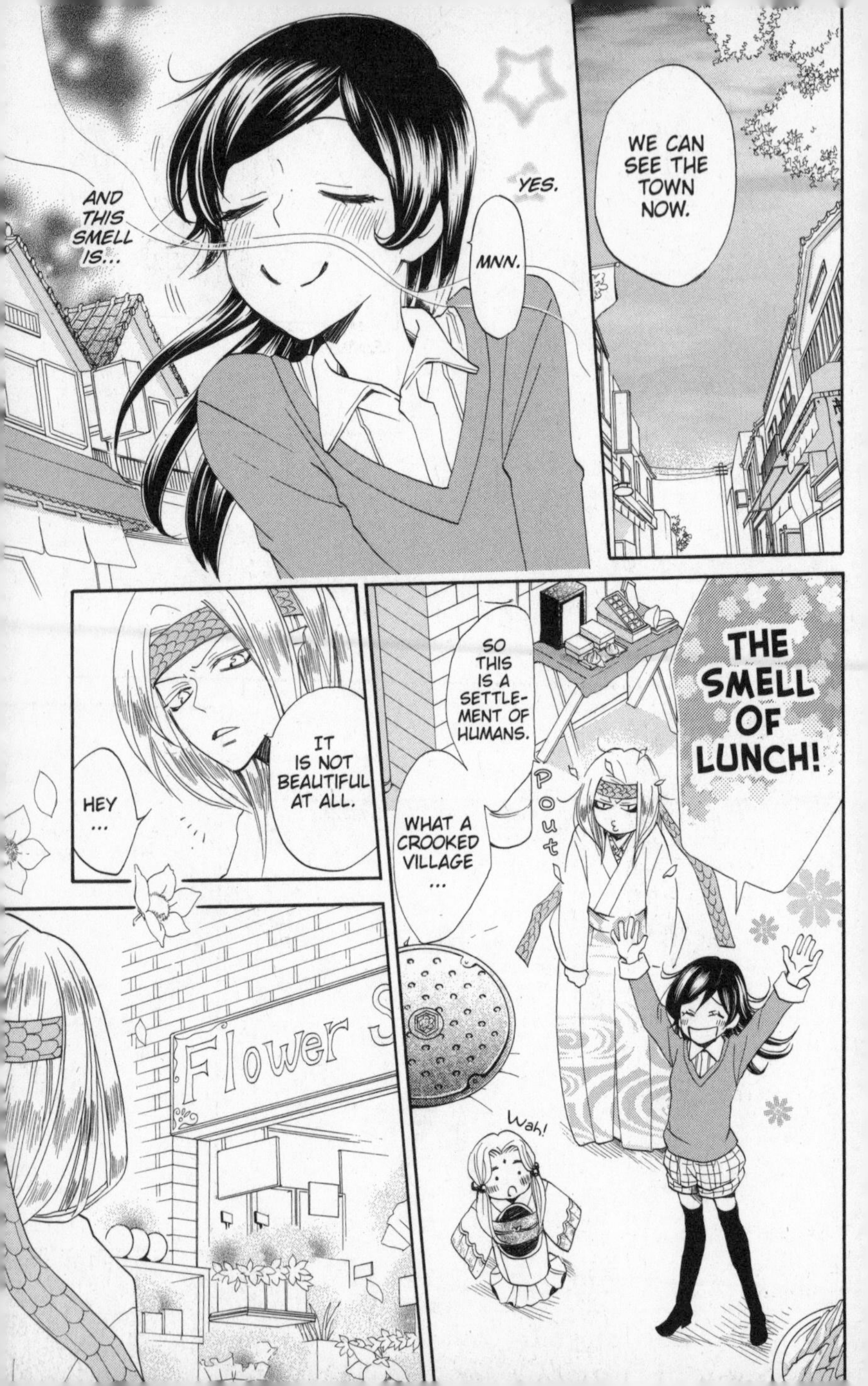
WE CAN SEE THE TOWN NOW.
YES.
MNN.
AND THIS SMELL IS...
THE SMELL OF LUNCH!
SO THIS IS A SETTLE-MENT OF HUMANS.
Pout
WHAT A CROOKED VILLAGE ...
Wah!
IT IS NOT BEAUTIFUL AT ALL.
HEY ...
Flower S

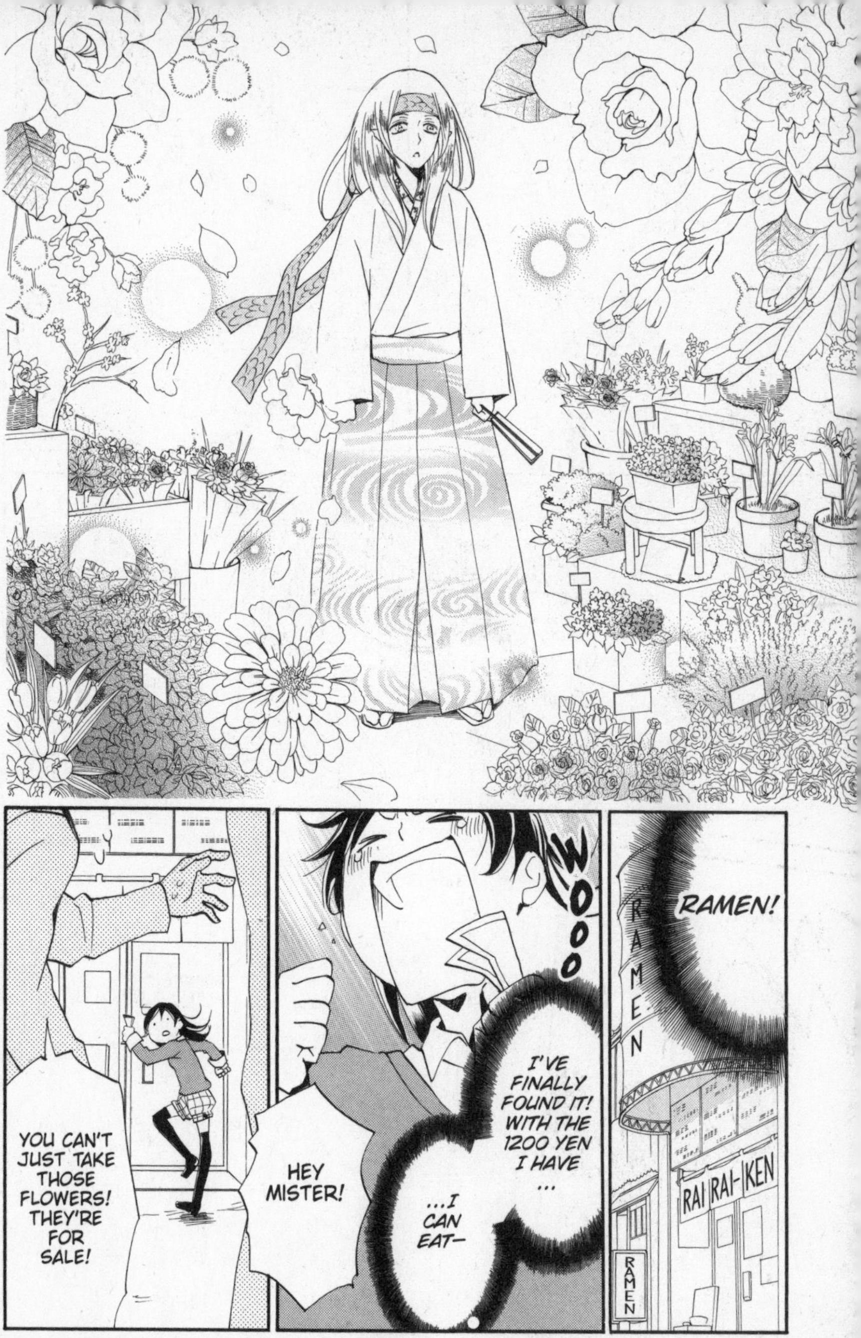
RAMEN!
RAMEN
RAI RAI-KEN
RAMEN
WOOOO
I'VE FINALLY FOUND IT! WITH THE 1200 YEN I HAVE ...
...I CAN EAT—
HEY MISTER!
YOU CAN'T JUST TAKE THOSE FLOWERS! THEY'RE FOR SALE!

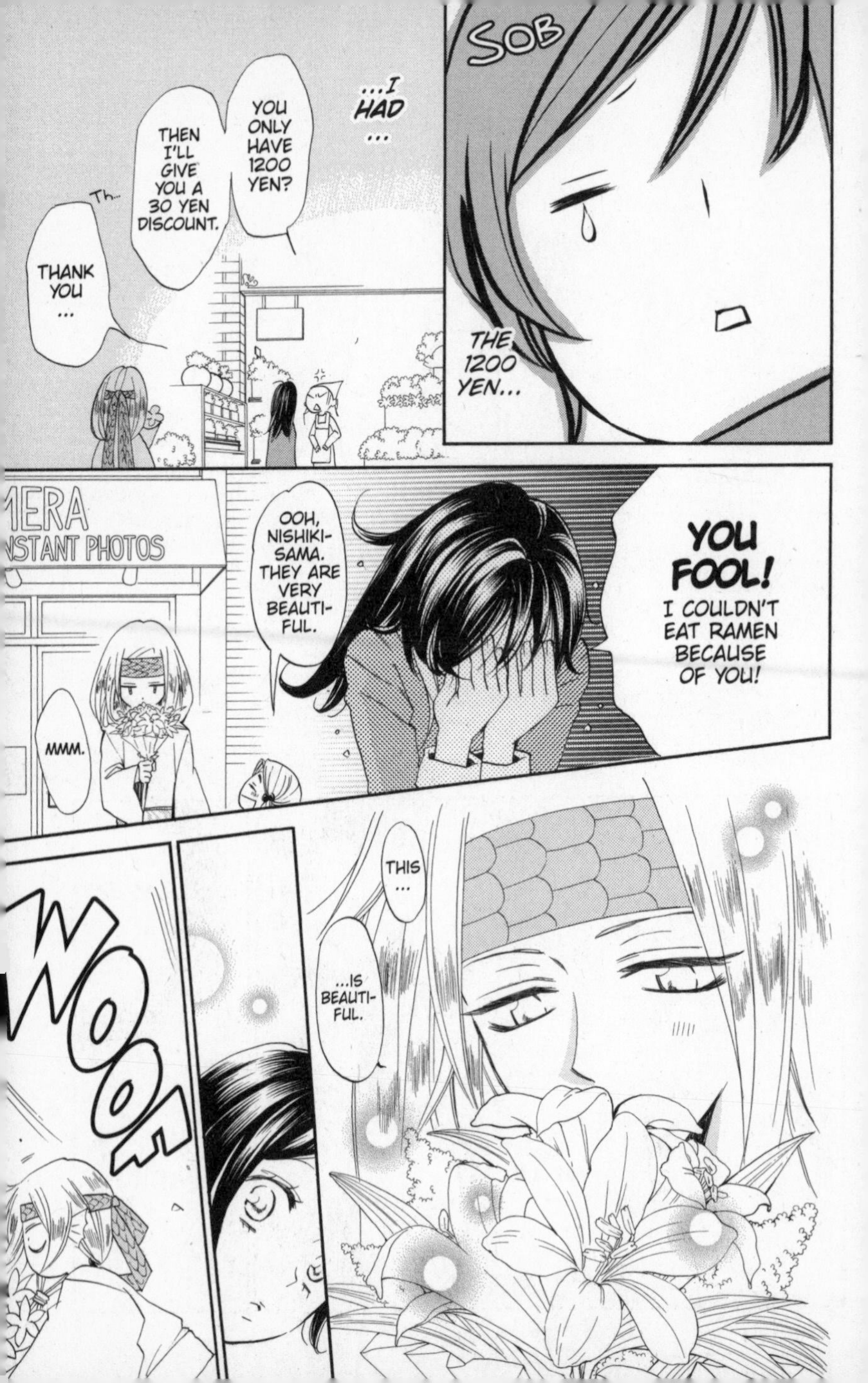
SOB
THE 1200 YEN...
...I HAD ...
YOU ONLY HAVE 1200 YEN?
THEN I'LL GIVE YOU A 30 YEN DISCOUNT.
Th...
THANK YOU ...
YOU FOOL! I COULDN'T EAT RAMEN BECAUSE OF YOU!
OOH, NISHIKI-SAMA. THEY ARE VERY BEAUTIFUL.
MERA
NSTANT PHOTOS
MMM.
THIS ...
...IS BEAUTIFUL.
WOOF

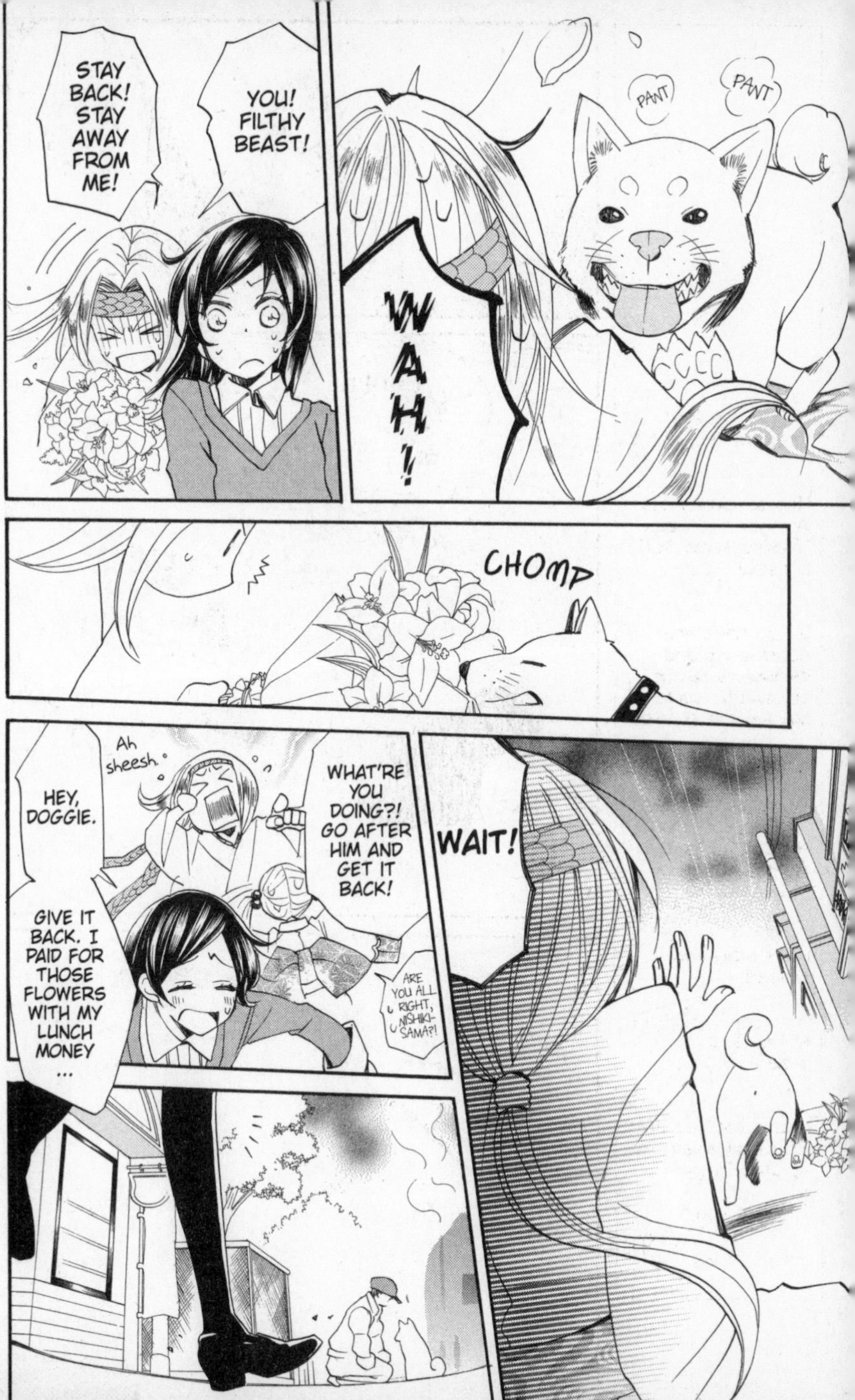
PANT
PANT
WAH!!
YOU! FILTHY BEAST!
STAY BACK! STAY AWAY FROM ME!
CHOMP
WAIT!
WHAT'RE YOU DOING?! GO AFTER HIM AND GET IT BACK!
Ah sheesh.
HEY, DOGGIE.
ARE YOU ALL RIGHT, NISHIKI-SAMA?!
GIVE IT BACK. I PAID FOR THOSE FLOWERS WITH MY LUNCH MONEY...

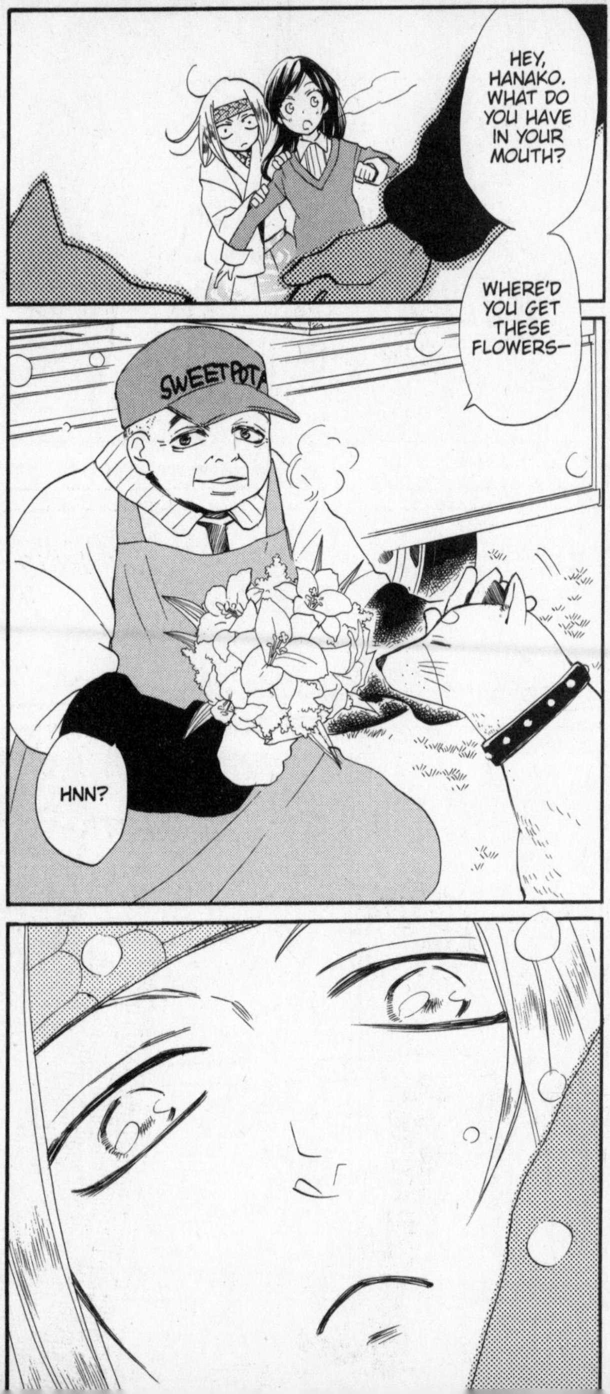
HEY, HANAKO. WHAT DO YOU HAVE IN YOUR MOUTH?
WHERE'D YOU GET THESE FLOWERS—
SWEETPOTA
HNN?

Thank you for reading this far! ♡

Thank you always for your letters. They're food for my soul.

If you have any comments and thoughts about volume 12, do let me hear from you.

Julietta Suzuki
c/o Shojo Beat
VIZ Media, LLC
P.O. Box 77010
San Francisco
CA 94107

I still blog and tweet.

My Blog

http://suzuju.jugem.jp/

I hope we'll be able to meet again in volume 13.

See you!

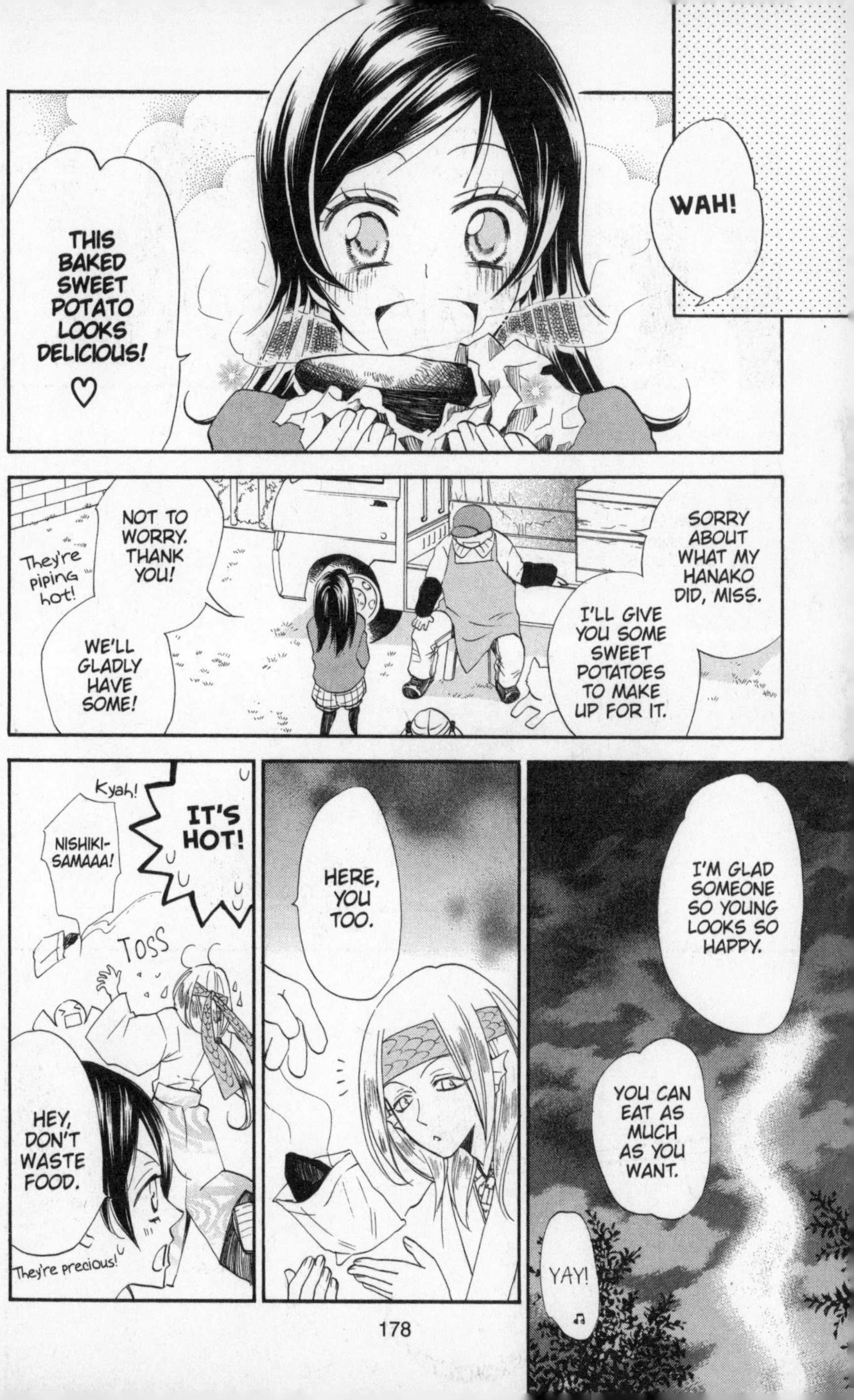
WAH!
THIS BAKED SWEET POTATO LOOKS DELICIOUS! ♡
SORRY ABOUT WHAT MY HANAKO DID, MISS.
I'LL GIVE YOU SOME SWEET POTATOES TO MAKE UP FOR IT.
NOT TO WORRY. THANK YOU!
They're piping hot!
WE'LL GLADLY HAVE SOME!
I'M GLAD SOMEONE SO YOUNG LOOKS SO HAPPY.
YOU CAN EAT AS MUCH AS YOU WANT.
YAY! ♫
HERE, YOU TOO.
IT'S HOT!
Kyah!
NISHIKI-SAMAAA!
TOSS
HEY, DON'T WASTE FOOD.
They're precious!

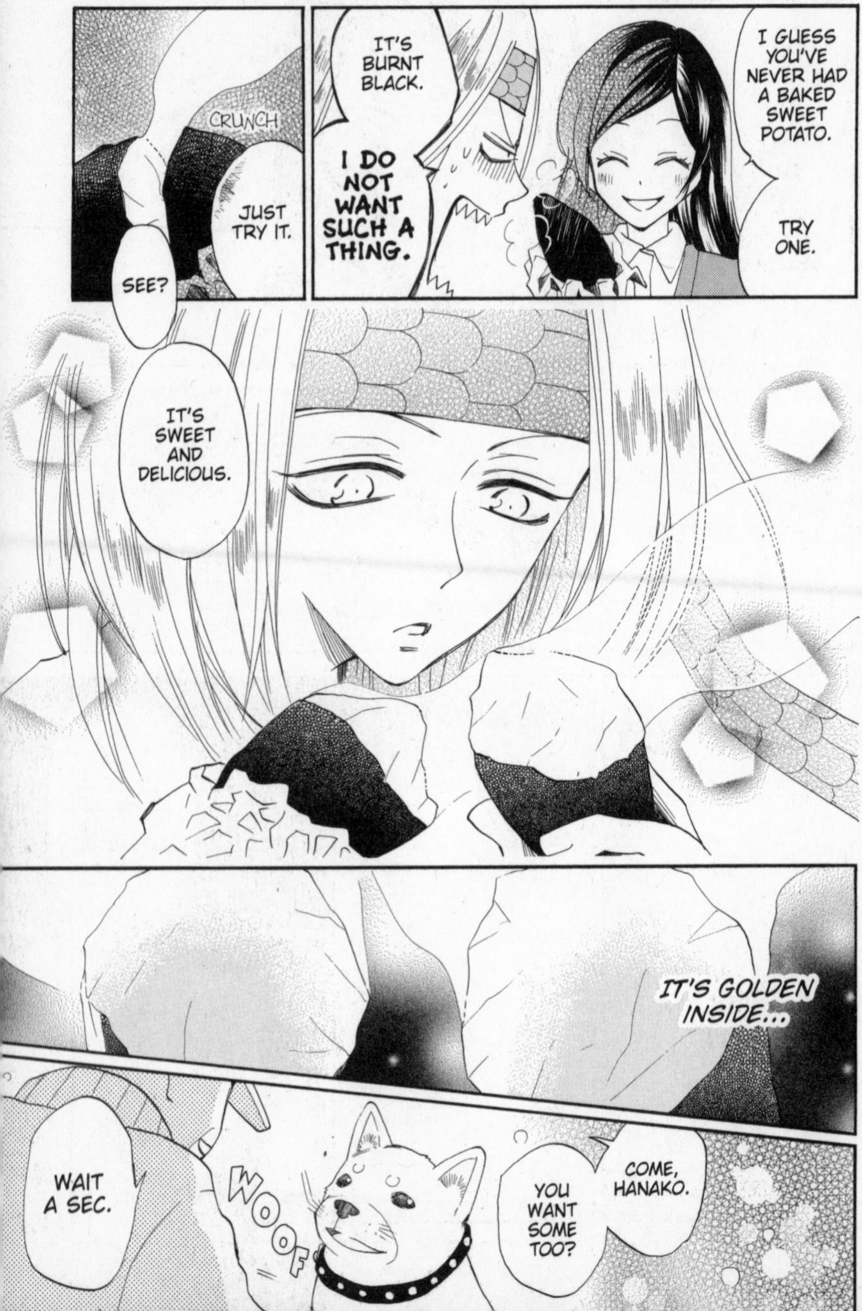
I GUESS YOU'VE NEVER HAD A BAKED SWEET POTATO.
TRY ONE.
IT'S BURNT BLACK.
I DO NOT WANT SUCH A THING.
CRUNCH
JUST TRY IT.
SEE?
IT'S SWEET AND DELICIOUS.
IT'S GOLDEN INSIDE...
COME, HANAKO.
YOU WANT SOME TOO?
WOOF
WAIT A SEC.

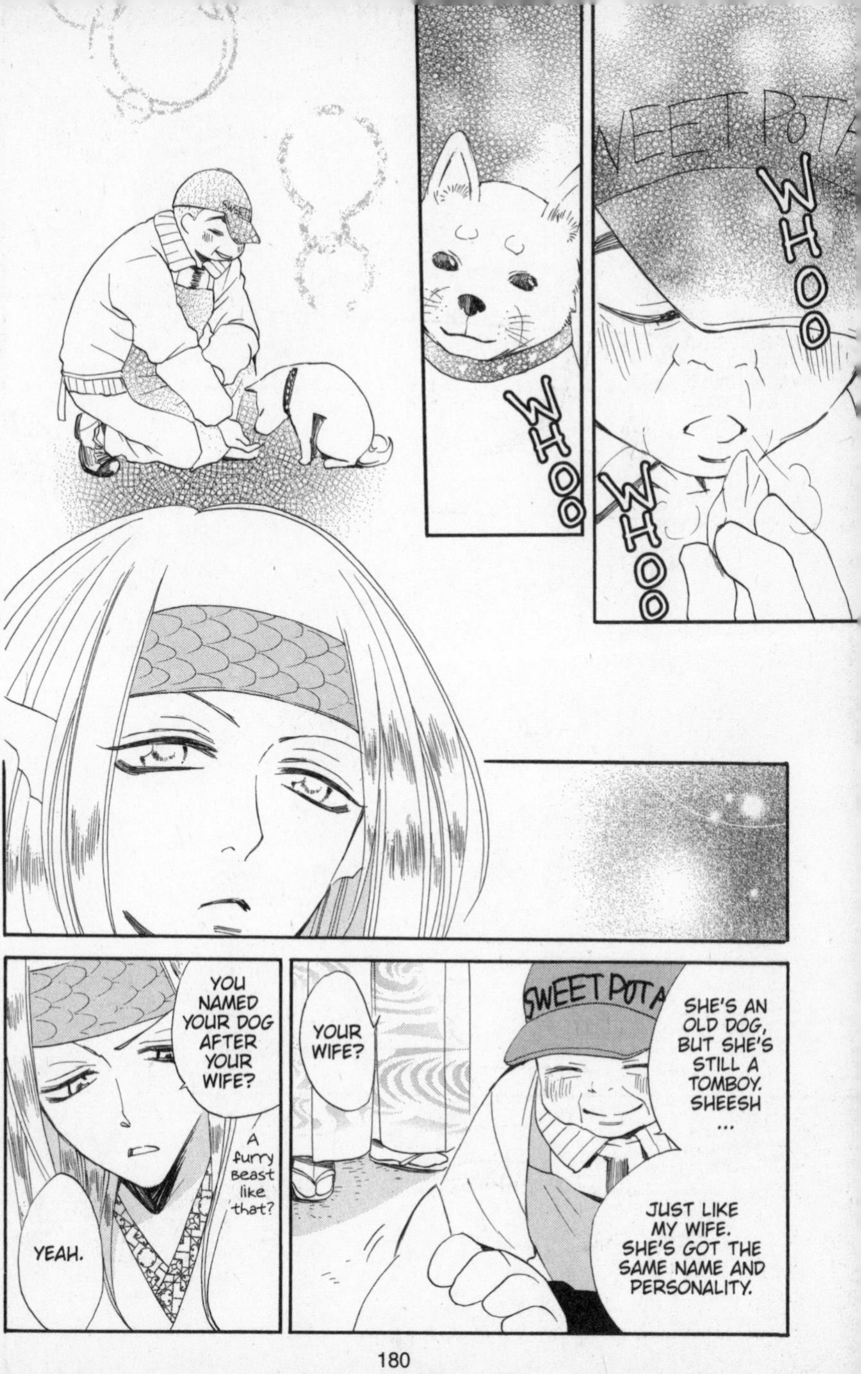
SWEET POTA
WHOO
WHOO
WHOO
SWEET POTA
SHE'S AN OLD DOG, BUT SHE'S STILL A TOMBOY. SHEESH ...
YOUR WIFE?
JUST LIKE MY WIFE. SHE'S GOT THE SAME NAME AND PERSONALITY.
YOU NAMED YOUR DOG AFTER YOUR WIFE?
A furry beast like that?
YEAH.

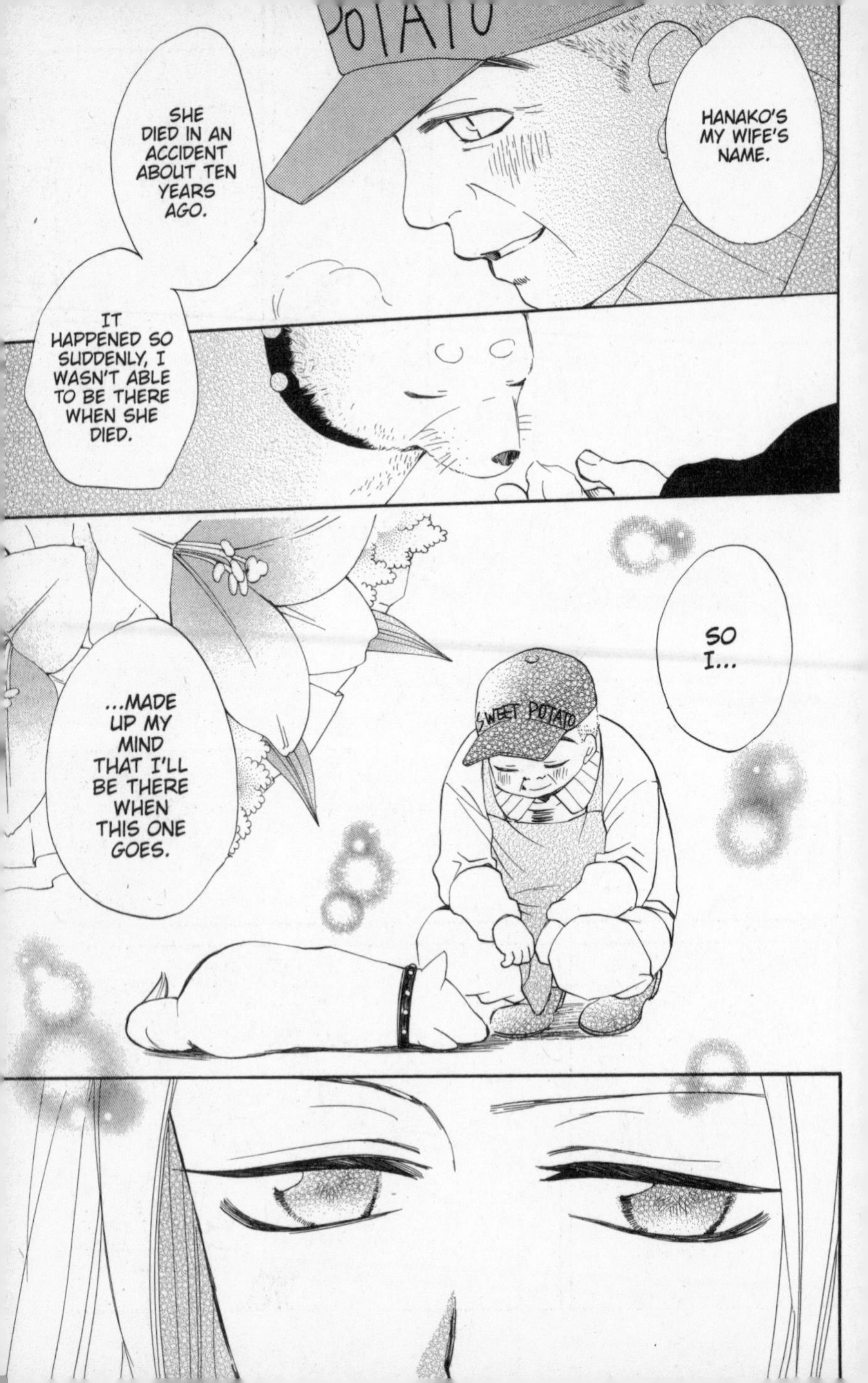
POTATO
HANAKO'S MY WIFE'S NAME.
SHE DIED IN AN ACCIDENT ABOUT TEN YEARS AGO.
IT HAPPENED SO SUDDENLY, I WASN'T ABLE TO BE THERE WHEN SHE DIED.
SO I...
SWEET POTATO
...MADE UP MY MIND THAT I'LL BE THERE WHEN THIS ONE GOES.

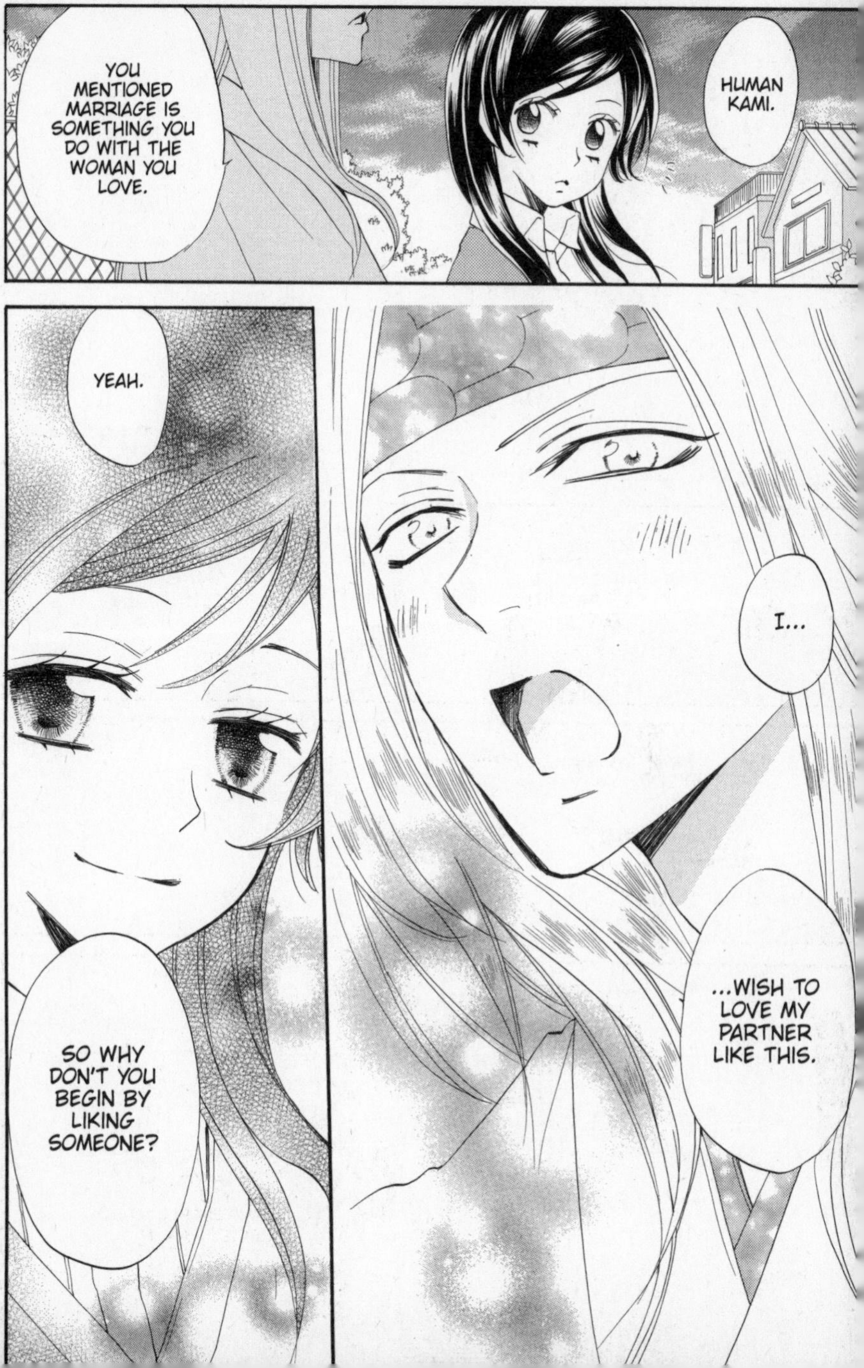
HUMAN KAMI.
YOU MENTIONED MARRIAGE IS SOMETHING YOU DO WITH THE WOMAN YOU LOVE.
I...
...WISH TO LOVE MY PARTNER LIKE THIS.
YEAH.
SO WHY DON'T YOU BEGIN BY LIKING SOMEONE?

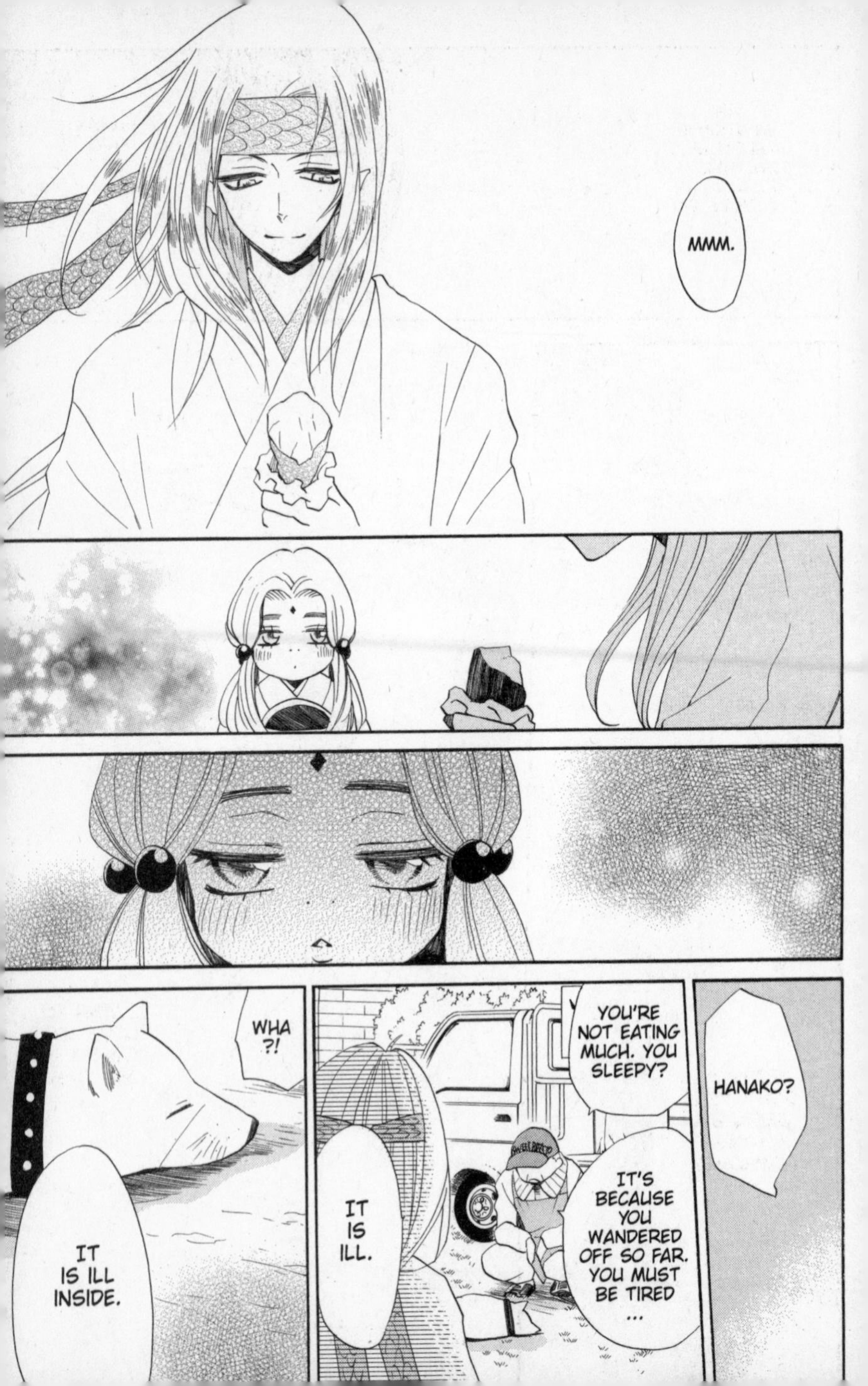
MMM.
HANAKO?
YOU'RE NOT EATING MUCH. YOU SLEEPY?
IT'S BECAUSE YOU WANDERED OFF SO FAR. YOU MUST BE TIRED ...
IT IS ILL.
WHA ?!
IT IS ILL INSIDE.

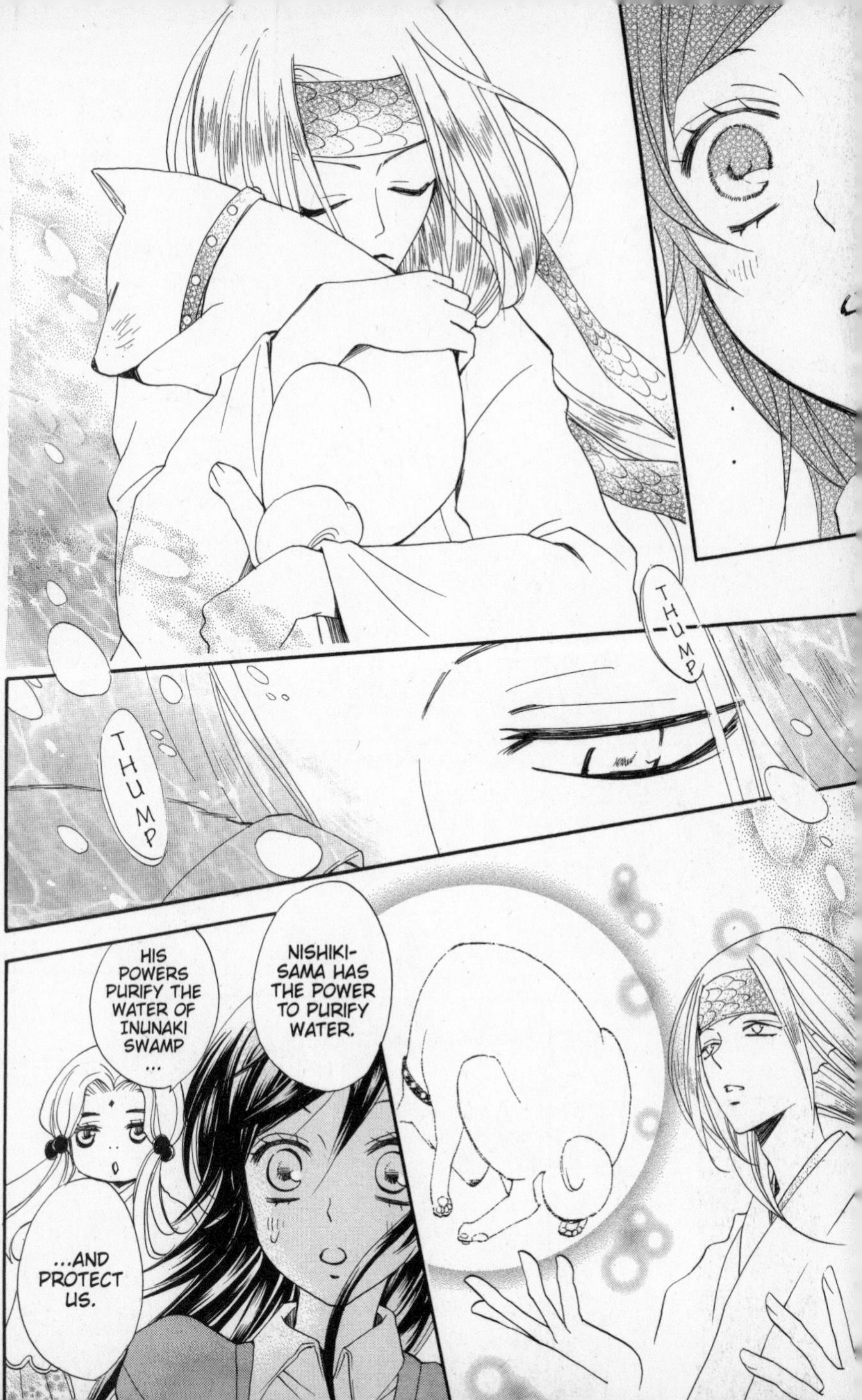
THUMP
THUMP
NISHIKI-SAMA HAS THE POWER TO PURIFY WATER.
HIS POWERS PURIFY THE WATER OF INUNAKI SWAMP ...
...AND PROTECT US.

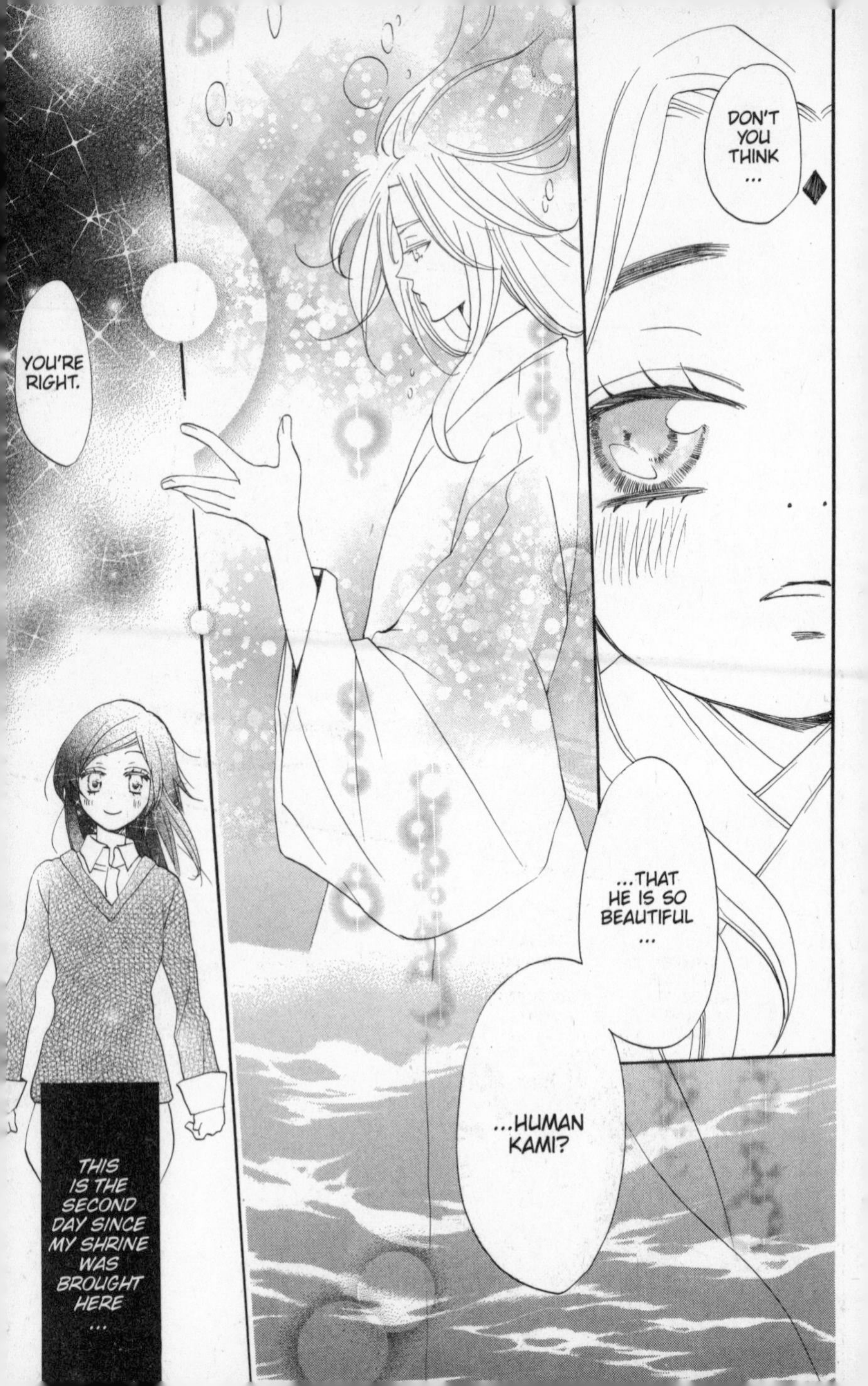
DON'T YOU THINK ...
...THAT HE IS SO BEAUTIFUL ...
...HUMAN KAMI?
YOU'RE RIGHT.
THIS IS THE SECOND DAY SINCE MY SHRINE WAS BROUGHT HERE ...

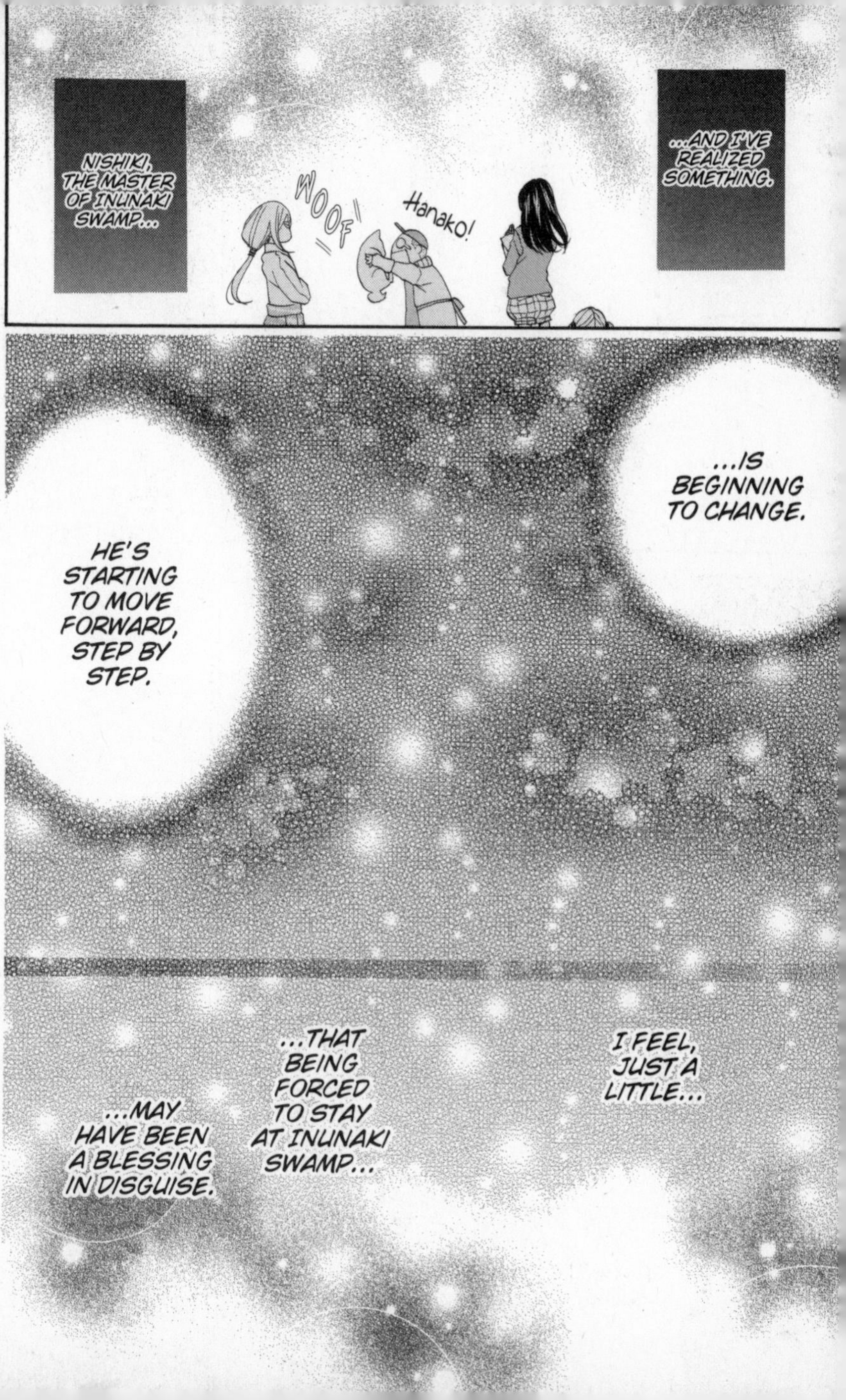
...AND I'VE REALIZED SOMETHING.
Hanako!
WOOF
NISHIKI, THE MASTER OF INUNAKI SWAMP...
...IS BEGINNING TO CHANGE.
HE'S STARTING TO MOVE FORWARD, STEP BY STEP.
I FEEL, JUST A LITTLE...
...THAT BEING FORCED TO STAY AT INUNAKI SWAMP...
...MAY HAVE BEEN A BLESSING IN DISGUISE.

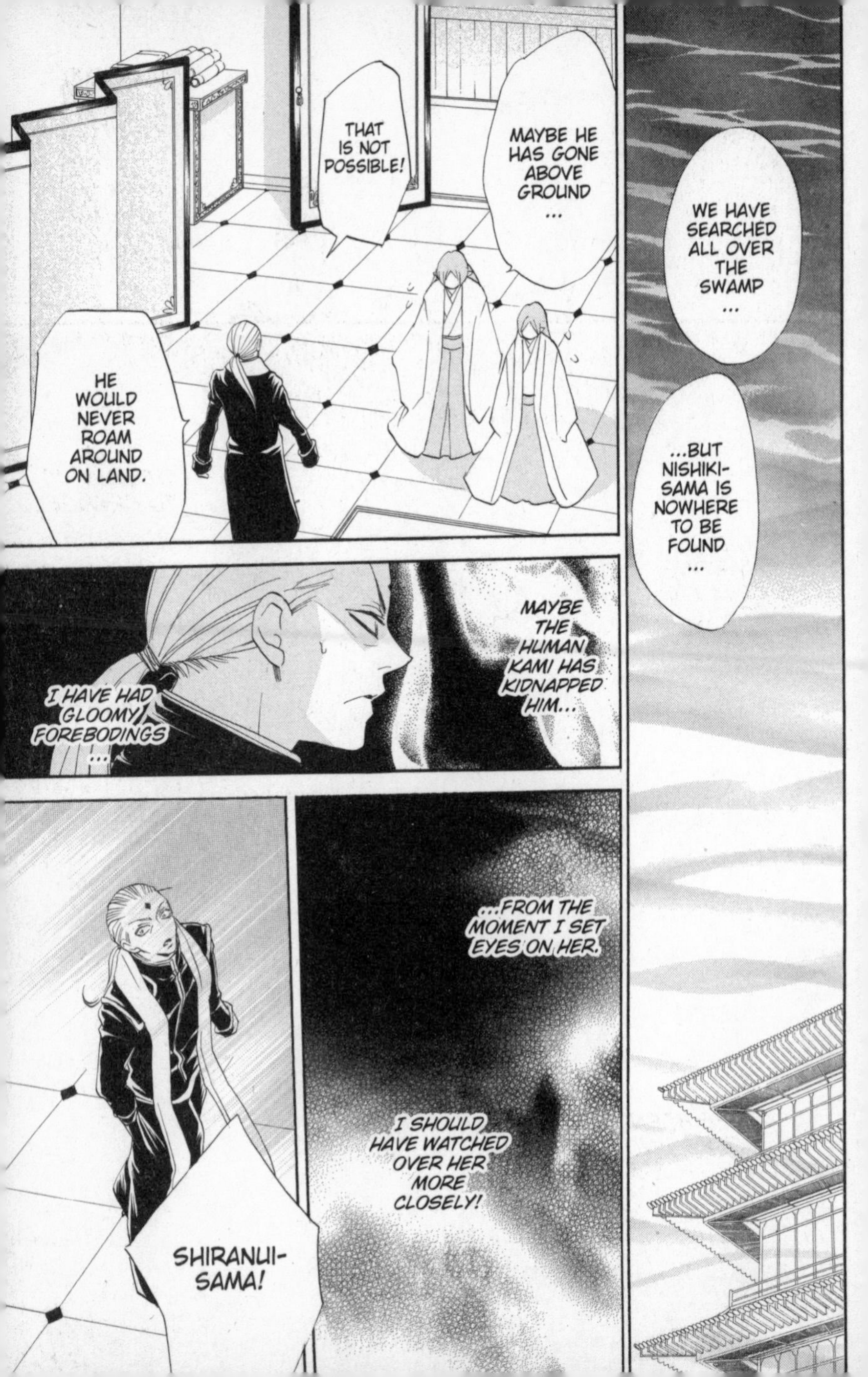
WE HAVE SEARCHED ALL OVER THE SWAMP...
...BUT NISHIKI-SAMA IS NOWHERE TO BE FOUND...
MAYBE HE HAS GONE ABOVE GROUND...
THAT IS NOT POSSIBLE!
HE WOULD NEVER ROAM AROUND ON LAND.
MAYBE THE HUMAN KAMI HAS KIDNAPPED HIM...
I HAVE HAD GLOOMY FOREBODINGS...
...FROM THE MOMENT I SET EYES ON HER.
I SHOULD HAVE WATCHED OVER HER MORE CLOSELY!
SHIRANUI-SAMA!

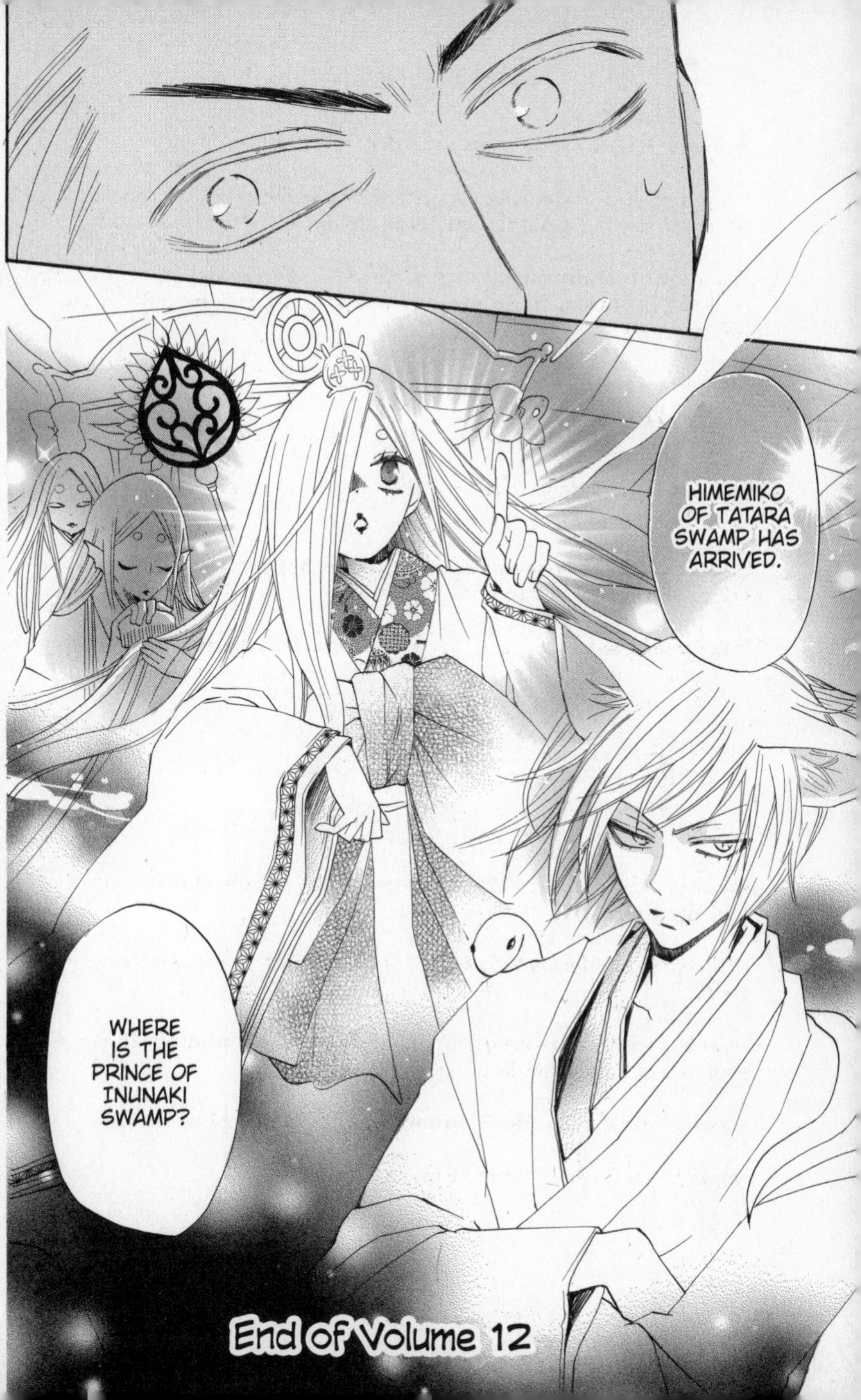
HIMEMIKO OF TATARA SWAMP HAS ARRIVED.
WHERE IS THE PRINCE OF INUNAKI SWAMP?
End of Volume 12

The Otherworld

Ayakashi is an archaic term for yokai.

Kami are Shinto deities or spirits. The word can be used for a range of creatures, from nature spirits to strong and dangerous gods.

Kotodama literally means "word spirit," the spiritual power believed to dwell in words. In Shinto, the words you speak are believed to affect reality.

Onibi-warashi are like will-o'-the-wisps.

Ryu-oh is a title that literally means "dragon king."

Shikigami are spirits that are summoned and employed by *onmyoji* (Yin-Yang sorcerers).

Shinshi are birds, beasts, insects or fish that have a special relationship with a kami.

Tochigami (or *jinushigami*) are deities of a specific area of land.

Honorifics

-chan is a diminutive most often used with babies, children or teenage girls.

-dono roughly means "my lord," although not in the aristocratic sense.

-kun is used by persons of superior rank to their juniors. It can sometimes have a familiar connotation.

-san is a standard honorific similar to Mr., Mrs., Miss, or Ms.

-sama is used with people of much higher rank.

Notes

Page 12, panel 4: All-white kimono
Worn at wedding ceremonies held at shrines.

Page 30, panel 1: Nishiki Ryori
The kanji for *Ryori* means "dragon-carp" and the kanji for *Nishiki* means "Japanese brocade." There is a type of carp called 錦鯉 (*nishikigoi*), or "fancy-colored carp."

Page 48, panel 2: Shiranui
Shiranui means "unknown fire," and refers to mysterious lights that appear at sea during the night.

Page 81, panel 4: Saikyo-miso
Miso is a fermented paste (usually from soybeans) used to make broths, sauces, spreads, and to pickle vegetables and meat. *Saikyo-miso* is a white miso commonly made in Kyoto.

Page 110, panel 3: A thousand ri
Ri is an old unit of measurement that was used in Japan, Korea, and China. In Japan, it was equivalent to about 2.4 miles. One thousand ri is about 2,440 miles.

Julietta Suzuki's debut manga *Hoshi ni Naru Hi* (The Day One Becomes a Star) appeared in the 2004 *Hana to Yume Plus*. Her other books include *Akuma to Dolce* (The Devil and Sweets) and *Karakuri Odette*. Born in December in Fukuoka Prefecture, she enjoys having movies play in the background while she works on her manga.

KAMISAMA KISS
VOL. 12
Shojo Beat Edition

STORY AND ART BY
Julietta Suzuki

English Translation & Adaptation/Tomo Kimura
Touch-up Art & Lettering/Joanna Estep
Design/Yukiko Whitley
Editor/Pancha Diaz

KAMISAMA HAJIMEMASHITA by Julietta Suzuki
© Julietta Suzuki 2012
All rights reserved.
First published in Japan in 2012 by HAKUSENSHA, Inc., Tokyo.
English language translation rights arranged with
HAKUSENSHA, Inc., Tokyo.

Printed in Canada

Published by VIZ Media, LLC
P.O. Box 77010
San Francisco, CA 94107

10 9 8 7 6 5 4
First printing, February 2013
Fourth printing, December 2017

www.viz.com   www.shojobeat.com

PARENTAL ADVISORY
KAMISAMA KISS is rated T for Teen and
is recommended for ages 13 and up. This
volume contains fantasy violence.
ratings.viz.com

W9-CLN-987